Human Resource Management in Small Business

NEW HORIZONS IN MANAGEMENT

Series Editor: Cary L. Cooper, CBE, *Distinguished Professor of Organizational Psychology and Health, Lancaster University, UK*

This important series makes a significant contribution to the development of management thought. This field has expanded dramatically in recent years and the series provides an invaluable forum for the publication of high quality work in management science, human resource management, organizational behaviour, marketing, management information systems, operations management, business ethics, strategic management and international management.

The main emphasis of the series is on the development and application of new original ideas. International in its approach, it will include some of the best theoretical and empirical work from both well-established researchers and the new generation of scholars.

Titles in the series include:

International Terrorism and Threats to Security
Managerial and Organizational Challenges
Edited by Ronald J. Burke and Cary L. Cooper

Women on Corporate Boards of Directors
International Research and Practice
Edited by Susan Vinnicombe, Val Singh, Ronald J. Burke, Diana Bilimoria and Morten Huse

Handbook of Managerial Behavior and Occupational Health
Edited by Alexander-Stamatios G. Antoniou, Cary L. Cooper, George P. Chrousos, Charles D. Spielberger and Michael William Eysenck

Workplace Psychological Health
Current Research and Practice
Paula Brough, Michael O'Driscoll, Thomas Kalliath, Cary L. Cooper and Steven A. Y. Poelmans

Research Companion to Corruption in Organizations
Edited by Ronald J. Burke and Cary L. Cooper

Self-Management and Leadership Development
Edited by Ronald J. Burke and Mitchell G. Rothstein

Handbook of Employee Engagement
Perspectives, Issues, Research and Practice
Edited by Simon Albrecht

Human Resource Management in Small Business
Achieving Peak Performance
Edited by Cary L. Cooper and Ronald J. Burke

Human Resource Management in Small Business

Achieving Peak Performance

Edited by

Cary L. Cooper, CBE

Distinguished Professor of Organizational Psychology and Health, Lancaster University, UK

Ronald J. Burke

Professor of Organizational Behavior, Schulich School of Business, York University, Canada

NEW HORIZONS IN MANAGEMENT

Edward Elgar

Cheltenham, UK • Northampton, MA, USA

Published by
Edward Elgar Publishing Limited
The Lypiatts
15 Lansdown Road
Cheltenham
Glos GL50 2JA
UK

Edward Elgar Publishing, Inc.
William Pratt House
9 Dewey Court
Northampton
Massachusetts 01060
USA

A catalogue record for this book
is available from the British Library

Library of Congress Control Number: 2010941487

ISBN 978 1 84980 121 8 (cased)

Typeset by Servis Filmsetting Ltd, Stockport, Cheshire
Printed and bound by MPG Books Group, UK

Contents

PART IV HUMAN RESOURCE MANAGEMENT AND INDIVIDUAL CHALLENGES

PART V IMPROVING HUMAN RESOURCE MANAGEMENT PRACTICES IN SMALL BUSINESSES

Contributors

Sarah Baillie Royal Veterinary College, University of London, UK

Ronald J. Burke Schulich School of Business, York University, Canada

Brad Carson Collins College of Business, The University of Tulsa, USA

Gary J. Castrogiovanni College of Business, Florida Atlantic University, USA

Sharon Clarke Manchester Business School, University of Manchester, UK

Christopher J. Collins School of Industrial and Labor Relations, Cornell University, USA

Cary L. Cooper Lancaster University Management School, Lancaster, UK

Eileen Drew School of Computer Science and Statistics, Trinity College Dublin, Ireland

Sandra Fielden Manchester Business School, University of Manchester, UK

Kyle Fuschetti Robins School of Business, University of Richmond, USA

Magnus George Lancaster University Management School, Lancaster, UK

Eleanor Hamilton Lancaster University Management School, Lancaster, UK

Colette Henry Royal Veterinary College, University of London, UK

Anne Laure Humbert Middlesex University Business School, London, UK

Carianne Hunt Manchester Business School, University of Manchester, UK

Denise Jepsen Department of Business, Macquarie University, Australia

Andrew Noblet Deakin Business School, Deakin University, Burwood, Australia

Timothy L. Pett W. Frank Barton School of Business, Wichita State University, Wichita, Kansas, USA

Jeffrey M. Pollack Robins School of Business, University of Richmond, USA

Andreas Rauch Rotterdam School of Management, Erasmus University, the Netherlands

Gerard H. Seijts Ivey School of Business, University of Western Ontario, Canada

Lorna Treanor Royal Veterinary College, University of London, UK

Michael Troilo Collins College of Business, The University of Tulsa, USA

James A. Wolff W. Frank Barton School of Business, Wichita State University, Wichita, Kansas, USA

Acknowledgements

Cary Cooper and I have previously written about the role of human capital in achieving organizational success, and the effects of human resource management policies and practices on the quality of life of managers, their employees and families. Given our training, and the fact we both have worked in schools of management, all of our efforts have focused on large organizations, reflecting a bias in our field.

As we continued on our research and writing programs, I became aware of emerging work on small- and medium-sized businesses, particularly short case studies of very successful firms. One observation I made was that many of these successful small businesses placed a high value on their people for their success, and many of the human resource practices they exhibited were similar to those employed by large organizations. This got us thinking about shifting some of our energy to the small business sector in terms of both filling a serious gap in our understanding of human resource policies and practices in this sector and looking at a major contributor to the economic success of all countries. Large organizations and small organizations share some similarities and some differences. Our intention was to take our understanding of what works in both to contribute to the improvement of performance in the latter. Hence this collection. Not surprisingly, Edward Elgar was delighted to work with us, proudly announcing the fact that it is a small business in its publication listings.

Cary and I continue to work productively. Thanks again Cary. Gerry Wood, at Lancaster, as always, provided outstanding support to our efforts by managing our relationships with both authors and Edward Elgar. I thank our international contributors for sharing their latest thinking on how we might better support small- and medium-sized businesses. My contributions were supported in part by York University.

Finally some thanks of a different kind to two individuals who have shaped me in different ways. First, my late mother, Anne Burke, provided a supportive home environment as I was growing up, which allowed me to pursue my education. Second, the late Norman R.F. Maier, of the

University of Michigan, provided me with an example of how professors lived their lives – and in Norm's case he was a maverick.

Ronald Burke
Toronto, Canada

PART I

Introduction

1. Overview of the book

Ronald J. Burke

In Chapter 2 of Part I, I provide an overview of important content relating to HRM and SMEs. This area has not received the research attention that it deserves given its importance to country economic fortunes. HRM is important to the success of both small and large firms. Unfortunately, despite considerable research and writing on HRM, SMEs have not changed their approach to HRM much over the years. I provide a summary of some of the uses of HRM in SMEs. I then consider the question of why managers in SMEs are satisfied, and look at work and family concerns, family-owned and managed businesses, SMEs and entrepreneurship activities for women and the additional challenges women face, why HRM has not been seen as important by entrepreneurs, owners and managers in SMEs, the recently emerging interest in HRM by managers of SMEs, technology adoption, and the management of change. Government policies can be supportive of the creation and management of SMEs. I conclude with suggestions for SMEs to more effectively utilize their human capital including obtaining coaching or mentoring assistance, advice seeking more generally, and the potential use of professional employer organizations for the outsourcing of some HRM functions.

Part II examines what is known about HRM contributions to SME effectiveness. Gary Castrogiovanni in Chapter 3 considers the importance of investing in human capital by small businesses. Human capital involves the education, training, experience, and health of a workforce. He reviews major human capital studies, pulling the findings together into an integrative model. The model considers external context concepts, founding team, and managing team characteristics. Human capital was found to influence aspects of venture creation, access to financial capital, growth, innovation, and firm performance. But human capital is only one of many factors affecting small business founding, outcomes, and long-term performance. Human capital combines with social, financial, and physical capital. And different types of human capital are relevant for new versus established small businesses. He illustrates various types of human capital: entrepreneurial, managerial, industry-specific, firm-specific, and the unique roles played by each.

Christopher Collins in Chapter 4 proposes a theoretical model for the way that HRM systems facilitate performance of entrepreneurial SMEs. He suggests, building on writing from the fields of both strategic HRM and organizational theory, that different HRM systems will be better matched to performance of SMEs depending on the growth strategy of the firms. Collins is advocating a contingency approach to strategic HRM. Thus, an engineering HR model will better fit SMEs pursuing an exploration strategy while a bureaucratic HR model will better fit SMEs pursuing an exploitation strategy. SMEs at the exploration stage emphasize innovation and creativity; SMEs at the exploitation stage need predictability and consistency. Employees and their management are at the heart of both HR strategies, however.

Andreas Rauch in Chapter 5 begins with the premise that SME success and survival is heavily dependent on HRM practices. We know that HRM practices in SMEs are less formal and receive fewer resources. He reviews 15 quantitative studies that address the relationship of HRM and performance in SMEs. He starts by indicating potential relationships between HRM practices and firm performance. Why should HRM practices matter to SMEs? He then considers whether HRM should be viewed in a "best practices" or a contingency way, raising the issues of types of HRM practices and types of performance assessment. He proceeds to examine the research evidence in these 15 studies. He finds that HRM practices were associated with performance assessments but more strongly with some types of assessments (e.g., subjective performance, growth of SMEs) than others. His meta-analytic review, while limited because of the sample size, provides preliminary support for the role of HRM practices in SME performance. It also calls out for more research on this important question.

Timothy Pett and James Wolff address in Chapter 6 the question of why some SMEs achieve high levels of performance while others fall short, failing to achieve management performance goals. They position learning – the integration, interpretation, and use of new knowledge for effective decision-making – as the answer to this question. Learning involves both exploration and exploitation. And organizational learning in SMEs is different from the way learning is undertaken in large firms. Adapting successfully to an ever-changing environment involves effective organizational learning. Learning results from having skilled people in the right place and jobs interested in contributing to the SME's success – basically the core challenges of HRM. Pett and Wolff then examine the role of organizational learning in the relationship of HRM and SME performance. They explain how organizational learning is a central factor in the

HRM and SME performance relationship. To learn successfully, SMEs need to develop a "learning orientation" or learning culture – a challenging assignment at the best of times. They conclude by offering suggestions on how organizational learning can be enhanced and linked to HRM practices.

The chapters in Part III consider some HRM challenges facing SMEs. Michael Troilo and Brad Carson address legal issues facing SMEs and their owners in Chapter 7. In a practical and engaging way, they lay out best practices in tackling legal issues in SMEs. Entrepreneurs at start-up *need* legal advice. SMEs *must* understand sources of their potential liability. They first offer guidance on the firm's legal counsel. Then they move to a consideration of the engagement of employees (e.g., worker health and safety, discrimination and harassment, incentive plans, termination). Then they move to a consideration of the ownership structure possibilities (e.g., sole proprietorship or sole trader, partnerships, corporations, limited liability arrangements). They conclude with a discussion of other relevant regulations (e.g., product safety, environmental regulations). SMEs must create and keep documentation supporting compliance with all relevant regulations. In addition, communication with employees is a sound basis for conveying SME processes and procedures, SME expectations, and addressing employee issues.

Sharon Clarke focuses on health and safety in SMEs in Chapter 8. SMEs experience higher accident and injury rates than do large organizations. Surprisingly little attention has been paid to health and safety concerns in SMEs. And small firms differ from medium-sized firms as well. Injury rates have fallen more slowly in SMEs than in larger firms. Small firms have a higher fatality rate than larger firms. SMEs are more likely to under-report injuries. Some risks to health and safety are particularly high in SMEs. These include less investment in health and safety, working in more hazardous environments, and a less formal management style. But SMEs also may have some advantages here such as higher employee work motivation. She collected data from managers of SMEs having health and safety responsibilities and found more themes that hindered than helped health and safety. Workplace safety was promoted by awareness, encouragement, and flexible management practices. Training was most often used to raise awareness and encourage safe behaviors. Barriers to safety included economic pressures, lack of communication and support, and excessive government regulations. But most UK SMEs had a basic safety management system in place. Clarke emphasizes a significantly stronger role for SME managers in improving their health and safety records with a focus on HRM and SME safety culture rather than solely on training and blaming human error.

The chapters in Part IV look at HRM opportunities supporting individual employees. Kyle Fuschetti and Jeffrey Pollack in Chapter 9 lay out human resource management practices that have proven effective in addressing personal and family transitions in small business. Two areas in which entrepreneurs face difficult transitions are examined: stress-related issues and family-related issues. They present "best practices" for dealing with these issues along with practical thoughts. An important stressor is the possibility of business failure. Stress can also have both positive and negative effects. Two problems can occur when family members are not involved in the business and when they are. They identify specific transitions (e.g., role overload, nepotism), note some consequences of each (e.g., work overload, unfairness towards non-family members), and offer advice (e.g., train others to do what you do, make family members earn their stripes). Company vignettes flesh out the application of these best practices in concrete situations.

Colette Henry, Lorna Treanor, and Sarah Baillie in Chapter 10 examine challenges of female SME owners and managers in veterinary medicine. They first review the literature on women entrepreneurs, business owners, and managers. Women continue to be under-represented as entrepreneurs and SME managers. The unique challenges women face here are indicated (e.g., gender stereotypes, work and family responsibilities, difficulties raising capital). Women report lower confidence in their business and management abilities and are more conservative risk takers. They then move into a consideration of the veterinary sector. The veterinary sector is dominated by SMEs, historically led by men. But women are increasingly moving into this sector, now comprising about half the workforce. Some have attributed this to the relatively lower salaries of veterinary professionals. Women in this sector face challenges common to women in the professions more generally. But the authors are optimistic about the future prospects for women here. Combining work and family will remain women's biggest challenge. In addition they suggest raising these challenges in undergraduate veterinary education will do much for women's future success.

Eileen Drew and Anne Laure Humbert in Chapter 11 consider how entrepreneurs manage their business and family commitments. Most managers talk about the importance of work–family balance or integration but rarely achieve it. They focus their research on the Irish experience. Men are more likely than women to engage in entrepreneurial activities but women are now starting their own businesses at a faster rate than men are. Having a family member in business was found to support entrepreneurship. Time pressures, having younger children, and support from one's spouse/partner relate to levels of work–family conflict. Women see entrepreneurship as a way to address work–family conflict but this view is often not borne out. Using a sample of men and women entrepreneurs in Ireland, they found significant structural differences and employment patterns in entrepreneurship that in themselves may influence work–family issues. Men tended to have children cared for by their spouses/partners while women more often used paid child care or cared for children themselves. Women had a stronger interest in flexible work hours. Men worked more hours per week as well. Women reported higher levels of work–family conflict. Women valued flexible work hours more than men did and were more likely to offer flexibility to their staff (which contained a higher percentage of women employees). Not surprisingly, women more than men reported more interference of family in their business than did men. Interestingly both women and men indicated having made similar levels of sacrifice (family, leisure) in their business lives. It is vital that responsibility for children and family be shared equally by women and men if this gendered imbalance is to be curtailed. They offer concrete policy proposals in this direction.

Magnus George and Eleanor Hamilton in Chapter 12 examine job stressors, coping, and well-being among SME owner managers and with SME performance. They review how entrepreneurship and SMEs differ from work and the workings of large organizations, the entrepreneurial lifestyle, and the SME owner/manager's job. They identify job stressors and factors that make SME owner managers more susceptible to them. They then consider the effects of job stress on job satisfaction, job crafting, and well-being. Very little is known about the effects of job stress among SME owner managers. They identify various job stressors that exist for SME owner managers as well as flesh out the concept of well-being. Entrepreneurial experiences contributing to flourishing and positive well-being are noted. Social support and coping have been found to have benefits in the stress–well-being relationship. They propose social capital, a network of personal ties, as a central resource in this regard. Respite has been increasingly seen to have recuperative value. They conclude with a description of a program supporting SME owner/managers, LEAD, offered by their institution that indirectly grapples with stress and well-being issues.

Part V concludes with suggestions for improving HRM in SMEs. Andrew Noblet and Denise Jepsen in Chapter 13 highlight the importance of organizational justice in SMEs and illustrate ways to improve levels of justice in them. Employee perceptions of organizational justice affect their behaviors and performance and ultimately the success of SMEs. They begin by describing various forms of organizational justice/injustice showing how these impact key employee and employer outcomes. SMEs are particularly prone to perceptions of injustice and factors associated with these are identified. SMEs should care about justice/injustice perceptions. SMEs lack the resources or slack to absorb costs of injustice. The authors then discuss interventions for enhancing justice in SMEs at primary, secondary, and tertiary levels. Primary-level interventions include increasing levels of social support to employees and employee involvement and engagement efforts. Secondary-level interventions include recognition and reward programs and performance feedback. Tertiary-level interventions include compensation and taking of corrective actions to increase organizational justice.

The evidence indicates that women small business owners and managers face unique challenges. Carianne Hunt and Sandra Fielden in Chapter 14 report results of an online coaching initiative designed to increase the success of women small business owners and managers. The evaluation compared the experiences of women who participated over a six-month period receiving online coaching from an experienced woman business owner with a control group of women entering small business ownership but not participating in the coaching program. They describe the coaching program in some detail covering its objectives, key elements, and its website. Small business owners and managers were "matched" with more experienced female business owners. The program also encouraged networking among the participants and the provision of social support. The recipients of the coaching reported greater self-efficacy, a stronger internal locus of control, and more positive entrepreneurial attitudes. Recipients believed they had benefited from the program and were satisfied with the support received from the coaches. Recipients also believed that they had improved their skills. Interestingly, coaches also reported benefits from their coaching of another. These data resulted in their revising the coaching program to make it better. Thus, telephone contact and face-to-face meetings will be incorporated into future online coaching programs. Men working in SMEs would also benefit from programs such as this one.

Shortly after 9/11, it was difficult for airlines to show a profit. Most airlines lost money and some declared bankruptcy. But WestJet, a Canadian airline, has thrived. WestJet's success has been attributed to its low-cost structure and focus on customer service. Gerard Seijts in Chapter 15, using a detailed case study of WestJet, shows the important role played by HRM practices and business strategy. WestJet has few passenger complaints and an award-winning corporate culture. Central HRM practices include employee selection, on-boarding processes, performance management, orientation and talent management, and profit sharing. The key strategic element for WestJet's success is the articulation of corporate culture values and its relentless efforts to inculcate these values into the daily behaviors of its employees. Seijts provides concrete examples using WestJet materials that offer a vivid picture of why WestJet flourishes while many of its competitors struggle.

2. Human resource management in small- and medium-sized enterprises: benefits and challenges*

Ronald J. Burke

INTRODUCTION

This chapter serves as a primer for the analysis of the benefits from and challenges of introducing sound human resource management (HRM) practices in small- and medium-sized enterprises (SMEs). It identifies central themes in this area and serves as an introduction to the more intensive chapters that make up the remainder of the volume.

The chapter addresses factors contributing to the success of SMEs. This area receives less attention than that devoted to large organizations. This is ironic since there are significantly more SMEs than large organizations, SMEs employ more people, SMEs exist in every country, SMEs seem to be weathering the current economic recession better, and some SMEs eventually become large organizations. More individuals are now in SMEs with the downsizing of large organizations, and the frustration many people feel, particularly women, with their careers in large organizations. In a nutshell, the economic performance of an economy is inextricably linked to the SME sector, and SMEs rely heavily on their people and on their HRM practices for their success (Brand & Bax, 2002; Way, 2002).

Consider these facts:

- Small businesses account for over 95 percent of all businesses in the US and Canada (Heneman et al., 2000).
- Small businesses represent 99 percent of employers (Williamson et al., 2002).
- Small businesses create 66 percent of new jobs and produce 39 percent of the gross national product (GNP) in the US.
- In Canada, small businesses, defined by the Federal Government as firms having 100 or fewer employees, account for about 98 percent

of firms, 43 percent of the private sector labor force and contribute 25 percent to GNP (Industry Canada, 2008).
- Only 2 percent of organizations in the US and Canada have more than 100 employees (Industry Canada, 2008; Wiatrowski, 1994).
- Hamilton and Dana (2003) highlight the key role played by SMEs in contributing to the economy of New Zealand.
- According to Challenger et al. (2010), more out of work managers and executives in the US are no longer looking for jobs but are starting their own businesses. This figure rose to 8.6 percent in 2009, the biggest increase coming among those older than 55.
- Online recruiters CareerBuilder (August, 2009) reported that 25 percent of the US workforce laid-off from full-time jobs found new jobs with small businesses. And another 59 percent would be interested in working for a small business, and 29 percent were considering starting a small business. Why this interest in small businesses? Fifty-six percent indicated that a "family-like" work environment was attractive and 48 percent indicated that they could make more of a difference in a small firm.

Why a volume on HRM in SMEs for entrepreneurs and managers, and for the development of management skills? The typical entrepreneurial venture starts small. For it to survive, prosper and grow, a number of skills are required, one of which is managing people and using HRM practices that support high performance.

This chapter has several objectives. First, it highlights why HRM practices are critical to entrepreneurs and the success of SMEs. Second, it provides concrete examples of specific HRM initiatives that contribute to the effectiveness of SMEs. Third, it indicates some of the personal and organizational challenges facing entrepreneurs/managers and their SMEs and how HRM practices are relevant to them. Finally, it cites recommended readings that provide practical suggestions for developing the management skills of entrepreneurs and SME managers.

WHAT IS HRM?

Tocher and Rutherford (2009, p. 457) define HRM as "a set of distinct but interrelated activities, functions, and processes that are directed at attracting, developing, and maintaining (or disposing of) a firm's human resources". Schermerhorn (2001) defines HRM as "the process of attracting, developing, and maintaining a talented and energetic workforce to support organizational mission, objectives and stragtegies" (p. 24). HRM policies and practices can help firms improve their performance. All SMEs use HRM practices, often informally. Most SMEs do not have a formal HR department or trained HR professionals on staff. SMEs generally do not use HR policies and practices to the same extent as large firms do (Kotey & Folker, 2007; Kotey & Slade, 2005). SMEs do use a mix of HRM practices such as recruiting, training, compensation, and motivating (Tocher & Rutherford, 2009). These HRM practices have a traditional role (e.g., job analysis, selection) and a strategic role (empowerment, TQM [total quality management], culture change). SMEs that use HRM policies and practices tend to perform at a higher level (Chandler & McEvoy, 2000; Hayton, 2003).

Carlson et al. (2006), in a study of 168 fast-growing family-owned firms, reported that faster-growing SMEs made greater use of the following HRM practices: training and development, recruitment packages, efforts to improve morale, the use of performance appraisals, and competitive compensation and incentive plans.

What do professional HRM practices look like? De Kok et al. (2003, 2006) provide the following illustrative examples (2006, p. 460):

- *recruitment* – recruitment and selection office, temporary employment agencies, magazines, Internet, referrals by employees, references from other sources, open houses;
- *selection* – use of written job descriptions, job analysis, psychological tests, and interview panels;
- *compensation* – performance pay, pay partly based on job evaluation, competitive wages, wages based on acquired skills, group incentive programs, individual incentive programs, profit sharing, annual bonus, other financial benefits such as insurance and savings plans;
- *training and development* – training provided to employees, formal training budget available, recent introduction of formal training programs, recent intensification of existing training programs, formal in-house training by internal staff, formal in-house training by external staff, external training, and management and development training;
- *appraisal* – rating scales, management by objectives, and appraisal conducted by line managers.

Entrepreneurs sometimes fail to see the importance of sound HRM practices or if they believe HRM practices to be critical for success, lack the time, patience, and skill to fully utilize these practices. Entrepreneurs are typically men and women of action; they get things done. They often lack the time to train, develop, and create the conditions that motivate staff by knowing their individual employees. HRM is often given lower priority than manufacturing and/or marketing. In addition, many entrepreneurs believe that HRM is common sense and being good with people (being liked). Sound HRM practices are much more than this. SMEs historically have not incorporated new developments in HRM.

SMEs are now facing significant challenges on several fronts. These include skills shortages and gaps in available and needed skills, low labor force growth, high levels of absenteeism, and high levels of employee turnover. HRM processes are important in addressing these real needs.

DIFFERENCES BETWEEN SMEs AND LARGE ORGANIZATIONS

There are unique aspects to working in and managing in an SME. SMEs differ from large organizations in fundamental ways. These include: less "slack" in SMEs, less formality and structure, less distance between the top and the bottom levels, fewer systems and administrators in place to handle HRM issues, and they are less hierarchical. De Kok et al. (2006), in a study of 736 family-owned SMEs, found that these family-owned SMEs made less use of professional HRM practices (less formal recruiting, less training, less use of performance appraisal). It should not be assumed that the research findings based on large firms can be directly applied to SMEs; large firms and SMEs differ in significant ways.

Newness and Smallness

Cardon and Stevens (2004) note that while SMEs differ from large firms in many ways, they indicate two important potential "liabilities", being both newness (age) and smallness (size). And SMEs, by definition, are small, but some are relatively new (young) while others are relatively well established (old). Some SMEs will eventually become large organizations while other SMEs will remain small, sometimes by choice.

As SMEs grow in size their HRM practices become more formal, and hopefully more professional. Changes include a greater division of labor, more hierarchical structures, increased bureaucratization, more administrative processes, and tendency for these to become more formal for employees than for managers. Some have suggested that this increased formalization may be a liability in decreasing the flexibility of HRM policies and practices.

WHY ARE ENTREPRENEURS AND CEOs/ MANAGERS OF SMEs SATISFIED?

Research evidence indicates that the self-employed and the creators of new ventures are more satisfied than employed individuals (Hundley, 2001). This has been attributed to greater autonomy and control, less bureaucracy, more varied challenges among owners/managers of SMEs, and personal relationships among employees of SMEs (Tsai et al., 2007).

Schjoedt (2009) studied the relationship of four core job characteristics (autonomy, variety, task identity, feedback) and job satisfaction of founders/initial partners of SME start-ups and non-founding top managers, the sample sizes being 429 and 118, respectively. Both groups of respondents were very highly job satisfied, likely reflecting their working in SMEs. Entrepreneurs (founders/initial partners) scored slightly but significantly higher on the four job characteristics and job satisfaction than did the non-founding managers. And the four job characteristics were significant predictors of job satisfaction in both groups of respondents. But some job characteristics (autonomy, variety, feedback) had different strengths in predicting job satisfaction in the two samples; autonomy and feedback has stronger relationships, and variety a smaller relationship, with job satisfaction in the founder sample.

BEING INDEPENDENT

An increasing number of women and men are now working solo as independents, sometimes termed self-employed or "micropreneurs". This sometimes happens following retirement or career changes, and the change from a manufacturing industrial economy to a service-based economy.

There are both pros and cons of working solo. The cons include a potentially unstable income and a need to be more self-reliant and disciplined. The pros include that since working solo there is no need for teams, individuals can pick and choose clients; as the solo enterprise grows the individual can smoothly move from doing to managing; individuals can spend time looking for the right people to add to staff; there are fewer financial risks that can be more carefully managed; and solo entrepreneurs can be more agile and more adaptive to changes in their external environment.

WHO IS AWARE OF HRM PROBLEMS IN SMEs?

Tocher and Rutherford (2009) collected data from 1693 SMEs in the US to investigate the effect of owner/manager and firm characteristics on the likelihood of perceiving acute HRM problems. This is important since failing to identify and address pressing HRM problems is a common cause of SME failure, while solving these problems likely contributes to SME success. SME owners and managers typically focus on HRM issues only when they become critical because of time constraints, inadequate planning, and a reactive stance. Respondents were asked to identify the single most important problem facing their business today. Twenty-one percent of respondents indicated HRM issues, the largest problem category.

SME owners and managers of high-performing SMEs were less likely to perceive HRM problems. But SME owners and managers who had more experience, more education, and worked or managed larger SMEs perceived more acute HRM problems. Gender, owner or manager age, firm age, and firm growth had no relationship to perceptions of acute HRM problems.

PERCEIVED VALUE OF HRM IN SMEs

HRM has historically been viewed as a peripheral function in both large and small organizations. McEvoy (1984) found that accounting, finance, production, and marketing were seen as more important than HRM. In SMEs, the owner/CEO likely handles HR matters, and full-time HR professionals are not employed. These informal approaches to HRM may lead to business failure and low productivity.

But Some SME Managers and Entrepreneurs Value HRM

Heneman et al. (2000) used information from focus groups with founders and managers of SMEs, surveys of young entrepreneurs and growth-oriented SME managers, and a review of leading HRM journals to examine HRM needs of SMEs and what HRM researchers were studying. It may be the case that the wider HRM research literature does not meet the needs of SMEs and new venture creators. Heneman et al. identified some gaps between the consumers and producers of HRM information for SMEs. Consumers wanted more information on labor shortages and recruiting strategies for SMEs, for example.

Founders/managers of SMEs, when asked to identify the biggest challenge facing their firms, had 17 percent of their responses related to HRM. These included: employee recruitment, retention, motivation, training, rewarding, compensation, and negotiations. Young entrepreneurs expressed a desire for HRM content that related to their firms as well as HRM information that had personal relevance (e.g., work hours and work–family balance). These findings suggest that there is a market for research and writing that addresses particular HRM issues in the SME context.

Heneman et al. also commented on the relatively little attention devoted by HRM researchers to SMEs. They offered some speculations on why this was the case:

- Owners/managers of SMEs do not have enough time to take part in research studies.
- Owners/managers in SMEs do not view HRM issues as important.
- HRM research in SMEs is not valued by the best academic and research outlets.
- There were small sample sizes in many SME studies, making the results tentative.

Signs of Progress?

Hornsby and Kuratko (2003) collected data on HRM policies and practices in 262 US small businesses replicating their 1990 study (Hornsby & Kuratko, 1990). There was little advancement in HRM functions of these small businesses over the ten-year period. Hornsby and Kuratko (1990) examined 247 SMEs and found that those having 50 or fewer employees had less formal HRM policies and practices, while larger firms (50–100, 100–150) had more formal HRM policies and practices. They concluded that HRM practices had not changed during the ten-year period, and the types of important HRM issues also had not changed. These were: obtaining quality staff, benefits, wages, and government regulations. Even though HRM issues became higher priority in some large-scale firms, little change in HRM functions in SMEs were observed.

EMPLOYEES AS A COMPETITIVE ADVANTAGE

Why does HRM matter? Research evidence has accumulated over the past 20 years, primarily from large firms, that employees and organizational culture represent the one unique competitive advantage in an economy that has become increasingly service and knowledge based (Katzenbach, 2000; Schwartz, 2010; Ulrich & Ulrich, 2010). Other sources of competitive advantage (e.g., access to capital, design of products, consulting advice) can be bought or copied. As a result, HRM functions and a changed role for the HR department emerge as important success factors for large firms. One might argue that employees and firm culture are likely even more important to the success of SMEs. SMEs do not have the capacity and slack to retain employees and practices that do not contribute to performance, cannot afford to underutilize human capital, and have to rely on staff for learning, innovation, and creativity.

One could make a convincing case that HRM is even more important now than ever. There are several reasons for this argument. These include:

- an increasingly knowledge-based economy;
- a more educated workforce – the most educated workforce the world has ever seen;
- higher employee expectations that they will have quality work in a positive environment;
- a staff shortage and an increasing war for talent making employee retention critical;
- an aging workforce making it imperative that training and development initiatives and performance incentives for keeping up-to-date be made available to fully utilize these people;
- clients and customers that are demanding higher-quality products and services.

PERSONAL AND SME CHALLENGES THAT COULD BENEFIT FROM HRM PRACTICES

There are many challenges facing individual entrepreneurs and managers of SMEs, both personal and organizational.

Personal challenges include:

- maintaining work hours and work intensity within reasonable bounds;
- work and family synergies and conflicts;
- stress management and recovery;
- maintaining focus and stamina;
- personal and family transitions;
- unique issues for female entrepreneurs.

SME start-up challenges include:

- business and strategic planning;
- legal issues;

- incorporating the latest technology;
- safety and health concerns;
- recruiting, selection, retaining, and motivating employees;
- the use of work teams;
- customer service and product quality;
- marketing;
- networking;
- building the SME brand.

Stability and growth challenges include:

- maintaining growth;
- succession planning;
- the hiring of professional managers;
- knowing when to let go;
- exiting the SME.

THEORETICAL FRAMEWORKS

There are three theories, borrowed from the large organization literature, that have been used/can be used to assess the effects and relevance of HRM in small businesses (see Burke & Singh, 2010). First, there are "universalistic" theoretical explanations of the use of HRM as bundles of practices. Universalistic explanations state that certain HRM "best practices" can be applied to any firm/across organizations because the effects are similar (see for example, Delaney et al., 1989; Dewar & Derbel, 1979; Morris et al., 2006; Ostroff & Bowen, 2000). These HR practices – such as careful hiring, training and development of quality employees, and performance-based pay – create value for the firm and, given their universal benefits, all organizations should adopt them as they provide a competitive advantage (Becker & Gerhart, 1996; Delery & Doty, 1996; MacDuffie, 1995; Martin-Alcazar et al., 2005; Morris et al., 2006). While universalistic explanations have been mainly used to explain the HRM–firm performance relationship in large firms, they can be applied to the SME and entrepreneurial firm environment. Arguably, given the general scarcity of resources and the inherent problems in refining many HR practices, the use of "best practices" in small businesses makes this approach more relevant and appealing for owners and managers.

Second, "behavioral" explanations may also be used to assess HRM in SMEs, especially as they affect firm outcomes. Behavioral theories suggest that HRM policies and practices influence employee behaviors – such as work engagement, organizational commitment, and creativity – which, in turn, affect productivity and performance. This chain extends to the firm level; that is, HRM practices affect organizational outcomes, including profitability (Becker & Gerhart, 1996; Becker & Huselid, 2006; Pfeffer, 1994, 1995, 1998). For instance, "expectancy theory" has been/can be used to explain the motivational impact of pay-for-performance compensation systems and employee benefits on employee productivity and firm performance (Lawler, 2000), including small businesses.

Third, "economic" explanations help with a key HRM-related issue – when should formal HR structures, including an HRM department, be adopted by an organization? Several writers have debated whether formal HR practices help or hinder small businesses (Cardon & Stevens, 2004; De Kok et al., 2006; Kaman et al., 2001). A key concern is the costs versus benefits of such formalization. Larger organizations benefit from economies of scale, thus are more likely to adopt formal practices; smaller firms generally have less financial resources to adopt and develop effective practices or to install permanent structures, such as a formal HRM unit/department (Bryson, 1999; De Kok et al., 2006). Some scholars and practitioners suggest that 100 employees is the critical size/point for implementing such a unit (Cardon & Stevens, 2004).

While these theories can be applied to SME and entrepreneurial environments, the context is fundamentally different (small business versus large organizations); thus, it should not be surprising if results of empirical research do not always conform to expectations. The dynamics of small businesses are quite different than their larger counterparts and consequently, different theoretical lenses may be needed.

CORE HRM ISSUES IN SMALL BUSINESSES

While there is an emerging body of literature on the HRM–firm performance relationship in small businesses, the research in the field has generally focused on a few traditional HRM practices and how they become formalized over time (see Cardon & Stevens, 2004, for an extensive review). Researchers have examined the way that employees are recruited and hired by SMEs (Deshpande & Golhar, 1994; Gatewood & Feild, 1987; Heneman & Berkley, 1999; Hornsby & Kuratko, 1990; McEvoy, 1984), the use of formal training programs in SMEs (Chandler & McEvoy, 2000; Curran, 1988; Fairfield-Sonn, 1987; Storey, 2004) and pay systems (Amba-Rao & Pendse, 1985; Balkin & Logan, 1988; Carr, 1997; Fowler & Murlis, 1987).

Given the space limitations in this chapter, Table 2.1 summarizes a

Table 2.1 Summary of HRM small business research findings

HRM Practices	Contribution/Key Findings
General/overall review of HRM Practices	
Wagar (1998)	Larger firms were more likely to have formal HR practices, including orientation program and training in total quality management
Kaman et al. (2001)	Larger firms use bureaucratic HRM practices more than smaller firms; high-commitment HRM practices were not correlated with organizational size
Kotey & Slade (2005)	Formalization of HRM practices increases with size
Recruitment and selection	
Julien (1998); Wilkinson (1999)	Higher internal referrals – recruitment done through networks of family and friends
Hornsby & Kuratko (1990)	Smaller firms are less likely to engage in expensive recruitment techniques
Heneman & Berkley (1999)	Recruitment strategies are ad hoc
King et al. (2001)	Recruitment decisions less likely to be based on a standardized set of performance criteria
Training and development	
Kotey & Slade (2005); Cardon & Stevens (2004)	Presence of formal training is related to the size of the business Training is done primarily on the job
Storey (2004)	Small firms are much less likely to provide employees and managers with formal training
Compensation and benefits	
Julien (1998)	Wages and fringe benefits are lower in small firms
Hornsby & Kuratko (1990)	Only one-fifth of small businesses offer pension plans
Brand & Bax (2002)	Lower employee benefits in small businesses
Wilkinson (1999)	Remuneration is subject to management choice Small firms are less likely to pay employees more due to working conditions
HRM and firm performance	
Chandler & McEvoy (2000)	Total quality management was most effective when used with training and group-based compensation practices

Table 2.1 (continued)

HRM Practices	Contribution/Key Findings
Storey (2004)	There is weak evidence that small firms that provide formal training perform better than those that do not
Way (2002)	High performance work systems (which included staffing, compensation, and training) reduced turnover but had no significant effect on labor productivity
Carlson et al. (2006)	HRM, including training and development, recruitment, and incentive compensation, have a positive impact on firm performance (measured as sales and sales growth

Source: Burke & Singh (2010).

sample of studies that cover core HRM areas (Burke & Singh, 2010). As can be seen in the table, while some of the findings are consistent, for instance wages and benefits are lower in smaller firms, training and development is less formal, and that formalization increases with size, one can still debate the effects of HRM on SME firm performance. Some studies find that HRM practices impose an unbearable cost on small businesses, thus decreasing their potential benefits (Storey, 1994); others report a positive effect on performance (Carlson et al., 2006).

RESEARCH ON HRM IN SMEs

There is an emerging body of compelling evidence that the effective management of an organization's human resources is vital to its success (Becker & Gerhart, 1996; Becker & Huselid, 1998, 2006; Birdi et al., 2008; Combs et al., 2006: Huselid, 1995; Morris et al., 2006). However, much of this literature focuses on large firms. As a result, several scholars and practitioners have called for more research on HRM in small businesses, especially given the role and pervasiveness of small entrepreneurial firms in the economy (Cassell et al., 2002; Golhar & Deshpande, 1997; Hornsby & Kuratko, 1990; Marlow, 1997; Ram, 1999; Wilkinson, 1999). As Katz et al. (2000, p. 7) in a recent review stated:

> . . . historically, entrepreneurship researchers have studied founding processes, entrepreneurs as individuals, and high growth firms. Scholars in human

> resource management have been studying the management of employees for many years. However, very little serious academic work on human resource management was carried out in smaller firms.

This situation is difficult to explain at first glance because small businesses account for over 95 percent of all businesses in free market economies worldwide (Heneman et al., 2000). For instance, small businesses – defined as organizations with fewer than 100 employees – represent between 90–99 percent of all employers, create more jobs than the private sector, and account for about 25–40 percent of the economy in the United States and Canada (Industry Canada, 2008; Williamson et al., 2002). In fact, it is estimated that only 2 percent of organizations in the two countries have more than 100 employees (Industry Canada, 2008; Wiatrowski, 1994). This lack of research prompted one author to refer to employees in small businesses as "the invisible workforce" (Curran, 1988).

HRM AND PEAK-PERFORMING SMEs

Galbraith and Nkwente-Zamcho (2005), in a study of three production-oriented SMEs (two in the US and one in Mexico) found that particular HRM practices were associated with higher performance. SMEs making greater use of job specialization and changes in organizational structures as firms grew indicated higher levels of productivity.

Atkinson (2007) describes the operation of an award-winning auto dealership in British Columbia and these characteristics were consistent with effective HRM practices in large organizations. These included:

- a charter of work ethics;
- the articulation of 15 climate goals (e.g., managers must lead by example, staff are encouraged to share new ideas and express their points of view);
- in-house training;
- encouragement of further education;
- the involvement of workers' families;
- promoting from within.

Jenkins et al. (2006), using Formula 1 motoring teams, show how peak performance at individual, team partnership, and organizational levels can be achieved. Central concepts in their analysis include speed, simplicity, boundaryless behavior, team work, leadership at all levels, unwavering commitment, clear and consistent communications, continual drive for improvement, knowledge, and attention to detail. The challenge in Formula 1 racing is how to manage in a highly competitive, fast-changing, high-technology business environment. Does this sound familiar?

The *Globe and Mail* (2007), a major national Canadian newspaper, profiled 25 firms that were very successful and distilled some common elements among them. These included:

- encouraging employee input (e.g., contact with the top managers, use of shared daily huddles, quarterly meetings to discuss company issues);
- promotion from within;
- keeping employees in the loop.

EXECUTIVE SKILLS FOR SME SUCCESS

While not the only factor important for SME success, leadership skills must be considered. Martin et al. (2010) identified 12 "executive skills" associated with high performing individuals. These were:

1. response inhibition – thinking before acting; taking time to assess a situation;
2. working memory – holding information in memory when undertaking complex tasks;
3. emotional control – managing emotions in order to reach goals;
4. sustained attention – focusing on a task despite tiredness and boredom;
5. task initiation – starting tasks without delay;
6. planning and prioritization – creating a roadmap to reach one's goals;
7. organization – arranging tasks in a systematic way;
8. time management – estimating and allocating time effectively;
9. goal-directed persistence – following paths to goals until they are reached;
10. flexibility – revising plans in the face of barriers and setbacks;
11. meta-cognition – monitoring and changing oneself to better address issues;
12. stress tolerance – thriving in stressful conditions.

Murphy (2010) found that executive leaders used challenge – pushing staff to achieve higher results and connection – development of a strong emotional bond with staff – to get results. Murphy, based on high and low levels of both challenge and connection, identified four types of leaders:

- intimidators – high on challenge and low on connection;
- appeasers – low on challenge and high on connection;
- avoiders – low on both challenge and connection;
- hundred percenters – high on both challenge and connection.

His research, based on 17000 leaders, showed that managers doing well on economic performance measures were typically hundred percenters with a few intimidators. Hundred percenters also had low turnover as did appeasers. Hundred percenters also had more innovation. Hundred percenters set challenging goals, made employees accountable and monitored their progress, and offered employees guidance when mistakes occurred (also see Silverstein, 2010). Murphy also found that the use of employee references was a very useful way to hire potential hundred percenters.

GETTING MORE VALUE FROM INVESTMENTS IN STAFF TRAINING

Cermack and McGurk (2010) indicated that training programs have greater value for SMEs when the content addresses important business metrics or measures. Based on research undertaken with the Boys and Girls Clubs of America (BGCAs), they found that providing leadership training that focused on a small number of leadership measures previously found to be associated with BGCA local clubs' performance, produced revenues at least four times greater than the cost of the training. The local clubs receiving this training performed better than control locations on all measures of performance that were considered.

FOCUSING ON EMPLOYEES OR CUSTOMERS? WHICH IS MORE IMPORTANT?

The world's more productive organizations (Coffman & Gonzalez-Molina, 2002) know that their most valuable resource lies in their employees *and* customers. I remember some writing in the 1990s that advocated putting customers first; I then wrote an article advocating putting one's employees first and satisfied customers would follow (Burke et al., 2005). Coffman and Gonzalez-Molina give high priority to both but with employee engagement coming before satisfied customers and clients.

Coffman and Gonzalez-Molina's work stems from results from the Gallup Organization's surveys of millions of employees in thousands of business units from hundreds of companies in several countries. The upshot of sophisticated analyses of these data is the "Gallup Path" to productivity as follows:

1. select employees based on strengths and utilize their strengths;
2. strive for the right fit of employees to jobs and their responsibilities;
3. hire and develop great managers;
4. create engaged employees;
5. leading to engaged customers and clients;
6. resulting in sustained growth;
7. increases in profits;
8. increases in stock prices.

The last three stages on the path are important business outcomes. The first three stages are important antecedents of two critical intermediate stages – engaged employees and engaged customers and clients.

Organizations, to be successful, need to develop an emotional connection with both employees and customers – these individuals need to become engaged with the organization and its products and services. Organizational roles that utilize and stretch the talents of employees result in talented staff. Skilled managers that take talented staff and develop and reward them appropriately create committed and engaged employees. These committed and engaged employees emotionally connect with customers and clients and provide them with a higher quality of service or product. Engaged customers lead to sustained organizational performance that produces valued reputational and financial outcomes.

How does an organization – small, medium, or large – increase employee engagement? Coffman and Gonzalez-Molina offer the following evidence-based suggestions:

- provide clear performance expectations;
- provide necessary support and resource for successful task completion;
- encourage and facilitate employees' use of their strengths;
- provide recognition and reward for job performance;
- consider and learn about employees as individuals;
- support staff development;
- encourage employee input;
- provide a compelling organizational mission;
- managers clarify expectations for performance, reward good performance, and build on employee strengths;
- build a workplace culture of quality;

- encourage social contacts between employees;
- provide opportunities to learn.

Coffman and Gonzalez-Molina report differences between organizations high on employee engagement and those low on employee engagement. Organizations higher on employee engagement were:

- 54 percent higher on customer loyalty;
- 44 percent higher on employee retention;
- 50 percent higher on productivity;
- 33 percent higher on profitability;
- 50 percent higher on stock prices.

In addition, engaged employees were more likely to recommend the company as a place to work, commented that their jobs built on their strengths, were more satisfied with their pay and benefits, were more likely to spend their entire career with their organizations, and were more satisfied with their lives as a whole.

But too many employees are "phoning it in". Their aggregate data indicated that only 33 percent of employees were engaged, about 50 percent were not engaged, and a full 20 percent were actively disengaged. The ratio of engaged to unengaged employees in an organization is an important determinant of organizational success.

Customer/client engagement was the product of four emotional states:

- confidence – the firm could be trusted, the firm delivered on promises;
- integrity – the firm fixes any problems that might arise, the firm treats its customers fairly;
- pride – proud to be a customer of this firm, feel respected by the firm;
- passion – positive feelings or love for the firm.

Their data for customers, however, was also not very encouraging. They report that 21 percent of customers/clients were fully engaged, 21 percent were engaged, 30 percent were not engaged, and a fully 28 percent of customers and clients were actively disengaged.

The good news is that these figures for both employees and customers were shown to change over time. Firms – small, medium, and large – can take steps to increase levels of engagement in both employees and customers.

SMEs need to meet their customers at least once a year. Failing SMEs tend to spend more time in their research and development or in their search for capital and not enough time contacting customers. A company's products must meet a need in a customer or solve a customer problem: SMEs need to know what these needs and problems are. Customers should be involved in all aspects of an SME's business for sales and service and product distribution.

SMEs should consider these questions:

1. Who are their top ten customers?
2. Are these customers satisfied with your products or services?
3 Are you satisfied with your prices or fees?

HRM, MOJO, AND MASLOW

Conley (2007), a successful entrepreneur and small business owner/executive in the hotel and hospitality sector, describes how he used the writing of Abraham Maslow to build a philosophy of management and organization. Conley distilled the five levels of Maslow's hierarchy of needs motivation theory into three levels: survival, success, and transformation. Employees have survival needs (e.g., compensation), which then move on to the social/esteem needs for recognition (e.g., success), moving on to meaning/aspirational needs at the top of the pyramid (transformation) to create what Maslow termed a "self-actualized person". Conley illustrates, in concrete ways, how he used the Employee Pyramid consisting of Money, Recognition/Meaning and the Transformation Pyramid corresponding to Sustain, Succeed, Transform to build his successful business. Individual growth and health, and firm success and health, go hand in hand here.

In interesting ways, Conley's approach is consistent with that taken by Katzenbach (2000), who builds on Maslow's notions of levels and types of motivational needs, coming to the same conclusions on the well-springs of peak performance. Kets de Vries and Florent-Treacy (2002) reported similar findings in an interview study of leaders of successful global businesses. They found that peak performance was achieved through meeting three motivational need systems of employees: community, pleasure, and meaning. Community referred to attachment and affiliation that resulted from high levels of trust within the organization; to increase levels of trust, leaders had to be accessible, and keep employees fully informed. Pleasure referred to employees enjoying themselves at work, having fun, and being happy. Meaning occurred when employees saw their jobs as transcending their own needs, as contributing to society, and helping others to lead better – higher quality – lives.

MANAGING STAFF

New Hires

It has been shown that about half of new hires will fail within their first 18 months on the job. Most failures are the result of "attitude", not skills. By attitude I mean not fitting into your SME culture, not being open to learning and coaching, not being motivated, not having the kind of temperament that would make them successful in your SME. Skilled interviewers can improve their batting average in hiring for "attitude".

Motivating Staff When Money is Tight

Most managers still believe that money is the best motivator of employee performance. They believe that financial incentives are effective and make frequent use of them when they can. But what about when money is tight? Non-financial incentives also work and have been found to work well (Akerloff & Kranton, 2010). The three most common non-financial incentives in a survey conducted by McKinsey & Company (2009) were:

- praise and commendations from immediate managers;
- receiving attention from senior executives;
- opportunities to lead projects or task forces.

Some SMEs have cut back on their use of financial motivators. Almost 75 percent of organizations have altered their financial incentive programs. Employees receiving a satisfactory rating are motivated more strongly by non-financial incentives than financial ones. Non-financial incentives make staff feel their SME values them, cares about their well-being and supports their career development.

Staff Motivation and Retention

Managers of SMEs spend a lot of time thinking about human resource issues. Underperforming employees are a problem for SMEs. Here are some thoughts on addressing underperforming employees.

- Communicate more with staff (Twitter, use of video-conferencing across different sites, and bi-monthly newsletters) to indicate where the SME is heading and expectations of staff. Li (2010) illustrates how the new technologies can increase leadership effectiveness.

- Provide higher levels of pay than competitors and employee reward programs (e.g., merchandise prizes).
- Hold management teams/managers accountable for both performance and turnover.
- Use retention-related bonuses (e.g., career planning services) for employees staying two years or longer.
- Use psychological rewards (e.g., raise).
- Encourage former staff to return.
- Hold exit interviews to find out why employees are leaving.
- Organize staff social events.
- Obtain staff input on how to improve the business.
- Terminate the employment of underperforming staff.

Motivating Staff During Slow Periods

SMEs occasionally may have a slow period such as a few weeks over the summer when customers are away. How might managers and staff get motivated during this time? Here are some suggestions:

For managers:

- Involve staff in a special project focusing them on a common goal.
- Meet one on one with staff to get their ideas on improving operations.
- Provide staff with flexible hours such as shorter Fridays.
- Build staff morale and relationships by organizing a picnic or outing.
- Allow/encourage staff to switch jobs.
- Review performance of staff by highlighting/reviewing performance against earlier set objectives.

For staff:

- Learn some new skills, take a course.
- Do different tasks.
- Take a bit of time off to recharge your energy.
- Spend more time with your co-workers and your managers getting to know them and their expectations better.

SME LEGITIMACY

SMEs have more difficulty in recruiting high-quality staff than do larger organizations and this has been identified as an important factor in the success of organizations. SMEs often have the liabilities of both smallness and newness. SMEs have less influence on applicant norms and expectations, and SMEs are less connected to colleges and universities. But relatively few writers have dealt with employee recruitment in SMEs. Williamson (2000) developed a framework of SME recruitment with the notion of legitimacy as a central element. He defines legitimacy as follows: "a generalized perception or assumption held by job applicants that an organization is a desirable, proper, or appropriate employer given the systems of norms, values, beliefs, and definitions that exist within an industry" (p. 28). SMEs have an image problem, for some job seekers.

To be successful in recruiting high-quality employees, SMEs need to become more legitimate. They need to increase their ability to successfully recruit high-quality job applicants. Williamson (2000) offers the following suggestions:

- Increase applicant awareness by making their firm name more recognizable.
- Copy the recruitment practices of large firms by using their forms of job advertisements and recruitment practices.
- Make use of Internet technology.
- Develop relationships with colleges and universities.
- Attend job fairs, industry trade shows, and job placement centers.
- Develop HR policies used by larger organizations such as flexible hours, flexible career options, and incentive pay.

SMEs also face a challenge in overcoming the liability of newness and smallness in establishing their legitimacy, with not only potential employees but also clients and customers. Rutherford et al. (2009) found that entrepreneurs and managers of SMEs tell "legitimacy lies". That is, they often indicate that they are larger than they are, have been around longer than they have, have taken on similar projects when they have not, and can deliver a project or product by a certain date when they know they can't. Rutherford and his colleagues offer this advice to SMEs struggling to gain legitimacy:

- Make every effort to only pass on appropriate and accurate information.
- Carefully reflect on their personal and their SME's strengths and weaknesses; this will likely temper over-selling.
- Telling legitimacy lies may undermine the character of the manager and the SME though bringing in short-term benefits.
- Create organizational support for ethical decision-making.

GROWING AN SME

Rottenberg and O'Meara (2010) identify seven ways to help SMEs to grow. These are:

1. Use your own life experiences. What products, services or issues can you improve upon?
2. Get information from and the perspective of customers and outsiders.
3. Zoom out – consider events in the wider environment of your business.
4. Zoom in – see which business sub-unit or product might be developed into a larger opportunity.
5. Borrow good ideas from others.
6. Get information from within your SME.
7. Identify barriers to product or service purchase and attempt to overcome them.

Spence (2010a) writes that SMEs go through two phases of growth. The first phase relies on the owner's skills, resources, and vision. Eventually SMEs will plateau or hit a wall. This situation leads to the second phase of SME growth. There are several possible growth strategies that might exist. But all rely on the business owner once again identifying challenges ahead and addressing them by learning from a range of sources. Successful SME growth is more likely to occur among SME executives who are life-long learners.

SMEs also need to know when to "stop" things or people that are no longer working or perhaps never did. This includes products, features of products, employees, meetings, reports, investors, processes, HR practices (e.g., forms new employees fill out), and software codes (e.g., clean up and streamline). SMEs need a person who spends part of their time "stopping" things or people.

SMEs also need to take time to stop "dysfunctional momentum". Barton and Sutcliffe (2010) discuss the importance of interruptions or pauses – an opportunity to stop momentum – as managers and their teams work through achieving an original goal without stopping to reconsider their goal or processes when obvious warning signs exist. Stopping dysfunctional momentum through pauses can avoid miscues and later failure. Pauses allow SMEs to identify potential or growing problems. Managers of SMEs need to understand that they may be unable to fully grasp their situation by themselves. And they then need to get additional information – during a pause – to re-examine their situation. Employees need to be encouraged to express concerns. Managers need to be skeptical of "experts". Managers need to solicit differing viewpoints. Finally, managers need to be open to changing direction should such a need arise.

SMEs in the developed world need to look at BRIC countries (Brazil, Russia, India, China) as a source of growth. BRIC countries, according to a recent McKinsey report (McKinsey & Company, 2010a) will become a source of capital, talent, and innovation. More BRIC countries now appear on the Fortune 500 and more are making patent applications.

Leaders of SMEs need to be more active in looking for international opportunities by making cold calls to potential clients, traveling to other countries to interact with potential clients, and being flexible enough to change a business plan as opportunities develop in different countries.

REPUTATION BUILDING AND HRM

A positive SME reputation can be significant to the success of an SME. Goldberg et al. (2003) review four strategies for developing a favorable corporate reputation: dynamic exploitation of existing assets, development of core competencies, image management, and strategic alliances. These strategies have either an internal or external focus or focus on the short term or the long term:

- Dynamic exploitation of existing assets – management exploits existing internal resources to quickly take advantage of market opportunities, focusing on short-term objectives and rapid growth.
- Develop core competencies – management adopts a long-term perspective making large investments in internal capabilities, building a strong system of skilled human resources, experienced managers and leading technologies, then developing a favorable reputation through marketing of high-quality products having high value and the provision of good service.
- Image management – management undertakes an externally focused strategy based on short-term use of symbols linked with successful firms or "borrowing/renting" the reputation of more established firms.
- Strategic alliances – managers develop alliances in which they can trade on the strong name of a partner or by linking up with high-profile customers who then connect the SME with a guaranteed market.

They undertook case studies of three Israeli software companies, and found that they differed not only in reputation-building strategies undertaken but their success in reputation building and success in the market place. These authors suggest that SMEs should ideally use each of the four strategies.

Fischer and Reuber (2007) offer some thoughts on how new SMEs develop reputations among internal and external stakeholders. Reputations of new SMEs begin to be formed based on signals, both positive and negative, they send. Based on these signals, insiders and outsiders begin to form beliefs about the attributes of the SME. These signals include the founder's track record, high-status business partners, obtaining designations (e.g., ISO 9000) or other certifications, quality of direct contact and experience with the SME, financial reports, media coverage, and word of mouth. Thus, SME reputation has several components, and internal and external stakeholders likely use different components in their assessment and may come to different conclusions about an SME's reputation. SME reputations exist at an overall/aggregate level and how the SME compares with other SMEs in its industry. To build a favorable SME reputation, SMEs need to send coherent, integrated, credible, and consistent signals.

SMEs also need to maintain their reputations in the face of a variety of potential threats to firm reputations. Company reputation matters today more than ever before. In addition, company reputations can be damaged in an instant by negative publicity. All it takes is one disgruntled client or customer to make his or her comments available on the Internet. More SMEs are now taking responsibility for reputation management (Beal & Strauss, 2006). This starts with a review of what people are saying about their SMEs on the Internet. SMEs don't have the luxury of large marketing and PR budgets to support their efforts at reputation management. SMEs should not panic if they get a negative review if the majority of their reviews are positive. SMEs should also try to identify unhappy clients or customers before they finish their transaction with the SME and try to "fix" the problem then and there. Individuals should respond to negative reviews with honesty, openness, and consistency, apologizing for an incident. Explaining how it happened, why this was not the typical way customers are treated, and what steps were being taken to make sure it doesn't happen again, are important. In addition, asking the client or customers for another chance to provide a positive experience is critical. It is important to have the client or customer leave with a somewhat positive impression of the firm. Asking satisfied clients or customers to provide their reviews is also helpful. But satisfied clients and customers are much less motivated to do this than are unhappy clients and customers.

Networking Dos and Don'ts

Various writers have championed the benefits of networking over the past two decades as a way of getting known, obtaining business, and developing an SME reputation. Zack (2010), in an easy to read practical book starts with the premise that traditional networking techniques do not work as well as their proponents suggest. She suggests that the following techniques *fall short*:

- Meet as many people as you possibly can at a given event or gathering.
- Get as many of your business cards into the hands of others as you can.
- Attend as many networking events as you possibly can since each may be an opportunity.
- Always have any meals you may be eating with someone else.
- It helps to have a drink or two to loosen up before meeting others.

Zack indicates why these networking approaches *do not* work very well and offers other more promising techniques.

CULTURES OF ENTITLEMENT

First some facts: 77 percent of managers believe their employees are not giving 100 percent and 72 percent of employees admit that they are not giving 100 percent (Murphy, 2010).

SMEs need, and employees want, to contribute. Entitled employees do not feel accountable for performance, do not feel personally responsible for the SME's success or failure or personal ownership over their jobs and results, and they are more likely to resist change. Entitled employees are typically young, likely long-serving, and working in a culture that treats them like children. I have also observed that family members sometimes feel entitled.

How can SMEs reduce a culture of entitlement? Managers need to meet with employees individually and encourage a greater sense of accountability and of responsibility and ownership. Managers need to become coaches and teachers more than parents. When your manager talks with you, do you learn something? Employees need to develop a more realistic view of the competitive business world and why doing a great job matters.

Nielson and Peterson (2009) believe that too much work in organizations is "fake" work rather than "real" work. Fake work includes pointless meetings, purposeless projects, meaningless paperwork, and useless e-mails. They write that about half the work individuals do each day is fake work, based on a survey of over 100 000 employees from 300 US organizations. Consider these findings:

- 87 percent are regularly unsatisfied with the results of their work;
- 70 percent duplicate efforts because of lack of coordination with others in their work unit;
- 68 percent of work unit goals are not translated into real work tasks;
- 56 percent do not know whether what they do contributes to their company's goals;
- 53 percent believe that at least half the work they do in a day doesn't accomplish anything.

Nielson and Peterson recommend the following for managers and their employees:

1. Provide clear short-term and long-term organizational needs and goals.
2. Clarify roles in work units and how each role contributes to work unit goals.
3. Encourage employees to ask questions about reasons for assignments and how these contribute to organizational goals.
4. Encourage employees to question tasks that may have little value and ask for more real work.
5. Only use meetings if they have a real work benefit.
6. Look for ways of doing things better.
7. Know what others in your work unit are doing and encourage people to help each other.
8. Clarify company goals and how your projects support them.
9. Communicate company goals to all members of your work unit.
10. Cut red tape as much as you can.
11. Talk to staff about "fake" work and barriers to "real" work.
12. Give your staff the freedom to do their work in their own way.
13. Develop rewards supportive of doing "real" work.

DOING MORE WITH LESS

SMEs and business start-ups usually face a squeeze on resources, making it important for them to do more with less. Spence (2010b) offers the following possibilities:

- Integrate programs and marketing for greater impact.
- Use external people – former employees, suppliers, customers – as goodwill ambassadors.
- Enlist customers in a cause you care about.
- Welcome newcomers to the firm – perhaps by a personal letter.
- Tell your success story at every opportunity.
- Think about how every dollar is spent by making itemized lists of expenses.

THE "DARK SIDE" OF CUSTOMER SERVICE

The service sector has grown in both size and economic importance over the past two decades. It is commonly assumed that providing a high-quality product or service to clients and customers is vital to success. Yet there is considerable evidence that customer service is too often falling short. Customer complaints have been identified as an important source of SME learning, with the successful dealing with complaints associated with customer satisfaction and loyalty. Suggestions have been offered to help SMEs deal with customer complaints and with poor service. Yet customer complaints are often concealed by both front-line service employees and their managers (Harris & Ogbonna, 2010).

Harris and Ogbonna (2010) interviewed managers, supervisors, and front-line service employees of UK general retailers/supermarkets and found the concealment of customer complaints to be widespread. Front-line workers concealed complaints by misleading customers, resolving the complaint without reporting it, hiding recorded complaints, and falsifying the recorded complaint. Supervisors and managers concealed complaints by resolving the complaint but not recording it, hiding recorded complaints, not recording complaints, and disregarding "minor" complaints. Causes or motivations for hiding complaints were: personal protection, seeing the customer as unpleasant, serial complainers, work alienation, potential personal gain, unfairness of the complaint, making more work, and a shortage of time. The concealment of customer complaints is a rational act on the part of front-line employees and their managers that unfortunately reduces both the levels of customer service and SME performance.

They suggest the following practical recommendations. SMEs need to examine their rules and regulations for handling customer complaints. Rewards and careers costs limit the reporting of customer complaints. Incentives for such reporting must be identified and made available. Instead, give rewards for successful resolution of complaints. All staff must be made aware of the negative outcomes for the SME as well as for both employees and customers. Managers need to develop ways of reducing those factors that increase the concealment of complaints. Employees and managers could be given a listing of common complaints and how best to deal with them. Issues of complaint concealment should be covered in new employee orientations and all training sessions.

FAMILY VERSUS NON-FAMILY SMEs

Family firms, on average, survive longer than non-family firms. But succession processes can undermine the longevity of family firms (Landes, 2006).

There are likely to be difficulties for the successor and the succession process if the founder leaves but still maintains influence on the SME, including:

- a focus on wealth preservation;
- predecessors' involvement post-succession;
- familiness – an agreement of values and goals;
- commitment to succession;
- political concerns.

Family businesses (FBs) are widespread; 80 to 90 percent of all businesses in the US are family-dominated, generating half of all employment and half of GDP. FBs face unique HRM challenges (King et al., 2001). An important issue for couples that work together in FBs is the effect of the business, and their home life, on the relationship of the couple. Danes and her colleagues (Danes et al., 1999; Danes & Olson, 2003; Danes & Morgan, 2004; Danes, 2006) have studied the way these factors create tensions within FB couples.

Another issue for family business is succession – the process when managerial control of the business is transferred from one generation to the next. This process includes time before and after the actual transition.

Family businesses are, unfortunately, very dependent on a single individual in matters of decision-making, influence, and control (Feltham et al., 2005). This creates difficulty in leadership succession, the use of professional HRM practices, and the development of employees. In addition, combining family members and management within SMEs adds another layer of complexity (Fritz, 2001; Kets de Vries, 1993). Many successions in FBs go badly; 70 percent of FBs fail to survive through the second generation and 90 percent through the third generation (Kets de Vries, 1999).

Succession is not necessarily the major cause of these failures however. The following have been shown to impact FB succession: the development of a formal succession plan, the interrelationships between family members, power and politics, and discrimination against daughters and women more generally.

FB owners often prefer not to address succession, however. Choosing a successor among one's children can be problematic, leading to competition, sabotage, and ill will. The succession process seems to work best when a formal plan for succession has been developed and the family members, over time, have created a set of shared values about the firm and its purposes.

Colleges and universities have attempted to be of service to FBs by creating and sponsoring family business programs (FBPs). To be of value, FBPs must address both family and business needs. Kaplan et al. (2000) undertook the first evaluation of university-sponsored FBPs. Data were collected from both program directors and members using surveys. The most valuable part of the FBPs was the sharing of experiences and gaining access to expert advice on both family and business issues. Dialogue, interaction, and information from their peers was highly valued. Using workshop formats was encouraged as was the development of mentoring programs. Formal presentation of content using lectures and the holding of brief breakfast meetings, for example, was seen as much less useful to FBP members.

Succession Planning

SME owners need to plan for succession. Succession planning typically involves the smooth transfer of a business from one generation to another in a way that meets the needs of the owner.

A key question is the value of the business. The Canadian Federation of Independent Business undertook a survey that found that two-thirds of business owners that responded planned to retire by 2005 but only 10 percent had a written succession plan in place.

A succession plan lays out the transfer of ownership and control of an SME to avoid succession issues. An effective succession plan also works to minimize taxes, plans for the owner's and family's future needs, protects the business owner's assets in the event of death or disability, and develops a planning strategy for the SME's future.

Succession planning should be part of an SME's business plan right from the start. But this rarely happens as the owner/manager is occupied with staying afloat. The founder/owner needs to begin serious thinking about the succession process no later than the five-year point. Only 10 percent of SMEs have written succession plans. About one-third say they have a succession plan but it is not written down.

The founder's children typically work or have worked for the SME. Some founders prefer that their children work for a different firm not run by their parents to obtain experience as an employee elsewhere.

Eighty-five percent of founders believe that their children will take over when they die or retire. But succession is not guaranteed. Only 30 percent of firms survive to the second generation, according to the Family Business Institute in the US. Most founders are hands-on and are not good at teaching their children. In addition, children of founders likely had access to more financial security than did the founder and might not be as "hungry" as the founder. It is also difficult to manage siblings that were taught and had perhaps been treated as equals. Sometimes siblings need to be fired.

Recommendations include: developing communication channels so issues about the future can be discussed; and giving children work experience both inside and outside the SME. Working for another firm is good preparation for entering their parents' business.

HRM AND LEGAL ISSUES

Small businesses sometimes lack HR resources, policies, and procedures for dealing with particular legal issues. Some SMEs may even be unaware of the relevant laws. Ignorance, however, is no defense.

In Toronto, former employers had to pay $20 000 to a cancer patient in a discrimination suit and undergo human rights training (see Hui, 2010). Elsa Torrejon was diagnosed with breast cancer, and upon hearing this, her employers asked her to provide written notice of when she would leave for treatment. She provided this believing it indicated an indefinite leave. Torrejon's employers took this as her resignation and asked her not to return. The employers indicated that they were unaware that they had to accommodate ill employees under the Ontario Human Rights Code.

OCCUPATIONAL HEALTH AND SAFETY IN SMEs

Relatively little research has been undertaken on the role of HRM practices and occupational health and safety in SMEs. Scholars have, however, examined rates of accidents, injuries, fatalities, and illness in both large organizations and SMEs (Eakin & MacEachern, 1998; Hasle et al., 2009;

Walters, 2004). Consider the following findings (Hasle & Limborg, 2006; Sorensen et al., 2007):

- SMEs experience higher accident and injury rates than do larger organizations.
- Injury and accident rates have fallen more slowly in SMEs than in larger organizations.
- SMEs have a higher fatality rate than do larger firms.
- SMEs are more likely to under-report accidents and injuries than are larger firms.
- Smaller SMEs fare more poorly in these areas than do larger SMEs.

Why do SMEs have higher rates of accidents, injuries, fatalities, and illnesses than larger firms? Some reasons for this include less investment in occupational health and safety, working in more hazardous environments, a less formal approach to management, poor management of risk, and the critical role of the owner/manager of the SME in establishing a safety culture (Hasle et al., 2009; Walters, 2004). Owners of SMEs see safety as an individual problem once necessary safety equipment is provided to them. SMEs do not have the resources to recognize risks and associated likelihood of injury.

Clarke and Flitcroft (2008), in a UK study involving both interviews and questionnaire surveys of SME owner/managers reported the following barriers to health and safety in their firms: economic pressures, lack of communication and support, and excessive government regulations. Yet almost all SMEs had some sort of health and safety system in place. It seems that the task facing managers in SMEs is to embed these systems into a functioning health and safety culture.

At a different level, Jorgensen et al. (2010) describe the application of a tool readily available for use in SMEs to reduce accidents and injury. They use an occupational risk model (ORM) developed in the Netherlands and apply it to three occupations in Denmark (e.g., carpenters, caretakers). The ORM can be applied to any job and these authors provide a detailed outline of how the ORM can be used.

Finally, Hasle et al. (2010) show how trained accountants can serve as occupational health and safety intermediaries to their SME employers. They found that their sample of trained accountants provided advice to their employing SMEs and the accountants felt positive about their contributions and experiences. The accountants did, however, find that since occupational health and safety was only a small part of their role they did not contribute as much as they might have and, in addition, they felt that having more health and safety information and better support from the

SME leadership would have helped them make an even greater contribution here.

HRM AND OTHER PERFORMANCE-RELATED PRACTICES

There is increasing evidence that SMEs that adopt sound HRM practices are more likely to be aware of and adopt other organizational practices that can increase productivity.

HRM, TQM, and SME Performance

A total quality management (TQM) strategy emphasizes customer satisfaction, quality management, just-in-time production, continuing improvement processes, and solving problems at their source before they mushroom. An effective TQM initiative rests on employee involvement and empowerment in the workplace.

Chandler and McEvoy (2000) examined the relationship of SMEs' adoption of a TQM strategy and performance, with training and use of group-based incentive systems as moderators of this relationship. They collected data from 66 US small manufacturing firms. Although TQM, training, and use of group-based pay stems had no association with firm performance (earnings), use of TQM and training, and use of TQM and group-based incentive pay, were both significantly related to firm performance.

SMEs, HRM, and the Balanced Scorecard

Kaplan and Norton (1992) introduced the notion of a Balanced Scorecard (BSC) following a study of the success of 12 companies. They concluded that financial measures alone were inadequate measures of firm performance. The BSC included four perspectives: financial, customer, operational efficiency and processes, and learning and growth (Kaplan & Norton, 1996a). Key success factors in each of the four perspectives are balanced between long term and short term, as well as including internal and external factors that contribute to business strategy. A BSC helps a firm link its mission to business strategy and then translates strategy to operational objectives and measures (Kaplan & Norton, 1993, 1996a, 1996b, 1996c).

BSCs are commonly used in large organizations but rarely used in SMEs. There is considerable evidence that the use of a BSC can improve firm performance. Gumbus and her colleagues (Gumbus & Lyons, 2002;

Gumbus & Johnson, 2003; Gumbus et al., 2003; Gumbus & Lussier, 2006), using case studies of SMEs, showed how use of BSCs contributed to success of these firms. They provide examples of these firms' BSCs, and indicated how SMEs can develop their own. BSCs promote growth, support the measurement of performance, provide focus on key indicators of performance, create measures aligned to goals, clarify goals, and assign accountabilities for achieving these goals.

Underlying these initiatives is the notion of those at the top levels of an SME to share the burden for performance and success. This involves, as a first step, making employees of an SME aware of the financial performance of the SME – a need for greater transparency. Making staff aware of the SME's priorities and sharing the burden of performance with them not only lightens the load at the top but is more likely to achieve desired results.

HRM and the Adoption of Technology in SMEs

In order to survive, organizations of all sizes need to adopt the latest technology related to their operations. What factors influence technology adoption? It has been shown that the behaviors of senior managers are important in this regard. Gagnon et al. (2000) examined senior managers' behaviors in SMEs and the decision to adopt new technology. Data were collected from 164 senior managers using questionnaires along with interviews of another 54 senior SME managers. About half behaved like administrators and half as entrepreneurs. SME managers who behaved like administrators had more successful technology adoptions. Administrative behaviors were more long term, made more use of teams in planning and implementing, and included more planning for needed resources.

SME Orientation versus Entrepreneurial Orientation and Firm Performance

Runyan et al. (2008), in a sample of 267 small business owners, examined the relationship of an entrepreneurial orientation (EO), and a small business orientation (SBO), and firm financial performance (compared with last year, compared with major competition, compared with similar firms in the industry). EO was measured by a sample of these items: "I stongly favor high-risk projects with chances of very high return" and "The changes in product or service lines have been quite dramatic" while SBO was measured by a sample of these items: "I established this business because it better fit my personal life than working for someone else" and "I consider this business to be an extension of my personality". They found that SBO was related to firm performance but EO was unrelated to firm performance. But they also observed that EO was related to firm performance in firms that were less than ten years old while SBO was related to firm performance among firms 20 years or older. They conclude that, for SME continuance, the more emotionally attached the owner is to the business and the more committed the owner is to balance work and family life, the more successful the owner. And this transition, from EO to SBO, may be a natural transition in the experiences of SME owners.

Protecting and Backing Up Information

Backing up and protecting important and/or sensitive information should be a high priority for SMEs – and all organizations. A Symantec 2010 SMB Information Protection report surveyed 2152 executives from 28 countries. Only 7 percent of Canadian respondents (n = 192) reported losing confidential data in the past versus a global average of 42 percent. Top Canadian losses due to cyber attacks were work down-time, theft of corporate data, and loss of personal information. For 2010, 78 percent of Canadian firms said that backup and recovery would be their top IT priority with 77 percent citing disaster recovery and 74 percent security.

SMEs and the Adoption of ISO 9000

Briscoe et al. (2005) examined the benefits and barriers to ISO 9000 (International Standards Organization) certification among SME manufacturers. They collected data from 275 SMEs in the manufacturing sector. They found that SMEs in manufacturing can successfully implement ISO 9000 programs if they internalize central ISO practices in managing their quality systems. But resource shortages make it more difficult for SMEs to achieve ISO 9000 certification (lack of time, limited training funds, lack of quality know-how).

Firms of all sizes need to deliver high-quality products and services to satisfy customer and client demands and compete successfully. ISO 9000 goals include: meeting customer quality requirements, meeting regulatory requirements, increasing customer satisfaction, continual improvement in performance in meeting these goals. Organizations seek ISO 9000 certification mainly for external reasons, in order to meet customer or government regulations. And customers would rather buy products or services from firms that are ISO 9000 certified. Thus, SMEs should be encouraged to seek this certification.

Successfully achieving this certification depends on several factors: a ready firm culture, substantial pre-implementation analysis, and the firm's ability to internalize and enact key ISO quality practices. And not all ISO 9000 implementation efforts show benefits. Briscoe et al. identified some characteristics common to successful SMEs: the development of a quality culture, ensuring that the necessary support structures were in place, implementing ISO 9000, and making ISO practices a part of the SMEs daily quality routines.

Use of the Web 2.0

It is increasingly important for SMEs to use the Internet to control both one's individual and SME firm brand. Funk (2009) indicates how SMEs can use online communication to increase SME visibility and reputation. He provides a case example of how Lake Champlain Chocolates of Vermont took this opportunity. Dushinski (2009) provides examples of how SMEs can use Web 2.0 to increase their marketing efforts and make them more successful.

For SMEs, use of the Internet opens up a cost-effective way of getting their companies out to customers. Social media tools (blogs, Facebook, Twitter) allow SMEs to engage in dialogue with customers. And customers can also talk with each other. SMEs can get a better understanding of what their customers want. A good strategy is to use social media to make information available to customers rather than try to sell directly to customers. And the use of LinkedIn is critical for presenting SMEs in a business-to-business environment.

McKinsey & Company (2010b) has found that word-of-mouth (WOM) has the largest impact when consumers decide which products to consider and when they are actively evaluating products in developed markets – about 20 percent see WOM as the single most important factor influencing them. This figure rises to 46 percent in developing markets.

Monitoring the Web also allows SMEs to find useful data that helps them find out what their competitors are doing and permits comparisons with other firms. This information can help identify future trends and predict what is going to happen down the road.

HRM AND THE DEVELOPMENT OF STRATEGIC PARTNERSHIPS

SMEs can develop strategic partnerships with large organizations. This is more likely to take place when the HRM capabilities of the SME are more sophisticated and thus more likely to be in line with the HRM practices of the large organization. These SMEs are more likely to be seen as part of the value chain of large organizations (e.g., a parts supplier to a large automaker, a consumer products supplier to Wal-Mart).

SMEs have often successfully developed relationships with social causes and high-profile individuals or events to promote themselves. For these to work out well, Southcott (2010) believes that SMEs need to connect with partners in deep and meaningful ways. She offers the following guidance:

- The partners must be complementary.
- The SME believes in what the partner is supporting.
- The partner shares similar values and world view with the SME.
- Both parties would benefit from the relationship.
- The relationship can be either simple and straightforward or more complex and still have benefits for both parties.

HRM AND THE MANAGEMENT OF CHANGE

Winn (2000), using a detailed case study of Kacey Fine Furniture in Colorado, showed how HRM practices helped this SME successfully manage significant change in its business environment. Key features of its HRM strategy were employee involvement, open-book management, and working to bring about a significant change in its culture.

When a Large Firm Acquires an SME

It occasionally happens that an SME (e.g., Stoneyfield Farm, Honest Tea) will either be acquired by a very large multinational organization or have a substantial investment made in it by a very large organization (e.g., Group Danone, Coca-Cola). Olson (2010) discusses challenges facing both the SME and the larger owners or financial investors. The key advice is for the SME to maintain operating as it was before the acquisition or investment. It is critical for the SME – and the larger owners/investors – to jointly develop a document that spells out their working relationship. The SME needs to retain its culture and be able to make independent decisions. Both sides are more likely to benefit from this document.

Learning from Bankruptcy

Bitti (2010) chronicles the journey of Pazazz, a printing company located in Montreal that had 18 years of growth but filed for bankruptcy on 8 March 2010 because of the effects of the worldwide economic recession on its business. The firm came out of bankruptcy on 18 May 2010. The firm's founder and CEO, Warren Werbitt, got through this transition by seeking outside advice, having a good relationship with his bank, having staff meetings in which he openly laid out the cuts in wages needed from everyone, and eventual acceptance of the reality of his situation but remaining optimistic that Pazazz would succeed. And it has so far.

BEING AN EXCEPTIONAL SME

It is not all that hard for a SME to be exceptional. All it takes to be exceptional is to have people who know what it takes to provide outstanding company service. This makes the hiring of such people critical. In addition, your people need to know what your SME is trying to accomplish.

Bell and Patterson (2009) provide practical suggestions on how an SME might distinguish itself from its competitors in providing high-quality customer service. They suggest the following:

- Invite a customer to an important staff meeting.
- Create special learning experiences for customers.
- Send a hand-written thank you note to an important customer.
- Send customers greetings cards on all important holidays.
- Provide a parking space for an important customer.
- Provide discounts to loyal customers.
- Remember a customer's birthday (or other significant event) in a personal way.
- Send customers a magazine subscription they value or a book.
- Invite customers to your workplace or home for a BBQ.
- Provide tickets to an event valued by a customer.
- Name a conference room in your building after a very important customer.
- Nominate your customer for a special award (e.g., a green workplace, excellence in diversity).

IMPORTANT ISSUES FACING MANAGERS/ ENTREPRENEURS AND SMEs

Given the nature of individuals and managers in SMEs, their personalities and motivations, and the historical nature of work and workplaces, managers in SMEs may face issues that have a unique twist to them.

Work and Family

Work and family may get intertwined to a greater extent in SMEs than in large organizations (Jennings & McDougald, 2007; Kim & Ling, 2001) Many SMEs are family businesses. Women often start their own ventures to better integrate work and family. Owners and managers of SMEs often work long hours – not unique to SMEs, however. SMEs do not have the resources to provide policies and practices allowing greater flexibility to their employees (e.g., flex-time, work at home).

Shelton et al. (2008) investigated the impact of role demands, difficulty in managing work–family conflict and business performance among minority entrepreneurs (African American, Mexican American, Korean American) and White business owners. Ethnic minorities tended to indicate more family role demands and more work demands than did Whites. In addition, difficulties in managing work–family conflict were associated with reduced business performance. Four measures of business performance were included: self-rated perceptions of success, success in reaching personal goals, and two financial measures – gross income of business and frequency of cash flow problems.

Niehm et al. (2009) identified 14 strategies employed by household and SME managers to cope with overlapping work and family demands. Comparing surviving and non-surviving family SMEs, both tended to bring household work to their businesses when times were demanding and hectic, and took care of family responsibilities while at their businesses. In non-surviving family SMEs, managers more often took work home; work intruded more into family for managers in these SMEs. Managers of surviving family SMEs were more likely to hire temporary help for either their SME or home, and were less likely to ask for unpaid help with their businesses. Managers of surviving family SMEs also spent more time on family matters and (unfortunately) spent less time sleeping in order to assist their SMEs.

Occupational Stress in SMEs

Some occupational stressors are common to both large firms and SMEs. These include long work hours, work–family conflict, poor supervision, role ambiguity and abusive colleagues. SMEs may also face some unique occupational stressors such as threats to survival because of changes in their economic environment, high levels of staff turnover, and difficulty in recruiting high-quality staff.

Villaneuva and Djurkovic (2009) examined the relationship of a composite measure of job pressures (a composite of six occupational stressors and work outcomes in a sample of 158 employees working in four SMEs. Job pressures included role ambiguity and lack of control over one's job. Employees indicating greater job pressures also reported less job satisfaction, lack of commitment, lower firm support, and greater intention to quit. Firm support mediated the effects of job pressures on intentions to quit; this relationship was absent among employees receiving higher levels of firm support.

Reducing all job pressures or stressors is unrealistic but some job stressors and pressures can be reduced. Providing employees with more control over their jobs, more clarity on job responsibilities and goals, offering more appreciation for jobs well done, and higher levels of firm support have been shown to be useful in this regard.

SMEs and Entrepreneurship for Women

A greater proportion of men than women are entrepreneurs, start SMEs, and then manage them (Langowitz & Minniti, 2007). Using data from a large sample of male and female respondents from 17 countries, Langowitz and Minniti show that subjective perceptual variables account for this difference. Women see both themselves and the entrepreneurial environment in a less favorable way in all 17 countries and this existed independent of their levels of entrepreneurial motivation. And the research evidence indicates that women have disadvantages (Fielden et al., 2000, 2006; Loscocco et al., 1991) as do other minority group members (Sullivan, 2007). Shelton (2006) indicates that work–family conflict is common among female entrepreneurs and has an impact on the SME performance.

But this picture seems to be slowly changing. Women are creating new businesses at a faster rate than men, and women's SMEs have been shown to have a higher survivor rate than men's. More women are leaving large organizations to either start their own businesses or to work in already established SMEs (Buttner & Moore, 1997; Heilman & Chen, 2003; Moore & Buttner, 1997). More women than men are graduating from high schools, obtaining undergraduate university degrees, and an increasing number of women are entering the professions (business, law, engineering, architecture). These highly trained, motivated, skilled, and ambitious women are now more likely to start their own ventures should they become frustrated with working in large organizations. Some governments have offered training in the start-up of new businesses targeted specifically to women (Moore, 2003).

Fielden and Davidson (2005), in an edited collection, examined women's motivations for entering SME ownership, women's characteristics, their career paths, constraints faced, conditions associated with their success, and government initiatives targeted at women in a number of countries. Fielden and Davidson (2010) followed up their 2005 volume with a description of women's global small business ownership and successful women entrepreneurs in 17 countries. Women small business owners are making an important contribution to the economic growth of both developing and emerging markets. Yet barriers facing women entrepreneurs and SME owners still exist. Women are less likely than men to plan to start an SME, to know an entrepreneur or SME owner, to identify viable business opportunities, or to believe they have the skills required to start an SME. Yet women entrepreneurs and SME owners seem to do better at managing financial resources.

Women's SMEs tend to be smaller, concentrated in the service sector, are part-time and operate from their homes, have lower levels of financial investment, less business support, and smaller business networks. Using financial indicators, women-owned and -operated SMEs "perform" at lower levels than do those operated by men (Watson, 2002). Women business owners, more than their men counterparts, have other important goals (e.g., autonomy, lifestyle choices). For women in several countries, SME creation and ownership is seen as a survival strategy providing personal and some financial freedom (also see Walker & Brown, 2004). The Fielden and Davidson (2010) collection focuses on how women overcome their disadvantages and are now managing successful SMEs.

Gupta at al. (2009) studied the role of gender stereotypes in perceptions of entrepreneurs and intention to become entrepreneurs in three countries (Turkey, India, and the US). Their findings were similar in all three countries. First, entrepreneurship was perceived as a masculine field and that entrepreneurs have masculine characteristics. Second, more women than men see women as having entrepreneurial characteristics. Third, women and men had similar levels of entrepreneurial motivation. Fourth, women and men seeing themselves as having more masculine characteristics had higher entrepreneurial motivations. Fifth, women may not pursue entrepreneurial interests because they do not see them as consistent with feminine characteristics. Thus, women may need additional support to overcome these perceptual barriers.

The Rotman School of Management at the University of Toronto has developed a course for women entrepreneurs. Rotman has created an intensive short program for established women entrepreneurs. This is a six-week course including both theory of entrepreneurship and entrepreneurial behavior and counseling from an established entrepreneur. Weekly sessions address the following topics:

1. negotiating for success;
2. growth strategies; the importance of finding a capable No. 2;

3. leading with authority; includes self-assessments addressing the questions of who you are and what you need to change;
4. business value; selling the SME; planning your exit early;
5. technology and demographics; working with different generations; leveraging technology;
6. action planning – developing a plan for their next stage.

Helping Women Entrepreneurs and SME Managers Make Connections

Women entrepreneurs and SME owners have a harder time than their male colleagues in getting government contracts and being a supplier to contracting agents in other sectors. An organization called WEConnect was started to connect women with these contract opportunities so they can grow their businesses. WEConnect was started in the US about 15 years ago by the Women Business Enterprise National Council. Female entrepreneurs wanting to join must prove that: the SME is at least 51 percent owned by women, women manage and control the business, the company is established, successful, growth-oriented and can supply products or services in any sector, the company has the capacity to sell to large organizations, it is a business-to-business operation not a business-to-customer operation, and it has at least $100 000 in sales to qualify. Members of WEConnect can form strategic alliances with other members when bidding on larger or more complex projects.

GOVERNMENT POLICIES SUPPORTING ENTREPRENEURSHIP AND SMEs

Minniti (2008) introduced a special issue on the role of government policy on entrepreneurial activity for entrepreneurship theory and practice. Government policies influence the institutional environment in which individuals decide or choose to start their own businesses. There is considerable debate on which government policies spur entrepreneurship and SME creation, however. Several levels of government – local, national, and international – have attempted to foster entrepreneurship and new venture creation. It seems to be clear that government policies targeting these activities will be different in different areas and regions of a country. Government policies include making financing more readily available, changing the tax structure, and embarking on both local and national interventions.

It has been observed that the relatively small country of Israel, surrounded by hostile neighbors and low in natural resources, produces more entrepreneurs and successful SMEs per capita than any other country in the world. How do they achieve this? Senor and Singer (2009) suggest several reasons for this. These include: personal factors such as a "can do" spirit (chutzpah) and high levels of education (human capital); cultural values of questioning authority and trying, failing but learning from failures, of leadership, and given the challenges Israel faced from its beginning, understanding risk management; a country history of adversity requiring inventiveness, resilience and early adoption of potentially useful ideas, services, and products; and country policies supporting immigration, compulsory military service, and research and development (R&D). Israel has the highest concentration of engineers and R&D spending of any country in the world. And a nation of immigrants is likely to be a nation of entrepreneurs and new business start-ups. And because Israel is a relatively small country, it has developed industrial clusters, a cluster being a geographic concentration of interconnected institutions in a specific and common field (business, government, universities). Israel fosters such clusters. Other countries also have clusters that have developed successfully, including Silicon Valley, Route 126 outside of Boston, the wine region north of San Francisco, the movie and television industries in Hollywood, the banking and financial services sectors on Wall Street, and the fashion industry in Milan. Military service also seems to have a particularly strong influence on new business creation. Military service builds leadership, team skills, provides a realistic training ground, an understanding of risk and risk management, and access to a network of other similarly-trained men and women.

IMPROVING THE SKILLS OF SME MANAGERS AND INCREASING SME SUCCESS

There are a range of activities that support the development of managerial skills that are associated with the success of SMEs.

Advice Seeking

The success of SMEs often depends on their owners/managers and their levels of skills. These individuals benefit from seeking advice – tapping into the knowledge and experiences of others. Sometimes advice can be sought from business advisors and at other times from friends and colleagues working in SMEs. But many owner/managers working in SMEs are reluctant to seek advice. Does advice seeking make a difference? The results on the benefits to SME managers of advice seeking are mixed. Dyer and Ross (2008) interviewed 158 small business owners to examine this question. They found that small business owners working in more dynamic environments, and those using more complex marketing activities, engaged in more advice seeking. Frequency of advice seeking, in turn, was positively related to small business owners' perceptions of business performance.

Chrisman and McMullan (2004) examined the benefits of a start-up counseling assistance effort provided by an outside government-supported small business development unit. SMEs received an average of 20 hours of counseling advice. Follow-up data were collected between four to eight years after the counseling. They collected data from 159 clients who had received counseling assistance several years before research data were collected. Firms receiving counseling survived at a higher rate than those in the general SME population They conclude that outsider assistance was likely to increase the implicit and explicit knowledge bases of the individuals during their preparatory efforts at start-up.

It is suggested that SME managers might benefit from seeking the advice of accountants, banks, consultants, government programs, and other SME owners and managers. In addition, there are a variety of HRM software tools on the market that address specific HR processes.

SME Owner Physical Fitness and Firm Success

Goldsby et al. (2005) found, in a study of 366 small business owners, that running was positively associated with three outcome measures (intrinsic rewards such as personal satisfaction, independence, and autonomy, extrinsic rewards such as financial results and family security, and company sales), while weight lifting was associated with two of these three outcomes (not company sales). Small business owners who were physically fit were better able to deal with their job and life stresses, had more productive lives, had more energy, and were mentally sharper.

Using Professional Employer Organizations

SMEs typically do not employ a full-time HR professional. As a result, managers add HR responsibilities to their regular job duties and in many cases these managers lack HR expertise. Professional employer organizations (PEOs) emerged in the US (and now exist in several other countries) to help SMEs address HR and other needs. SMEs contract with PEOs to provide HR programs and services to their firms. Large PEOs work with several SMEs, sometimes in the hundreds, and cover tens of thousands of SME employees. PEOs use different approaches to working with their SME clients. Some use a call centre approach where SMEs call a number when they have a HR problem and this problem is addressed by whichever representative is then available. Other PEOs use a customer service team approach where SMEs only work with a designated team member who is responsible for that SME.

Klaas et al. (2000) studied how characteristics of SMEs and of the SME–PEO relationship influence SMEs' overall satisfaction with the PEO and with the PEOs' efforts to control HR costs. Data were collected from 763 SMEs, with a 30 percent response rate, all clients of a large PEO. SME firm growth was associated with more overall PEO satisfaction and with satisfaction with PEOs' efforts to contain HR costs. SMEs having more prior HR problems were also more satisfied in these two areas. Larger SMEs were less satisfied with their PEOs. Firms having more specific contracts with their PEOs indicated more satisfaction in both areas. SMEs having a "better" (higher-quality) relationship with their PEOs indicated more overall satisfaction with them but not more satisfaction with PEO efforts to control HR costs. SMEs having greater value congruence with their PEO, and SMEs making greater use of the PEOs' services were also more satisfied in both areas. Length of the SME–PEO relationship was unrelated to both satisfaction measures. Interestingly, larger SMEs were less satisfied with the services of their PEOs.

Thus, this research indicated that the SME outsourcing of HR functions to a PEO generally had benefits for the SME (Klaas et al., 1999). This was not always the case, however, so SMEs need to develop a specific contract with their HR provider, make use of their services, and work to develop a high-quality relationship with their PEO representatives.

A Toronto-based organization, Presidents of Enterprising Organizations (PEO) helps SME leaders achieve success by connecting with, discussing with, learning from, and growing with each other. SME leaders have four-person advising teams that meet monthly to address situations, opportunities, and decisions that he/she faces. Most issues involve business strategy, people, and culture – the HRM side of SMEs. PEO leaders commit to three hours a month with the advising team, six hours a year with an executive advisor, and attendance at a two-day retreat. PEO also offers seminars throughout each year. In 2010 PEO had about 100 members in Toronto. Fees to join range from \$6000 to \$15 000 per year. The PEO model exists in other countries as well.

Carniol (2010) describes another Toronto-based organization, Maven Business Matchmakers, a newly created consulting firm whose objective is to match start-ups and small businesses with its network of professionals. The network of professionals includes freelance consultants and small firms specializing in public relations, HR, and financial funding. Maven gets income from the "suppliers" of services. Maven had about 100 professionals on its roster in July 2010. Maven first meets potential clients to determine their needs and help Maven find a match. Clients are then told who their "consultant" will be. Then clients meet with a potential "consultant" with a Maven representative present. If all goes well, a deal is struck.

Improving Franchisee Success

Individuals sometimes begin to own and manage an SME by buying a franchise. Franchisees sometimes work out well and sometimes turn out to be a disaster. Some franchisors grow too rapidly and run into trouble (e.g., Krispy Kreme). Franchises fail because the franchisor selects the wrong people to own and manage their franchise. All franchisors have systems for selecting franchisees typically using criteria such as being qualified, motivated, having some business and managerial experience, and adequate financing, but still sometimes mistakes are made. Such mistakes have a cost to both franchisor and franchisee. Many franchisors are trying to learn from both past successes and failures to develop a better assessment process. In addition, a few consulting companies (e.g., Matchpoint) have begun to fill a gap in the franchisee selection process. They typically work for franchisors and get paid for each successful franchisee placed.

IMPLICATIONS FOR THE ROLE OF HRM

This review suggests the following implications for furthering the role of HRM in SME performance and success:

- There is need for greater advocacy on the key role of HRM in SME success in the popular media and business outlets.
- Consultants to SMEs need to devote more attention to HR issues.
- HRM associations should devote more attention to HR issues in SMEs.
- SME/entrepreneurship programs in colleges and universities need to offer more course work related to HRM issues.
- More research is needed to confirm what we think we know and what we don't yet know about HRM practices and SME performance.

FROM THE TRENCHES

Fortunately, there are now an increasing number of detailed case studies of efforts by SMEs to transform their firms by adopting new HRM strategies and practices. SMEs in a variety of sectors have embarked on this journey. Here are some recent examples.

Grigg (2010) describes the efforts of a 175-person baking company to move from a traditional hierarchical command-and-control structure to employee empowerment and the use of self-directed work teams (SDWTs). A new organizational owner wanted the bakery to develop a culture more in line with the new owner's SMEs. Grigg believes that the key issue for success involves the reasons why the SME wants to move in this direction. It has to be strategically related to SME business objectives. The institutionalized culture proved to be the biggest obstacle to overcome, requiring considerable time, effort, costs, and disruption. Most such change efforts fail due to a lack of commitment from senior SME management. Grigg's example took place over a three-year period, beginning with employee training followed by infrastructure change and support to encourage the characteristics and behaviors of an employee empowerment culture.

Desai (2009) describes his founding of his law firm in Mumbai, India, now with offices in both the US and Singapore, a process that took a few years in itself. He wanted his firm to be based on trust, democratic management, non-hierarchical relationships and structure, and the use of knowledge and research to provide high-quality service to clients. His firm seems to be dramatically different than most other law firms around the world. His law firm has about 100 employees. HRM and organizational behavior concepts were at the core of his developing firm. Employees are seen as co-owners. Intellectual capital is the term used to describe human resources. Rewards are given for high levels of job performance as well as being trustworthy and loyal. Challenging jobs and opportunities for learning and development through mentoring are encouraged and supported. A Balanced Scorecard having four dimensions each with associated metrics (financial, service to clients, learning and growth, internal processes) integrates short- and long-term planning, firm culture, and associated firm values.

Borden (2010) outlines the creation of a branded intranet to convey information to all employees of American Eagle Outfitters (AEO). Based on the results of an employee survey conducted in 2004, AEO decided that its internal communication efforts (a printed newsletter, an intranet service) needed improving. It created an inter-departmental task force to design a more effective intranet platform, incorporating AEO's first-ever communication strategy. The task force developed AE Life to meet this need. AEO's intranet platform allowed almost immediate posting of material, did not require extensive IT experience to use, and was representative of the style and brands of AEO. It both helped to brand the employee experience at AEO and provided information and opportunities for AEO employees to convey the AEO culture and brand.

Spence (2010c) describes a mentoring session conducted using "telepreneur" technologies involving three young entrepreneurs in Toronto in a meeting with three Silicon Valley veterans in a US location. The organizers of these events, C100, is a cross-border association of high-tech entrepreneurs mostly from Silicon Valley and mostly Canadian, who want to shorten the learning curve for Canadian entrepreneurs. These "telepreneur" events will be held every three months. Each Canadian entrepreneur had 45 minutes to "make their pitch" and received candid feedback in return.

For the past few years, a Canadian newspaper, the *National Post*, has had a competition to identify and profile the 50 best SMEs. SMEs either self-nominate or are nominated by someone else, and the 50 best are selected by a team of five judges. The judges are a varied group consisting of a business writer, a marketing professor, a senior bank executive and two consultants. The 2010 winners were profiled in a Special Issue in the *National Post* on 16 February 2010. I encourage interested readers to look at the entire Special Issue.

The writers of the Special Issue identified some factors common to the success of these SMEs over the past year. The SMEs:

- were investors and builders initiating acquisitions, joint ventures, and structured alliances that were global in nature;
- looked more closely at their balance sheets;
- paid more attention to succession planning;
- strengthened trust of various stakeholders (customers, employees, advisors)
- increasingly looked to outsiders through networks to gain insights and ideas to broaden their horizons;
- undertook new strategies to deal with the volatile US dollar;
- worked with employees and vendors to cut costs to better meet demands of customers for lower prices;
- needed to innovate;
- relied on HRM and employee commitment, energy, and creativity.

Several of these 50 "best managed" SMEs paid special attention to their HRM practices. Here is a selected sample of these SMEs. Again, interested readers should consult the Special Issue to gain additional information on these highly successful SMEs as well as contact details:

- *Ames Tile & Stone Ltd – 100 employees – wholesale distribution of stone and tile products* Operates with a family culture, encourages education, practices decentralized decision-making, fosters a sense of belonging at all levels, invests 5 percent of profits to support staff education, has a profit-sharing plan paying out 10 percent of its profits to staff, emphasizes customer relationships, and marketing via e-commerce;

- *Bayshore Home Health – 8000 employees – home health care* Emphasizes a service-oriented culture, makes substantial use of teams, and encourages decentralization so that decisions are made at the bedside;
- *Bragg/Eastlink – 1600 employees – media and communications* Emphasizes the development of internal talent necessary for its recent growth;
- *Evans Consoles Corp – 210 employees – design and manufacturing* Leverages a highly skilled staff by investing in experience and expertise of employees;
- *Focenco/Colemans Food Centers – 800 employees – food retail and distribution* Outstanding succession planning with the firm being now in its third generation of family ownership and management with a fourth on the way;
- *Harry Rosen Inc. – 700 employees – clothing retailer* Superb customer service, emphasis on relationship management, very low staff turnover, long-term relationships with customers and suppliers;
- *Morgan Mitchell Group – 90 employees – human resources* Financial rewards for sales staff;
- *United Van Lines Canada – 85 employees – household goods transportation* Incorporates high standards of customer service, a focus on employee engagement, the use of Internet task forces to identify problems and solutions, supporting the exchange of information and learning among member firms;
- *Upside Software Inc – 100 employees – technology* Focuses on hiring the right people and trusting them; leaders emphasize trust and accountability.

We encourage anyone interested in one or more of these company examples to contact the relevant SMEs for additional information and help. We noted earlier in this chapter that SME managers find this kind of personal contact to be the most valuable source of ideas.

CONCLUSIONS

We need to devote considerably more attention to the needs of SMEs. There are significantly more SMEs than large organizations; SMEs employ more people than do large organizations; SMEs exist in all countries; SMEs seem to be weathering the current economic storm better than large organizations; the economic performance of a country is inextricably linked to the SME sector; more women and more university-educated women and men are either starting or working in SMEs, and SMEs rely heavily on their employees and as a result, SME HRM policies and practices. More colleges and universities are offering courses or degrees linking SMEs with concentrations in business, engineering, law, architecture, science, medicine, and high technology. More research, consulting and advising activities have been devoted to SMEs, leading to a solid basis of understanding of some of the unique aspects of working in and managing an SME. The media in several countries have created annual surveys of the 50 best SMEs in which they not only list the names of these outstanding SMEs but also provide contact information. We encourage managers of SMEs to contact some of these outstanding firms to learn more about what works for them. In addition, there is a variety of information available on the Internet on best HRM practices for SMEs. Sometimes this information is provided by relevant government departments as well as by industry or sector associations. Various sector councils (e.g., IT, food industry) are encouraging the sharing of HR tools (e.g., measures of the costs of turnover) and HRM best practices as their sectors attempt to upgrade skills and produce more effective workplaces. Yet in spite of this evidence, HRM practices in SMEs have not changed or improved much over the past decade. This is the challenge that this volume addresses.

Senior managers of SMEs also need to take other actions to be productive. These include investing in machinery and equipment, training, research and development, and information and communication technology.

It is imperative that entrepreneurs, small business owners, and managers act diligently in steering their organizations, especially in the current business climate. The workplace today is different from what it used to be. People, organizational structures, and the work itself has changed (Benko & Anderson, 2010). Their management actions and strategies will very likely determine if small businesses survive and succeed in the future. As Katz et al. (2000, p. 7) state, "at a time of unparalleled technological development, it is the human resources that paradoxically spell success or failure for all firms, and especially entrepreneurial ones". The research in the field, already limited, has focused mainly on the degree or extent of HR practices such as recruitment, selection, and compensation (Heneman et al., 2000). Future work should go beyond this scope. Hopefully, this volume provides a few areas for such research that will then inform SME HRM practice.

NOTE

* Preparation of the manuscript was supported in part by York University, Canada. I acknowledge the contributions of my colleague, Parbudyal Singh, to this chapter.

REFERENCES

Akerloff, G.A. & Kranton, R. (2010). *Identity Economics: How Our Identities Shape our Work, Wages and Well-being*, Princeton, NJ: Princeton University Press.

Amba-Rao, S. & Pendse, D. (1985). Human resources, compensation and maintenance practices. *American Journal of Small Business*, **10**(2), 19–29.

Atkinson, C. (2007). The secret of a 90-percent retention rate: BC auto dealership puts its employees first with training and development and strong workplace ethics. *Globe and Mail*, Tuesday, 16 Oct., B12.

Balkin, D.B. & Logan, J.W. (1988). Reward policies that support entrepreneurship. *Compensation and Benefits Review*, **20**(1), 18–25.

Barton, M.A. & Sutcliffe, K.M. (2010). Learning when to stop momentum. *MIT Sloan Management Review*, **51**(3), 34–41.

Beal, A. & Strauss, J. (2006). *Radically Transparent: Monitoring and Managing Reputations Online*, Indianapolis, IN: Wiley Publishing.

Becker, B. & Gerhart, B. (1996). The impact of human resource management on organizational performance: Progress and prospects. *Academy of Management Journal*, **39**(4), 779–801.

Becker, B. & Huselid, M. (1998). High performance work systems and firm performance: Synthesis of research and managerial implications. *Research in Personnel and Human Resources Management*, **16**, 53–101.

Becker, B. & Huselid, M. (2006). Strategic human resource management: Where do we go from here? *Journal of Management*, **32**(6), 898–925.

Bell, C. & Patterson, J. (2009). *Take their Breath Away: How Imaginative Service Creates Devoted Customers*. New York: John Wiley.

Benko, C. & Anderson, M. (2010). *Corporate Lattice: Achieving High Performance in the Changing World of Work*. Boston: Harvard Business School Press.

Birdi, K., Clegg, C., Patterson, M., Robinson, A., Stride, C., Wall, T. & Wood, S. (2008). The impact of human resource and operational management practices on company productivity: A longitudinal study. *Personnel Psychology*, **61**(3), 467–501.

Bitti, M.T. (2010). Bankruptcy protection made Pazazz leaner, more focussed. *National Post*, Tues. 13 July, FP7.

Borden, R. (2010). American Eagle Outfitters creates a branded intranet that unites its associates. *Global Business and Organizational Excellence*, **29**(2), 40–46.

Brand, M. & Bax, E. (2002). Strategic HRM for SMEs: Implications for firms and policy. *Education and Training*, **44**(8/9), 451–63.

Briscoe, J.A., Fawcett, S.E. & Todd, R.H. (2005). The implementation and impact of ISO 9000 among small manufacturing enterprises. *Journal of Small Business Management*, **43**(3), 309–30.

Bryson, A. (1999). The impact of employee involvement on small firms' financial performance. *National Institute of Economic Review*, **169**(1), 78–96.

Burke, R.J. & Singh, P. (2010). The importance of human resource management in small- and medium-sized enterprises: Entrepreneurs take note. *MBA Review*, March, 49–52.
Burke, R.J., Graham, J. & Smith, F.J. (2005). Putting the customer second. *The TQM Magazine*, **17**, 86–91.
Buttner, E.H. & Moore, D.P. (1997). Women's organizational exodus to entrepreneurship: Self-reported motivations and correlates with success. *Journal of Small Business Management*, **35**(1), 33–46.
Cardon, M. & Stevens, C. (2004). Managing human resources in small organizations: What do we know? *Human Resource Management Review*, **14**(3), 295–323.
Carlson, D., Upton, N. & Seaman, S. (2006). The impact of human resource practices and compensation design on performance: An analysis of family-owned SMEs. *Journal of Small Business Management*, **44**(4), 531–43.
Carniol, N. (2010). Find the perfect match. *Toronto Star*, Mon. 19 July, B1.
Carr, L. (1997). Strategic determinants of executive compensation in small publicly traded firms. *Journal of Small Business Management*, **35**(2), 1–12.
Cassell, C., Nadin, S., Gray, M. & Clegg, C. (2002). Exploring human resources management practices in small and medium sized enterprises. *Personnel Review*, **31**(6), 671–92.
Cermack, J. & McGurk, M. (2010). Putting a value on training. *McKinsey Quarterly*, July, McKinsey & Company.
Challenger, Gray & Christmas, Inc. (2010). *Lowest Start-up Rates on Record as Jobs, Fragile Economy Deter Entrepreneurism.* Chicago: Challenger, Gray & Christmas, Inc.
Chandler, G. & McEvoy, G. (2000). Human resource management, TQM, and firm performance in small and medium-size enterprises. *Entrepreneurship Theory and Practice*, **25**(1), 43–58.
Chrisman, J.J. & McMullan, W.E. (2004). Outsider assistance as a knowledge resource for new venture survival. *Journal of Small Business Management*, **42**(3), 229–44.
Clarke, S. & Flitcroft, C. (2008). Regulation of safety in UK-based SMEs: A managerial perspective. The annual Conference of the British Psychological Society's division of Occupational Psychology, Stratford-Upon-Avon, UK. January, 2008.
Coffman, C. & Gonzalez-Molina, G. (2002). *Follow this Path: How the World's Greatest Organizations Drive Growth by Unleashing Human Potential.* New York: Warner Business Books.
Combs, J., Lui, Y., Hall, A. & Ketchen, D. (2006). How much do high-performance work practices matter? A meta-analysis of their effects on firm performance. *Personnel Psychology*, **59**(3), 501–28.
Conley, C. (2007). *Peak: How Great Companies Get Their Mojo From Maslow*. San Francisco: Jossey-Bass.
Curran, J. (1988). Training and research strategies for small businesses. *Journal of General Management*, **13**(3), 24–37.
Danes, S.M. (2006). Tensions within family business-owning couples over time. *Stress, Trauma and Crisis*, **9**(3/4), 237–46.
Danes, S.M. & Morgan, E.A. (2004). Tensions within family business-owning couples: An EFT view into their unique conflict culture. *Contemporary Family Therapy*, **26**(3), 241–60.
Danes, S.M. & Olson, P.D. (2003). Women's role involvement in family

businesses, business tensions, and business success. *Family Business Review*, **16**(1), 53–68.
Danes, S.M., Zuiker, V., Kean, R. & Arbuthnot, J. (1999). Predictors of family business tensions and goal achievements, *Family Business Review*, **12**(3), 75–86.
DeKok, J.M.P., Uhlalner, L.M. & Thurik, A.R. (2003). Human resource management with small and medium-sized enterprises: Facts and explanations. ERIM Report Series ERS 2003-015. Rotterdam: Erasmus University.
De Kok, J.M.P., Uhlaner, L.M. & Thurik, A.R. (2006). Professional HRM practices in family owned-managed enterprises. *Journal of Small Business Management*, **44**(3), 444–60.
Delaney, J., Lewin, D. & Ichniowski, C. (1989). *Human Resource Policies and Practices in American Firms*. Washington, DC: US Government Printing Office.
Delery, J. & Doty, D. (1996). Modes of theorizing in strategic human resource management: Test of universalistic, contingency and configurational performance predictions. *Academy of Management Journal*, **39**(4), 802–35.
Desai, N. (2009). Management by trust in a democratic enterprise: A law firm shapes organizational behavior to create competitive advantage. *Global Business and Organizational Excellence*, **28**(6), 7–21.
Deshpande, S. & Golhar, D. (1994). HRM practices in large and small manufacturing firms: A comparative study. *Journal of Small Business Management*, **32**(2), 49–55.
Dewar, R. & Derbel, J. (1979). Universalistic and contingency predictions of employee satisfaction and conflict. *Administrative Science Quarterly*, **24**(4), 426–48.
Dushinski, K. (2009). *The Mobile Marketing Handbook: A Step-by-step Guide to Creating Dynamic Mobile Marketing Campaigns*. Medford, NJ: CyberAge Books.
Dyer, L.M. & Ross, C.A. (2008). Seeking advice in a dynamic and complex business environment: Impact on the success of small firms. *Journal of Entrepreneurship Development*, **13**(2), 133–49.
Eakin, J.M. & MacEachern, E. (1998). Health and the social relations of work: A study of the health-related experience of employees in small workplaces. *Sociology of Health and Illness*, **20**(6), 896–914.
Fairfield-Sonn, J. (1987). A strategic process model for small business training and development. *Journal of Small Business Management*, **25**(1), 11–18.
Feltham, T.S., Feltham, G. & Barnett, J.J. (2005). The dependence of family businesses on a single decision-maker. *Journal of Small Business Management*, **43**(1), 1–14.
Fielden, S.L. & Davidson, M.J. (2005). *International Handbook of Women and Small Business Entrepreneurship*. Cheltenham, UK and Northampton, MA, USA: Edward Elgar.
Fielden, S.L. & Davidson, M.J. (2010). *International Research Handbook on Successful Women Entrepreneurs*. Cheltenham, UK and Northampton, MA, USA: Edward Elgar.
Fielden, S.L., Davidson, M.J. & Makin, P.J. (2000). Barriers encountered during micro and small business start-up. *Journal of Small Business and Enterprise Development*, **7**(4), 295–304.
Fielden, S.L., Dawe, A.J. & Woolnough, H.M. (2006). Government small business finance initiatives: Social inclusion or discrimination? *Equal Opportunities International*, **25**(1), 104–12.

Fischer, E. & Reuber, R. (2007). The good, the bad, and the unfamiliar: The challenges of reputation formation facing new firms. *Entrepreneurship Theory and Practice*, **31**(1), 53–75.
Fowler, A. & Murlis, H. (1987). Salary systems for small businesses. *Personnel Management*, **21**, 27–8.
Fritz, R. (2001). *Family Ties and Business Binds: How to Solve the Inevitable Problems of Family Business*. Bloomington, IN: Unlimited Publishing.
Funk, T. (2009). *Web 2.0 and Beyond: Understanding the New Online Business Models, Trends, and Technologies*. Westport, CT: Praeger Publishers.
Gagnon, Y.C., Sicotte, H. & Posada, E. (2000). Impact of SME manager's behavior on the adoption of technology. *Entrepreneurship Theory and Practice*, **25**(4), 43–57.
Galbraith, C.S. & Nkwenti-Zamcho, E. (2005). The effect of management policies on plant-level productivity: A longitudinal study of three US and Mexican small businesses. *Journal of Small Business Management*, **43**(4), 418–31.
Gatewood, R. & Feild, H. (1987). A personnel selection program for small business. *Journal of Small Business Management*, **25**(4), 16–24.
Globe and Mail (2007). What characterizes successful small businesses? Report on Business, B2.
Goldberg, A.I., Cohen, G. & Fiegenbaum, A. (2003). Reputation building: Small business strategies for successful venture development. *Journal of Small Business Management*, **41**(2), 168–86.
Goldsby, M.G., Kuratko, D.F. & Bishop, J.W. (2005). Entrepreneurship and fitness: An examination of rigorous exercise and goal attainment among small business owners. *Journal of Small Business Management*, **43**(1), 78–92.
Golhar, D. & Deshpande, S. (1997). HRM practices of large and small Canadian manufacturing firms. *Journal of Small Business Management*, **35**(3), 30–38.
Grigg, A. (2010). Employee empowerment is the main ingredient in a baking company's competitive strategy. *Global Business and Organizational Excellence*, **29**(2), 6–18.
Gumbus, A. & Johnson, S. (2003). The Balanced Scorecard at Futura Industries: Relentless commitment to employees' results in company success. *Strategic Finance*, **85**(1), 37–41.
Gumbus, A. & Lussier, R.N. (2006). Entrepreneurs use a Balanced Scorecard to translate strategy into performance measures. *Journal of Small Business Management*, **44**(3), 407–25.
Gumbus, A. & Lyons, B. (2002). The Balanced Scorecard at Philips Electronics. *Strategic Finance*, **84**(5), 45–9.
Gumbus, A., Bellhouse, D. & Lyons, B. (2003). A three-year journey to organizational and financial health using the Balanced Scorecard: A case study at a Yale New Haven Health Systems Hospital. *Journal of Business and Economic Studies*, **9**(2), 54–64.
Gupta, V.K., Turban, D.B., Wasti, S.A. & Sikdar, A. (2009). The role of gender stereotypes in perceptions of entrepreneurs and intentions to become an entrepreneur. *Entrepreneurship Theory and Practice*, **33**(2), 397–417.
Hamilton, R.T. & Dana, L.P. (2003). An increasing role for small business in New Zealand. *Journal of Small Business Management*, **41**(4), 402–8.
Harris, L.C. & Ogbonna, E. (2010), Hiding customer complaints: Studying the motivations and forms of service employees' complaint concealment behaviours. *British Journal of Management*, **21**(2), 262–79.

Hasle, P. & Limborg, H.J. (2006). A review of the literature on preventative occupational health and safety activities in small enterprises. *Industrial Health*, **44**(1), 6–12.
Hasle, P., Bager, B. & Granerud, L. (2010). Small enterprises – accountants as occupational health and safety intermediaries. *Safety Science*, **48**(3), 404–9.
Hasle, P., Kines, P. & Andersen, L.P. (2009). Small enterprise owners' accident causation attribution and prevention. *Safety Science*, **47**(1), 9–19.
Hayton, J. (2003). Strategic human capital management in SMEs: An empirical study of entrepreneurial performance. *Human Resource Management*, **42**(4), 375–93.
Heilman, M.E. & Chen, J.K. (2003). Entrepreneurship as a solution: The allure of self-employment for women and minorities. *Human Resource Management Review*, **13**(2), 347–64.
Heneman, H. & Berkley, R. (1999). Applicant attraction practices and outcomes among small businesses. *Journal of Small Business Management*, **37**(1), 53–74.
Heneman, R., Tansky, J. & Camp, S. (2000). Human resource management practices in small and medium-sized enterprises: Unanswered questions and future research perspectives. *Entrepreneurship Theory and Practice*, **25**(1), 11–26.
Hornsby, J. & Kuratko, D. (1990). Human resource management in small business: Critical issues for the 1990s. *Journal of Small Business Management*, **28**(3), 9–18.
Hornsby, J. & Kuratko, D. (2003). Human resource management in US small businesses: A replication and extension. *Journal of Developmental Entrepreneurship*, **8**(1), 73–92.
Hui, A. (2010). Cancer patient wins discrimination suit. *Globe and Mail*, Wed. 14 July, A2.
Hundley, G. (2001). Why and when are the self-employed more satisfied with their work? *Industrial Relations*, **40**(2), 293–316.
Huselid, M. (1995). The impact of human resource management practices on turnover, productivity, and corporate financial performance. *Academy of Management Journal*, **38**(3), 635–72.
Industry Canada (2008). Key small business statistics in Canada. Available at: http://strategis.ic.gc.ca/; accessed 11 November 2010.
Jenkins, M., Pasternak, K. & West, R. (2005). *Performance at the Limit: Business Lessons from Formula 1 Motor Racing*. Cambridge, UK: Cambridge University Press.
Jennings, J.E. & McDougald, M.S. (2007). Work–family interface experiences and coping strategies: Implications for entrepreneurship research and practice. *Academy of Management Review*, **32**(3), 747–57.
Jorgensen, K., Duijm, N.J. & Troen, H. (2010). Accident prevention in SME using ORM. *Safety Science*, **48**(8), 1036–43.
Julien, P. (1998). *The Star of the Art in Small Business and Entrepreneurship*. Aldershot: Ashgate.
Kaman, V., McCarthy, A., Gulbro, R. & Tucker, M. (2001). Bureaucratic and high commitment HRM in small service firms. *Human Resource Planning*, **24**(1), 33–44.
Kaplan, R.S. & Norton, D.P. (1992) The Balanced Scorecard: Measures that drive performance. *Harvard Business Review*, **70**(1), 71–9.
Kaplan, R.S. & Norton, D.P. (1993). Putting the Balanced Scorecard to work. *Harvard Business Review*, **71**(5), 134–47.

Kaplan, R.S. & Norton, D.P. (1996a). *The Balanced Scorecard: Translating Strategy into Action*. Boston: Harvard Business School Press.
Kaplan, R.S. & Norton, D.P. (1996b). The Balanced Scorecard is more than a new measurement system. *Harvard Business Review*, **74**(3), 4–7.
Kaplan, R.S. & Norton, D.P. (1996c). Using the Balanced Scorecard as a strategic management system. *Harvard Business Review*, **74**(1), 75–86.
Kaplan, T., George, G. & Rimler, G.W. (2000). University-sponsored family business programs: Program characteristics, perceived quality and member satisfaction. *Entrepreneurship Theory and Practice*, **25**, 65–75.
Katz, J., Aldrich, H., Welbourne, T. & Williams, P. (2000). Human resource management and the SME: Toward a new synthesis. *Entrepreneurship Theory and Practice*, **25**(1), 7–10.
Katzenbach, J.R. (2000). *Peak Performance: Aligning the Hearts and Minds of Your Employees*. Boston: Harvard Business School Press.
Kets de Vries, M.F.R. (1993). The dynamics of family controlled firms: The good and the bad news. *Organizational Dynamics*, **21**(3), 59–71.
Kets de Vries, M.F.R. (1999). *Family Business: Human Dilemmas in the Family Firm*. London: Thompson Business Press.
Kets de Vries, M.F.R. & Florent-Treacy, E. (2002). Global leadership from A to Z: Creating high commitment organizations. *Organizational Dynamics*, **30**(4), 295–309.
Kim, J.L.S. & Ling, C.S. (2001), Work–family conflict of women entrepreneurs in Singapore. *Women in Management Review*, **16**(5), 204–21.
King, S., Solomon, G. & Fernald, L. (2001). Issues in growing a family business: A strategic human resource model. *Journal of Small Business Management*, **39**(1), 3–13.
Klaas, B.S., McClendon, J. & Gainey, T.W. (1999). HR outsourcing and its impact: The role of transaction costs. *Personnel Psychology*, **52**(1), 113–36.
Klaas, B.S., McClendon, J. & Gainey, T.W. (2000). Managing HR in the small and medium enterprise: The impact of professional employer organizations. *Entrepreneurship Theory and Practice*, **25**(1), 107–24.
Kotey, B. & Folker, C. (2007). Employee training in SMEs: Effect of size and firm type – family and nonfamily. *Journal of Small Business Management*, **45**(2), 214–38.
Kotey, B. & Slade, P. (2005). Formal human resources management practices in small growing firms. *Journal of Small Business Management*, **43**(1), 16–40.
Landes, D.S. (2006). *Dynasties: Fortunes and Misfortunes of the World's Great Family Businesses*. New York: Viking.
Langowitz, N. & Minniti, M. (2007). The entrepreneurial propensity of women. *Entrepreneurship Theory and Practice*, **31**(3), 341–64.
Lawler, E. (2000). Pay strategy: New thinking for a new millennium. *Compensation and Benefits Review*, **32**(1), 7–13.
Li, C. (2010). *Open Leadership: How Social Technology Can Transform the Way You Lead*. San Francisco: Jossey-Bass.
Loscocco, K.J., Robinson, J., Hall, R. & Allen, J. (1991). Gender and small business success: An inquiry into women's relative disadvantage. *Social Forces*, **70**(1), 65–85.
MacDuffie, J. (1995). Human resources bundles and manufacturing performance. *Industrial and Labor Relations Review*, **48**(2), 197–221.

Marlow, S. (1997). The employment environment and smaller firms. *International Journal of Entrepreneurial Behavior and Research*, **3**(4), 143–50.
Martin, C., Guare, R. & Dawson, P. (2010). *Work Your Strengths*. New York: AMACOM.
Martin-Alcazar, F., Romero-Fernandez, P. & Sanchez-Gardey, G. (2005). Strategic human resource management: Integrating the universalistic, contingent, configurational and contextual perspectives. *International Journal of Human Resource Management*, **16**(5), 633–59.
McEvoy, G. (1984). Small business personnel practices. *Journal of Small Business Management*, **22**(4), 1–8.
McKinsey & Company (2009). Motivating people: Getting beyond money. Global Survey, New York: McKinsey & Company.
McKinsey & Company (2010a). *The Great Rebalancing*. New York: McKinsey & Company.
McKinsey & Company (2010b). *A New Way to Measure Word-of-mouth Marketing*. New York: McKinsey & Company.
Minniti, M. (2008). The role of government policy on entrepreneurial activity: Productive, unproductive, or destructive. *Entrepreneurship Theory and Practice*, **32**(5), 779–90.
Moore, D.P. (2003). Women: Are you ready to be entrepreneurs? *Business and Economic Review*, **49**(2), 15–21.
Moore, D.P. & Buttner, E.H. (1997). *Women Entrepreneurs: Moving Beyond the Glass Ceiling*. Thousand Oaks, CA: Sage Publications.
Morris, S.S., Snell, S.A. & Wright, P.M. (2006). A resource-based view of international human resources: Toward a framework of integrative and creative capabilities. In I. Bjorkman (ed.), *Handbook of Research in International Human Resource Management*, Cheltenham, UK and Northampton, MA, USA: Edward Elgar.
Murphy, M. (2010). *Hundred Percenters: Challenge Your Employees to Give Their All and They'll Give You Even More*. New York: McGraw-Hill.
National Post (2010). Canada's 50 best. Toronto: *National Post*, 16 February, SR1–SR32.
Niehm, L.S., Miller, N.J., Shelley, M.C. & Fitzgerald, M.A. (2009). Small family business survival: Strategies for coping with overlapping family and business demands. *Journal of Developmental Entrepreneurship*, **14**(3), 209–32.
Nielson, G. & Peterson, B. (2009). *Fake Work: Why People are Working Harder Than Ever But Accomplishing Less, and How to Fix the Problem*. New York: Simon Spotlight Entertainment.
Olson, E. (2010). Honest marketing key. *National Post*, Tues. 13 July, FP9.
Ostroff, C. & Bowen, E.E. (2000). Moving HR to a higher level: HR practices and organizational effectiveness. In K.J. Klein & S.W.J. Koslowski (eds), *Multilevel Theory, Research and Methods in Organizations*. San Francisco, CA: Jossey-Bass, pp. 211–65.
Pfeffer, J. (1994). *Competitive Advantage Through People*. Cambridge, MA: Harvard Business School Press.
Pfeffer, J. (1995). Producing sustainable competitive advantage through the effective management of people. *Academy of Management Executive*, **9**(1), 55–72.
Pfeffer, J. (1998). *The Human Equation: Building Profits by Putting People First*. Boston: Harvard Business School Press.

Ram, M. (1999). Managing autonomy: Employment relations in small professional service firms. *International Small Business Journal*, **17**(2), 1–5.
Rottenberg, S. & O'Meara, I. (2010). The art of looking. *Rotman Magazine*, May, 19–24.
Runyan, R., Droge, C. & Swinney, J. (2008). Entrepreneurial orientation versus small business orientation: What are their relationships to firm performance? *Journal of Small Business Management*, **46**(4), 567–88.
Rutherford, M.W., Buller, P.F. & Stebbins, J.M. (2009). Ethical considerations of the legitimacy lie. *Entrepreneurship Theory and Practice*, **33**(4), 949–64.
Schermerhorn, J.R. (2001). *Management Update 2001*. 6th edn. New York: John Wiley.
Schjoedt, L. (2009). Entrepreneurial job characteristics: An examination of their effect on entrepreneurial satisfaction. *Entrepreneurship Theory and Practice*, **34**(5), 619–44.
Schwartz, T. (2010). *The Way We're Working Isn't Working*. New York: Free Press.
Senor, D. & Singer, S. (2009). *Start-up Nation: The Story of Israel's Economic Miracle*. Toronto: McClelland & Stewart.
Shelton, L.M. (2006). Female entrepreneurs, work–family conflict, and venture performance: New insights into the work–family interface. *Journal of Small Business Management*, **44**(2), 285–97.
Shelton, L.M., Danes, S.M. & Eisenman, M. (2008). Role demands, difficulty in managing work–family conflict, and minority entrepreneurship. *Journal of Developmental Entrepreneurship*, **13**(3), 315–42.
Silverstein, S. (2010). *No Excuses*. New York: John Wiley.
Sorensen, G.H., Hasle, P. & Bach, E. (2007). Working in small enterprises – is there a special risk? *Safety Science*, **45**(10), 1044–59.
Southcott, A. (2010). There's power in partnerships for your brand. *Globe and Mail*, Mon. 21 June, B6.
Spence, R. (2010a). Take your oreo beyond "double-stuff". *National Post*, Tues. 13 July, FP6.
Spence, R. (2010b). How to do plenty with "zilch". *National Post*, Tues. 20 July, FP6.
Spence, R. (2010c). Start-ups get face-time with Valley veterans. *National Post*, Tues. 17 Aug, FP8.
Storey, D. (1994). *Understanding the Small Business Sector*. London: Routledge.
Storey, D. (2004). Exploring the link, among small firms between management training and firm performance: A comparison between the UK and OECD countries. *International Journal of Human Resource Management*, **15**(1), 112–30.
Sullivan, D.M. (2007). Minority entrepreneurs: More likely to try, but less likely to succeed. *Academy of Management Perspectives*, **21**(1), 78–9.
Tocher, N. & Rutherford, M.W. (2009). Perceived acute human resource management problems in small and medium firms: An empirical examination. *Entrepreneurship Theory and Practice*, **33**(2), 455–79.
Tsai, C.-J., Sengupta, S. & Edwards, P. (2007). When and why is small beautiful? The experience of work in the small firm. *Human Relations*, **60**(12), 1779–807.
Ulrich, D. & Ulrich, W. (2010). *The Why of Work*. New York: McGraw Hill.
Villanueva, D. & Djurkovic, N. (2009). Occupational stress and intention to leave among employees in small and medium enterprises. *International Journal of Stress Management*, **16**(2), 124–37.

Wagar, T. (1998). Is labor–management climate important? Some Canadian evidence. *Journal of Labor Research*, **18**(1), 163–74.
Walker, A. & Brown, A. (2004). What success factors are important to small business owners? *International Small Business Journal*, **22**(6), 577–91.
Walters, D. (2004). Representation in health and safety in small enterprises in Europe. *Industrial Relations Journal*, **35**(2), 169–86.
Watson, J. (2002). Comparing the performance of male and female controlled businesses: Relating to outputs and inputs. *Entrepreneurship Theory and Practice*, **26**(3), 91–100.
Way, S. (2002). High performance work systems and intermediate indicators of firm performance within the US small business sector. *Journal of Management*, **28**(6), 765–85.
Wiatrowski, W. (1994). Small businesses and their employees. *Monthly Labor Review*, October, 29–35.
Wilkinson, A. (1999). Employment relations in SMEs. *Employee Relations*, **21**(3), 206–20.
Williamson, I.O. (2000). Employer legitimacy and recruitment success in small businesses. *Entrepreneurship Theory and Practice*, **25**(1), 27–42.
Williamson, I.O., Cable, D.M. & Aldrich, H.E. (2002). Smaller but not necessarily weaker: How small businesses can overcome barriers to recruitment. In J. Katz & T.M. Welbourne (eds), *Managing People in Entrepreneurial Organizations: Learning from the Merger of Entrepreneurship and Human Resource Management*. Amsterdam: JAI Press, pp. 83–106.
Winn, J. (2000). Kacey Fine Furniture: Human resource management in the face of change. *Entrepreneurship Theory and Practice*, **25**(2), 95–107.
Zack, D. (2010). *Networking for People Who Hate Networking: A Field Guide for Introverts, the Overwhelmed, and the Underconnected*. San Francisco: Berret-Koehler.

PART II

Human resource management and small business effectiveness

3. The role of human capital factors in small business performance and success

Gary J. Castrogiovanni

Though similar notions had probably been around for centuries, the concept of "human capital" was popularized by Becker (1964). Accordingly, the education, training, experience, and health of the workforce affect worker productivity and economic performance. Government and businesses can invest in human capital, just as they invest in other resources, with the hope of generating satisfactory returns on that investment through the resulting performance gains.

In the United States, small businesses employ roughly half of the private sector workforce and create most new jobs in the country. Small businesses are at least as important in many other countries as well. Thus, the economic benefits of human capital investment envisioned by Becker and other economists cannot be significant unless they accrue to the small business sector. National or local government investment in human capital must facilitate small business creation and growth within the targeted geographic areas, and human capital investment within small business firms must be related to firm performance.

This chapter examines those linkages. Literature dealing with effects of human capital on small businesses is reviewed. Then, an integrative perspective is offered, with conclusions and implications for creating, developing, and managing small firms. Businesses may be small because they are new and have not yet had time to grow or because there are no advantages to growth like scale or scope economies. Investment in human capital contributes to economic development primarily in the former case because new businesses tend to have more growth potential than established ones. Consequently, this chapter is focused more on the role of human capital in the creation and development of new, small businesses than in the performance of established small businesses. Some findings and conclusions about long-term performance, however, may generalize across both types.

HUMAN CAPITAL AND SMALL BUSINESSES

Though definitions and measures vary across authors and studies, human capital is defined here as the knowledge, skill, and experience that top management brings to a venture, which influences venture success. As noted above, the focus is on new ventures that have not yet had time to grow, though some studies reviewed and conclusions offered fit established small businesses as well. Human capital is defined here in terms of that possessed by the top management team because top management plays a very dominant role in both new and small businesses (Mintzberg, 1979).

This review summarizes relevant research within roughly the past 20 years. Topics are discussed in the approximate sequential order of relevance to a given firm. First, studies dealing with external conditions favoring economic development through firm creation are examined. Whereas the focus there is on general conditions, emphasis then shifts to research focused on specific firms, dealing with business founding and early-stage outcomes such as survival, venture capital (VC) funding, and initial public offerings (IPOs). Next, intermediate outcomes of human capital investment are examined, such as various firm characteristics, financial structure, and patenting activity. Finally, effects of human capital on profit, growth, and other long-term performance outcomes are reviewed.

External Conditions

Audretsch and Keilbach (2004) argued that development of human capital will not in itself have much impact on the formation of new businesses and resulting economic growth in a geographic region unless there is sufficient "entrepreneurship capital". They defined the latter as a subset of social capital that reflects legal, institutional, and relational factors conducive to entrepreneurship. Though their findings showed that entrepreneurship capital indeed contributed to regional economic development in Germany, they acknowledged that these were only preliminary, and that more research is needed to clarify exactly what constitutes entrepreneurship capital and its role in economic development.

Focusing on academic entrepreneurship, Powers and McDougall (2005) identified a set of financial, organizational, and human capital resources that related to technology commercialization of universities. The key human capital variable was faculty quality, measured by faculty citations in leading journals. Examining 120 research institutions, they found that faculty quality was positively related to both (1) startups formed and (2) licensing to IPOs.

Allen et al. (2007) also studied academic entrepreneurship, sampling 200 men and 200 women from a variety of disciplines. They found that university faculty members are more likely to work with industry to develop and patent innovations when they are (1) older and (2) tenured. Thus, although investment of human capital in the form of support for faculty research increases the likelihood of innovative new ventures, another human capital factor, namely the experience associated with age and tenure, enhances that effect.

Majumdar (2007) compared growth of government and corporate firms in India from the early 1970s to the late 1990s. A significant increase in human capital productivity across all ownership categories of industry was associated with growth of private firms and shrinking government ownership. Thus, investment in human capital resulted in greater privatization in the Indian economy.

Sine and Lee (2009) examined the wind-energy business in the US over the 1978–92 interval. Their focus was not on human capital *per se*, but rather on how social movements influence entrepreneurial endeavors. They found that, while natural resources, market conditions, and skilled human capital positively influenced entrepreneurial activity, those effects were enhanced by increasing social movement membership.

Braunerhjelm et al. (2010) examined gross domestic product (GDP) growth of Organisation for Economic Co-operation and Development (OECD) countries during 1981 to 2002. The countries examined were Australia, Austria, Belgium, Canada, Denmark, Finland, France, Germany, Ireland, Italy, Japan, the Netherlands, Norway, Spain, Sweden, the United Kingdom, and the United States. They proposed and found that human capital is a necessary but insufficient condition for economic development. Government investments in research and technical knowledge do not in themselves lead to business creation and economic development. Rather, government policies should also be directed toward fostering entrepreneurship by providing incentives and mechanisms for creating new ventures.

These studies suggest that in recent years emphasis has shifted away from simple investment in human capital to stimulate venture creation and economic development toward more nuanced views. Majumdar's (2007) findings followed the traditional view of human capital and economic development since investment in human capital in India resulted in more private ventures. Likewise Powers and McDougall's (2005) study supported the traditional view since there was a direct link between their human capital indicator (faculty quality) and entrepreneurial activity (startups and IPOs). The findings by Audretsch and Keilbach (2004), Allen et al. (2007), Sine and Lee (2009), and Braunerhjelm et al. (2010)

suggest that specific mechanisms are needed to stimulate venture creation. Audretsch and Keilbach (2004) offered entrepreneurial capacity as that specific mechanism. For Allen et al. (2007), the mechanism was the absorptive capacity that comes with age and tenure. For Sine and Lee (2009), the mechanism was social concerns coupled with the appeal of sustainable energy sources. For Braunerhjelm et al. (2010), the mechanism was government policies that would create incentives for entrepreneurial endeavors.

Business Founding

Analyzing a national, longitudinal sample of women in the United States, Dolinsky et al. (1993) found that education level affected the likelihood of entering, continuing, and re-entering self-employment. They suggested that this is due to both the greater human capital and greater financial capital of more highly educated individuals.

Castrogiovanni (1996) offered a model spelling out the potential impacts of pre-startup planning on new venture survival. In that model, human capital was represented by the knowledge that founders bring to their ventures and on the learning founders gain through the business planning process. Though he suggested that founder knowledge and learning both impact survival, he also suggested that substitution is possible. More knowledgeable founders, for example, might have less need for learning. Moreover, financial slack may enable founders to cope with deficiencies in their knowledge.

Cyr et al. (2000) examined human capital among 402 IPOs in 1993 to determine whether venture capital (VC) backing made a difference. They found that firms with VC backing were more likely to have a vice-president of human resources (VPHR), thus indicating that VCs influence human capital somewhat, though it is unclear whether VCs tend to (1) back firms with VPHRs, (2) influence firms they back to create VPHR positions, or (3) both. Having a VPHR, however, did not seem to impact IPO stock price performance. The VPHR effect on stock price was insignificant, as was the VPHR–VC interaction effect on stock price.

In a study of entrepreneurial activity in Sweden, Honig (2001) found that human capital had little impact on nascent entrepreneurs and intrapreneurs. In that study, human capital was assessed by three variables (1) years in school, (2) business school coursework, and (3) prior startup experience. Honig found that learning strategy was much more important, with intrapreneurs using learning strategies geared toward organizational consensus and entrepreneurs employing more flexible and adaptive learning strategies.

Davidsson and Honig (2003) examined the influence of human and social capital on two aspects of business creation – recognizing and exploiting opportunities. They found that human capital influenced nascent entrepreneurs' recognition of opportunities, but had little effect on exploitation. Thus, greater levels of education and experience made it more likely that someone would start a business, but did not affect subsequent business sales and profit. In contrast, social capital had a significant impact on opportunity exploitation and resulting sales and profit.

Baum and Silverman (2004) looked at whether VCs focus on picking winners or building them, in part, by comparing human capital characteristics of startups before and after they received VC backing. They found that VCs tended to back startups strong in technology but weak in managerial expertise. Thus, technology-related human capital was more important than managerial-related human capital for receiving VC backing. Presumably, this is because the VCs bring considerable managerial-related human capital of their own to the startup, which VCs can then use to develop the managerial-related human capital of the startup venture. Interestingly, Baum and Silverman (2004) found, however, that human capital had little effect on venture startup performance. Thus, VCs seem to give greater weight to human capital in their decisions to back startups than is warranted.

Cassar (2006) posited a relationship between opportunity costs and the intended scale of new ventures. Thus, he argued that nascent entrepreneurs with greater opportunity costs would require greater returns from a new venture. Suggesting that some opportunity costs were associated with human capital and using data from the Panel Study of Entrepreneurial Dynamics, he measured the effects of several human capital variables on intended venture scale. Controlling for industry and location, age, education, and gender were insignificant, whereas ethnicity and managerial work experience were significant.

Packalen (2007) offered a model suggesting that human capital (i.e., founding team status within the industry and founding team demographics) and social capital affect a venture's initial legitimacy, which in turn affects its initial resource endowment. She suggested that these different factors could substitute for one another to some extent. She also noted, however, that interactions among them create complementarities. Thus, though Packalen did not offer empirical results, it seems plausible that each of these factors needs to be present at least to some minimal degree.

In a longitudinal study of 161 high-technology ventures, Beckman et al. (2007) examined linkages between top management team (TMT) characteristics and desirable early-stage venture outcomes. They found that human capital diversity (indicated by company affiliations, management functions, TMT turnover, and founder exit) is positively associated with VC funding and IPO. Thus, it appears that investors value top management teams with broad knowledge and skill sets.

While prior experience is often examined as a key human capital factor, researchers typically assume the experience is in legitimate, legal ventures. In contrast, Aidis and van Praag (2007) focused on whether illegal entrepreneurship experience yields similar effects. Surveying business owners in Lithuania, they found that illegal entrepreneurship experience was positively related to motivation to stay in business and motivation to grow, but it was not significantly related to organization size, business revenue, or profit.

Keep in mind, however, that prior experience – legal, illegal, startup, managerial, or some other kind – is more than merely putting effort into some activity for a certain amount of time. Experience can vary in quality as well as degree. Since it is difficult to assess experience quality, however, researchers typically assume that people are more capable of starting a business if they have engaged in certain relevant activities in the past, presumably because of the learning gained while conducting those other activities. Corbett et al. (2007) sought insights on how that learning occurs. In a longitudinal, qualitative study of technology-based ventures, they focused on the learning gained from new venture failures, and they found that learning depended on the approach used to terminate the venture.

DeTienne and Chandler (2007) examined the effect of gender on opportunity recognition. They found that men and women assess opportunities differently, presumably because of their different backgrounds and experiences. This does not necessarily lead to different results, however. For example, no differences between men and women were found in the innovativeness of the opportunities recognized.

General forms of human capital (education and work experience) were distinguished from entrepreneurship-specific forms of human capital (business ownership experience, managerial capabilities, entrepreneurial capabilities, and technical capabilities) by Ucbasaran et al. (2008). In a study of 588 business owners, they found that more variance in terms of business opportunities recognized and pursued was associated with entrepreneurship-specific human capital than general human capital. When human capital variables were considered together, only one of six general variables was at least marginally significant (education, $p \leq 0.10$). In contrast, three of four entrepreneurship-specific variables were significant (ownership experience, $p \leq 0.001$; managerial capability, $p \leq 0.01$; and entrepreneurial capability, $p \leq 0.10$).

Wiklund and Shepherd (2008) made a similar distinction between general and entrepreneurship-specific human capital in a study of portfolio entrepreneurship. Focusing on persons starting ventures in Sweden in 1994, education was the indicator of general human capital, and startup experience in 1994 (i.e., novice versus habitual entrepreneur in terms of whether or not they had started another venture) indicated entrepreneurship-specific human capital. Measuring portfolio entrepreneurship as new ventures after 1994, they found that both forms of human capital and two indicators of social capital had positive effects on portfolio entrepreneurship. In addition, they found that, of those variables, only startup experience was related to the organizing mode for the new venture (i.e., creating a new organization or using their existing organization). Habitual entrepreneurs were more likely than novice entrepreneurs to create new organizations when pursuing new venture opportunities.

Studying master weavers in India, Bhagavatula et al. (2010) hypothesized that three human capital variables – experience, skills, and languages spoken – affect both opportunity recognition and resource mobilization. In addition, however, they argued that social capital mediates those relationships. Thus, as their findings showed, human capital has both direct and indirect (mediated) effects.

In sum, this literature suggests that human capital does indeed influence venture creation and early-stage outcomes. The kind of human capital stock, however, may be more important than the overall level. For example, entrepreneurship-specific human capital may have a greater impact than general human capital (Ucbasaran et al., 2008) and breadth may be more important than depth (Beckman et al., 2007) – at least in some contexts. Moreover, the value of human capital may be influenced by social capital or other factors (e.g., Davidsson & Honig, 2003).

Intermediate Outcomes

Chaganti et al. (1995) examined linkages of human capital with the financial capital structure of 903 small businesses. They found that businesses where the owner and unpaid family members worked long hours relied more on debt obtained from external sources than small businesses where owners and unpaid family members worked less. In addition, businesses with many partners relied more on debt financing than small businesses with fewer partners.

Westhead et al. (2001) considered whether human capital and other factors influenced subsequent exporting behavior among 621 British small and medium enterprises (SMEs). Four categories of human capital were examined: (1) general human capital, (2) management know-how, (3) specific industry know-how, and (4) ability to acquire financial capital.

Westhead et al. (2001) found that businesses with older principal founders, considerable management know-how, principal founders who had considerable industry-specific knowledge, and previous experience of selling goods or services abroad were more likely to be exporters. The significant human capital variables pertained to management and specific industry know-how. Surprisingly, general human capital and ability to acquire financial capital did not have much effect.

Sirmon and Hitt (2003) presented a resource management model as an organizing framework for studying family businesses. Accordingly, five key sets of resources were argued to affect wealth creation: (1) human capital, (2) social capital, (3) patient capital, (4) survivability capital, and (5) governance structure. Regarding human capital, they noted that family firms often favor family members over more qualified individuals in their hiring and promotion decisions. Moreover, because of such tendencies, they often find it difficult to attract and hire highly qualified candidates.

In a study of 90 owner-managed ventures over the 1990–2000 interval, Ucbasaran et al. (2003) found that human capital factors associated with member entry to the top management team differed from those associated with member exit. Size of the founding team was negatively related to subsequent entry. Team heterogeneity in terms of both functional background and entrepreneurial experience was positively related to exit.

Decision speed was the focus of a study by Forbes (2005). Survey data on 98 Internet startups and their founders revealed that older entrepreneurs and those with prior entrepreneurial experience tend to make quicker decisions. Forbes suggested, however, that these findings might be contextually bounded.

Intermediate outcomes examined by Branzei and Vertinsky (2006) were the external absorption and internal emergence of product innovation capabilities among SMEs. Focusing on Canadian manufacturing establishments with 100 or fewer employees, they found that human capital contributed to SME acquisition and transformation processes. Thus, they argued that human capital development plays a critical role in SME innovation.

Manolova et al. (2007) looked at effects of human and social capital on the venture growth expectancies among male and female entrepreneurs in Bulgaria. Effects varied by gender. Growth expectancies of females were influenced more by human capital (i.e., prior experience) whereas the growth expectancies of males were influenced more by social capital (i.e., interpersonal networks).

Marvel and Lumpkin (2007) investigated the effects of technology entrepreneurs' education level and prior knowledge on degree of innovation. They found that degree of innovation was positively influenced by both education level and prior technological knowledge, but negatively influenced by prior market knowledge. Thus, both general human capital (education level) and specific human capital (technological and market knowledge) affect entrepreneurial abilities to generate radical innovations.

In a longitudinal, theory-building study of 24 academic entrepreneurs, Mosey and Wright (2007) examined influences of human capital on the development of social capital needed for venture creation. They proposed that prior business ownership experience affects an entrepreneur's social network and development of network ties. Moreover, they concluded that business ownership experience seems essential for building relationships with experienced managers and potential investors.

Toole and Czarnitzki (2009) also considered the human capital of academics, but they distinguished between the scientific versus commercial content of the knowledge and experience. They found that those two components of the academic's human capital have differential effects on the research and invention tasks of their ventures. Thus, they argued that academic human capital is heterogeneous.

Drawing on the similarity–attraction paradigm, Bruns et al. (2008) found that parallels between loan officers' human capital and applicants' human capital can predict loan approval. Interestingly, their study of Swedish loan officers and small business loan requests failed to uncover relationships between general and specific human capital and loan approval, however. Thus, at least among this sample, loan officers seemed to favor entrepreneurs with backgrounds similar to their own over those with backgrounds more suited to the needs of the venture.

Hallen (2008) observed that new organizations differ from old ones in the manner in which their positions evolve within their interorganizational networks. In a study of 92 Internet security ventures, he found that human capital plays a role when new organizations first form network ties early on, but organizational accomplishments are more important when organizations first form network ties later on. Thus, it appears that human capital should be developed prior to early round financing so that the new organization can establish the necessary relationships with financiers.

Nevertheless, the kind of human capital matters. Zhang et al. (2008) found that two human capital factors (occupational status and industry experience) have positive effects on the use of existing network ties when approaching early investors, whereas prior management or marketing experience had a negative effect. In addition, management or marketing experience moderated the occupational status and industry experience effects. Zhang et al. (2008) suggested that managerial and marketing experience provide entrepreneurs with the confidence and skill needed to initiate new ties with strangers rather than to simply rely on their existing ties.

Wright et al. (2008) looked at relationships of human capital with (university versus non-university) science park location decisions. They found that Chinese entrepreneurs who obtained practical business knowledge or business ownership experience abroad were more likely to locate in university science parks upon their return to China. Of those two human capital variables, however, only practical business knowledge was related to subsequent employment growth – and only among ventures located in non-university parks – and neither variable was related to managerial perceptions of performance.

Aside from the benefits described in the various studies mentioned thus far, human capital can have certain drawbacks. Arthurs et al. (2009) observed that, although the firm-specific knowledge, skills, and experience developed and possessed by founding entrepreneurs can be a source of competitive advantage, they can also pose a threat to potential investors since they increase the potential for a "hold-up" agency problem whereby the entrepreneurs seek to appropriate a larger share of the economic rents generated by the venture than what they previously negotiated. In their study of 313 IPOs, they argued and found evidence that this threat could be mitigated by greater outsider ownership and startup experience by the board as well as greater use of contingent compensation and involuntary departure agreements.

Audretsch et al. (2009) also highlighted the agency issues associated with the human capital that entrepreneurs bring to their ventures. They argued that firms are especially vulnerable to hold-up by their entrepreneur-CEOs when the number of patents held by the entrepreneur is high relative to the total number held by the venture. This view was supported in their study of 127 German IPOs, which found that the percentage of equity held by the entrepreneur-CEO was positively related to the number of patents held by that individual and negatively related to the number held by the firm.

Although human capital considerations have helped to explain differences in propensities to franchise the outlets of retail, restaurant, and service chains, they have been largely ignored in discussions of the internal management of those chains. Addressing this gap, Castrogiovanni and Kidwell (2010) highlighted differences in the human capital brought to new outlets within chains by franchisees and employee-managers, respectively. Specifically, they argued that franchisees tend to bring more general business knowledge to their outlets, whereas employee-managers tend to bring more chain-specific operational knowledge. Consequently, chains with franchisee-managed outlets need to emphasize operational training, and those with employee-managed outlets should emphasize general managerial development.

Together, these studies illustrate that there is no clear, cohesive theory of the intermediate effects of human capital. Studies have tended to focus on particular intermediate outcomes, and human capital factors were some of the variables used to explain those outcomes. This suggests that human capital contributes to a wide range of organizational phenomena. For example, human capital can affect the financial structure of new and small businesses (Chaganti et al., 1995), decision speed (Forbes, 2005), and innovation (Marvel & Lumpkin, 2007). Moreover, different types of human capital can have different effects (Toole & Czarnitzki, 2009).

Long-term Performance

Interest in the effects of human capital on the long-term performance of new ventures was stimulated by the seminal work of Cooper et al. (1994). In addition to financial capital, three types of human capital were considered – (1) general human capital (education, gender, and race), (2) management know-how (without regard to industry), and (3) industry know-how. In a longitudinal study of 1053 new ventures, the initial stock of general human capital affected both venture survival and growth, as did industry know-how.

Building on that same theme, Gimeno et al. (1997) argued that survival is not strictly a function of economic performance but also reflects a performance threshold determined by human capital characteristics. When the human capital that an entrepreneur brings to a venture can generate more economic rents elsewhere, the entrepreneur may exit that venture even though it seems successful in some absolute sense. Conversely, an entrepreneur may persist with a current venture when alternative uses of his/her human capital are inferior, and so the venture may persist despite relatively weak performance. Strong support was obtained for this view, using a sample of 1547 entrepreneurs in the United States.

DeTienne et al. (2008) also found that human capital influences the performance threshold above which a firm will persist. Using an experimental design, they found that decisions to continue a business reflect in part the other opportunities and options available to the entrepreneur. These in turn depend on the human capital possessed by the entrepreneur.

Honig (1998) examined human, financial, and social capital determinants of successful Jamaican entrepreneurs. In his study of 215 informal micro-enterprises, human capital associated with vocational training and years of experience was positively related to micro-enterprise performance. Those effects, however, were moderated by environmental structure.

Watson et al. (2003) examined how venture profit and growth were impacted by human capital, interpersonal processes, and organizational demography. They found that, in terms of human capital, education and work experience were positively correlated with growth perceptions of venture partners. Thus, they argued that human capital considerations should be important in decisions about venture initiation and direction.

Dimov and Shepherd (2005) examined relationships between the education and experience of the TMTs of venture capital firms and the performance of those firms. They found that general human capital was positively related to performance in terms of the proportion of ventures in the firm's portfolio that went public, while specific human capital was negatively associated with the proportion of portfolio ventures that went bankrupt. Thus, general human capital of TMTs seemed to help the venture capital firms pick winners, whereas specific human capital helped them avoid losers.

In another study of venture capital firms, Zarutskie (2010) examined relationships between TMT human capital and venture portfolio performance in terms of the proportion of portfolio exits (IPOs or acquisitions). She found that the number of managers having past experience as venture capitalists and the number having past experience in startup ventures was positively linked to venture portfolio performance. In addition, she found some evidence that industry-specific human capital (e.g., industry consulting experience) is positively related to venture portfolio performance, whereas general human capital (e.g., MBA degree) is negatively related.

Rauch et al. (2005) studied the effects of human capital on performance in terms of employment growth. Examining a sample of young, small businesses in Germany, they found that both the business owners' human capital and human resource development activities were positively linked to growth. In addition, employee human capital moderated the relationship between human resource development and growth. That is, the human resource development effect was stronger when employee human capital was greater.

In contrast to studies viewing performance in terms of growth, Haber and Reichel (2007) sought to examine the impact of human capital on "lifestyle" firms where the owners are not actively pursuing growth. Focusing on 305 tourism businesses in Israel, they found that the owner's human capital in terms of managerial skills was positively linked to both short- and long-term performance. Thus, they concluded that managerial skills are crucial to small business success.

Whereas human capital discussions of prior work experience tend to focus on or assume that the experience was legitimate, Aidis and van Praag (2007) examined the effects of illegal entrepreneurship experience. Specifically, they looked at whether black or gray market experience in a planned economy would be valuable once private enterprise was legalized in that country. Based on a survey of 399 entrepreneurs in Lithuania, they found that illegal entrepreneurship experience was positively related to performance for younger entrepreneurs and those who started completely new, legal businesses.

In a study of 198 new high-technology ventures, Shrader and Siegel (2007) examined the links between the human capital of the founding top management team, the venture's competitive strategy, and both sales and profit performance. Founding team human capital was assessed in terms of total years of previous experience in the industry, in functional areas, and in prior startups. They found that there is a strong relationship between team experience and venture strategy, but only a weak link between team experience and venture performance.

In a study of 2713 SMEs within the European Union, Soriano and Castrogiovanni (2010) considered effects of general and industry-specific human capital of CEO-entrepreneurs, acquired before and after their business startups, on SME profitability and productivity. They found that both profitability and productivity are positively related to industry-specific knowledge possessed by the CEO-owner prior to starting the firm and the general business knowledge acquired once the firm is up and running. Prior industry experience was related to productivity but not profitability.

In these studies of the relationship between human capital and performance, both variables have been conceptualized in many ways. Human capital, for example, has been examined in terms of being general versus industry-, firm- or task-specific (e.g., Cooper et al., 1994) and legal versus illegal (Aidis & van Praag, 2007). Performance has been assessed in terms of profitability (e.g., Soriano & Castrogiovanni, 2010), employment growth (Rauch et al., 2005), and business-specific considerations (e.g., Zarutskie, 2010). Despite all these differences, the overall conclusion is robust – *human capital is positively related to long-term small business performance.* Still, there are nuances that small businesses need to consider as they assemble or develop their own human capital. These are discussed below.

AN INTEGRATIVE PERSPECTIVE

The preceding review showed that human capital is seldom considered in isolation – and rightfully so. Human capital is just one of many sets of factors affecting business founding, intermediate outcomes, and long-term performance. Figure 3.1 illustrates an integrative perspective on human capital and small business performance. Two key premises form the foundation of that perspective. First is a configuration view that human capital

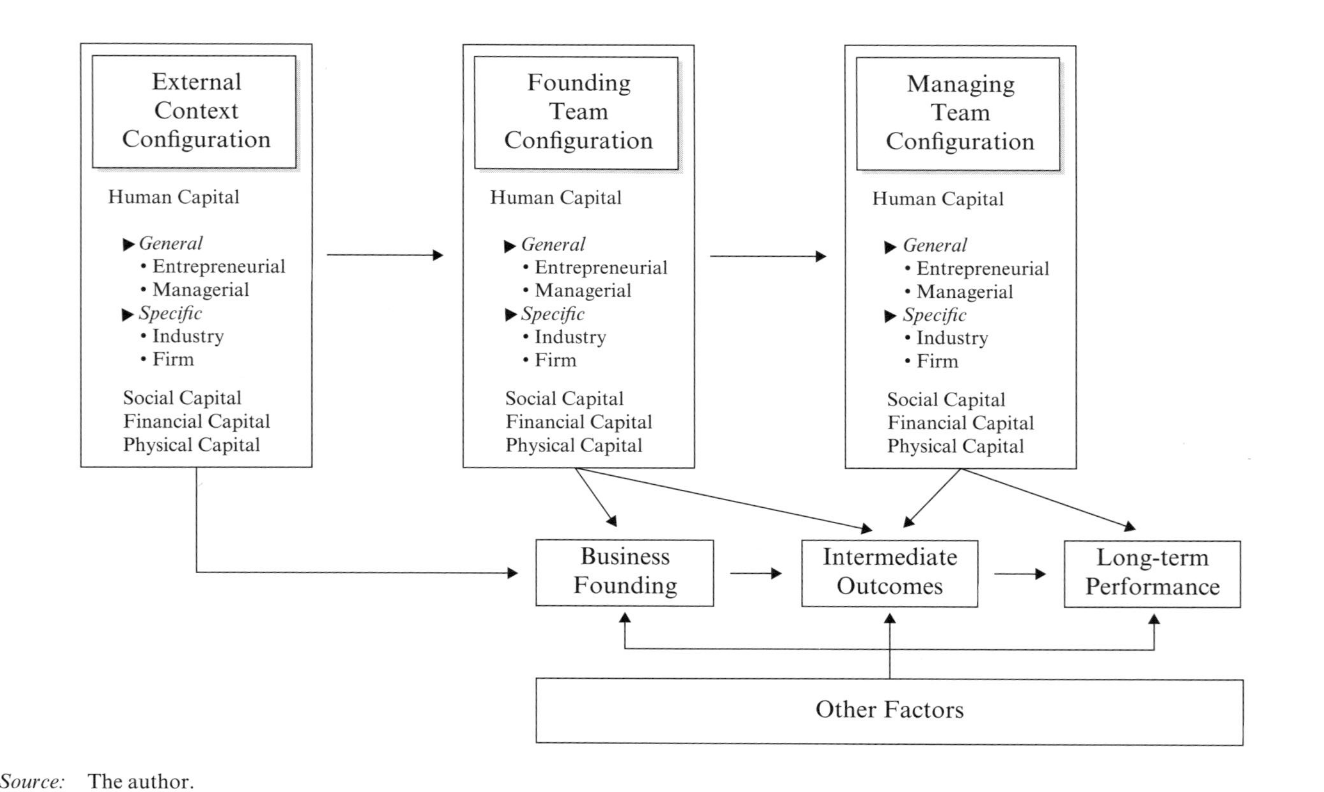

Source: The author.

Figure 3.1 Integrative perspective of human capital and entrepreneurial success

combines with other forms of capital (e.g., social, financial, and physical capital) in complex ways to affect business founding and both intermediate and long-term results. Second is the contention that different types of general and specific human capital affect business founding and results in different ways.

Three Configurations

Human capital is just one type of resource contributing to economic activity. Social, financial, and physical capital are among the other types often discussed (cf. Audretsch & Keilbach, 2004; Sine & Lee, 2009). These various types of resources interact in complex ways. For example, human capital may have limited value by itself when other types of resources are lacking. Thus, Audretsch and Keilbach (2004) found that a particular type of social capital, which they labeled "entrepreneurial capital", moderated the relationship between human capital and economic development. To some extent, different types of resources may be substitutable. If they have sufficient financial capital, for example, business founders may be able to compensate for their own limitations by hiring others to provide the expertise that they themselves lack. Thus, we cannot consider effects of human capital in isolation, but rather we need to consider how the configuration of human capital and other types of resources contributes to desired results.

In Figure 3.1, human capital is part of three resource configurations associated with three points in the business development process. The "external context configuration" consists of the stocks and flows of resources such as human, social, financial, and physical capital used in economic activity within a geographic area. When governments seek to promote economic development in an area, they do so by investing in human capital or other resources in this configuration (Becker, 1964). The external context configuration, in turn, influences the "founding team configuration" to the extent that team members and other resources are drawn from the external context. Consistent with this configuration perspective, for example, the findings by Audretsch and Keilbach (2004) suggest that the interaction between human capital and a particular form of social capital (which they called entrepreneurial capital) results in founders teaming together to start new ventures. Likewise, the research by Sine and Lee (2009) suggests that founding teams were formed as the result of the interplay between market conditions, human capital, key natural resources, and social movement trends. Once the founding team is formed, the study by Davidsson and Honig (2003) suggests that its success largely depends on how its human and social capital are utilized together.

Whereas each form of capital, along with other resources within or available to a founding team, may be sufficient for venture creation, the founding team configuration may be deficient for growing or maintaining the venture over the long run. Thus, as Figure 3.1 suggests, the founding team must evolve into a "managing team configuration". Human capital is enhanced as founding team members gain new knowledge and experience (Corbett et al., 2007; Soriano & Castrogiovanni, 2010), and as they are replaced or as team size is increased (cf. Cyr et al., 2000; Ucbasaran et al., 2003) with new top management team members having the knowledge, skills, and experience needed to guide the venture after its early stages of development.

These three configurations give rise to the kinds of outcomes discussed previously, as indicated in Figure 3.1. The external context configuration makes it more or less likely that businesses will be founded (e.g., Allen et al., 2007; Braunerhjelm et al., 2010). Businesses are unlikely to emerge spontaneously and unintentionally, however, and so a founding team is needed to initiate the startup effort (cf. Davidsson & Honig, 2003). The founding team is also responsible for the early development and intermediate outcomes of the venture such as capital structure (Chaganti et al., 1995), decision speed (Forbes, 2005), and innovation (Marvel & Lumpkin, 2007). As the founding team evolves into the managing team, some intermediate outcomes may be achieved by the managing team configuration. Then, it is the managing team configuration that shapes growth (Rauch et al., 2005), productivity (Soriano & Castrogiovanni, 2010), and other aspects of long-term performance (e.g., Dimov & Shepherd, 2005; Shrader & Siegel, 2007). Finally, as Figure 3.1 shows, other factors (e.g., industry conditions) influence these various results, and earlier results (e.g., intermediate outcomes) influence later results (e.g., long-term performance).

General and Specific Human Capital

As noted, Figure 3.1 also shows the basic distinction between general and specific human capital often made in the literature (e.g., Cooper et al., 1994; Westhead et al., 2001). Recall that human capital was defined earlier as the knowledge, skill, and experience that top management brings to a venture, which influences venture success. It follows then that general human capital is the knowledge, skill, and experience relevant for any kind of venture, whereas specific human capital is that which is particularly relevant for a given venture.

This differs somewhat from prior views of general and specific human capital. Cooper et al. (1994), for example, viewed general human capital in terms of an entrepreneur's education level, gender, and race. Thus, they were considering attributes of entrepreneurs that might correlate with entrepreneurial success. In contrast, the focus here is on variables that can be manipulated in human capital development efforts. In efforts to stimulate economic activity in a particular area, for example, it is hard to imagine national or local governments manipulating gender or racial balances.

General human capital

Accordingly, general human capital as viewed here more closely resembles what Cooper et al. (1994) described as management know-how. In Figure 3.1, two forms are distinguished – entrepreneurial and managerial. Entrepreneurial human capital is the knowledge, skills, and experience relevant for starting businesses (cf. Ucbasaran et al., 2008; Wiklund & Shepherd, 2008). In the external context, it may be stimulated in part by entrepreneurial education and assistance programs offered by universities or government agencies. Among top management teams, entrepreneurial human capital is largely determined by the education and experiences of team members. A serial entrepreneur who started several ventures in the past, for example, would possess more entrepreneurial human capital than a novice entrepreneur.

Whereas entrepreneurial human capital is relevant for starting businesses, managerial human capital is the knowledge, skills, and experience relevant for developing and maintaining businesses after the startup. As noted in the preceding review, venture capital firms often provide managerial capital to firms in their portfolios (Baum & Silverman, 2004) or otherwise seek to ensure that a venture has the managerial skills needed after the startup (Cyr et al., 2000). In fact, managerial skills may influence long-term performance more than entrepreneurial skills (Haber & Reichel, 2007).

Specific human capital

Finally, Figure 3.1 shows that specific human capital can be either industry- or firm-specific. Industry-specific human capital can help entrepreneurs to define opportunities, and to understand customer needs, technological possibilities, and critical success factors (Soriano & Castrogiovanni, 2010). Firm-specific human capital accrues from top managers' experiences with the particular venture, giving them in-depth understanding of the venture's capabilities, risks, and inner-workings (Arthurs et al., 2009).

PRACTICAL IMPLICATIONS

As discussed previously, the configuration perspective suggests that firms, institutions, and governments seeking to stimulate economic activity should strive for an appropriate balance between human, social, financial,

	Founding Team	*Managing Team*
General Human Capital	Entrepreneurial	Managerial
Specific Human Capital	Industry	Firm
	New Venture	*Established Venture*

Source: The author.

Figure 3.2 Key forms of human capital for new versus established ventures

and physical capital. Thus, although human capital is the focus here, we should not ignore the other forms of capital. The value of human capital in fostering economic development may be very limited, for example, if social mechanisms for bringing people together are lacking (Audretsch & Keilbach, 2004).

In addition, timing considerations may be critical. The value of different types of general and specific human capital may shift as a venture matures. Regarding general human capital, entrepreneurial capital may be more important for the founding teams creating new ventures, whereas managerial capital may be more important for the managing teams overseeing established ventures. Regarding specific human capital, industry capital may be more critical for founding teams whereas firm capital may be more important for managing teams. These relationships are depicted in Figure 3.2, and they suggest the conclusions that follow.

Entrepreneurial human capital

Since entrepreneurial human capital is needed to create new ventures it is more crucial to the external context and founding team configurations than to the managing team configuration. It can be fostered in the external context through government-, university-, or community-sponsored entrepreneurial education and assistance programs. In the founding team, entrepreneurial human capital can be enhanced by including one or more experienced entrepreneurs among the team members, or by drawing on the expertise of experienced entrepreneurs in paid or unpaid advisory roles. As a venture matures, entrepreneurial human capital becomes less important.

Managerial human capital

Since managerial human capital is needed to develop and maintain established ventures, it is more important to the managing team configuration than to the founding team configuration. In the external context, it can be fostered in part by university degree programs (e.g., MBA programs) or relevant continuing education programs. In the managing team configuration, it can be developed by hiring individuals with needed managerial skills and experience. In addition, firms might send existing TMT members back to school to further their managerial education.

Industry-specific human capital

Though it certainly is relevant for established ventures, industry-specific human capital is critical for the founding team. As noted above, this form of human capital helps entrepreneurs spot and tap opportunities. It should be developed and infused into the founding team prior to the venture startup, mainly by including members in the team who possess the relevant industry training and experience. In the external context, choices most likely need to be made to target certain industries in a given area, depending on such considerations as local customs and preferences, or comparative advantages.

Firm-specific human capital

By definition, there can be no firm-specific human capital until a new firm is created through a business startup. Thus, little firm-specific human capital exists among the founding team in a new venture. Through their experiences guiding the firm after its inception, top managers develop valuable insights that can be preserved by compensation systems and other mechanisms geared toward retaining key people. In addition, tacit firm-specific knowledge can be made explicit to the extent possible, such as by formalizing in writing the policies and practices found to be effective.

CONCLUSION

In reviewing major studies within the past two decades pertaining to human capital in small businesses, this chapter highlights the various antecedents and consequences of human capital development efforts. In doing so, insights on the role of human capital factors in small business performance and success were offered. In addition, an integrative perspective was presented.

REFERENCES

Aidis, R. & van Praag, M. (2007). Illegal entrepreneurship experience: Does it make a difference for business performance and motivation? *Journal of Business Venturing*, **22**(2): 283–310.

Allen, S., Link, A. & Rosenbaum, D. (2007). Entrepreneurship and human capital: Evidence of patenting activity from the academic sector. *Entrepreneurship Theory & Practice*, **31**(6): 937–51.

Arthurs, J., Busenitz, L., Hoskisson, R. & Johnson, R. (2009). Firm-specific human capital and governance in IPO firms: Addressing agency and resource dependence concerns. *Entrepreneurship Theory & Practice*, **33**(4): 845–65.

Audretsch, D., & Keilbach, M. (2004). Does entrepreneurship capital matter? *Entrepreneurship Theory & Practice*, **28**(5): 419–29.

Audretsch, D., Lehmann, E. & Plummer, L. (2009). Agency and governance in strategic entrepreneurship. *Entrepreneurship Theory & Practice*, **33**(1): 149–66.

Baum, J. & Silverman, B. (2004). Picking winners or building them? Alliance, intellectual, and human capital as selection criteria in venture financing and performance of biotechnology startups. *Journal of Business Venturing*, **19**(3): 411–36.

Becker, G. (1964). *Human Capital: A Theoretical and Empirical Analysis, with Special Reference to Education*. Chicago: University of Chicago Press.

Beckman, C., Burton, M. & O'Reilly, C. (2007). Early teams: The impact of team demography on VC financing and going public. *Journal of Business Venturing*, **22**(2): 147–73.

Bhagavatula, S., Elfring, T., van Tilburg, A. & van de Bunt, G. (2010). How social and human capital influence opportunity recognition and resource mobilization in India's handloom industry. *Journal of Business Venturing*, **25**(3): 245–60.

Branzei, O. & Vertinsky, I. (2006). Strategic pathways to product innovation capabilities in SMEs. *Journal of Business Venturing*, **21**(1): 75–105.

Braunerhjelm, P., Acs, Z., Audretsch, D. & Carlsson, B. (2010). The missing link: Knowledge diffusion and entrepreneurship in endogenous growth. *Small Business Economics*, **34**(2): 105–25.

Bruns, V., Holland, D., Shepherd, D. & Wiklund, J. (2008). The role of human capital in loan officers' decision policies. *Entrepreneurship Theory & Practice*, **32**(3): 485–506.

Cassar, G. (2006). Entrepreneur opportunity costs and intended venture growth. *Journal of Business Venturing*, **21**(5): 610–32.

Castrogiovanni, G. (1996). Pre-startup planning and the survival of new small businesses: Theoretical linkages. *Journal of Management*, **22**(6): 801–22.

Castrogiovanni, G.J. & Kidwell, R.E. (2010). Human resource management practices affecting unit managers in franchise networks. *Human Resource Management*, **49**(2): 225–40.

Chaganti, R., DeCarolis, D. & Deeds, D. (1995). Predictors of capital structure in small ventures. *Entrepreneurship Theory & Practice*, **20**(2): 7–18.

Cooper, A., Gimeno-Gascon, F. & Woo, C. (1994). Initial human and financial

capital as predictors of new venture performance. *Journal of Business Venturing*, **9**(5): 371–95.
Corbett, A., Neck, H. & DeTienne, D. (2007). How corporate entrepreneurs learn from fledgling innovation initiatives: Cognition and the development of a termination script. *Entrepreneurship Theory & Practice*, **31**(6): 829–52.
Cyr, L., Johnson, D. & Welbourne, T. (2000). Human resources in initial public offering firms: Do venture capitalists make a difference? *Entrepreneurship Theory & Practice*, **25**(1): 77–91.
Davidsson, P. & Honig, B. (2003). The role of social and human capital among nascent entrepreneurs. *Journal of Business Venturing*, **18**(3): 301–31.
DeTienne, D. & Chandler, G. (2007). The role of gender in opportunity identification. *Entrepreneurship Theory & Practice*, **31**(3): 365–86.
DeTienne, D., Shepherd, D. & De Castro, J. (2008). The fallacy of "only the strong survive": The effects of extrinsic motivation on the persistence decisions for under-performing firms. *Journal of Business Venturing*, **23**(5): 528–46.
Dimov, D. & Shepherd, D. (2005). Human capital theory and venture capital firms: Exploring "home runs" and "strike outs". *Journal of Business Venturing*, **20**(1): 1–21.
Dolinsky, A., Caputo, R., Pasumarty, K. & Quazi, H. (1993). The effects of education on business ownership: A longitudinal study of women. *Entrepreneurship Theory & Practice*, **18**(1): 43–53.
Forbes, D. (2005). Managerial determinants of decision speed in new ventures. *Strategic Management Journal*, **26**(4): 355–66.
Gimeno, J., Folta, T., Cooper, A. & Woo, C. (1997). Survival of the fittest? Entrepreneurial human capital and the persistence of underperforming firms. *Administrative Science Quarterly*, **42**(4): 750–83.
Haber, S. & Reichel, A. (2007). The cumulative nature of the entrepreneurial process: The contribution of human capital, planning and environment resources to small venture performance. *Journal of Business Venturing*, **22**(1): 119–45.
Hallen, B. (2008). The causes and consequences of the initial network positions of new organizations: From whom do entrepreneurs receive investments? *Administrative Science Quarterly*, **53**(4): 685–718.
Honig, B. (1998). What determines success? Examining the human, financial, and social capital of Jamaican entrepreneurs. *Journal of Business Venturing*, **13**(5): 371–94.
Honig, B. (2001). Learning strategies and resources for entrepreneurs and intrapreneurs. *Entrepreneurship Theory & Practice*, **26**(1): 21–35.
Majumdar, S. (2007). Private enterprise growth and human capital productivity in India. *Entrepreneurship Theory & Practice*, **31**(6): 853–72.
Manolova, T., Carter, N., Manev, I. & Gyoshev, B. (2007). The differential effect of men and women entrepreneurs' human capital and networking on growth expectancies in Bulgaria. *Entrepreneurship Theory & Practice*, **31**(3): 407–26.
Marvel, M. & Lumpkin, G. (2007). Technology entrepreneurs' human capital and its effects on innovation radicalness. *Entrepreneurship Theory & Practice*, **31**(6): 807–28.
Mintzberg, H. (1979). *The Structuring of Organizations*. Englewood Cliffs, NJ: Prentice Hall.
Mosey, S. & Wright, M. (2007). From human capital to social capital: A longitudinal study of technology-based academic entrepreneurs. *Entrepreneurship Theory & Practice*, **31**(6): 909–35.

Packalen, K. (2007). Complementing capital: The role of status, demographic features, and social capital in founding teams' abilities to obtain resources. *Entrepreneurship Theory & Practice*, **31**(6): 873–91.

Powers, J. & McDougall, P. (2005). University start-up formation and technology licensing with firms that go public: A resource-based view of academic entrepreneurship. *Journal of Business Venturing*, **20**(3): 291–311.

Rauch, A., Frese, M. & Utsch, A. (2005). Effects of human capital and long-term human resources development and utilization on employment growth of small-scale businesses: A causal analysis. *Entrepreneurship Theory & Practice*, **29**(6): 681–98.

Shrader, R. & Siegel, D. (2007). Assessing the relationship between human capital and firm performance: Evidence from technology-based new ventures. *Entrepreneurship Theory & Practice*, **31**(6): 893–908.

Sine, W. & Lee, B. (2009). Tilting at windmills? The environmental movement and the emergence of the US wind energy sector. *Administrative Science Quarterly*, **54**(1): 123–55.

Sirmon, D. & Hitt, M. (2003). Managing resources: Linking unique resources, management, and wealth creation in family firms. *Entrepreneurship Theory & Practice*, **27**(4): 339–58.

Soriano, D.R. & Castrogiovanni, G. (2010). The impact of education, experience, and inner circle advisors on SME performance: Insights from a study in public development centers. *Small Business Economics*. DOI 10.1007/s11187-010-9278-3.

Toole, A. & Czarnitzki, D. (2009). Exploring the relationship between scientist human capital and firm performance: The case of biomedical academic entrepreneurs in the SBIR program. *Management Science*, **55**(1): 101–14.

Ucbasaran, D., Westhead, P. & Wright, M. (2008). Opportunity identification and pursuit: Does an entrepreneur's human capital matter? *Small Business Economics*, **30**(2): 153–73.

Ucbasaran, D., Lockett, A., Wright, M. & Westhead, P. (2003). Entrepreneurial founder teams: Factors associated with member entry and exit. *Entrepreneurship Theory & Practice*, **28**(2): 107–27.

Watson, W., Stewart Jr., W. & BarNir, A. (2003). The effects of human capital, organizational demography, and interpersonal processes on venture partner perceptions of firm profit and growth. *Journal of Business Venturing*, **18**(2): 145–64.

Westhead, P., Wright, M. & Ucbasaran, D. (2001). The internationalization of new and small firms: A resource-based view. *Journal of Business Venturing*, **16**(4): 333–58.

Wiklund, J. & Shepherd, D. (2008). Portfolio entrepreneurship: Habitual and novice founders, new entry, and mode of organizing. *Entrepreneurship Theory & Practice*, **32**(4): 701–25.

Wright, M., Liu, X., Buck, T. & Filatotchev, I. (2008). Returnee entrepreneurs, science park location choice and performance: An analysis of high-technology SMEs in China. *Entrepreneurship Theory & Practice*, **32**(1): 131–55.

Zarutskie, R. (2010). The role of top management team human capital in venture capital markets: Evidence from first-time funds. *Journal of Business Venturing*, **25**(1): 155–72.

Zhang, J., Souitaris, V., Soh, P. & Wong, P. (2008). A contingent model of network utilization in early financing of technology ventures. *Entrepreneurship Theory & Practice*, **32**(4): 593–613.

4. Alternative systems of human resources practices and performance in small entrepreneurial organizations

Christopher J. Collins

Small businesses, defined as independent businesses with fewer than 500 employees, play an important role in our economy. It is estimated that there are over 23 million small businesses in the US making up over 99 percent of all US businesses, and small businesses employ 50 percent of all private sector employees (US Small Business Administration, 2004). Small, entrepreneurial firms are an important subset of small firms because they are frequently cited as being the key drivers of economic growth job creation (Shane & Venkataraman, 2000). Further, entrepreneurial firms play an essential role in creating new knowledge and converting knowledge into new products and services (Christensen, 1998; Shane & Venkataraman, 2000). Given the importance of these firms, it is important for researchers to understand how small, entrepreneurial businesses can improve their performance and increase their impact on the general economy.

Following the definition of entrepreneurship provided by Shane and Venkataraman (2000), I define entrepreneurial organizations as those firms that create market opportunities through the discovery, evaluation, and exploitation of new goods and services. Inherent in this definition is the notion that firms may be on one end of the entrepreneurship spectrum or the other – that is, some will be in the exploration stage while others will be in the exploitation stage. Firms in the exploration stage are focused on creative processes around the discovery of new ideas and innovations; whereas, firms in the exploitation stage are focused on competitive advantage based on consistent execution of existing processes and incremental improvement of existing products and services (March, 1991). While it is possible for firms to be simultaneously pursuing exploration and exploitation, I take the position that smaller entrepreneurial firms will be resource constrained in a way that senior leaders are likely to focus the bulk of their resources on one of these strategic orientations at a particular point in time.

Over the past 10–15 years, entrepreneurship research has tended to focus on how environmental characteristics (Aldrich, 2000), characteristics of entrepreneurial opportunities (Christensen, 1998), or characteristics of the entrepreneur (Baum et al., 2001) affect the founding and performance of entrepreneurial organizations. While each of these factors have been found to be important for informing models of entrepreneurship, they each seem to ignore a critical resource that is likely to also have a substantial role in driving the success and survival of entrepreneurial firms – employees. In fact, an emerging body of research suggests that employees are the key organizational resource that leads to sustainable competitive advantage because the knowledge that they create enables firms to adapt and survive (Nahapiet & Ghoshal, 1998; Smith et al., 2005). Thus, research that examines how small, entrepreneurial firms can better manage employees may lead to a more complete model of entrepreneurial performance and survival.

Employees and employee management practices appear to be one way that companies are able to improve their performance. Strategic human resource management (SHRM) scholars have argued that an organization's success is at least partially dependent on its employees and their behaviors in carrying out the strategies of the business (Becker & Huselid, 2006; Wright et al., 2001). Organizations that can effectively influence the behaviors and motivation of their employees through human resource management systems will be able to increase their performance and viability (Collins & Smith, 2006; Wright et al., 2001). Like other organizations, entrepreneurial firms should also be able to leverage their employees through human resource management (HRM) to improve their performance.

SHRM researchers, however, have focused almost exclusively on the study of HRM in large organizations in an effort to understand the role that HRM plays in firm performance. Little if any research has addressed the role of SHRM in small businesses (Collins et al., 2004). The majority of empirical studies on HR practices in small, entrepreneurial firms have surveyed firms to identify the frequency with which they use different practices (Cardon & Stevens, 2004). These broad-based surveys have shown that small, entrepreneurial firms implement a wide array of recruitment, selection, training, and compensation practices (Heneman et al., 2000; Hornsby & Kuratko, 1990), and these smaller firms are more sophisticated in their use of HR practices than originally thought (Cardon & Stevens, 2004; Heneman et al., 2000). While these studies help to identify the range of practices used by smaller firms, they are limited in the useful advice that they can provide managers and researchers. Importantly these papers do not help determine which of these practices are likely to be effective for small, entrepreneurial firms nor have they taken into account the research on SHRM that points to examining systems of practices and the alignment of those systems to the strategy of the organization.

One important way to address this shortcoming is to identify the contextual factors of small firms and draw on organizational theories to suggest when specific types of practices are likely to be more or less effective. This follows recent calls by SHRM researchers who have argued that researchers need to carefully match the systems of HRM practices to the strategic context being studied in order to advance the field of SHRM (Becker & Huselid, 2006; Collins & Smith, 2006). While small businesses depend on their human capital for competitive advantage, they also face resource constraints that make it essential that they wisely invest in HR practices that drive the employee outcomes that are most critical for success. Unlike larger organizations that may have slack resources to overinvest in HR activities, small firms may not see an appropriate return from an HR investment unless the investment is fully aligned with the strategy of the organization (Way, 2002). Thus, I look to contribute to the literature on small entrepreneurial organizations by identifying HR systems that are a theoretical match to the growth strategy of the business.

In this chapter, I focus on alternative models of HR management that entrepreneurial firms may implement depending on whether the firm is at a stage of exploring new opportunities or exploiting an existing innovation or idea. First, I briefly review the literature on SHRM with a particular focus on the contingency perspective. Next, I outline two alternative approaches for entrepreneurial growth – exploration and exploitation – noting the employee requirements to support both. Third, I theoretically link systems of HR practices to each of the approaches to growth. Specifically, based on the work of Baron and colleagues (Baron et al., 2001; Baron & Hannan, 2002), I focus on elaborating how an engineering model of HR practices can support an exploration strategy and how a bureaucratic model of HR practices is the best support for an exploitation strategy. Finally, I discuss the implications for future research on the link between HR practices and firm performance in small, entrepreneurial companies.

THEORY AND HYPOTHESES

HRM and Firm Performance: The Contingency Approach

Research suggests that HRM systems as a resource can lead to competitive advantage (Becker & Huselid, 2006; Wright et al., 2001), and there is a growing body of empirical studies that have demonstrated relationships between different bundles of HR practices and firm performance in larger firms (see Wright et al., 2005 for a review). Researchers working in the area of SHRM have argued that an organization's human resource management system can lead to improved organizational performance and provide a source of competitive advantage when successfully aligned with the strategic needs of the organization (e.g., Dyer, 1984; Wright et al., 2001). Specifically, when a human resource management system elicits the workforce characteristics leading to organizational competencies that drive competitive advantage in the market, firm performance will be positively affected (Collins & Smith, 2006). Consequently, SHRM scholars have called for research to identify the specific competencies required for success in different strategic contexts and to determine the human resource management approaches that will elicit and support these competencies within organizations (Collins & Smith, 2006; Wright et al., 2001).

Following research on contingency theory, SHRM researchers have argued that organizations can drive competitive advantage and higher performance by implementing systems of HR practices that create and reinforce the workforce characteristics consistent with a particular organizational strategy (Becker & Huselid, 2006; Wright et al., 2001). In effect, different organizational strategies require different employee knowledge, skills, and behaviors and, thus, different underlying HR systems that are most likely to produce these workforce characteristics (Dyer, 1984). Similarly, following the behavioral approach, Schuler and Jackson (1987) argued that firms should first look to determine the role behaviors needed to meet the demands of their strategy and then develop the system of HR practices most likely to induce and support these behaviors. Consistent with SHRM theory, the behavioral perspective argues that an organization can elicit the workforce characteristics necessary for successfully competing with its business strategy through appropriate HR initiatives.

Taken together, there are two underlying premises of the contingency-based approach to SHRM. First, different business strategies require unique sets of organizational and workforce competencies and behaviors, and managers must identify the competencies that are required by a strategy and develop an HR system that effectively elicits and supports these competencies (Collins & Smith, 2006; Wright et al., 2001). Second, there is a strong focus on the entire HR system rather than on individual practices (Becker & Huselid, 2006; Schuler & Jackson, 1987). Consistent with the theme of this chapter, I identify the systems of HR practices most likely to support the underlying workforce characteristics needed to drive and sustain both the exploration and exploitation strategies.

Alternative Strategies for Entrepreneurial Performance

There has been a relatively long-held belief that firms seek to take advantage of market opportunities for growth and survival through the ability to explore and exploit their knowledge and capabilities (March, 1991). Companies that follow an exploration strategy pursue advantage and growth through a learning orientation focused on variation and experimentation (He & Wong, 2004), and these firms focus on the innovation of novel technologies, products, or services (Gupta et al., 2006; Hage, 1980). Organizations following an exploration strategy often face an uncertain, dynamic environment, characterized by technological races among competitors and changing consumer demands (Hage, 1980). In contrast, firms following an exploitation strategy are characterized by competitive advantage and learning based on incremental improvements around existing technologies, products, or services (Gupta et al. 2006; He & Wong, 2004). Firms following the exploitation strategy are typically characterized by competition based in established product domains within new and established consumer markets that are relatively stable and more predictable (Hage, 1980).

While organizations may need to pursue both exploration and exploitation to adapt to changes in the external environment and survive, firms are likely to be oriented to one strategy or the other based on the firm's history, structure, and leadership orientation (Benner & Tushman, 2003; March, 1991). This is particularly true for small entrepreneurial firms that face constrained resources and may not have the capacity to pursue both strategies simultaneously. Given the context of small entrepreneurial firms, I follow a punctuated equilibrium approach (Gupta et al., 2006) and argue that these firms will likely be following one or the other strategy at any point in time and not be simultaneously pursuing both exploration and exploitation strategies.

Scholars have recognized that the competitive demands of the exploitation and exploration strategies require markedly different organizational processes and competencies and firms that are able to create organizational structures aligned with their strategies are more likely to achieve a successful approach to competition (Gupta et al., 2006). Organizational structure has been conceptually identified as a plan for coordination and control within the firm, and firms ideally employ activities and implement practices that support structural characteristics that are conducive to the firm's competitive strategy (Hage, 1980). I argue that small entrepreneurial firms can create structure through HR systems because HR practices shape the relationships between employees and managers and influence how work is completed. In the following sections, I outline the learning and employee workforce demands to support both exploration and exploitation strategies, outline the required organizational structure to support both, and then identify the HR systems that are a theoretical match to these requirements.

Exploration Strategy and the Engineering HR Model

Requirements of the exploration strategy

Organizations following an exploration strategy compete through novel innovation aimed at new product or service domains (Gupta et al., 2006; March, 1991). Exploration-oriented firms seek to create radical innovations that shift the technology trajectory rather than incrementally refine technologies (Benner & Tushman, 2003). Firms following this strategy tend to be characterized with a learning orientation focused on experimentation and seeking variation from existing patterns or technologies (He & Wong, 2004). Because of rapid technological advancements and changing consumer preferences, the competitive environment for explorative firms is characterized by instability and a lack of predictability (Hage, 1980; March, 1991). Explorative organizations need to be highly flexible in order to adapt to the changing demands of their environments, meet the changing needs of consumers, and strategically react to the innovations of competitors (Zammuto & O'Connor, 1992).

To successfully pursue the exploration strategy, firms need access to new knowledge and do so through a broad and wide-ranging search (He & Wong, 2004). Further, these firms need to instill a climate of creativity that is dependent on both broad knowledge search and a willingness to experiment in the ways of combining knowledge to produce novel ideas (He & Wong, 2004; Nahapiet & Ghoshal, 1998). To increase creativity, firms pursuing this strategy must also create a willingness to take risks and experience failures in the pursuit of doing things in novel ways or shifting the technology trajectory (Benner & Tushman, 2003). The learning orientation for explorative organizations involves more open-ended research and exploration, investment in experimentation, and a focus on outcomes that are often larger in scope but less predictable than the steady outputs in the exploitative firm (March, 1991; Tushman & O'Reilly, 1996). Thus, the explorative organization must be tolerant of uncertain outcomes and the regular possibility of project failure, as well as possess the ability to evaluate employee and team performance in the absence of immediate production feedback. Finally, to increase the spread of knowledge and increase the climate for experimentation and risk-taking, firms pursuing this strategy should loosen coordination and control of employees (Gupta et al., 2006).

The workforce characteristics desirable in an explorative firm also differ from those needed in the exploitative organization. Specifically, ideal employees in an organization following an exploration strategy are flexible, willing to collaborate, diverse, and risk-taking (Benner & Tushman, 2003; Hage, 1980). Flexible employees are likely to be better able to switch directions, trade roles, or desert obsolete projects in response to environmental changes, which is particularly important in explorative firms since task stability tends to be low as consumers change preferences and competitors switch directions (Amabile, 1996; Benner & Tushman, 2003). In order to broadly search for and access knowledge, employees must have expansive external ties (Collins & Smith, 2006). Further, employees must have a strong sense of trust in one another and opportunities to meet and interact with organizational colleagues to facilitate the exchange and combination of knowledge within the firm (Collins & Smith, 2006; Nahapiet & Ghoshal, 1998). Hence, employees' willingness and ability to collaborate and create ties with others are important attributes in an organization pursuing an exploration strategy. To further increase rewards from collaboration, explorative organizations can also encourage employees to take active roles in projects in multiple departments (Rousseau, 1988). This boundary-spanning is likely to be most productive when employees across the organization possess diverse areas of expertise, thus maximizing the gains from skill and knowledge exchange.

In addition to striving for free and open collaboration across departments, it is beneficial for the workforce of an explorative firm to embrace risk-taking attitudes (March, 1991; Smith et al., 2005). Employees who feel comfortable taking risks are more likely to propose and exchange unusual ideas and experiment with new knowledge (Smith et al., 2005). Not surprisingly then, risk-taking climates that promote experimentation and tolerate failure in organizations have been linked to increased knowledge creation capability (Nahapiet & Ghoshal, 1998; Smith et al., 2005). Further, the exploration strategy requires creativity and creative individuals who are typically motivated through intrinsic rather than extrinsic motivation (Amabile, 1996).

In sum, the workforce characteristics most advantageous to a firm pursuing an exploration strategy are flexibility, open and active cross-departmental communication networks, the possession of unique and diverse skill sets by many employees, and a risk-taking culture that facilitates creative experimentation. Thus, to maximize knowledge exchange and creation, it is important for firms following an exploration strategy to create a structure that best supports these employee outcomes. An organic organizational structure – characterized by low centralization, low formalization, high specialization, and the regular use of horizontal communication – is the best fitting structure to support the exploration strategy (Gupta et al., 2006).

A decentralized system is characterized by the empowerment of employees at multiple levels of an organization's hierarchy. Employees in departments throughout the decentralized firm frequently make key decisions independently and without the direct supervision of top managers (Hage, 1980). The low formalization in the organic structure is reflected in the constant adjustment and redefinition of individuals' task assignments (Damanpour, 1991; Hage, 1980), which promote the flexibility required by the uncertain environment characteristic of the exploration strategy. The loose definition of work roles also allows for open boundaries with the outside environment and fosters an openness for exchange and collaboration between employees within the organization (Hage, 1999).

Organizations with high specialization employ specialists from several functional backgrounds, providing for a broader knowledge base among employees and leading to greater potential returns from collaboration (Damanpour, 1991; Hage, 1980). Additionally, high specialization in organizations is likely to increase the likelihood of breakthrough innovation as exchange of knowledge between employees with diverse and broad knowledge will spur unique and novel recombinations (Nahapiet & Ghoshal, 1998). Finally, horizontal communication – the communication between employees across the same level of an organization – will increase the sharing of information and advice throughout the organization and increase knowledge flows (Zammuto & O'Connor, 1992). An emphasis on horizontal communication facilitates the dispersion, cross-fertilization, and survival of new ideas (Damanpour, 1991). Additionally, a focus on horizontal communication is likely to be conducive to social control of employees, with information and advice communicated between peers regularly (Tushman & O'Reilly, 1996).

Importantly, the characteristics of the organic structure complement each other and their implementation supports the requirements of the exploration strategy. Specifically, the decentralization of power allows for more department-level decision-making, enabling employees at non-managerial levels to contribute more directly to decisions regarding the products and processes on which they have the most expertise and in meeting the changing demands of the respective competitive environments (Damanpour, 1991; Hage, 1999). An emphasis on horizontal communication combined with high levels of employee specialization fosters a creative, collaborative environment where employees with diverse skill sets can combine and create knowledge freely (Hage, 1999; Zammuto & O'Connor, 1992). The low level of formalization also contributes to the flexible movement of employees and employee knowledge across departmental boundaries and promotes an organization-wide environment of collaboration. In sum, implementation of the organic structure facilitates the flexibility, skill mobilization, and tolerance for uncertainty required to drive knowledge exchange and creation in an exploration strategy, and next I argue that the engineering model of HR is the best fitting HR system to an organic structure and exploration strategy.

The engineering model

Baron and colleagues (Baron et al., 2001; Baron & Hannan, 2002) described the engineering model as the "default culture" in the high-tech industry and noted that this system of HR practices is characterized by selection for specific task abilities, peer-based coordination and control, and employment attachment based on challenging work. I argue that many aspects of this HR model promote an organic organizational structure and support the underlying workforce characteristics demanded by firms pursuing the exploration strategy.

The first dimension of the engineering model – selecting and retaining employees based on their specific skills and abilities – will help small entrepreneurial firms promote high levels of specialization characteristic of an organic structure. Specifically, companies following the engineering model think of employment as an open market where the firm looks to bring in new employees that fit specific organizational needs in terms of skills, capabilities, or knowledge, adding new points of specialized knowledge to broaden the overall knowledge portfolio of the firm (Baron & Hannan, 2002). Further, by hiring employees with advanced and specialized skill sets, the engineering model supports the implementation of low formalization in the form of loose definition of job roles that support the boundary spanning required by the exploration strategy (Baron & Kreps, 1999). In line with the engineering model and with respect to their specialized skills, employees receive general guidelines and goals to guide their work and are left to make determinations of how to complete tasks and make decisions based on their own discretion rather than direct supervision (Baron et al., 2001). These practices, in effect, combine to create a climate of loose controls and self-guided work and are consistent with the organic structure and supportive of the broad knowledge flexibility necessitated by the exploration strategy.

A second aspect of the engineering model – the frequent utilization of cross-functional employee teams (Baron & Kreps, 1999) – supports both horizontal communication and flexibility to respond to market changes or opportunities. Specifically, movement of employees between cross-functional teams increases the sharing and spreading of knowledge as the employees from highly specialized and varied functional backgrounds collaborate to tackle new problems or explore new opportunities (Collins & Smith, 2006; Hage, 1999). Further, the active participation of employees in projects across departments and functional domains, promotes the creation and maintenance of diverse cross-functional networks among employees across the organization (Collins & Smith, 2006). The resulting cross-fertilization of ideas provides the opportunity for unique recombination of specialized knowledge that is a precursor to novel innovation fundamental to the exploration strategy. In particular, the exchange between employees working from different educational and functional backgrounds will increase employees' exposure to diverse perspectives and increase the likelihood that previously uncombined knowledge may be connected in unique ways (Nahapiet & Ghoshal, 1998).

A third aspect of the engineering model – control and coordination based on self-management and peer input – also matches with the organic model and will help support the exploration strategy. Loose guidelines, high levels of coordination, and reliance on attracting highly skilled professionals combine to create a climate in which employees adhere to professional standards and monitor their own as well as their peers' performance (Baron et al., 2001). The freedom to make decisions, decide how to best accomplish the job, and self-management also reinforce a job environment high in intrinsic motivation. Thus, the high degree of autonomy inherent in the engineering model creates the form of employee motivation (i.e., intrinsic motivation) most closely tied to creativity (Amabile, 1996). Managing performance through self-regulation also promotes horizontal communication and decentralization of power implicit in an organic structure. Finally, employees are more likely to experiment with new ideas and take risks on trying things in new ways when they are empowered to make decisions and determine how to best accomplish their job (ibid.).

The final aspect of the engineering model – attachment to the organization based on challenging work – is also complementary to the creation of novel innovation inherent to the exploration strategy. In particular, the focus on increasing attachment by providing employees with exciting and challenging work will create intrinsic motivation in the form of job involvement. Specifically, employees in these firms are responsible for keeping their own job-specific knowledge up-to-date – and are rewarded for doing so in the form of skill-based pay (Baron & Kreps, 1999). It is likely that employees who take responsibility for and are rewarded based on development within their roles will feel and express higher levels of involvement in their jobs. This is likely to lead employees to exert greater effort in their work-related tasks and increased creativity enabling the organization to find unique solutions to market opportunities and challenges (Amabile, 1996).

Overall, organizations following an engineering model attract employees with specialized knowledge, increase the flow of knowledge through cross-functional teams and horizontal communication, increase intrinsic motivation for creativity resulting in the exchange of diverse knowledge and unique recombinations of knowledge supportive of the exploration strategy.

Exploitation Strategy and the Bureaucratic Model of HR

Requirements of the exploitation strategy

As noted above, organizations following an exploitation strategy compete through advantages in quality and/or efficiency and follow a learning orientation anchored in incremental improvements on current technologies and processes (March, 1991). Because competition through the exploitation strategy depends on quality and efficiency in production, exploitative organizations can benefit from depth in knowledge in a particular area, which enables the firm to refine and improve existing activities (He & Wong, 2004). Indeed, firms focusing on the exploitation strategy benefit most from a narrow rather than broad knowledge acquisition strategy (Baum et al., 2000). The goal of exploitation is to reduce variability and this may be best achieved through tight coordination and controls (Gupta et al., 2006). Tight supervision and control also increases employees' focus on the consistent repeated execution of processes and procedures (Benner & Tushman, 2003).

Organizations can achieve a consistently high level of process and quality improvement through institutionalism and the standardization of work routines (Hannan and Freeman, 1984). By standardizing work routines, organizations are likely to increase both efficiency and proficiency in production processes. Specifically, Levinthal and March (1993) argued that by repeating standardized routines, employees complete tasks faster (reflecting increased efficiency) and have less variance in performance (reflecting increased proficiency). Additionally, Benner and Tushman (2003) noted that standardization can be used as a form of tighter coordination of routines, which is also likely to result in increased efficiency and quality in performance.

Consistent with institutionalism and standardization, firms following the exploitation strategy must be able to attract and manage employees who are willing and able to carefully and consistently follow rules and routines (Hage, 1980) and closely comply with managerial direction and rules (Hannan & Freeman, 1984). Specifically, employees must be committed to following routines, rules, processes, and procedures in order for the firm to maximize the production benefits of standardization (Levinthal &

March, 1993). Employees that are rules oriented and motivated to closely comply with processes and procedures are most likely extrinsically motivated (Amabile, 1996). Further, exploitation-oriented firms can facilitate incremental improvement by attracting an employee base with deep rather than broad knowledge. As employees focus their deep knowledge on the tasks and technology at hand, they will be able to identify the incremental improvements and marginal shifts in the existing technology inherent in the exploitation strategy (Baum et al., 2000).

Given the importance of institutionalism and work routine standardization and associated employee attributes for firms following an exploitation strategy, it is important to identify how exploitative organizations can be structured to increase institutionalism and standardization and the aligning workforce characteristics effectively. I argue that a mechanistic organizational structure is the best fitting structure to meet the requirements of the exploitation strategy. The mechanistic structure is characterized by high centralization, high formalization, and an emphasis on vertical communication (Hage, 1980).

Under high centralization, decision-making power and information flows are tightly controlled by the highest-ranking managers, and the tight control increases the standardization of processes, improves efficiency, and reduces errors in production (Benner & Tushman, 2003). Aspects of high formalization, such as tight adherence to job descriptions and rules, support the precise replication of processes and reduces the chance for variation in behaviors and actions across employees (Hage, 1980). Further, these aspects of formalization also enhance the development of narrow and deep expertise, enabling employees to focus on incremental enhancements to technology and processes within their narrow work roles. Finally, the mechanistic structure is characterized by vertical communication in which instructions and orders flow from the top down throughout the organization (Zammuto & O'Connor, 1992), enabling tighter coordination of activities and increasing repetition and replication of activities (Benner & Tushman, 2003).

The components of the mechanistic structure also complement each other to support the requirements of the exploitation strategy. Specifically, by centralizing authority, emphasizing vertical communication, and formalizing work roles, organizations can create a work environment consistent with the standardization of routines. For example, high centralization allows a few individuals at the top of the organizational hierarchy to determine the standard processes that will be implemented throughout the organization (Burns & Stalker, 1994). Then, by using vertical communication and tight management control, mechanistic organizations can drive uniform processes and procedures throughout the organization (Hage,

1980). Further, employees in highly formalized work roles are likely to quickly master the standardized practices as each employee has a narrow scope of responsibility and is likely to repeat the same routinized practice regularly without the distraction of other tasks (Benner & Tushman, 2003; Hage, 1980).

Different aspects of the mechanistic structure also work together to achieve an institutionalization of norms favorable to the exploitation strategy. Specifically, the centralization and communication characteristics of the mechanistic structure are conducive to norms promoting deference to authority and established organizational purposes. For example, the concentration of power among top management leaves little room for lower-level organizational members to effectively challenge management's decisions (Hage, 1999). Finally, by implementing a mechanistic structure, organizations can more effectively respond to the stability of the competitive environment faced by exploitative firms, enabling streamlined and consistent decision-making in a context where efficiency and quality are critical (Hage, 1980).

Through supporting the standardization and mastery of work processes, the institutionalization of relevant norms, and the processing of stable environmental demands, the creation of a mechanistic structure provides for the efficient and consistent reproduction of processes and procedures required for success in the exploitation strategy. Below, I argue that a bureaucratic model of HR will be an effective system of HR practices for creating a mechanistic environment and creating the climate and workforce characteristics necessitated by the exploitation strategy.

Mechanistic structure and the bureaucratic model of HR

Consistent with a mechanistic structure, the bureaucratic model is guided by a managerial philosophy characterized by formal rules, narrow jobs, tightly held standards, and top down communication and decision-making (Baron et al., 2001). As with the other models of HR systems, organizations following the bureaucratic HR model follow specific patterns in terms of how they select employees, control employee behaviors and performance, and create employee attachment to the organization, and these elements of the bureaucratic HR system will work to support the requirement of the exploitation strategy.

First, organizations following this model select employees to fit into the existing production processes based on a narrow set of specific skills, enabling employees to immediately carry out the narrow set of responsibilities tied to a particular job role (ibid.). Further, in this model of HR, employees are assigned specific tasks with tightly delineated responsibilities, resulting in little room for variability in the completion of tasks and assignments (Baron & Hannan, 2002). Consistent with this effort, formal rules are likely to dictate training specifications for each job role in the bureaucratic model (ibid.). With this narrow approach, organizations can ensure that employees in any given role are experts with regard to the requirements of their particular job and are therefore more able to efficiently and consistently carry out their standardized tasks independently and focus learning efforts on incremental improvement.

Second, organizations using a bureaucratic model control employee actions and behaviors through formal management systems, with tight supervision based on rules and documentation (Baron et al., 2001). This model uses a standardized performance evaluation system, with which managers can regularly track employee performance, which can help to ensure that employees are completing tasks correctly, efficiently, and according to regulations. Further, decision-making is controlled centrally, leaving little room for discretion and variability at the individual worker level (Baron & Hannan, 2002), increasing the consistent execution of activities. By concentrating knowledge flows at the top of the organization (Baron et al., 2001), the bureaucratic model reduces the exchange of broad and diverse knowledge across employees lower in the organization. Instead, this model focuses on the exchange of knowledge within functions or work units in a manner that will support incremental improvements in technologies, products, or processes (Benner & Tushman, 2003). Further, the top down communication helps to streamline information dissemination, increasing the consistency and efficiency with which information is communicated throughout the firm.

Finally, the bureaucratic model stresses rewards and employee attachment based on pay and other forms of extrinsic motivation (Baron et al., 2001). For example, in this model of HR, promotions and pay raises are tied to employee performance over time, rewarding and retaining those employees who have been most compliant in following the strict processes and procedures set for their job. Further, pay and promotion-based rewards help firms attract and retain the extrinsically oriented employees who are most likely to be willing and motivated to comply with strict rules and procedures (Amabile, 1996). Additionally, bureaucratic organizations often attract experienced employees by paying higher salaries than competitors, and as stated, promotions provide incentive and rewards for employee performance and development in a particular task domain (Baron & Kreps, 1999). For these reasons, highly-involved employees who are committed to their organization's goals are likely to remain with bureaucratic firms (ibid.), further supporting consistent execution and incremental improvements over time.

Thus, I argue that the bureaucratic model will support the requirements of the exploitation strategy and mechanistic organizational structure by creating an environment in which employees are more likely to comply with tight rules and procedures and look to direct learning towards incremental improvements based on HR practices oriented toward narrowly defined and tightly controlled job roles, narrow and task-specific job skills, vertically controlled decision-making and information flows, and extrinsically oriented rewards.

CONCLUSION

At the outset of the chapter, I noted the importance of entrepreneurial organizations to economies and noted the idea that employees may play a crucial role in the success of these organizations. Further, I argued that HR systems may play an essential role in driving the performance of small entrepreneurial organizations. Because there is little to no research that has examined the role of HR systems and performance in these types of organizations, I set out a goal for this chapter of identifying HR models that would best support firm performance under two alternative strategies followed by small entrepreneurial firms: exploration and exploitation. In the ensuing sections I went on to briefly outline the existing thinking on SHRM, with a particular focus on (1) a systems approach and (2) closely matching the HR system to the underlying workforce characteristics of the strategy of the organization. I then went on to differentiate the pattern of activities, workforce requirements, and structural needs for both the exploration and exploitation strategies. Finally, I argued that an engineering model of HR is the best fit for the exploration strategy and a bureaucratic model the best fit for the exploitation strategy.

Specifically, research on the exploration strategy suggests that firms following this learning orientation depend on broad access to new knowledge, collaboration, and the free flow of knowledge between employees, environment of experimentation and risk-taking organizations, and creativity and unique recombinations of knowledge. Further, I argued that an engineering model enables organizations to attract employees with specialized knowledge, increases the flow of knowledge through cross-functional teams and horizontal communication, increases intrinsic motivation for creativity, resulting in the exchange of diverse knowledge and unique recombinations of knowledge supportive of the exploration strategy, and facilitates risk-taking and experimentation. In contrast, research on the exploitation strategy suggests that firms following this learning orientation depend on close compliance with rules and regulations, strict adherence to processes and procedures, employees with deep knowledge in narrow areas of expertise, vertical communication and decision-making, and a commitment to incremental improvements. I argued that the bureaucratic model will support the requirements of the exploitation strategy by creating an environment in which employees are more likely to comply with tight rules and procedures and look to direct learning towards incremental improvements based on HR practices oriented toward narrowly defined and tightly controlled job roles, narrow and task-specific job skills, vertically controlled decision-making and information flows, and extrinsically oriented rewards.

Overall, this chapter adds to the literature on small business performance and SHRM by helping to clarify a more complex relationship between alternative HR systems and firm performance in small entrepreneurial companies. Additionally, I believe that this chapter points out a number of important areas for future research in these areas. First, there is a great need for continuing theoretical development of our understanding of how to improve the performance of entrepreneurial firms beyond examining the characteristics of the entrepreneur and the environment in which the firm is embedded. I hope that this chapter adds to this literature by introducing the importance of the rest of the employee base and identifying the specific workforce characteristics and organizational structure requirements needed to drive two alternative entrepreneurial growth strategies.

Second, while there has been a great deal of research examining the effects of high-commitment HR systems, there has been little empirical work that has examined the potential effectiveness of other HR systems. In fact, the bulk of the work in this area has simply examined the effectiveness of the high-commitment system or strategic equivalent (e.g., high-performance HR system) or has looked at the relative merit of the high-commitment system versus the non-strategic traditional alternative. To better understand the complexity of the relationship between HR systems and firm performance and to help the field provide better advice to practitioners regarding the variety of choices regarding how to manage employees, we as a field need to conduct more research that examines a much wider array of HR systems. Through the development of the theoretical logic of this chapter, I argued that it is crucial to identify the strategic choices that are specific to a particular industry in order to better understand the workforce requirements inherent to the strategies in that industry.

REFERENCES

Aldrich, H. (2000). *Organizations Evolving*. Beverly Hills: Sage.
Amabile, T.M. (1996). *Creativity in Context*. Boulder: Westview Press.

Baron, J.N. & Hannan, M.T. (2002). Organizational blueprints for success in high-tech start-ups: Lessons from the Stanford Project on Emerging Companies. *California Management Review*, **44**(3): 8–36.
Baron, J.N. & Kreps, D.M. (1999). *Strategic Human Resources: Frameworks for General Managers*. New York: John Wiley & Sons.
Baron, J.N., Hannan, M.T. & Burton, D.M. (2001). Labor pains: Change in organizational models and employee turnover in young, high-tech firms. *American Journal of Sociology*, **106**(4): 960–1012.
Baum, J.A.C., Li, S.X. & Usher, J.M. (2000). Making the next move: How experiential and vicarious learning shape the locations of chains' acquisitions. *Administrative Science Quarterly*, **45**(4): 766–801.
Baum, J.R., Locke, E.A. & Smith, K.G. (2001). A multidimensional model of venture growth. *Academy of Management Journal*, **44**(2): 292–303.
Becker, B.E. & Huselid, M.A. (2006). Strategic human resources management: Where do we go from here? *Journal of Management*, **32**(6): 898–925.
Benner, M.J. & Tushman, M.L. (2003). Exploitation, exploration, and process management: The productivity dilemma revisited. *Academy of Management Review*, **28**, 238–56.
Burns, T. & Stalker, G.M. (1961). *The Management of Innovation*. London: Tavistock.
Cardon, M.S. & Stevens, C.E. (2004). Managing human resources in small organizations: What do we know? *Human Resource Management Review*, **14**(3): 295–323.
Christensen, C.M. (1998). *The Innovator's Dilemma*. Boston: Harvard Business School Press.
Collins, C.J. & Smith, K.G. (2006). Knowledge exchange and combination: The role of human resource practices in the performance of high-technology firms. *Academy of Management Journal*, **49**(3): 544–60.
Collins, C.J., Allen, M. & Snell, S.S. (2004). Entrepreneurial human resource strategy. In M.A. Hitt (ed.), *Entrepreneurship Encyclopedia*. Oxford, UK: Blackwell Publishers.
Damanpour, F. (1991). Organizational innovation: A meta-analysis of effects of determinants and moderators. *Academy of Management Journal*, **34**(3): 555–90.
Dyer, L. (1984). Studying human resource strategy. *Industrial Relations*, **23**(2), 156–69.
Gupta, A.K., Smith, K.G. & Shalley, C.E. (2006). The interplay between exploration and exploitation. *Academy of Management Journal*, **49**(4): 693–706.
Hage, J. (1980). *Theories of Organizations: Form, Process, and Transformation*. New York: Wiley.
Hage, J. (1999). Organizational innovation and organizational change. *Annual Review of Sociology*, **25**(7), 597–622.
Hannan, M.T. & Freeman, J. (1984). Structural inertia and organizational change. *American Sociological Review*, **49**(2): 149–64.
He, Z.L. & Wong, P.K. (2004). Exploration vs. exploitation: An empirical test of the ambidexterity hypothesis. *Organization Science*, **15**(4): 481–94.
Heneman, R.L., Tansky, J.W. & Camp, S.M. (2000). Human resource management practices in small and medium-sized enterprises: Unanswered questions and future research perspectives. *Entrepreneurship Theory & Practice*, **25**(1): 11–26.
Hornsby, J.S. & Kuratko, D.F. (1990). Human resource management in small

business: Critical issues for the 1990's. *Journal of Small Business Management*, **28**(3): 9–18.
Levinthal, D.A. & March, J.G. (1993). The myopia of learning. *Strategic Management Journal*, **14** (Special Issue): 95–112.
March, J.G. (1991). Exploration and exploitation in organizational learning. *Organization Science*, **2**(1): 71–87.
Nahapiet, J. & Ghoshal, S. (1998). Social capital, intellectual capital, and the firm advantage. *Academy of Management Review*, **23**(2): 242–66.
Rousseau, D.M. (1988). Human resource planning for the future. In J. Hage (ed.), *Futures of Organizations*. Lexington, MA: Lexington, pp. 245–66.
Schuler, R.S. & Jackson, S.E. (1987). Linking competitive strategies with human resource management practices. *Academy of Management Executive*, **1**(3): 207–19.
Shane, S. & Venkataraman, S. (2000). The promise of entrepreneurship as a field of research. *Academy of Management Review*, **25**(1): 217–26.
Smith, K.G., Collins, C.J. & Clark, K.D. (2005). Existing knowledge, knowledge creation capability, and the rate of new product introduction in high-technology firms. *Academy of Management Journal*, **48**(2): 346–57.
Tushman, M.L. & O'Reilly, C.A. III. (1996). Ambidextrous organizations: Managing evolutionary and revolutionary change. *California Management Review*, **38**(4): 8–30.
United States Small Business Administration (2004). Small Business Profile, US. SBA Office of Advocacy. See also www.sba.gov.
Way, S.A. (2002). High performance work systems and intermediate indicators of firm performance within the US small business sector. *Journal of Management*, **28**(6): 765–85.
Wright, P.M., Dunford, B.B. & Snell, S.A. (2001). Human resources and the resource based view of the firm. *Journal of Management*, **27**(6): 701–22.
Wright, P.M., Gardner, T.M., Moynihan, L.M. & Allen, M.R. (2005). The relationship between HR practices and firm performance: Examining causal order. *Personnel Psychology*, **58**(2): 409–46.
Zammuto R.F. & O'Connor E.J. (1992). Gaining advanced manufacturing technologies benefits: The role of organizational design and culture. *Academy of Management Review*, **17**(7): 701–28.

5. The human resource practices of small businesses: an examination of performance implications

Andreas Rauch

INTRODUCTION

It is widely recognized that the success and survival of small firms depends to a large extent on their human resources, which is why a number of studies have addressed the human resource management (HRM) practices in small firms (e.g., Tocher & Rutherford, 2009). In general, these studies indicate that the human resource practices of small and new firms are less sophisticated and more informal than those employed by larger enterprises (Cardon & Stevens, 2004). The more interesting question, however, is whether or not the HRM practices of small enterprises are related to their performance. Unfortunately, this is a relationship that has been addressed less frequently in empirical studies. Moreover, some scholars argue that HRM practices are less important in small firms as compared with larger firms, because their scarce resources make it more difficult for them to invest in human resources. The aim of this review is to contribute to this debate by investigating the relationship between the HRM practices and performance of small and medium-sized enterprises.

Most studies investigating HRM practices focus on large firms. However, several special issues of well-recognized journals have called for more research on HRM in small enterprises (e.g., *Entrepreneurship Theory and Practice*, 2000, Vol. 25, Issue 1; *Human Resource Management Review*, 2003, Vol. 13, Issue 2; *Human Resource Management*, 2010, Vol. 49, Issue 2). The majority of papers published in these special issues argue that the HRM practices of small and new firms differ from those in large firms (e.g., Cardon & Stevens, 2004), which makes it necessary to combine knowledge in the areas of HRM and entrepreneurship.

New and small firms actually provide a unique context for studying HRM. For example, small firms usually do not have a human resource department or different subunits with their own traditions of human resources practices (Rauch et al., 2005). Moreover, small and new firms face unique challenges caused by liabilities of size and newness, and their human resources practices can help them deal with these liabilities and gain legitimacy in the industry in which they operate (Cardon & Stevens, 2004). Additionally, employees in small enterprises are paid less than employees in larger enterprises, which means that they have to be motivated in other ways. Finally, employees in small enterprises are less specialized than employees in bigger companies. They have to accept multiple roles and remain flexible to what the business demands. As a result, the human resource practices in small firms are likely to be different from those in larger organizations (Messersmith & Guthrie, 2010).

Although there are a number of reviews concerning HRM practices in the entrepreneurship domain, this review is different. First, its purpose is to review research into the relationship between HRM and performance in small and new enterprises. This is an important issue, because some approaches to HRM argue that HRM may not be important for new and small firms. Therefore, the starting point of this review is the theoretical frameworks that are used to explain the relationship between HRM and performance. Next, I look at whether this relationship depends on the size of business ventures, on different types of HRM interventions, and on different outcome variables. Finally, I discuss the theoretical and practical implications for small businesses. The review focuses on the empirical evidence regarding the HRM–performance relationship. Wherever possible, I use quantitative techniques for the review, which makes it possible to assess the practical utility of HRM interventions as well as of the boundaries of HRM.

Unfortunately, it is difficult to arrive at a complete overview of HRM-oriented literature in the entrepreneurship domain. Relevant literature was published in a variety of journals in the domains of entrepreneurship, HRM, and vocational behavior. Consequently, my starting point was to conduct a keyword search in EconLit, complemented by a search in the corresponding entrepreneurship journals (*Entrepreneurship Theory and Practice, Journal of Business Venturing, Small Business Economics*, and *Journal of Small Business Management*). Finally, I examined the references that were used in these articles. This approach made it possible to identify a total of 28 studies addressing the relationship between HRM practices and performance. Unfortunately, 13 of these studies relied either on a qualitative design (three studies), were theoretical in nature (two articles) or did not report the bivariate statistics necessary to be included in a quantitative review (eight articles). As a result, only 15 studies could be analyzed quantitatively (see asterisked entries in the bibliography). Although this is obviously a small sample size for a quantitative review, a careful analysis of such a small number of studies can also provide insightful results (compare e.g., Schwenk & Shrader, 1993).

THEORETICAL FOUNDATIONS OF HRM IN SMALL-SCALE BUSINESSES

Human resources management involves practices that ensure that the human capital (i.e., employees' knowledge, skills, and abilities) of firms contributes to their business results (Huselid et al., 1997, p. 171). Unfortunately, the existing empirical literature does not agree on how to define human resource practices specifically (Chandler & McEvoy, 2000, p. 45). In fact, no two studies included the same set of HRM practices in their conceptualization of HRM. Given this conceptual ambiguity, Marlow (2006) concluded that almost anything can be studied and that HRM has become a fuzzy concept. Additionally, the descriptive nature of most studies on the HRM of small companies (see e.g., Golhar & Deshpande, 1997; Heneman et al., 2000; Hornsby & Kuratko, 1990; McEvoy, 1984) may have contributed to the conceptual ambiguity in this area. However, there are key themes that reappear in the HRM literature, for example staffing, compensation, training and development, performance management, organizational change, and labor relations (Cardon & Stevens, 2004).

Fortunately, some studies have used theoretical frameworks to explain how HRM should relate to business performance. A majority of these studies relied on the resource-based view (RBV) of the firm (e.g., Barrett & Mayson, 2007; Way, 2002), which assumes that firms generate a competitive advantage by resources that are rare, valuable, inimitable, and non-substitutable (Barney, 1991). Traditional resources, such as financial capital and access to technology, are less important because they are easier to imitate than human resources (Neal & Hesketh, 2002). Thus, in order to achieve a competitive advantage and success, new firms should generate firm-specific resources by implementing specific HRM practices (Lepack & Snell, 1999). Strategic human resource management (SHRM) is an extension of the traditional HRM literature that integrates strategy and HRM (Dyer & Reeves, 1995). According to SHRM, firms need to develop internally consistent human resource practices that are adapted to the organizational context and business strategies. For example, a cost-efficient strategy requires operational efficiency, which calls for the selection of well-trained employees (Changanti et al., 2002). SHRM has contributed to existing literature by stimulating a debate about whether or not firms should adopt "best" HRM practices, HRM practices that "best fit" to a company's strategy or specific configurations of HRM practices that enhance business outcomes. Each of these perspectives seems to provide theoretical as well as empirical evidence that HRM is related to the performance of firms (Delery & Doty, 1996). Moreover, SHRM has stimulated attempts to develop taxonomies of HRM strategies, for example the distinction between commitment and control HR systems (Arthur, 1994). The various taxonomies published in the SHRM literature broadly reflect either more traditional HRM practices, which are characterized by fixed job designs, low levels of training, and minimal participation, or innovative HRM systems, which focus on participation, training and development, and flexible work designs (Dyer & Reeves, 1995). These innovative HRM systems are particularly important, because they are useful when it comes to developing human resources that are valuable and unique to a specific firm (Lepack & Snell, 1999). These unique assets have to be developed internally, for example, by human resource development and utilization (Rauch et al., 2005). The uniqueness required to achieve a competitive advantage is also pronounced in high-performance work systems (Way, 2002), which focus on practices that motivate people to apply their superior abilities in their work-related activities. Such practices include extensive staffing, group-based pay, job rotation, team work, training, and communication (ibid.). Most empirical studies that adopted the RBV found evidence in favor of a positive relationship between HRM and venture performance both in large firms (Huselid, 1995; Welbourne & Andrews, 1996) and in small enterprises (Messersmith & Guthrie, 2010; Rauch et al., 2005). However, both RBV and SHRM have been used predominantly as a broad justification for arguments rather than as a basis for specific hypotheses (Chadwick & Dabu, 2009). Accordingly, many studies on strategic HRM in small companies are tautological by nature (Mayson & Barrett, 2006).

A second stream of research on HRM relies on the life cycle theory (Dodge & Robbins, 1992), which assumes that firms develop through a sequence of stages, for example birth, growth, maturity, and decline (Ciaverella, 2003). Each of these stages is associated with specific activities and challenges. Managing these challenges successfully improves a firm's performance over time. HRM-related problems typically vary across the life cycle stages and become more important over time. In general, life cycle approaches assume that HRM is not important in the early stages and becomes increasingly important during the growth and maturity stages (Ciaverella, 2003; Rutherford et al., 2003). While life cycle approaches appear to be valid at face value because they explain why small and new companies use different HRM practices compared with large companies, empirical studies disagree on the number of stages as well as on the elements that are essential when it comes to defining the stages of the life cycle. For example, some studies used size (Hornsby & Kuratko, 1990), others relied on the firm's age (Kazanjian & Drazin, 1989), or growth (Rutherford et al., 2003) to define the stages of a firm's life cycle. Moreover, many studies that address the life cycle of small firms do not measure business performance, although the theory assumes that managing the challenges associated with the different stages should improve a firm's performance. Moreover, studies relying on growth to define the life cycle stages may even confound venture performance with the stage of the life cycle, making it impossible to evaluate the relationship between HRM and performance. Finally, the suggestion that HRM is less important in the early stages of business ventures contradicts the perceived problems associated with the business start-up. For example, both Hornsby and Kuratko (1990) and Tocher and Rutherford (2009) reported that perceived HRM-related problems are critically important to new and emerging firms.

A more recent conceptualization of HRM practices argues that the characteristics of HRM interventions depend on the type of rents being realized by firms (Chadwick & Dabu, 2009). Entrepreneurial rents depend on entrepreneurial alertness and decision-making in the face of uncertainty. In order to reduce the uncertainty, entrepreneurial firms need to coordinate and utilize the knowledge held by employees in the firm. Accordingly, HRM interventions that enforce entrepreneurial rents focus on learning processes and employee development in order to create and exploit firm-specific human capital. Ricardian rents depend on scarcity at one point of time and realizing Ricardian rents requires owning a production factor that makes it possible to exploit the scarcity. Since human resource mobility is high, selection strategies are more important than training when it comes to realizing Ricardian rents. While this framework has thus far not been verified empirically, it makes it possible to draw some specific hypotheses regarding the effectiveness of HRM practices in entrepreneurial firms. For example, a commitment-based HRM system may be particularly important for new entrepreneurial firms because it helps reduce the uncertainty associated with entrepreneurial rents and thus achieve a competitive advantage.

In summary, only the classic RBV assumes a direct relationship between HRM and performance. The other approaches assume that the effectiveness of HRM depends on other variables. The life cycle approach assumes that HRM practices are less important to the performance of new and small business start-ups, in contrast to Baron et al. (1999), who argue that the development of a firm is path-dependent, which means that HRM-related problems that are addressed (or ignored) at an early stage determine the future development of a company. Resource-based theories do not focus on the role of age, but rather on the competitive advantage firms aim to achieve. Both HRM best practices and certain types of HRM practices are discussed in existing literature.

THE EFFECTIVENESS OF HRM: BEST PRACTICE VERSUS SIZE, TYPE OF HRM INTERVENTION, AND TYPE OF PERFORMANCE ASSESSMENT

Despite the fact that HRM literature provides a great deal of evidence in favor of a "best practice" perspective, reviewing HRM literature in the context of SMEs logically implies a contingency perspective, because otherwise the literature on SMEs could simply rely on the evidence found in general management literature. This review specifically addresses the role of size, type of HRM assessment, and type of performance assessment.

Size is an important variable in this review, simply because the role of HRM has been discussed with regard to firm size. For example, small firms may not be able to afford expensive HRM practices and, moreover, they may find it hard to attract a skilled and talented workforce (Cardon & Stevens, 2004). Moreover, HRM practices may be more important and different once an enterprise grows to a certain size (Rutherford et al., 2003). Therefore, many authors argued that small firms either rely to a lesser extent on HRM or use other, more traditional HRM practices (Heneman & Tansky, 2002). However, HRM practices may well lead to advantages that have a positive effect on the performance of small and medium-sized enterprises. For example, HRM practices may create the legitimacy small firms need to grow and attract employees (Cardon & Stevens, 2004). Moreover, early HRM-related decisions may have long-term consequences (Aldrich & Marsden, 1988). Finally, a talented and motivated workforce should be effective even if the enterprise is comparatively small. Notably, different HRM practices require different amounts of resources and investments, which means that some specific HRM practices may be implemented relatively easily even if companies cannot afford to make major investments in HRM.

Therefore, one might assume that the type of HRM intervention matters in small and medium-sized enterprises. However, as yet there is no commonly accepted categorization of HRM interventions (Dyer & Reeves, 1995), partially because HRM practices may depend on a certain context (compare above). For example, small and new firms are more innovative than larger companies (Drucker, 1993). Moreover, small companies do not have the bureaucratic and formal structure that is usually found in large established companies. There is less specialization and employees have to play a variety of roles in small enterprises (Messersmith & Guthrie, 2010). As a consequence, traditional and formal HRM practices may not work well in small enterprises. For example, it is difficult to develop a formal job analysis when employees are involved in multiple tasks. Thus, in small enterprises, HRM practices that promote the flexibility and adaptability of the employees and that create a safe environment for experimentation and innovation should be effective and HRM practices should increase commitment, trust, and a climate for cooperation (Collins & Smith, 2006). More specifically, innovative HRM practices rely on commitment (Muse et al., 2005), training and development (Rauch et al., 2005), participation, and high-performance work systems (Way, 2002). Since these practices enable employees to work effectively in small enterprises, innovative HRM practices should be positively related to performance.

Empirical studies addressing the relationship between HRM and performance in small enterprises use a number of different ways to assess performance. The question remains whether or not HRM is specifically related to certain performance criteria. Unfortunately, existing entrepreneurship literature also uses a variety of ways to assess business performance (cf. reviews by Combs et al., 2005; Venkatraman & Ramanujam, 1986) and there is little consensus about what the most important criteria are. A distinction is usually drawn between financial and operational performance (Venkatraman & Ramanujam, 1986). Financial performance includes factors like sales growth and return on investments. With regard to financial performance, there is often a low convergence between different indicators (Murphy et al., 1996). At a conceptual level, one can distinguish between growth measures and measures of profitability (Combs et al., 2005). Operational performance addresses a broad category of non-financial performance criteria that may lead to financial performance (Venkatraman & Ramanujam, 1986), for example new product development and product quality. In the context of this review, one could categorize human resources outcomes (employee turnover, complaints, sales per employee) as being part of the operational performance, because HR outcomes are concerned with HR efficiency, which may improve the financial performance of business firms.

Regarding the relationship between HRM and performance, there is probably a higher convergence between HRM and operational performance compared with financial performance. For example, implementing innovations in an organization requires the commitment of multiple employees in the firm (Klein & Sorra, 1996). HRM can directly increase the skills and motivation of employees and thus affect the implementation of innovation (Hayton, 2004). Similarly, HRM should directly affect

HRM outcomes, such as labor turnover or employee productivity. As a result, HRM outcomes have a close relationship to HRM interventions, which means that there should be a close relationship between HRM and HRM outcomes. However, HRM outcomes are deficit outcomes, because they may not fully reflect the financial goals of an organization (Dyer & Reeves, 1995). On the other hand, financial performance depends on multiple factors and not just HRM (such a criterion is therefore contaminated; Smith, 1976). However, it is reasonable to assume that at least some business owners implement HRM to achieve financial results. One would probably expect that HRM investments do not immediately affect financial performance, because the effects of HRM are delayed (Boxall & Steeneveld, 1999; Welbourne & Andrews, 1996). Thus, there may be only a small relationship between HRM and current profitability. On the other hand, HRM should be positively related to growth because growth reflects lagged performance (Delmar, 1997). Moreover, HRM practices may be implemented to enable growth. However, reversed causality is possible, for instance when a growing company decides to invest in HRM as a consequence of growth. These arguments imply the necessity to address HRM in longitudinal studies, with specific attention to the long-term consequences of HRM (Rauch et al., 2005).

EMPIRICAL EVIDENCE

Because, in this review, the focus is on small and medium-sized enterprises, I used the definition suggested by the OECD and selected only studies including enterprises with up to 500 employees. The unit of analysis is the entire firm. Thus, the review included only studies that investigated firm-level HRM and performance. The quantitative analysis was based on 15 studies.

The quantitative review was based on the methodology suggested by Hunter and Schmidt (2004). The results of the analysis are presented in Table 5.1. The results indicated that there is a positive relationship between HRM and success ($r = .111$). Because the confidence interval does not include zero, this relationship was significant. While this relationship is small by statistical standards (Cohen, 1977), the effect size is comparable with other effect sizes reported in literature. For example, one meta-analysis reported a relationship between planning and performance of $r = .10$ (Brinckmann et al., 2010). Moreover, the relationship between human capital of business owners and performance is $r = .098$ (Unger et al., 2011). These results indicate that HRM is as important as other indicators when it comes to measuring business performance. At the same time, the size of

Table 5.1 *The relationship between HRM and success: quantitative analysis*

Correlations	*K*	*N*	*Rw*	*So*	*Q* Value	95% Confidence Interval
HRM	15	11039	.111	.082	96.43**	.052 to .170
Small	8	2450	.126	.033	16.18*	.072 to .180
Medium-sized enterprises	5	7991	.103	.042	62.33**	−.018 to .201
Innovative HRM	10	5442	.159	.041	71.29**	.072 to .275
Traditional HRM	5	8458	.078	.011	70.06**	−.031 to .185
Growth	5	8239	.082	.016	23.64**	.011 to .152
Profitability	4	5428	.042	.034	6.40	−.029 to .112
HRM outcomes	9	6935	.122	.056	127.86**	−.005 to .245
Subjective performance	3	807	.251	.013	21.18**	.021 to .455

Note: *K*= number of studies; N = overall number of observations; *Rw* = sample weighted mean correlation; *So* = observed variance; *Q* value = test for heterogeneity; $*p < .05$; $** p < .01$.

Source: Author's calculations.

the reported relationship between HRM and success varied considerably between the different studies. This significant *Q*-value indicated that this variation is noteworthy. This in turn indicates the need to look for variables that affect the size of the relationship between HRM and success.

Our database included eight studies that investigated small enterprises with up to 100 employees and five studies that tested medium-sized enterprises (with up to 500 employees). The results presented in Table 5.1 indicate that the relationship between HRM and success is slightly higher in small enterprises ($r = .126$) than it is in medium-sized enterprises (r = .103). More importantly, the relationship between HRM and success was not significant for enterprises with more than 100 employees, which is predominantly due to the high variance in the size of reported relationship between HRM and performance in medium-sized enterprises. By contrast, the relationship between HRM and performance was significant for the subsample of studies examining HRM in small-scale enterprises. Thus, the proposition that HRM is not important for small enterprises was not supported in our analysis.

When analyzing the effect of the type of HRM interventions, I divided the studies into two categories: innovative HRM and traditional HRM. Innovative HRM included training and development, participation, and high-performance work system. Studies that were coded as traditional HRM focused on selection, compensation, and the presence of professional HRM staff. An initial inspection of the results (Table 5.1) indicated that innovative HRM interventions have been studied more often than traditional HRM. Eventually, researchers expect that innovative HRM is particularly important in the context of small and medium-sized companies. The results confirmed this importance: the correlation between HRM and performance was $r = .159$ for innovative HRM practices. Because the confidence interval does not include zero, this relationship is significant. The relationship between traditional HRM was only $r = .078$ and the effect size was not significant.

The final part of the analysis focused on different types of performance assessment. To test the effect of different performance categories, I divided venture performance into four categories: growth, profitability, HRM-related outcomes and subjective performance. Growth was operationalized in the primary studies by calculating the increase (decrease) in the firm's number of employees, sales levels or profit. Profitability referred to accountant-based assessments (e.g., return on investment, return on sales). HRM outcomes include an assessment of, for example, labor-related turnover and profit levels related to the number of employees. Finally, subjective performance includes ratings by the business owners with regard to performance, for example profitability compared with their most important competitors (Wiklund & Shepherd, 2003). Although subjective performance measures may be subject to various reporting biases, they do exhibit a relatively high correlation with objective measures (Dess & Robinson, 1984).

Our results indicated that the effectiveness of HRM interventions may depend on the type of performance assessment that is used. An initial observation is that HRM was most strongly correlated with subjective performance ($r = .251$). Moreover, HRM proved to be related to HRM outcomes, with a mean correlation of $r = .122$. However, this effect size was not significant, due to the high variance of effect sizes reported in the nine studies included in this review. Thus, HRM may sometimes, but not always, affect HRM outcomes. As expected, HRM practices were positively correlated with the growth of enterprises ($r =.082$). This effect was significant, although it is a small effect size by statistical standards. Moreover, the *Q*-test indicated that the relationship between HRM and growth was moderated by other variables. Finally, four studies examined the relationship between HRM using profitability as a criterion. Across these studies, the relationship between HRM and profitability was small and insignificant ($r =.042$). In general, one has to be careful when interpreting these findings, because the number of studies is quite small with regard to some of the performance assessments. However, there is some preliminary evidence that the effectiveness of HRM in small and medium-sized enterprises depends on the performance criterion being used.

DISCUSSION

Despite repeated calls for studying the role of HRM in small and entrepreneurial firms (Baron, 2003) HRM has remained a relatively neglected topic in entrepreneurship research. The few studies that have examined HRM in small and medium-sized companies tend to focus on the differences in HRM practices between small and large firms, which means that little is known about which type of HRM practices is correlated with the success of small and medium-sized enterprises. The present review was motivated by the question of whether or not HRM has an impact on the performance of small firms. Based on the literature examined, several observations can be made.

First, it became obvious that few attempts have been made to study the connection between HRM and performance in small firms, which is surprising, given the fact that the role of knowledge and information is a conceptual cornerstone in the theory of entrepreneurship (Kirzner, 1997; McMullen & Shepherd, 2006). Knowledge and information are important elements in the whole entrepreneurial process. Knowledge is important for opportunity recognition (Shane, 2000), it supports successful opportunity exploitation (Unger et al., 2011), and is related to the growth and survival of small firms (Cooper et al., 1994). In entrepreneurship research, most studies address the role of human resources by investigating either the owner and manager (Unger et al., 2011) or the management team of the small firm (Ruef et al., 2003). However, because human resource-related advantages depend on the knowledge and information of the entire firm, they include HRM. In fact, the effect size found in the quantitative part of this review was as high as the effect size of the relationship between the owner's human capital and performance (cf. Unger et al., 2011), which indicates that it is important for small firms to use HRM practices.

A second observation is that HRM practices benefit small firms as well, which means that HRM is important for enterprises of different sizes. Accordingly, the assumption that HRM is less important for small enterprises is not valid. HRM practices enable small firms to become and remain competitive, and skilled and motivated employees improve a firm's performance. Moreover, the results presented here are in line with strategic human resource management, because the analysis indicates that innovative HRM practices are more effective than traditional HRM management.

Innovative HRM practices are probably quite useful for small enterprises, because training, HR development, and high-performance work systems can effectively increase the flexibility of employees required to adapt to the multiple roles they have to play in small enterprises (Messersmith & Guthrie, 2010).

Several limitations must be addressed when interpreting the findings of this review. In general, the analysis presented here is based on only 15 studies. The small number of studies included in the quantitative review seriously challenges the generalization of the results. For that reason, I used only basic quantitative techniques to aggregate the results without testing for the significance of moderator variables or correcting for attenuation factors (e.g., reliabilities), as suggested by Hunter and Schmidt (2004). However, this type of analysis provides more reliable information compared with the count of significant results that is usually employed in narrative reviews (which, for example, do not take sampling error into account; ibid.). Moreover, the small number of existing studies identified indicates that there is a need for additional studies testing the relationship between HRM and performance in small and medium-sized enterprises.

Moreover, most studies included in the review did not address the causality of effects. For example, HRM may very well be a consequence of growth and performance, because the owners of growing enterprises may not be able to control their workforce directly and, therefore, implement more sophisticated HRM practices. On the other hand, HRM practices may affect the subsequent performance of a firm, because employees are highly motivated and able to carry out their tasks. The few longitudinal studies included in our sample showed that the former path is present: HRM practices affect subsequent growth (Rauch et al., 2005).

Finally, the review focused on small enterprises. However, empirically, business size is confounded with business age, because most new firms start small. Theoretically, however, small and new businesses face distinct HRM-related issues, for example because small firms lack resources, while new firms have yet to attain legitimacy within a given market. Thus, small and new firms face different challenges that impact their HRM practices (Cardon & Stevens, 2004).

Despite these limitations, the results of this review allow for some theoretical and practical conclusions. Theoretically, entrepreneurship needs to move toward a theory of the entrepreneurial firm rather than focusing on the entrepreneur. Knowledge and resources need to be conceptualized at the level of the firm, which includes the entrepreneur, the founding team, and the employees of the firm. Thus, firm-level human resources are a unique source providing competitive advantages.

Moreover, it would be interesting to study the mechanism by which these human resource-related advantages lead to performance. HRM may simply motivate employees to work harder and more effectively. However, HRM may also increase the stock of human resources and create intangible resource advantages that may support differentiation and success. Thus, future research should investigate the outcomes of investments in human resources and the way these outcomes affect business success (Unger et al., 2011). This would move HRM literature away from a static view of HRM towards a process-based view, making it possible to investigate the processes by which HRM affects performance. Such processes may include, for example, the learning environment and learning processes by which small enterprises achieve competitive advantages (Reuber & Fisher, 1999).

In practical terms, entrepreneurs running small enterprises are advised to address HRM at an early stage. However, it may not be necessary to establish a formal HRM department, to employ professional HRM staff or to invest in expensive selection procedures in small enterprises. Instead, the entrepreneur should acquire HRM skills that help develop human resources internally (Rauch et al., 2005). Skills and knowledge developed internally enable employees to learn and grow with their company. In this way, entrepreneurs may create valuable and firm-specific human resource advantages and increase their ability to compete in a market successfully.

BIBLIOGRAPHY

Aldrich, H.E. & Marsden, P.V. (1988). Environments and organizations. In N.J. Semelser (ed.), *Handbook of Sociology*. Newbury Pearl, CA: Sage, pp. 361–92.

Arthur, J.B. (1994). Effects of human resource systems on manufacturing performance and turnover. *Academy of Management Journal*, **37**(3), 670–87.

Barney, J.B. (1991). Firm resources and sustained competitive advantage. *Journal of Management*, **17**(1), 99–129.

Baron, J.N., Hannan, M.T. & Burton, D.M. (1999). Building the iron cage: Determinants of managerial intensity in early years of organizations. *American Sociological Review*, **64**(4), 527–47.

Baron, R.A. (2003). Editorial: Human resources management and entrepreneurship: Some reciprocal benefits of closer links. *Human Resource Management Review*, **13**(2), 253–6.

Barrett, R. & Mayson, S. (2007). Human resource management in growing small firms. *Journal of Small Business and Enterprise Development*, **14**(2), 307–20.

Boxall, P. & Steeneveld, M. (1999). Human resource strategy and competitive advantage: A longitudinal study of engineering consultancies. *Journal of Management Studies*, **36**(4), 443–63.

Brinckmann, J., Grichnik, D. & Kapsa, D. (2010). Should entrepreneurs plan or just storm the castle? A meta-analysis on contextual factors impacting the business planning–performance relationship in small firms. *Journal of Business Venturing*, **24**(1), 24–40.

*Burton, M.D. & O'Reilly, C. (2004). *Walking the Talk: The Impact of High Commitment Values and Practices on Technology Start-ups.* Technical report: Cornell University, School of Industrial and Labor Relations.

Cardon, M.S. & Stevens, C.E. (2004). Managing human resources in small organizations. *Human Resources Management Review*, **14**(3), 295–323.

Chadwick, C. & Dabu, A. (2009). Human resources, human resources management, and competitive advantage of firms: Toward a more comprehensive model of causal linkages. *Organization Science*, **20**(1), 253–72.

Chandler, G. & McEvoy, G. (2000). Human resources management, TQM and firm performance in small and medium-sized enterprises. *Entrepreneurship Theory & Practice*, **25**(1), 43–58.

*Changanti, R., Cook, R.G. & Smeltz, W.J. (2002). Effects of styles, strategies, and systems and the growth of small businesses. *Journal of Developmental Entrepreneurship*, **7**(2), 175–92.

Ciaverella, M.A. (2003). The adoption of high-involvement practices and processes in emergent and developing firms: A descriptive and prescriptive approach. *Human Resource Management*, **42**(4), 337–56.

Cohen, J. (1977). *Statistical Power Analysis for the Behavioral Sciences*. New York: Academic Press.

Collins, C.J. & Smith, K.G. (2006). Knowledge exchange and combination: The role of human resource practices in the performance of high-technology firms. *Academy of Management Journal*, **49**(3), 544–60.

Combs, J.G., Crook, T.R. & Shook, C.L. (2005). The dimensionality of organizational performance and its implications for strategic management research. In D.J. Ketchen & D.D. Bergh (eds), *Research Methodology in Strategic Management*. San Diego, CA: Elsevier, pp. 259–86.

Cooper, A.C., Gimeno-Gascon, F.J. & Woo, C.Y. (1994). Initial human and financial capital as predictors of new venture performance. *Journal of Business Venturing*, **9**(5), 371–95.

*De Kok, J.M.P. & Den Hartog, D. (2006). *Is Human Resource Management Profitable for Small Firms?* Scales Research Reports H200621, EIM Business and Policy Research.

Delery, J.E. & Doty, H. (1996). Modes of theorizing in strategic human resource management: Tests of universalistic, contingency, and configurational performance predictions. *Academy of Management Journal*, **39**(4), 802–35.

Delmar, F. (1997). Measuring growth: Methodological considerations and empirical results. In R. Donkels & A. Miettinen (eds), *Entrepreneurship and SME research: On its Way to the New Millennium*. Aldershot, UK: Ashgate, pp. 190–216.

Dess, G.G. & Robinson Jr., R.B. (1984). Measuring organizational performance in the absence of objective measures: The case of the privately-held firm and conglomerate business unit. *Strategic Management Journal*, **5**(3), 265–73.

Dodge, H.R. & Robbins, H.E. (1992). An empirical investigation of the organizational life cycle model for small business development and survival. *Journal of Small Business Management*, **30**(1), 27–38.

Drucker, P.F. (1993). *Innovation and Entrepreneurship*. New York: Harper Business.

Dyer, L. & Reeves, T. (1995). Human resources strategies and firm performance:

What do we know and where do we need to go? *International Journal of Human Resource Management*, **6**(3), 656–70.

Golhar, D.Y. & Deshpande, S.P. (1997). HRM practices of large and small Canadian manufacturing firms. *Journal of Small Business Management*, **35**(3), 30–38.

Hayton, J.C. (2004). Strategic human capital management in SME's: An empirical study of entrepreneurial performance. *Human Resource Management*, **42**(4), 375–91.

Heneman, R.L. & Tansky, J.W. (2002). Human resource management models for entrepreneurial opportunity: Existing knowledge and new directions. In J. Katz & T.M. Welbourne (eds), *Managing People in Entrepreneurial Organizations*, Vol. 5. Amsterdam: JAI Press, pp. 55–82.

Heneman, R.L., Tansky, J.W., & Camp, S.M. (2000). Human resource management practices in small and medium-sized enterprises: Unanswered questions and future research perspectives. *Entrepreneurship Theory & Practice*, **25**(1), 11–26.

Hornsby, J.E. & Kuratko, D.F. (1990). Human resource management in small business: Critical issues for the 1990s. *Journal of Small Business Management*, **28**(3), 9–18.

Hunter, J.E. & Schmidt, F.L. (2004). *Methods for Meta-analysis: Correcting Error and Bias in Research Findings*. Newbury Park, CA: Sage.

Huselid, M.A. (1995). The impact of human resource management practices on turnover, productivity, and corporate financial performance. *Academy of Management Journal*, **38**(3), 635–72.

Huselid, M.A., Jackson, S.E. & Schuler, R.S. (1997). Technical and strategic human resource management effectiveness as determinants of firm performance. *Academy of Management Journal*, **40**(1), 171–88.

*Jennings, J.E., Jennings, P.D. & Greenwood, R. (2009). Novelty and firm performance: The case of employment systems in knowledge-intensive service organizations. *Journal of Business Venturing*, **24**(3), 338–59.

*Kaman, V., McCarthy, A.M., Gulbro, R.D. & Tucker, M.L. (2001). Bureaucratic and high commitment human resource practices in small service firms. *Human Resource Planning*, **24**(1), 33–43.

*Kasturi, P., Orlov, A.G. & Roufagalas, J. (2006). HRM systems architecture and firm performance: Evidence from SMEs in a developing country. *International Journal of Commerce & Management*, **16**(3/4), 178–96.

Kazanjian, R.K. & Drazin, R. (1989). An empirical test of a stage and growth progression model. *Management Science*, **35**(12), 1489–1504.

*King-Kauanui, S., Ngoc, S.D. & Ashley-Cotleur, C. (2006). Impact of human resource management: SME performance in Vietnam. *Journal of Developmental Entrepreneurship*, **11**(1), 79–95.

Kirzner, I.M. (1997). Entrepreneurial discovery and the competitive market process: An Austrian approach. *Journal of Economic Literature*, **35**(1), 60–85.

Klein, K.J. & Sorra, J.S. (1996). The challenge of innovation implementation. *Academy of Management Review*, **21**(4), 1055–80.

Lepack, D.P. & Snell, S.A. (1999). The human resource architecture: Toward a theory of human capital allocation and development. *Academy of Management Review*, **24**, 31–48.

*Litz, R.A. & Stewart, A.C. (2000). Research note: Trade name franchise membership as a human resource management strategy: Does buying group training

deliver "true" value for small retailers? *Entrepreneurship Theory & Practice*, **25**(3), 125–35.
Marlow, S. (2006). Human resource management in small firms: A contradiction in terms? *Human Resources Management Review*, **16**(4), 467–77.
Mayson, S. & Barrett, R. (2006). The "science" and "practice" of HRM in small firms. *Human Resources Management Review*, **16**(4), 447–55.
McEvoy, G.M. (1984). Small business personnel practices. *Journal of Small Business Management*, **22**(4), 1–8.
McMullen, J.S. & Shepherd, D.A. (2006). Entrepreneurial action and the role of uncertainty in the theory of the entrepreneur. *Academy of Management Review*, **31**(1), 132–52.
*Messersmith, J.G. & Guthrie, J.P. (2010). High performance work systems in emergent organizations: Implications for firm performance. *Human Resource Management*, **49**(2), 241–64.
Murphy, G.B., Trailer, J.W. & Hill, R.C. (1996). Measuring performance in entrepreneurship research. *Journal of Business Research*, **36**(1), 15–23.
*Muse, L.A., Rutherford, M.W., Oswald, S.L. & Raymond, J.E. (2005). Commitment to employees: Does it help or hinder small business performance? *Small Business Economics*, **24**(2), 97–111.
Neal, A. & Hesketh, B. (2002). Productivity in organizations. In N. Anderson, D.S. Ones, H.K. Sinangil & C. Viswesvaran (eds), *Handbook of Industrial, Work, and Organizational Psychology*, Vol. 2. Thousand Oaks, CA: Sage, pp. 7–24.
*Patel, P.C. & Cardon, M.S. (2010). Adopting HRM practices and their effectiveness in small firms facing product-market competition. *Human Resource Management*, **49**(2), 265–90.
Rauch, A. & Frese, M. (2007). Let's put the person back into entrepreneurship research: A meta-analysis of the relationship between business owners' personality traits, business creation and success. *European Journal of Work and Organizational Psychology*, **16**(4), 353–85.
*Rauch, A., Frese, M. & Utsch, A. (2005). Effects of human capital and long-term human resources development and utilization on employment growth of small-scale businesses. *Entrepreneurship Theory & Practice*, **29**(6), 681–9.
Reuber, A.R., Fisher, E. (1999). Understanding the consequences of founders' experience. *Journal of Small Business Management*, **37**(2), 30–45.
Ruef, M., Aldrich, H.E. & Carter, N.M. (2003). The structure of founding teams: Homophily, strong ties, and isolation among U.S. entrepreneurs. *American Sociological Review*, **68**(2), 195–222.
*Rutherford, M.W., Buller, P.F. & McMullen, P.R. (2003). Human resource management problems over the life cycle of small to medium-sized firms. *Human Resource Management*, **42**(4), 321–35.
Schwenk, C.R. & Shrader, C.B. (1993). Effects of formal planning on financial performance in small firms: A meta-analysis. *Entrepreneurship Theory and Practice*, **17**(3), 53–64.
*Sels, L., De Winne, S., Delmotte, J., Maes, J., Faems, D. & Forrier, A. (2006). Linking HRM and small business performance: An examination of the impact of HRM intensity on the productivity and financial performance of small businesses. *Small Business Economics*, **26**(1), 83–101.
Shane, S. (2000). Prior knowledge and the discovery of entrepreneurial opportunities. *Organization Science*, **11**(4), 448–69.
Smith, P.C. (1976). Behaviors, results, and organizational effectiveness: The

problem of criteria. In M.D. Dunnette (ed.), *Handbook of Industrial and Organizational Psychology*. Chicago: Rand McNally, pp. 745–75.

Tocher, N. & Rutherford, M.W. (2009). Perceived acute human resource management problems in small and medium firms: An empirical examination. *Entrepreneurship Theory & Practice*, **33**(2), 455–79.

Unger, J., Rauch, A., Rosenbusch, N. & Frese, M. (2011). Human capital and entrepreneurial success: A meta-analytic review. *Journal of Business Venturing*, **26**(3), 341–58.

Venkatraman, N. & Ramanujam, V. (1986). Measurement of business performance in strategy research: A comparison of approaches. *Academy of Management Review*, **11**(4), 801–14.

*Way, S.A. (2002). High performance work systems and intermediate indicators of firm performance within the US small business sector. *Journal of Management*, **28**(6), 765–85.

Welbourne, T.M. & Andrews, A.O. (1996). Predicting the performance of initial public offerings. Should human resource management be in the equation? *Academy of Management Journal*, **39**(4), 891–919.

Wiklund, J. & Shepherd, D. (2003). Knowledge-based resources, entrepreneurial orientation, and the performance of small and medium-sized businesses. *Strategic Management Journal*, **24**(13), 1307–14.

Note: * Included in the quantitative review.

6. On learning in high-performing small and medium-sized businesses and the relationship to HR practices

Timothy L. Pett and James A. Wolff

INTRODUCTION

There has been growing interest in small and medium-sized enterprises (henceforth SMEs) during the last two decades. SMEs have been recognized as a key element for economic development in developed and developing economies. As examination into large-scale enterprise becomes finer grained and advances in understanding are at the margin, many investigators have begun to apply the concepts employed in large firm study to the realm of SMEs. This is not to say that SMEs are simply smaller versions of their larger counterparts. Indeed, there is ample evidence to the contrary. However, applying large firm conceptual models to the examination of SMEs is an important start in the process through which greater understanding can be gained. In this process research has shown the SMEs are not a homogeneous cluster of entities to which common conclusions apply and common practices can be ascribed.

SMEs represent the vast majority of business entities in developed (in excess of 95 percent of businesses in the US and the EU) and developing economies and have a significant impact upon those economies. As such they are fertile ground for the application of research effort to gain an understanding of how SMEs work.

A key area in understanding SMEs has been performance related with the primary question being why some SMEs are able to achieve high levels of performance while others are unable to achieve the goals established by their owners or managers. One theme in the research literature is that of organization–environment fit where the general premise is that the better the fit with environmental conditions, the better will be the performance of the enterprise. This premise makes intuitive sense until one considers that business environments are dynamic and constantly in flux. Therefore, for a firm to consistently perform at high levels there must be a mechanism by which it is able to adapt itself to dynamic and uncertain conditions. A key mechanism to facilitate adaptation is through learning – the integration of new knowledge and information into the enterprise, interpreting the new knowledge and information, drawing inferences for what it means for the firm, and disseminating the knowledge and inferences throughout the organization for effective decision-making. At a fundamental level successful adaptation implies effective organizational learning.

In turn effective organizational learning to yield high levels of firm performance requires having the right people, with the right skills, in the right places at the time they are needed. Getting the right people with the right skills in the right places within the organization is the purview of human resource (HR) practices. Although there are many reasons forwarded regarding why certain SMEs seem to outperform others, the linkage to and managerial direction for human resource practices is very limited. In this chapter our goal is to link HR practices to high performance in SMEs by exploring the role of organizational learning within that relationship. With the linkage explained we offer suggestions to SME managers regarding the HR practices that may help drive their organization to higher levels of performance.

We begin the discussion with a general overview designed to provide the underlying premise connecting organizational learning and high performance in the SME context and the importance of HR practices that contribute to effective learning and hence high performance. Next the definition and description of what is meant by high performance in SMEs is developed followed by discussion that explains organizational learning, what comprises organizational learning, and how learning is related to high performance in SMEs. The final section contains some discussions on how to connect HR practices to organizational learning for high-performance SMEs and provide practical recommendations for what managers would be wise to consider in their quest for high performance. The chapter concludes with a summary of the rationale presented and the prescriptive recommendations made with respect to SME HR practice.

HIGH-PERFORMING SMEs

The subject of performance has been an important cornerstone topic for business owners as well as researchers for decades and is *the* central issue for strategic management researchers. The fundamental question in this area is "Why do some firms outperform others?" While there is general agreement on the importance of performance in work to gain understanding about business organizations and thereby prescribe normative recommendations to practicing managers, there is significant disparity on how to define performance and what measures are appropriate to gain meaningful insights. This seems especially vexing in the area of SME research where much of the discussion distills to two dimensions by which performance is measured: growth and profitability.

Growth

The importance of growth as a key performance dimension in SMEs is rooted in the very practical issue that SMEs (especially very small firms) are resource challenged and their survival may depend heavily upon their ability to attain sufficient size to overcome competitive marketplace challenges. Stinchcombe's (1965) "liability of newness" and Freeman et al.'s (1983) "liability of smallness" are terms grounded in research that are illustrative of the difficulties that small firms may face in dynamic competitive markets. Hence, for small firms, growth may be a particularly desirable goal to attract or generate through business activity the resources that will sustain them into the future.

Several well-known theoretical frameworks have been used to underpin the notion that growth is important for SMEs. Among the theoretical bases for the premise is research that pertains to economies of scale (Besanko et al., 2004), learning-curve effects (Stern & Stalk, 1998), and first-mover advantage (Lieberman & Montgomery, 1988). Each of these theories proposes that size may translate to greater profitability at a later point in the life cycle of the firm and it is, therefore, desirable for the SME to generate significant growth to achieve future profitability. Therefore, especially in entrepreneurship and SME research, growth has been used as a primary performance dimension (Davidsson et al., 2008).

Academicians employing growth as the dependent variable support the usage of the measure by making the valid argument that small firms are much more willing to provide data about growth metrics than they are about profitability (Chandler & Hanks, 1994). Small firms are overwhelmingly private closely-held firms with owner/managers reticent to disclose profitability metrics. They are more open to providing numbers of employees, sales growth rates, geographic spread, and other growth-related measures to other business owners and researchers. In those research studies that use data on both the growth and profitability dimensions of performance, the association between the two has been decidedly mixed, with some reporting strong positive associations, some reporting weak (but statistically significant) positive associations, and still others reporting no or negative correlations between growth and profit. According to Davidsson et al. (2009) these outcomes provide reason to question whether growth as a performance measure is overdone.

Profitability

According to much strategic management research, profitability is the defining measure of performance. If business activity is the quest for competitive advantage (Porter, 1985), profitability is the generally accepted measure that demonstrates a firm's competitive advantage or lack thereof. The "bottom line" is a key indicator of performance to owners and business managers to validate past decisions and provide the necessary resources for future initiatives. Therefore, measures of profitability are the gold standard for research and practice.

However, profitability alone may be insufficient for long-term prospects in SMEs. Given the difficulties of the liability of newness or smallness in SMEs, growth may be a very necessary element in the overall performance issue. Indeed, there are those (Davidsson et al., 2009) that effectively argue that it is profitable growth that is desirable and from a theoretical perspective, profitability drives growth and not the reverse. Steffens et al. (2009) provide a very useful conceptualization of the relationship between profitability and growth in defining high performance in SMEs. These researchers specify nine performance classes by dividing the growth dimension (horizontal axis) and the profitability dimension (vertical axis) into three equal divisions each. The resulting nine-cell grid yields three cells of low performance, three of mid-level performance, and three of high performance. The three high-performing categories are high-profit SMEs (mid-level growth), high-growth SMEs (mid-level profit), and stars (both high profit and high growth).

While any classification scheme is subject to criticism and debate, the case for defining high-performing SMEs as those firms that demonstrate high levels of profitability *and* high levels of growth is reasonable. Therefore, in the following discussions we adopt the notion that high-performing SMEs are those firms that have demonstrably higher levels of profitability and growth than most of their industry counterparts. Now we turn our attention to a rationale for why some SMEs will be high performing and some will not.

ORGANIZATIONAL LEARNING

At a conceptual level organizational learning can be thought of quite simply as the ability for an organization to successfully adapt to a dynamic world (Cohen & Levinthal, 1990; Hedberg, 1981; Huber, 1991). Learning is a stepwise process (i.e., Kolb's (1984) learning cycle). The learning process begins when firms observe events and gather information from customers, suppliers, and other external entities through experience. Next, firms interpret or draw inferences and conclusions from observations and experiences. Third, ideas are generated about what actions to take regarding interpretations and conclusions and decisions are made and tested regarding those ideas. Last, the decisions likely to have desirable outcomes are stored in the institutional memory of the organization to be drawn upon through time. Although we present learning as a continuous event, it is much more dynamic and free-flowing than the four steps. The ability of a firm to leverage its learning may be a large contributor to what sets high-performing SMEs apart from competitors (Pett & Wolff, 2007).

In our discussion it is important to distinguish the role of learning in SMEs compared with the much larger businesses in a competitive marketplace. Large enterprises with significant horizontal and vertical differentiation in their structures may become significantly "hidebound" and thus inflexible due to their size. The size of large enterprises may lead them to attempt to manipulate their external environment rather than flexibly adapt (i.e., learn) to changing conditions. Hence large firms may be less likely to exhibit a predisposition toward learning and adaptive action.

SMEs on the other hand usually are not large enough or influential enough to exert pressures externally that will materially change their environmental situation. SMEs are also likely to be much more tightly coupled (meaning fewer organizational structure layers vertically and horizontally) such that channels of communication are more open to the integration, adaptation, and application of information and new knowledge to their operational situation. This suggests that although SMEs on their own cannot modify their environment to any noticeable degree, what they do have is succinct communication channels and possibly richer information about customers, competitors, and suppliers. Thus, SMEs may be much more likely to exhibit the elements of organizational learning in their effort to flexibly adapt to changing environmental and business conditions over time. SMEs adept at learning and implementing the actions necessary for successful adaptation may therefore exhibit high performance levels relative to their peers. Central to successful adaptation of organizations to environmental change is the relationship between exploration of the possible and exploitation of the known (March, 1991; Schumpeter, 1934).

Exploration

To learn, one necessary step in the process is exploration and discovery of that which is new, helpful, and of importance regarding a firm's product or service offerings. In terms of the learning cycle discussed above, for individuals or organizations, a first step in the process is observation and gathering information. With respect to organizational learning, new information must be discovered by those individuals or groups in direct contact with the source (i.e., a marketing group). Once the information is gathered it must be consistently transferred across boundaries into the organization for translation, interpretation, and ultimately decisions regarding meaning and subsequent action. The information may be new or existing technologies, new or existing product features and customer needs, new means of distribution, or other relevant information not previously considered or incorporated into organizational plans or actions.

Following the discovery and transference of information, innovations are derived from new knowledge and creative insights that are dependent upon experimentation by organizational members using the acquired information. For example, an SME research and development group may learn of a new technology with potential useful application in the firm's industry. This information when combined with a marketing and sales group's knowledge of customer needs could lead to the development of a new product or service from which the firm could potentially benefit. The key word in the discussion is potential. The realization of potential is an iterative process that requires time with very uncertain outcomes. In the management of business organizations time and risk are two sometimes costly elements that management may be unwilling to undertake yet explorative learning requires both time and risk taking.

Exploitation

While exploration encompasses the activities of search, discovery, and experimentation, exploitation includes refinement, efficiency, implementation, and execution (March, 1991). Exploitative learning involves some of the same steps in the learning process that exploration employs but the focus of exploitative learning is to improve upon the existing knowledge or know-how. The essence of exploitation is to improve the efficiency of operational or production processes through better execution of organizational activities. For example, while exploration may yield an entirely new product as discussed above, exploitation may yield the original product more efficiently. Hence, exploitative organizational learning can be exemplified by effort to absorb knowledge about lean manufacturing systems or six-sigma processes to make the organization more effective and efficient within the current product markets.

In an organization's effort to survive and prosper the issue is not whether exploration should be pursued over exploitation or vice versa. As March (1991) explains, maintaining a balance between exploration and exploitation is necessary for high levels of sustained organizational performance. However, maintaining balance between the two forms of organizational learning is not a straightforward exercise. The difficulties can be illustrated by the managerial decisions surrounding invention and commercialization of new technology versus the refinement of an existing technology. Organizational resources devoted to new technology development are resources that cannot be directed to refinement and improvement of a firm's current production systems and product lines. The reverse is also apparent. Therefore, organizational managers may face a set of mutually exclusive resource allocation decisions. This condition may be particularly problematic in SMEs because of the resource constraints they face as stated above. The ability of a firm to find a balance requires ambidexterity with respect to organizational learning (i.e., explorative and exploitative learning) and in part may help explain high-performing SMEs.

A significant and growing dialogue in organizational learning seeks to understand the notion of ambidexterity in organizations. A number of areas show promise with respect to the idea that ambidextrous firms exist – those firms are very good at explorative and exploitative learning, and are found to be on average higher-performing firms than their less capable counterparts (Morgan & Berthon, 2008; Raisch et al., 2009). Studies in this stream posit that organizations with a well-understood and specified organizational context are conducive to explorative and exploitative ambidexterity. For example, some have successfully illustrated that vision, values, and flexibility in a firm are supporting conditions for ambidexterity (O'Reilly & Tushman, 2008). Still others have proposed that organizational context – operationalized as cooperation, autonomy, and reward structure – are effective elements in achieving organizational ambidexterity (Gibson & Birkinshaw, 2004). Drawing from the research on ambidexterity, one can conclude that organizations exhibiting a common vision and strong values with respect to learning – a culture of learning – coupled with the organizational practices of cooperation, responsibility through autonomy, and appropriate reward structures yields an effective balance between explorative and exploitative learning. In turn, balance yields higher performance levels for the organization.

Learning Orientation

Ideally, a culture of learning or what scholars have termed a "learning orientation" may serve to establish the necessary balance in SMEs, which could lead to high levels of performance:

> Organizational learning occurs when members of the organization act as learning agents for the organization, responding to changes in the internal and

> external environments of the organization by detecting and correcting errors in organizational theory in use, and embedding the results of their inquiry in private images and shared maps of the organization. (Argyris & Schön, 1978, p. 23)

Conceptually, organizational learning is a meta-construct comprised of three constituent elements: a predisposition to learn; learning facilitation; and application of learning to facilitate organizational adaptation (Sinkula et al., 1997). A predisposition to learn at the organization level is expressed by the philosophy-in-use and culture regarding learning. Proponents (ibid.) articulated this predisposition as a values-based cultural construct and termed it a "learning orientation". Organization-level learning begins with the commonly held firm values of open-mindedness, commitment to learning, and shared vision, which researchers (ibid.) articulated as the elements of a learning orientation.

The combination of these three dimensions as the predisposition to learn is the focal point in understanding the linkage between the human resource practices of an SME and the performance levels experienced by that SME. The first dimension, open-mindedness, is a precondition to the learning process because firms must be willing to question routines and assumptions that comprise the mental models (Senge, 1990) that drive thought and action. The willingness to question deeply held assumptions and beliefs may facilitate heuristics and non-routine mechanisms by which new insights and counterintuitive patterns can be devised to solve ambiguous challenges, that is, double-loop learning (Lei et al., 1996).

Associated with open-mindedness is the value that the collective of individuals comprising a firm places on learning, in other words a commitment to learning (Sinkula et al., 1997). Just as firms are not homogeneous with respect to structural organization they are likely to have very different views with respect to learning. The culture dimension can be visualized as a continuum anchored by hierarchical mechanistic organizations on one end and non-hierarchical and loosely configured network organizations at the other. The cultural values related to learning – especially explorative learning – in a mechanistic organization are likely much weaker than in the more organic network organization (Gibson & Birkinshaw, 2004). The mechanistic organization is likely to be much more attuned culturally to generating efficiencies with learning focused primarily on exploitation. Absent the values and context that reflect a commitment to the full learning spectrum, balanced learning and adaptation by the SME may not be fully successful.

Finally, creating a shared vision within the organization is essential for balanced learning to prosper. Research suggests that organizational learning's underlying principle is to create a shared vision, which in turn creates a proactive learning culture while providing direction to stakeholders. Further, having a shared vision is a vital focus of learning because it provides for a sense of commitment and resolve for the organizational participants (Day, 1994). Some have argued that without commitment and an understanding of organizational direction people will in general be less motivated to learn (Senge, 1990). Therefore, by fostering an atmosphere of shared vision organizational participants are empowered to act knowing the expectations and metrics by which they and the organization are to be measured. An effectively communicated and shared vision is likely to enhance learning within an organization.

When enterprise leaders fail to create a shared vision, organizational members are left to their own interpretation of what might be important, thus creating the potential for individuals or groups to work at cross-purposes, duplicate effort, or to devolve into apathy waiting for leaders to dictate rather than seeking the initiative. Such business organizations are much more likely to find themselves on the lower side of the performance dimension. The opposite is more likely in those firms that continually share the vision through communications and managerial actions. Members of any organization can easily become focused on their activities and unit while missing the bigger picture of the organization. In sum, a learning orientation comprised of open-mindedness, an organizational commitment to learning, and shared vision in SMEs can yield high performance levels related to the balance of explorative and exploitative learning. In other words, with the appropriate blend of values, leadership, and organizationally embedded capability for learning, the likelihood of successful exploration and exploitation increases, which, in turn, enhances the probability of an SME achieving the highest levels of performance. It is to the organizationally embedded capability for learning that we now turn our attention.

HUMAN RESOURCE PRACTICES, LEARNING, AND SME PERFORMANCE

The resource-based view of the firm proposes that valuable, rare, non-imitable, and organizationally embedded resources are the source of firm's sustainable competitive advantage (Barney, 1991). The knowledge-based view conceptualizes the firm as a knowledge-integrating institution (Grant, 1996) that coordinates and applies the knowledge from individuals to the productive tasks of the organization. Thus, knowledge at the individual level is proposed to become know-how (a potentially rare, valuable, non-imitable, organizationally embedded resource or capability) at the organization level, which can impart competitive advantage, and thus higher levels of performance, to the firm. The key elements in this discussion are the individuals that comprise the organization. SMEs have limited resources (Hornsby & Kuratko, 2003) and rely on fewer people in their organization to perform vitally important functions that have a major impact on the current and future prospects of the firm. Hence, people, while important in all organizations, are vitally important to the functioning and performance of SMEs.

HR practices are "A set of distinct but interrelated activities, functions, and processes that are directed at attracting, developing, and maintaining (or disposing of) a firm's human resources" (Lado & Wilson, 1994). HR practices have been proposed to have both a technical/functional and a strategic role in the operation and performance of firms of all sizes (Huselid et al., 1997). While SME HR practices do not rise to the level of functionality and formalization found in larger firms, studies have found that small firms do engage in a mix of HR practices that include recruiting, selection, training, and compensation (Hornsby & Kuratko, 2003; Kotey & Slade, 2005). Furthermore, there is evidence that SMEs have seen improved performance levels resulting from the effective implementation of these HR practices (Chandler & McEvoy 2000).

In SMEs, when it comes to collective organizational learning for ambidexterity the HR practices of recruiting, selection, training, and compensation can play a pivotal role in the performance and growth of the firm (Hayton, 2003). However, although conceptually we can make the argument that HR practices are vitally important, in practice SME owners and managers do not focus their time and effort on what is perceived as mundane administration until they perceive the HR issues as critically important to the firm (Tocher & Rutherford, 2009). In practice, again due to resource constraints in the SME, managers tend to prioritize in triage fashion the elements of the business that need their attention in the moment (Jawahar & McLaughlin, 2001). Therefore, until the HR issues reach potentially acute levels in the SME, managers tend not to devote sufficient time to them. This situation becomes problematic because it plays into the development of the culture of the organization over time. If HR practices are not valued consistently by the leaders of the organization and are important only in times of crisis, organizational members will also tend to adopt this view.

A recent study (Atkinson, 2007) illustrates the attitudinal divide between organizational leaders and those charged with carrying out the important functional work for the organization that can occur if HR practices do not rise to the level of strategic importance in the SME. The study focuses upon the employment relationship in small firms. Contrasts are drawn between three firms that each have distinct dimensions to the psychological contract and thus illustrate three different types of employment relationships between SME managers and employees. The results of the work illustrate three distinct types of employment relationship: transactional; relational with the firm; and relational with the profession. Transactional and relational with the firm are particularly appropriate for our discussion.

Firms that have developed a highly transactional employment relationship are likely to experience a lack of mutual trust, lack of buy-in to the goals of the organization, perceptions of very limited mutual obligation, and conditions in which employees perform at minimum levels of expectation and the principal motivator is pay. Simply put, employees "put in their time" in return for a paycheck at the end of the period. Firm performance outcomes will be low because of the lack of investment and initiative present in the activities of the collective. When employees are not engaged in and identify with the goals and objectives of the firm, learning and adaptation may be blocked. In the absence of learning the SME is left on a trajectory pointing downward in terms of firm performance and could be in a very difficult self-reinforcing downward spiral.

In contrast to the transactional employment psychological contract, a relational employment contract is characterized by a strong sense of mutual reciprocity, loyalty, and trust. In a very real sense the psychological contract between the firm and the employee emulates the internal environment of a benevolent and supportive family. In such an environment organizational members are willing to voluntarily go beyond their expected role for the organization and the organization (owners/managers) is willing to reciprocate, going well beyond the minimal transactional (pay for time) expectations. For an SME seeking high levels of performance such a relational setting may be a required antecedent condition for learning and the resulting high performance that can result. Indeed, it may be the sense of community that can be created in SMEs versus larger firms that may facilitate higher levels of performance (profitability and growth). With that said, embracing sound HR practices is vitally important for the creation of a community of individuals capable of working together to absorb knowledge and create the know-how that can lead to high levels of performance.

Implications for SME Management Practice

In the discussion above we have argued for a logical connection between high-performing SMEs, their ability to learn – organizational learning – and the role that HR can play in facilitating learning that can lead to high levels of performance (Kang et al., 2007). We now turn our attention to the very practical aspects of how owners or managers of SMEs may be able to effectuate learning and high performance, both profitability and growth, in their firms. In this discussion we specifically focus on professional and managerial positions (exemplified by MBA, CPA, IT, and engineering professionals) as those most appropriate to yield high performance through learning. This is consistent with the strategic aspect of HR practices in SMEs. With respect to the strategic relevance of HR practices in SME learning and performance there are four specific areas from which SME owners/managers may derive the greatest benefit: recruitment, selection, training, and compensation/retention.

Recruitment

Finding qualified individuals to staff key organizational positions has consistently been at the top or near the top of concerns identified by SME managers in national US surveys (Conference Board 2000 survey; National Federation of Independent Business 1998 survey). Williamson et al. (2002) point out that what a prospective employee knows about potential employers will usually determine whether they will seek employment with the firm. Two elements are identified as important in this discussion: "organizational knowledge" and "organizational legitimacy". Each of the elements will be discussed in turn.

Organizational knowledge is defined as the level of knowledge prospective employees possess about the SME and its activities in the business community. To attract interest on the part of potential employees there must be a baseline level of knowledge about a firm and what it does. Williamson et al. further subdivided the notion of organizational knowledge into two different types of knowledge: "the *familiarity* of an organization to job seekers, and job seekers' beliefs about an employer's *image*" (2002, p. 86; italics added). On both of these dimensions SMEs may be disadvantaged with respect to larger employers. Newer and smaller firms are unlikely to attract a significant amount of attention consistently while larger firms are more likely to have a greater impact in the business community, draw attention from the public at large, and be viewed as important to community leaders simply because of size. There is also a significantly greater network effect for larger firms due to the quantity of employee connection opportunities, resulting in greater and faster spread of information about the firm. Hence there is less opportunity for job seeker familiarity with SMEs, and a smaller chance that job seekers have formed beliefs about the SME's image.

In addition to possessing knowledge about the SME organization, prospective job seekers must view the SME as a legitimate and attractive organization likely to be beneficial to career prospects. Organizational legitimacy is defined as a prospective employee's view that a potential employer is desirable, proper, and appropriate given the norms and expectations within an industry (Suchman, 1995). Further, Suchman argues that legitimacy helps a firm to attract resources due to strengthened credibility and expectations that the firm can help to achieve organizational participants' goals and objectives. High-potential employees seek out organizations that are best able to provide them job security, growth and advancement, and challenge. Thus, legitimacy regarding accepted industry practices, trustworthiness, and future career growth opportunities can be a deciding factor in whether a job seeker will pursue a position with any specific firm. Again the advantage may go to larger firms primarily as a result of track record, institutionalized HR practices, and their ability to set the norms and expectations within an industry (Williamson et al., 2002).

Though SMEs may be disadvantaged in recruitment there are specific actions with respect to recruitment that can increase organizational knowledge and organizational legitimacy by prospective job seekers that can help to achieve the strategic goals of the small firm. First with respect to organizational knowledge, SMEs are well advised to take a page from their marketing playbook and undertake brand building with respect to their organization. In this instance rather than build the brand with respect to prospective customers, the target group is prospective job seekers. To improve the chances of recruitment success, SMEs must effectively manage the information flow to the target audience by capturing awareness and motivation prior to communicating organizational image. Williamson et al. (2002) suggest that an avenue to accomplish this is to access the places where job seekers tend to cluster such as universities, professional organizations, job fairs, and so on. Building relationships with professors in relevant disciplines at universities, developing links to university placement centers, attending professional organization social mixers, and exhibiting organizational information at job fairs are all relatively low-cost mechanisms for raising the level of organizational knowledge with job seekers.

To improve perceptions of organizational legitimacy in prospective employees the more an SME can imitate the practices of larger firms the more they are likely to be perceived as legitimate players in the market for talent. Imitating the practices generally accepted as the norms and expectations for behavior of legitimized firms is termed strategic isomorphism (DiMaggio & Powell, 1983). The underlying premise for strategic isomorphism is that legitimized practices communicate positive perceptions to a particular population about the firms that are using them (ibid.). Hence

SMEs that emulate practices used by larger firms may be viewed as more legitimate in the eyes of job seekers. Activities as straightforward as imitating the job advertisement formats and recruitment brochure practices of larger firms can enhance the legitimacy of SMEs in the minds of potential job seekers (Aldrich & Fiol, 1994). An HR practice deserving attention by SMEs is the use of the Internet to inform. Most large firms have a significant Internet presence with a prominent feature of their site focused on job seekers and potential employment. While most SMEs have recognized the potential of the Internet to gain new customers or provide information to existing customers, the use of the firm's website to recruit prospective employees is a practice that can enhance organizational legitimacy to this important group.

Another means to communicate an SME's legitimacy to job seekers is to highlight the "company the firm keeps". Developing and communicating an SME's inter-organizational ties are mechanisms to legitimize the firm to constituents. In general job seekers are looking for ways to start a career, transition to a new career, or grow in their current career path. As such they are looking for what a firm can do for them regarding their career. Part of the job seeker's calculus is security and opportunity. Prospective employees want positions in organizations that are or are likely to be stable over time and that provide opportunity for experiential and responsibility growth. SMEs may be viewed as limited on both these dimensions unless they can associate themselves closely with other stable firms with a history of opportunity. Hence SMEs can promote "legitimacy by association" that is attractive to job seekers by publicizing their association with other firms in a supply chain, industry network, or community of businesses that may represent these qualities to prospective employees.

Selection

Attracting interest from high-quality and high-potential prospective employees is a necessary first step that high-performing SMEs must undertake to establish a qualified pool of candidates. Selecting the best candidate from the pool is the next step of vital importance to SMEs in their quest for high performance. In the early stages of firm growth the selection process is of critical importance because of the relative impact that the new hire may have on the development of the firm. For example, the individual brought into a firm of ten people will have a significantly greater impact on the prospects for the firm than will the individual brought into a firm of 100 people. As Cassell et al. (2002) point out, while our understanding of HR practices in SMEs is woefully inadequate, it is apparent that as a firm grows from a few employees to many employees the HR practices employed become more formalized and structured. However, if formalization and structure in the selection process yield better-quality hiring decisions, SMEs seeking to achieve high performance may be well advised to adopt such practices early in their development. Indeed Cassel et al. (2002) report that of SMEs using formalized selection procedures it is the view of managers that the procedures aid the firm in achieving organizational objectives in most cases.

Caution should be used when interpreting the notion of formalized selection procedures. It is not the intent of this chapter to advocate establishing a formal HR function in the very small firm. However, top management and owners should have a sound understanding of how HR practices could pay dividends to their firm and how they may expand their knowledge base with respect to the HR practices initiated. In effect, in very small SMEs the activities of the HR professional must be rolled into the general manager. The "jack-of-all-trades" nature of the general manager in SMEs can lead to management by exception or management by crisis for the firm. Such situations are reactionary stances by the top management and can preclude the notion of the learning organization and the development of ambidexterity. For an early-stage SME to become a high-performing SME, selecting the right individual to help develop the firm requires the right mindset and skills regarding HR selection on the part of the general manager. The best individual for positions in SMEs will likely be heavily dependent upon the correct balance between attitude and skill.

Formalizing the selection criteria against which prospective new hires can be measured is a positive first step for SMEs. This action entails not only establishing the criteria but also communicating the criteria to key SME personnel involved in the selection process and decisions as well. Effort to establish selection criteria necessarily must be an ongoing process due to the dynamic nature of a growing enterprise. With every addition to the organizational team the future needs of the enterprise in terms of the skills and task responsibilities are likely to change. Therefore, the selection criteria for key positions should be revisited by top managers on a regular basis to tailor the criteria to the particular needs of the SME at any point in time.

Included in the selection criteria should be non-negotiable "must have" qualities and more flexible "nice-to-have" qualities. For SMEs striving for high performance growth and profitability through ambidextrous organizational learning attitudinal elements of the selection criteria may dominate the "must have" category. Learning requires qualities of open-mindedness, cooperativeness, confidence, the ability to effectively communicate, humility, and a willingness to take calculated risks to name a few. Absent these soft attitudinal dimensions a prospective key employee with significant technical capability may not be able to cope with the ambiguity and fluid business environment that is characteristic of many high-potential SME firms. Hence, though difficult, selection of new hires based on soft-skill criteria may be significantly important in the development of high-performing SMEs.

Training

The exhortation for managers to "hire for attitude and train for skill" may be especially appropriate for SME firms seeking high performance levels through ambidextrous learning. Attitude necessarily encompasses a willingness to learn with respect to SMEs. Firms with sound prospects for high levels of growth and profitability are very dynamic environments in which to work. As is common for SMEs, on-the-job training is the most common form of training provided (Kotey & Slade, 2005) and is a very important component in the SME arsenal. However, on-the-job training is likely insufficient for high-potential individuals successfully selected into an SME and, according to research, more formal training in SMEs is generally not an element provided (Barrett & Mayson, 2007). Therefore, a gap exists between the need for training in SMEs and the likelihood that training, in addition to that provided on the job, is part of the HR practice repertoire.

To resolve this gap between need and HR practice in SMEs it is instructive to examine the limited evidence that research provides regarding the organizational payoff from a more formalized training regimen in SMEs. In a study of Australian SMEs Barrett and Mayson (2007) found that faster-growing SMEs used more formalized HR practices than their no-growth counterparts including tailored training programs for select individuals. In another examination of SMEs by Kotey and Slade (2005) more formalized HR practices are adopted as SMEs grow from micro through medium-size. However, the analysis also revealed a much greater pattern of usage of HR practices at the operational level irrespective of size than the use of HR practices at the managerial level, especially in the realm of training. Training at the managerial level increased significantly with firm size, indicating the recognition on the part of managers that as the firm grows middle management becomes increasingly important. Combined, these two studies may indicate an opportunity for SMEs to adopt more formalized management talent development training at early stages if they aspire to high performance and growth through learning.

Compensation/retention

The final HR practice to be discussed in the implications for practice section of this chapter is compensation. The issue of key personnel compensation in SMEs is a difficult one due to the resource-constrained nature of SMEs. To obtain and retain qualified key personnel in an SME requires attention to the issue of compensation. However, the term compensation needs to be considered in a broad sense versus the narrow sense of salary or monetary remuneration. Compensation is an area where SME owners/managers may have to be or become creative and innovate to keep quality people. At minimum the issue of compensation should be viewed as a package of benefits that is changeable over time and heavily dependent upon both individual and organizational performance. Growing SMEs have been shown to use the benefits package approach while non-growing SMEs are more one-dimensional with respect to compensation (Barrett & Mayson, 2007).

Compensation packages in growing SMEs necessarily include salary as a major component with a variety of elements added to increase the attractiveness and retention power of the package. Chief among these elements is an incentive system tied to individual and organizational performance. Well-conceived and implemented incentive systems (such as bonuses) may be used in SMEs to enhance compensation in a number of ways. While many incentive systems are based on monetary reward, SME managers can be innovative and complement monetary incentives with non-monetary components. Included in the non-monetary elements of a reward system can be company-wide recognition of performance; extra vacation time or personal days; and special privileges or other perks that the individual may value. In addition to the non-monetary elements that can be included SMEs may consider lower-cost monetary alternatives such as US Savings Bonds, increased company contribution to 401 (k) plans, education fund contributions, and/or life insurance contributions. Such combinations of incentives for key individuals in the SME reward for exceeding target performance goals that help to drive the firm toward its goals and at the same time the combinations can reduce the pressure on the firm's resource base.

There are also a few less often utilized elements to SME compensation packages that should be considered. One such element is some form of firm ownership share plan. While ownership should be reserved for key individuals with the ability to contribute in major ways to the success of the SME, it can be a powerful message that performance is rewarded and retention of key players to the firm is important. The message may extend well beyond the individual to whom the incentive is provided as well and generate consequential loyalty and dedication to what the SME is striving to accomplish. In addition, other incentive elements such as sponsored off-site training and education benefits, succession planning, or promotional opportunities can be used to reward and retain individuals that are significant contributors to goal accomplishment in SMEs. As one can see from the above discussion there are a number of mechanisms to construct a compensation package with the goal of rewarding performance and retaining strong performers in the firm. Success in creating the compensation package in SMEs requires creativity and innovation on the part of SME owners and managers along with a more formalized and strategic approach to HR practices by the firm.

CONCLUSION

The goal of this chapter was to discuss and illustrate the relationship between HR practice, organizational learning, and high levels of performance in SMEs. While there has been significant work done to understand these elements in large organizations, the application to SMEs has only begun to scratch the surface. This is primarily due to the sheer number and great variety of firms that comprise the category of business firms known collectively as SMEs. What is obvious from the current research effort in the areas of SME performance, learning and HR practice is the heterogeneity that exists among SMEs. As a result of the significant heterogeneity, a cautionary note must be provided. The intent of the work was to present the logic that certain HR practices may be appropriate for SME firms seeking to establish ambidextrous organizational learning as the basis for achieving very high levels of profit and growth rate performance. Outside this relatively narrow segment of the SME landscape the recommendations above may not apply.

In summary, Atkinson (2007) argued effectively that high-performing SMEs may require that owners/managers build high-performing employment relationships. The logic of building solid employment relationships through specific and targeted HR practices in SMEs to achieve high levels of performance is sound. Furthermore, strong employment relationships derived from reasoned HR practices can build into the SME a capability for ambidextrous learning, which, in turn, enables an SME to generate higher levels of profitability and growth.

REFERENCES

Aldrich, H. & Fiol, C.M. 1994. Fools rush in? The institutional context of industry creation. *Academy of Management Review*, **19**(4): 645–70.

Argyris, C. & Schön, D. 1978. *Organizational Learning: A Theory in Action Perspective*. New York, Addison-Wesley.

Atkinson, C. 2007. Building high-performance employment relationships in small firms. *Employee Relations*, **29**(5): 506–19.

Barney, J.B. 1991. Firm resources and sustained competitive advantage. *Journal of Management*, **17**(1): 99–120.

Barrett, R. & Mayson, S. 2007. Human resource management in growing small firms. *Journal of Small Business and Enterprise Development*, **14**(2): 307–20.
Besanko, D., Dranove, D., Shanley, M. & Schlaeter, S. 2004. *Economics of Strategy* (3rd edition). New York: Wiley.
Cassell, C., Nadin, S., Gray, M. & Clegg, C. 2002. Exploring human resource management practices in small and medium-sized enterprises. *Personnel Review*, **31**(6): 671–92.
Chandler, G. & Hanks, S. 1994. Market attractiveness, resource-based capabilities, and venture performance. *Journal of Business Venturing*, **9**(4): 331–49.
Chandler, G.N. & McEvoy, G.M. 2000. Human resource management, TQM, and firm performance in small- and medium-sized enterprises. *Entrepreneurship Theory and Practice*, **25**(3): 43–57.
Cohen, W.M. & Levinthal, D.A. 1990. Absorptive capacity: A new perspective on learning and innovation. *Administrative Science Quarterly*, **35**(1): 128–52.
Davidsson, P., Steffens, P.R. & Fitzsimmons, J.R. 2008. Performance assessment in entrepreneurship and management research: Is there a pro-growth bias? Queensland University of Technology ePrints, available at: http://eprints.qut.edu.au/archive/00012040/; accessed 16 November 2010.
Davidsson, P., Steffens, P.R. & Fitzsimmons, J.R. 2009. Growing profitable or growing from profits: Putting the horse in front of the cart? *Journal of Business Venturing*, **24**(4): 388–406.
Day, G.S. 1994. The capabilities of market-driven organizations. *Journal of Marketing*, **58**(4): 37–52.
DiMaggio, P.J. & Powell, W.W. (1983). The iron cage revisited: Institutional isomorphism and collective rationality in organizational fields. *American Sociological Review*, **48**(2): 147–60.
Freeman, J., Carroll, G.R. & Hannan, M.T. 1983. The liability of newness: Age dependence in organizational death rates. *American Sociological Review*, **48**(5): 692–710.
Gibson, C.B. & Birkinshaw, J. 2004. The antecedents, consequences, and mediating role of organizational ambidexterity. *Academy of Management Journal*, **47**(2): 209–226.
Grant, R.M. 1996. Toward a knowledge-based theory of the firm. *Strategic Management Journal*, **17**(Winter Special Issue): 109–22.
Hayton, J. 2003. Strategic human capital management in SMEs: An empirical study of entrepreneurial performance. *Human Resource Management*, **42**(4): 375–93.
Hedberg, B. 1981. How organizations learn and unlearn. In P.C. Nystrom and W.H. Starbuck (eds), *Handbook of Organizational Design*. London: Oxford University Press, pp. 3–27.
Hornsby, J.S. & Kuratko, D.F. 2003. Human resource management in U.S. small business: A replication and extension. *Journal of Developmental Entrepreneurship*, **8**(1): 73–89.
Huber, G.P. 1991. Organizational learning: The contributing processes and the literatures. *Organization Science*, **2**(1): 88–115.
Huselid, M.A., Jackson, S.E. & Schuler, R.S. 1997. Technical and strategic human resource management effectiveness as determinants of firm performance. *Academy of Management Journal*, **40**(1): 171–88.
Jawahar, I.M. & McLaughlin, G. (2001). Toward a descriptive stakeholder theory: An organizational lifecycle approach. *Academy of Management Review*, **26**(3): 397–415.

Kang, S.C., Morris, S.S. & Snell, S.A. 2007. Relational archetypes, organizational learning, and value creation: Extending the human resource architecture. *Academy of Management Review*, **32**(1): 236–56.
Kolb, D. 1984. *Experiential Learning*. Englewood Cliffs, NJ: Prentice Hall.
Kotey, B. & Slade, P. 2005. Formal human resource management practices in small growing firms. *Journal of Small Business Management*, **43**(1): 16–40.
Lado, A.A. & Wilson, M.C. 1994. Human resource systems and sustained competitive advantage: A competency-based perspective. *Academy of Management Review*, **19**(4): 699–727.
Lei, D., Hitt, M.A. & Bettis, R. 1996. Dynamic core competencies through meta-learning and strategic context. *Journal of Management*, **22**(4): 549–69.
Lieberman, M.B. & Montgomery, D.B. 1988. First-mover advantages. *Strategic Management Journal*, **9**(Special Issue): 41–58.
March, J.G. 1991. Exploration and exploitation in organizational learning. *Organization Science*, **2**(1): 71–87.
Morgan, R.E. & Berthon, P.R. 2008. Market orientation, generative learning, innovation strategy and business performance inter-relationships in bioscience firms. *Journal of Management Studies*, **45**(8): 1329–53.
O'Reilly, C.A. & Tushman, M.L. 2008. Ambidexterity as a dynamic capability: Resolving the innovator's dilemma. *Research in Organizational Behavior*, **28**(1), 185–206.
Pett, T.L. & Wolff, J. 2007. SME performance: The case for internal consistency. *Journal of Small Business Strategy*, **18**(1): 16–32.
Porter, M.E. 1985. *Competitive Advantage: Creating and Sustaining Superior Performance*. New York: Free Press.
Raisch, S., Birkinshaw, J., Probst, G. & Tushman, M.L. 2009. Organizational ambidexterity: Balancing exploitation and exploration for sustained performance. *Organization Science*, **20**(3): 685–95.
Schumpeter, J.A. 1934. *The Theory of Economic Development*. Cambridge, MA: Harvard University Press.
Senge, P.M. 1990. *The Fifth Discipline: The Art and Practice of the Learning Organization*. New York: Doubleday.
Sinkula, J.M., Baker, W.E. & Noordewier, T. 1997. A framework for market-based organizational learning: Linking values, knowledge and behavior. *Journal of the Academy of Marketing Science*, **25**(4): 305–18.
Steffens, P., Davidsson, P. & Fitzsimmons, J. 2009. Performance configurations over time: Implications for growth- and profit-oriented strategies. *Entrepreneurship Theory and Practice*, **33**(1): 125–48.
Stinchcombe, A.L. 1965. Social structure and organizations. In J.G. March (ed.), *Handbook of Organizations*. Chicago: Rand McNally, pp. 153–93.
Suchman, M.C. 1995. Managing legitimacy: Strategic and institutional approaches. *Academy of Management Review*, **20**(3): 571–610.
Tocher, N. & Rutherford, M.W. 2009. Perceived acute human resource management in small and medium firms: An empirical examination. *Entrepreneurship Theory and Practice*, **33**(2): 455–79.
Williamson, I.O., Cable, D.M. & Aldrich, H.E. 2002. Smaller but not necessarily weaker: How small businesses can overcome barriers to recruitment. In J.A. Katz & T.M. Welbourne (eds) *Managing People in Entrepreneurial Organizations: Learning From the Merger of Entrepreneurship and Human Resource Management*, Volume 5. Amsterdam: JAI Press, pp. 83–106.

PART III

Human resource management and small business challenges

7. Legal issues facing small businesses and their owners

Michael Troilo and Brad Carson

INTRODUCTION

One of the defining characteristics of small businesses is their lack of resources relative to larger firms. This is most acute in the start-up phase, when entrepreneurs are scrambling to survive. Among the expenses that may be postponed is legal counsel. The entrepreneur may rationalize that legal advice, while desirable, is a luxury that can be afforded later in the firm's life-cycle.

We beg to differ. Our purpose in this chapter is to highlight the myriad areas of business operations that require legal attention if one is to avoid catastrophic liability. As one lawyer we interviewed said, "You can pay me now, or you can pay much more later" (Jurgensen, 2010). Understanding the sources of potential legal liability is critical for all businesses, small as well as large, new, and established.

This chapter is more than an admonishment to hire legal counsel early; it is a guide for best practices in legal issues among small firms. It is written with both the practitioner and the student of entrepreneurship in mind, and contains not only the common legal pitfalls of operating a business but also tactics to anticipate and avoid them. There is particular emphasis on pragmatism as opposed to theory. We present some legal concepts and cases for context but do not explore them in depth. A person wishing to explore the legal nuances of the principal–agent relationship, for example, would be better served by any number of law textbooks examining this subject.

One caveat about this chapter is that we approach these issues from a broad common-law perspective. Our advice, while practical, is general in nature and is in no way a substitute for hiring a lawyer competent in a particular locale's codes. This chapter assumes a developed-country context, and doesn't capture all the differences between countries, let alone within a given country. A preliminary reading of Mandel (2010) gave us initial topics to discuss. Interviews with lawyers with decades of experience representing small firms and secondary sources such as scholarly articles, books, and cases constitute our research.

We begin with a brief overview of hiring legal counsel. We then divide the chapter into several major components of legal liability for businesses: (1) issues arising from employment and employees, (2) issues arising from ownership structure, and (3) issues arising from other regulations. Within employment, we treat mandatory deductions/accruals for payroll taxes, vacation, and so on, discrimination and harassment, worker health and safety, employee incentive plans, termination, and employees as agents of the company. For ownership structure, we discuss the taxation and governance issues that differ among sole proprietorships, partnerships, and corporations, as well as within the categories of partnership and corporation, for example, "S" corporation v. limited liability corporation "LLC". Other sources of legal liability beyond these first two broad categories include product safety, securities issuances regulations, and environmental regulations. We discuss insurance as a best practice separately and offer final thoughts to conclude the chapter.

HIRING LEGAL COUNSEL

According to Petillon and Hull (2009), "the most important thing that a lawyer representing small and growing businesses can recognize is that entrepreneurs usually have extremely limited resources and must use legal assistance sparingly" (Vol. 1, pp 1-1). It is due to these limited resources that entrepreneurs tend to postpone the hiring of legal counsel, as we highlighted initially. Given this fact, what should entrepreneurs do? We put this question to the lawyers we interviewed, and here is the response from Tom Jurgensen:

Q: What advice would you give to an entrepreneur regarding the selection of legal counsel? What's the best way of going about this?

Tom: My first thought would be to ask other entrepreneurs. I wouldn't rely on advertising, rather, I would want referrals from other business owners. You want to get a good business attorney, and I would also avoid some of the big firms.

Q: Why would you avoid the big firms?

Tom: Well, think about the cost. A person just starting their business can't afford the fees. Sometimes the big firms will offer to defer the fees. That sounds good from a cash flow perspective, but before you know it you've racked up a huge debt. Another issue is that many of the lawyers from the big firms aren't entrepreneurial. Don't get me wrong; I have many friends who work or have worked in the big firms. They're fine for training lawyers in certain specialties, but most of them have never owned or managed a business. As an entrepreneur, you really want to find someone who is both knowledgeable about law and who is also business-savvy. Now the big firms may offer you several people each with his or her own specialty: this one does tax, that one does securities, etc. but think again about the cost: you'll have each of these people billing at $700/hour. As an entrepreneur you can't afford that. You want to have someone who is a great business attorney. If they haven't run their own business, they should at least have had significant experience helping other start-up ventures. I do have some bias favoring the smaller law firms, but my experience as an entrepreneur shapes my opinion.

Mandel (2010) also notes that, at least in the US context, the legal profession is highly specialized, yet there are no official designations for specialties. Once a person passes the bar he or she is simply a lawyer. It is a matter of caveat emptor; the small business owner must search for a lawyer who is knowledgeable about small businesses as opposed to litigation, and so on. Perhaps as important as technical competence is empathy for the daily constraints the entrepreneur faces.

LEGAL ISSUES RELATING TO EMPLOYMENT

Mandatory Deductions and Accruals

There are a myriad of issues revolving around employment: hiring, retention, and termination. The first topic is mandatory deductions and accruals that employers make for social welfare purposes, for example, Medicare and Social Security in the US, as well as benefits such as vacation and sick leave. Entrepreneurs are generally aware of some of these payroll expenses, but rarely are conversant with all of the statutes surrounding deductions and accruals, for example, the Family and Medical Leave Act of 1993 (Eschels & Brown, 2005). This lack of familiarity has legal consequences. Here is an excerpt from the conversation with Tom Jurgensen:

Q: Can you identify some of the legal issues with regard to hiring employees and payroll taxes? Most people know about Social Security and Medicare; what are some of the other issues?

Tom: Oh, well, where do we start? There are just so many things involved. Not only do you have Social Security and Medicare, you also have worker's compensation and unemployment insurance that you have to consider. Many times entrepreneurs get loosey-goosey with the payroll deductions, and that's how they get in trouble. Let me tell you what I see all the time: entrepreneurs want to make their employees exempt. You know that there can be non-exempt employees, for whom deductions for payroll are necessary, and exempt employees, right? Well, entrepreneurs figure they will make employees exempt, then they also aren't required to pay overtime. So here's what happens. The entrepreneur has the employee working crazy hours. Maybe the employee gets burned out, or there's a falling out. Do you know what's the first thing they do?

Q: Complain to the state?

Tom: Exactly. The employee then reports to the state what the situation is, and then the entrepreneur is in big trouble.

Q: Why do you think entrepreneurs do this? Do they not know the law? I understand that ignorance isn't a defense, but is it ignorance or is it willful? Is it a matter of being so focused on the business that they just don't bother?

Tom: There are a couple of things involved. First, many entrepreneurs don't have procedures for making the right payroll deductions. Next, even if they do have policies, they don't file paperwork. They don't keep track of it. Many entrepreneurs want to cut corners: they don't hire lawyers, they don't hire HR, and they figure they'll save money that way. Now with regards to knowing, I say there are three categories. The first category is the folks who don't know. They may be so hyper-focused on their business, as you say, that they don't pay attention to it. The second category does know, but they just plan around it. They know exactly what they should do and they are trying to get away with it. The third type doesn't know, and doesn't want to know. They want to pretend that they are unaware. When I start telling them what the requirements are, they'll actually ask me to stop telling them.

Q: Why is that? The penalties can be so high.

Tom: Entrepreneurs are gamblers. They figure they will take that risk. You have a guy who has money for building a prototype or for compliance. He goes for the prototype and then is subject to violations.

Q: What other areas of payroll also present liability?

Tom: There are benefits, vacation time, sick leave, etc. Those are also areas where entrepreneurs just kind of reassure their employees that they have them, but where the entrepreneurs also don't keep track. All of a sudden when an employee resigns the entrepreneur says "You have this much time" and the employee says "I thought I had more vacation time" and the problems start. You know that you're supposed to keep track of this throughout, and you have to pay it upon termination?

Q: Right. The employee would be accruing the vacation.

Tom: Right, well, the entrepreneur doesn't do that. He doesn't have a system in place to keep track of these things. There should be a manual or a handbook specifying what the policies are, and then a means of tracking it. Many entrepreneurs lack both. The good ones have an HR manual and follow it.

There are two best practices concerning legal practices and small businesses that deserve reiteration. The first is that entrepreneurs need to codify human resources policies and procedures in an employee handbook. In the rush to create and run a business this is overlooked, and becomes a potential source of legal liability. Other sources already cited such as Mandel (2010), Petillon and Hull (2009), and Eschels and Brown (2005) also mention the need to create and maintain a human resources manual.

The second best practice is just as important: small business owners need to have systems for tracking these employee-related liabilities. Beyond accruing vacation and sick leave, these systems should also have notifications and reminders for owners to file the paperwork for items such as workers' compensation that governments require. Too often entrepreneurs ignore these mundane details and procrastinate, thinking that once the business is running smoothly they will make the necessary investment to account for these items.

Worker Health and Safety

The owner is responsible for creating a reasonably safe working environment: physically, emotionally, and psychologically; legal ramifications arise from both willful violation of this principle as well as negligence in maintaining appropriate standards of behavior (Gregory, 2002). The common-law tradition emphasizes the responsibility of the owner for maintenance of his or her site; the obligation arises from ownership as opposed to a specific relationship, for example, master–servant or employer–employee (Patrizia et al., 2002). As a consequence, the issues surrounding worker health and safety extend to other persons on site, such as visitors and customers (ibid.).

As with payroll taxes, the paperwork demands for compliance with worker health and safety are strenuous. For example, in the United States the federal law known as The Occupational Safety and Health Act (OSHA) "requires that employers must provide records to any OSHA compliance officer who requests them" (Brown & Gutterman, 2005, p. 102). Beyond this, there is the Department of Labor with its myriad regulations, and state and local ordinances as well. It can be dizzying for an entrepreneur to keep current with all of them, which is why legal counsel is so essential. Best practices for this area include strong executive leadership, attention to detail such as specifying the worker's rights under the law in the HR manual, and frequent training. In the words of Jurgensen (2010):

> The good companies have leadership that pays attention to these issues. They hire attorneys to keep them abreast of the regulations, they have employee manuals with the policies, and they follow them. They don't cut corners. Here in California we have both federal and state agencies responsible for worker health and safety. It's important to maintain compliance with both.

Discrimination and Harassment

Another area of potential liability for the small business owner concerns discrimination and harassment of employees. To be proactive, entrepreneurs should screen prospective employees carefully. In terms of best practices, Chris White, a management consultant with small businesses for over three decades, had this to say:

> We have two rules for hiring people. Find people who have integrity, and find people who are smart. The background checks are important. There has to be someone to do that. There has to be a process in place for adding the next employee.

His partner, David Holden, himself a lawyer and management consultant with 40 years of practice counseling small firms, added the following:

> It's so important to hire the right people first, and to have a strong culture. I mean if I hire a guy who's honest and smart, I'm not expecting him to be involved in sexual harassment unless he's got a screw loose somewhere. It's also imperative to educate employees about these things, not just to have an HR manual. You need to imprint the culture, fire difficult people fast if you have to.

> For most businesses, rehabilitation is not a core competency. If someone has a psychological problem where they're not acting appropriately at the office then you need to get them to treatment, yes, but you also have to let them go to show that this type of behavior is not going to be tolerated.

The need for a strong culture of integrity is the first and best line of defense for small business owners to avoid legal problems in this and other areas of business. This was the consensus of the three experts we interviewed. Beyond this, several tactics are important:

- Codify policies and procedures for handling discrimination and harassment in a human resources manual that is provided to every employee.
- Have employees sign a form indicating that they've received the manual, read it, and understood the policies.
- Hold training courses for employees to emphasize these policies. As David Holden put it: "A manual is fine, as long as you don't just hand it to an employee and forget about it. It's just going to sit on the shelf and gather dust. Everyone says, 'read the manual', but who does? They're only going to read it if you tell them to read. Give them lunch and tell them what's important in the manual".

Employee Incentive Plans

Employee incentive plans can be a powerful tool to motivate business performance. Nonetheless, incentive plans can be complex and cumbersome. It is important to consult with benefit specialists in designing such plans. Irrespective of design, the paramount desire for such plans, one rarely met in practice, is that they in fact incentivize employees. To this end, an incentive compensation plan must meet several criteria. First, it must be easily communicated to employees, who can then act accordingly. Second, the plan must incentivize or reward activities that are actually within the control of the employee. If the rewards are not based on acts within the employees' control – such as overall corporate profitability – then the plan becomes an alternative form of profit-sharing, which may well be justified and advisable, although it is not an incentive plan and should not be recognized as such. Stock option plans are an example of a profit-sharing plan. The smaller the business or the fewer the number of employees, the more likely it is that a profit-sharing plan and an employee incentive plan resemble one another.

For small businesses, an elaborate incentive plan may be more trouble than it is worth. Alternatively, such businesses might want to develop simple but effective plans that reward increases in sales or a similar benchmark. A stock option plan in particular assumes that there will be a market for the stock at some point (or else, as in an employee stock ownership plan, a commitment by the company to redeem it from the employee). It is possible, though still somewhat involved, for small, privately-held businesses to supplement an amalgam of job-specific incentives with a phantom stock plan or stock appreciation rights, which award employees based on company performance without ever involving the actual transfer of shares. A benefits advisor, as well as books by organizations like the National Center for Employee Ownership, can assist in the design of these many different types of incentive plan.

For those businesses in the United States contemplating stock option plans, they should be aware that these programs come in two varieties: the incentive stock option (ISO) and the non-qualified stock option (NQSO). ISOs must have an exercise price equal or greater to the fair market value of the stock at the time of grant; NQSOs do not face this requirement. ISOs are not taxed at the time the employee exercises the option, while NQSOs are taxed (at the ordinary income rate) on the difference between their fair market value at the time of exercise and the exercise price. ISOs are taxed instead at the capital gains rate on the difference between the exercise price and the fair market value at the time of sale; NQSOs are taxed again upon sale of the stock – at the capital gains tax rate – on the difference between the exercise price and the fair market value at the time of sale. Significantly for the company, ISOs are tax-deductible as compensation, while NQSOs are not. For a start-up company, with little tax liability and a very low stock value, ISOs are often preferred, as employees benefit while the tax deduction is worth little to the company. For companies with significant tax liability, the deductibility of NQSOs is a powerful attraction.

Employee Termination

Terminating an employee should be done with utmost care, and then only with advice from legal counsel or qualified human resources specialists. Most US jurisdictions hold that employment is, as a rule, terminable at will – the doctrine of employment-at-will; that is, for good reason, bad reason, or no reason at all a job can be ended. Nevertheless, most jurisdictions also have laws that restrict or modify the rights to terminate a worker. Laws might also give employees certain pre-termination rights, and union contracts may specify a termination procedure that cannot be ignored. Employers must proceed with peril when handling terminations lest they face substantial legal risk.

In the United States, it is important to be aware of two sources of employment protections that modify the usual presumption toward employment-at-will. First, municipal, state, or federal law can restrict employers' right to terminate workers. Examples would be the federal prohibitions against race, gender, and age discrimination. Most states have similar protections, and these regulations are often much more restrictive on employers than their federal models. Cities also increasingly provide safeguards to employees who are members of a protected class, ranging from ethnic and racial minorities to women to gays and lesbians. Second, employees might have a contractual right to employment that supersedes employment-at-will. A union contract would be a paradigmatic example. But employment contracts are not uncommon in general, and it is even possible that an implicit employment contract is created through a course of dealing or through the provisions of an employee handbook.

Much legal anxiety around terminations can be prevented through proper employment practices in general. It is essential to communicate employment policies and procedures throughout the business, and also to document the communication. For all companies, these policies and procedures should be periodically re-examined and, for larger companies, audits should be used to verify compliance. It is equally essential that employers inform employees of work expectations. If performance is at issue, a review of past appraisals is in order before terminating an employee, with an expectation that both failure to meet expectations and a remediation plan be noted in the record. Being candid with employees about workplace inadequacies is recommended, and this frankness will be better received – both by employees and in later challenges – if problems have been recorded in the employee's personnel file long before termination. As a final matter, severance should be considered; in exchange, employees should be asked to sign a release waiving all future claims against the business.

Agency and Torts

There are two basic ways that either an employee or an independent contractor (I/C) might create legal liability for a small business owner in the ordinary course of business: agency or torts (Mandel, 2010). According to Presser, "an agent is one who is authorized to conduct business for a principal and can enter into contracts which bind the principal if they act with sufficient authority" (2005, p. 35). It is also possible for an agent to bind the small business owner legally if a customer can reasonably believe that the agent has sufficient authority, even if in fact the agent does not (Mandel, 2010). We posed the question of how entrepreneurs could prevent legal liability from agency to our experts. Here are their thoughts:

Chris: For independent contractors, it's imperative to have well-written contracts that specify the parameters. We sign two agreements. The first is an agreement specifying the relationship. It gives the scope of what is permissible and what is not in the relationship. The second contract is for the project itself. It sets the boundaries for the job. Sometimes entrepreneurs want to outsource: payroll companies are a good example. If you bind the independent contractor to specific parameters you will be okay. The biggest exposure for entrepreneurs is a fuzzy contract; there are gray areas that become sources of potential conflict and litigation.

Tom: In addition to being a lawyer I also was involved in starting four separate businesses. The way we handled this, and the way I've seen other good small firms handle it, is to be very clear about authority. Decide who does what; have very clear communications. Actually *tell* people what they can and cannot do; don't leave them guessing. When I was an entrepreneur we had set rules about what each position could do, what sorts of transactions needed the assent of more than one officer, or of the president, or required review by legal counsel or the board before they could be completed. Now where that gets tricky is with middle management. Someone may think they have the authority, but in any case the customer wouldn't know. The courts would rule in favor of the customer.

Clarity and communication are the keys. Roles have to be well-defined and explained to both employees and independent contractors. For independent contractors, these roles must be carefully specified in contracts with the small business owner.

Civil wrongdoings, or torts, on the part of employees and independent contractors can also bind entrepreneurs. According to Mandel (2010), "the employer, under the doctrine of *respondent superior* (or *vicarious liability*), is responsible for any actions of the employee occurring within the scope of her employment" (p. 286, italics his). The typical instance of this, which Mandel uses, is a traffic accident. If such occurs in the course of business, then the small business owner will be held responsible for the action of the employee. For independent contractors, a distinction is made between delegable and non-delegable duties; for the former the employer will not be found liable (ibid.).

There is a difference, however, between not being found liable and not being sued in the first place. Our interviews made it clear that victims of torts would sue all parties, regardless of whether the culprit is an employee or an independent contractor:

Q: Let's talk about torts. What's the difference between an I/C and an employee here? If I'm driving my car in the course of business, whether I'm an I/C or an employee, and I hit someone, does it matter?

David: The people who can be sued are those responsible for the accident. If you are a truck driver for a company, and you hit me, then I'm going to sue you and I'm going to sue the company. There's a cause-and-effect relationship for torts; both that person and the company will be sued.

Q: But if I'm an independent contractor, can the entrepreneur protect himself? Is there some sort of indemnification?

David: This area of law is one where the courts have found joint and several liability for the parties involved. The classic case is the operating room where the patient has the wrong leg amputated. Now everyone in that room is going to get sued. The parties can then sue each other and sort it out that way.

The response from Tom Jurgensen:

Q: What about torts? Say I'm an employee and I'm involved in a car wreck.

Tom: If it happened while the employee was doing something business-related you can expect to be sued.

Q: OK, but how does the situation differ if an independent contractor is involved?

Tom: Not that much. If something goes wrong, whether your employee did it or an independent contractor did it you're still going to get sued. One way a small firm might protect itself is to sign an indemnification contract with independent contractors, specifying that for instances where the I/C was to blame the firm can recoup damages from the I/C. That option isn't available for employees.

Q: So, basically, the injured party will sue both the I/C and the small firm, and then the small firm will sue the I/C if necessary? The theory behind all of this is that even if the firm isn't at fault it is in the best position to pay for damages?

Tom: That's right. It's just "deep pockets"; the firm is assumed to have the wherewithal to pay.

Between two of our experts, there was some slight difference of opinion about the scope of tasks that could not be delegated to independent contractors by small business owners. David Holden felt that the contract would dictate this, while Tom Jurgensen stipulated executive roles as a boundary. Both acknowledged that regulatory compliance cannot be delegated, and Tom specified the need for supervision as a best practice:

Q: What about non-delegable and delegable tasks for I/Cs? What can and cannot be delegated?

David: That would be a function of the contract between the entrepreneur and the I/C. What's in the contract? Normally the entrepreneur hires additional help, but a contractor can subcontract. You see that all the time with general contractors; that's what they do. A good example is the construction business.

Q: Is there anything non-delegable?

David: Let me think. Concerning contracts and torts, no, I don't think so. Perhaps in the area of compliance with regulations, for example, environmental, you may have non-delegable activities. An entrepreneur wouldn't be able to hide behind an I/C.

Q: With regards to independent contractors, what sorts of activities are non-delegable? I'm sure innumerable activities can be delegated, but what cannot be?

Tom: I would say that corporate functions that normally require an officer's approval cannot be delegated. If you need an officer's signature for something then you cannot ask an I/C to do it. It gets interesting when you have a contract CEO; in those instances you'd want board approval for some functions that otherwise could be delegated.

Q: What are best practices for avoiding some of these legal issues with I/Cs? You've said that the small firm could have indemnification contracts with I/Cs and could sue them, but obviously litigation is costly. What should entrepreneurs do?

Tom: Supervision is needed. If you have I/Cs, you have to check and make sure that they're not cutting corners on safety, the environment, etc.

Q: OK, but these firms are small. Are you saying that if you are the CEO of a micro-firm of ten employees, you'd still make time to supervise I/Cs?

Tom: I may not have time to do it as CEO, but I'd make sure that one of my officers was double-checking the work of our I/Cs. You have to evaluate their work even if the firm is small. That's the best way to avoid legal issues.

To recapitulate, there are several best practices for small business owners with regard to agency and torts for employees and independent contractors. Clear demarcation of authority and communication are important, and for independent contractors there should be specific contracts for both the general relationship and each project. Close supervision of both employees and independent contractors is required. Insurance is also a best practice, as will be discussed below.

LEGAL ISSUES RELATING TO OWNERSHIP STRUCTURE: GOVERNANCE AND TAXATION

The Structure of Business

A small closely-held business can be organized in the same way as any very large business, even publicly-traded ones, although the converse is not necessary true, as some of the options appealing to the former may be less attractive to the latter. Specifically, four primary options present themselves in structuring any business. First, a business can be organized by what in the United States is known as a sole proprietorship and in some other countries as a sole trader. Second, a business can be organized as a corporation or what is sometimes called a public limited company. Third, a business can be organized as a general or limited partnership. Fourth, a business can take advantage of hybrid structures, such as the limited liability corporation or limited partnership, which combines in one form the most appealing aspects of corporations and partnerships. The choice among these four alternative structures will depend both on governing law and on the size, type, and scope of the business. Issues of personal liability, taxation, capital formation, and ease of operation are paramount considerations.

Sole proprietorship or sole trader

A sole proprietorship is the simplest, fastest, and least expensive way to organize a business. As its name implies, a sole proprietorship has a single owner, who manages the business and is responsible for all of its transactions; in the United Kingdom, this business form is known as a sole trader. A key advantage of the sole proprietorship model is that it is attended to by very few formal requirements. There are typically no required legal filings necessary to form a sole proprietorship, although, as with any endeavor, zoning and licensure requirements must still be satisfied. This simple establishment is in contrast to other business forms, for which legal documents must typically be filed with the government (in the United States, the state of incorporation, and in the United Kingdom, Companies House). There are also no corporate income tax requirements on a sole proprietorship; all income generated by the sole proprietorship is treated as income to the business owner on his or her personal tax return. This is in especially marked contrast to the C corporation in the United States or the public limited company in the United Kingdom, whose income is taxed separately from the company owners. So, as business losses (and gains) from the sole proprietorship are part of the personal tax return, they can be used to offset other personal income, too.

Despite its relative simplicity, a sole proprietorship does have several disadvantages compared with other business forms. A sole proprietorship can borrow funds, like any business, but borrowing ability will likely depend on the owner's personal financial status, and, in most cases, the owner will have to personally guarantee all borrowings. Raising capital is also difficult for sole proprietorships, as there are no shares to issue in exchange for investment. Another key disadvantage, perhaps the most significant, of the sole proprietorship is the owner's personal liability for debts and obligations of the business, including liabilities associated with acts or omissions of the business's employees. In other words, if an employee acting within the scope of his or her duties does something to incur liability for the business – such as commit a tortious act – the sole proprietor can be held personally responsible for the debt. Sole proprietorships also cease to exist if the owner dies or sells the business; unlike shares of a corporation, interest in a sole proprietorship cannot be passed down from one generation to the next.

The choice of any business entity often comes down to tax considerations, and the sole proprietorship does have three tax implications that should be noted. First, as all of the business's income will be attributed to the owner, it is possible that the sole proprietor's personal income tax rate will increase, even to a level in excess of the corporate tax rate. Second, in the United States, corporations can deduct 100 percent of the cost of employee health insurance premiums, while sole proprietorships can only deduct 25 percent of health insurance costs. Third, and finally, sole proprietors are responsible for self-employment tax (FICA in the United States) based on 100 percent of the profits of the business, rather than on the salary paid by a corporate entity. If a sole proprietorship, for example, earns $50000 in profits, all of this amount would be subject to the combined 15.3 percent Social Security and Medicare taxes. On the other hand, if a limited liability corporation had $50000 in profits and paid its sole member a salary of $25000, only this latter amount would be subject to self-employment tax. This illustration shows the importance of obtaining good financial advice when forming a business and the importance of tax considerations in organizational choice.

Partnerships

A partnership is a business in which two or more owners agree to share profits. Like a sole proprietorship, rules can be minimal for this business form, and a partnership can be thought of as essentially a multi-person analogue to the sole proprietorship. Simply entering a business arrangement with another person is, in most cases, sufficient to create a general partnership. Indeed, a general partnership can be established through as little as a handshake or through a course of dealing; it can also be governed by a lengthy and complicated partnership agreement. But, whether formed by explicit or implicit mutual agreement, a partnership contemplates all partners participating in the decision-making of the business and sharing profits and losses among themselves.

In the United States, the law of the state in which the partnership is located will govern the business. These partnership laws, usually based on the Uniform Partnership Act, confer rights and impose obligations on the partners. One key obligation for any partnership is the fiduciary duty of all partners toward one another. This common-law duty requires a partner to act in the best interests of the partnership, while subordinating any conflicting personal ambition. While the fiduciary standard arises from well-established common law and cannot be negotiated away, a partnership will in most cases be governed by a formal partnership agreement. These written agreements allow partners to structure their relationship in ways best suitable to the business and in ways that may otherwise conflict with common law or the default provisions of statute. Common provisions in a partnership agreement address the share of profits and losses going to each partner, the management responsibilities and authority of the partner, and the effect of a partner's withdrawal or death on the business.

A general partnership has three especially important characteristics. First, partners, irrespective of their ownership interest, are jointly liable for all of the debts and obligations of the business. This means that partners can be sued as a group for company debts. In some jurisdictions in the United States, the liability of partners is even joint and several, meaning that one partner can be held individually responsible for the entirety of a company's liabilities. In England, Wales, and Northern Ireland, partners are jointly liable for debts, while, in Scotland, that liability is joint and several. Second, partners have the individual ability to contractually bind the partnership; in other words, every partner is considered an agent of the entity, capable of entering into contracts. Third, much like the sole proprietorship or sole trader, a general partnership does not pay taxes itself. Instead the profits and losses of the partnership are passed on to the partners themselves who claim those profits and losses on their own individual tax returns. Nevertheless, in nearly every jurisdiction, the partnership must file at least an information return each year. In the United States, this type of return is called the IRS Schedule K-1 and details the amount of profits and losses being claimed by each partner on his or her individual tax return. In the United Kingdom, the partnership must make annual self-assessment returns to HM Revenue & Customs for the same purpose.

To avoid the severity of joint or even joint and several liability among general partners, a limited partnership can be formed. This business form is often used for venture capital funds and other investments, especially where tax credits or other innovative financing is involved. The limited partners contribute capital, but are not involved in the day-to-day operations of the business, while the general partners operate the business and retain all liability among themselves. The limited partners meanwhile enjoy limited liability and are obligated for the business's indebtedness only to the extent of their investment. This division into those managing the business – general partners – and those outside the management – limited partners – is the hallmark of this business form. In most US states, limited partners are in fact prohibited from joining the management of the business in exchange for this limited liability, although some states are beginning to change this requirement.

In addition to the obvious liability benefits, limited partnerships have an appeal that is largely driven from tax considerations, at least in the United States. Unlike limited liability corporations, limited partnerships in the US can deduct vehicles and entertainment expenses from income that is passed along to the partners. Limited partnerships can also provide numerous tax deductions to employees, something unallowed to corporations or limited liability corporations. Limited partnerships have indefinite lifespans; the death or withdrawal of a limited partner does not end the entity, unlike the case with a sole proprietorship, general partnership, or a limited liability corporation.

Corporations

The corporation has four distinctive legal characteristics: legal personality, transferability of ownership interests, a functional managerial hierarchy, and limited shareholder liability (Hickson & Turner, 2005). In the United Kingdom, this type of entity is called a limited liability company, and can be either publicly-traded or privately-held. In the United States, there are, in fact, two types of corporations, at times having very different implications, advantages, and detriments. The first, and the most common, of these corporate forms is the so-called C corporation, the federal tax consequences of which are governed by Subchapter C of the Internal Revenue Code. A C corporation, the US equivalent to the British limited liability company, can be also be publicly-traded or privately-held. The C corporation (or the limited liability company) is a legal entity separate from the people who own or control it; in this way, the corporation is fundamentally different than the sole proprietorship. Put slightly differently, a C corporation is considered to be a legal "person" in its own right and to be capable as such of entering into contracts, incurring liabilities, and paying taxes on its own account. The most significant benefit of the corporate form follows naturally from this: owners are insulated from the debts and liabilities affecting the C corporation. The most significant disadvantage of the C corporation also springs from its status as a legal "person": C corporations are subject to double taxation.

The complexity of a C corporation, at least in comparison to the sole proprietorship, starts with formation of the entity. While a sole proprietorship requires no particular legal work, creation of a C corporation starts with the filing of articles of incorporation with state government, usually at the office of the Secretary of State (and, in the United Kingdom, the limited liability company is registered with Companies House). Among other things, the articles of incorporation must list the C corporation's board of directors, who have authority over the corporation subject to limitations set forth in the articles of incorporating themselves; state laws vary, but many – such as Delaware – will permit a single director of the corporation, and all states allow for a single corporate owner. The articles of incorporation – sometimes known also as a corporate charter or certificate of incorporation – must also list the corporation's registered agent, who will rcccive official mail or legal papers. The newly-formed corporation is required to pay initial taxes and registration fees as well. To complete the entity's formation, corporate by-laws are usually drafted, although these do not usually have to be filed with any unit of government.

As a separate legal "person", corporations shield owners – shareholders in the corporation – from personal liability for the company's debts and obligations. The only risk for shareholders is the extent of their investment itself, which could be compromised or even wiped out through corporate failure; the individual assets of shareholders usually cannot be reached. This is in marked contrast to the sole proprietorship, whose owner is fully responsible for business obligations, and partnerships too, which are seen in the common law merely as an agglomeration of individuals, with the same obligations as the sole proprietor.

An essential concern for the C corporation is the double taxation of profits. In the United States, corporate profits are taxed by the federal government, and often state governments, too. The after-tax profits can then be used to pay dividends to shareholders, who then must pay tax on the distribution. As a result, the effective tax rate on the profits of a C corporation can be 15 percent or higher than that on a sole proprietorship or on a partnership. In truth, the emphasis in much discussions of corporate law on the double taxation of corporations is overblown. In the United States, the federal corporate tax rate for income below $75 000 is lower than the comparable individual rate. So, if taxable income can be managed to not exceed that level, it is possible that a C corporation could achieve significant tax savings. And, for smaller, closely-held corporations, there are ways of minimizing if not avoiding the tax burden. If shareholders are also employees of the corporation, salary can replace dividends, and the salary has the additional benefit of being a tax-deductible expense. So, too, shareholders can provide capital to the small corporation not through equity investments but through loans, the repayment of which is tax-deductible to the corporation and taxed only as ordinary income to the shareholder/lender. Another approach still is for the shareholder of the small corporation to lease property or plant to the company, receiving in return rental payments that are tax-deductible to the company and ordinary income to the shareholder. A word of caution: while retaining profits within the company might seem an attractive option, shareholders must be wary of the accumulated earnings tax, which imposes a levy on retained income deemed unreasonable.

Despite the threat of double taxation and some administrative hassle, there are significant advantages to the C corporation or the limited liability company. The C corporation is arguably the most flexible of business organizations. There are no limits on the number or type of shareholders in a C corporation. C corporations can also have multiple classes of stock. Stock options and other equity incentives can easily be incorporated into the C corporation. There is also considerable case law around the rights and responsibilities of the C corporation, giving predictability to the form. It is for these latter reasons that large companies prefer the C organization.

In the United States, there is an alternative corporate form to the C corporation. Subchapter S of the Internal Revenue code provides that a small business corporation may elect not to be taxed at the corporate level but to have its income, regardless of whether the income is distributed to shareholders, passed through to its shareholders and taxed as ordinary personal income. The Subchapter S corporation in effect turns, for tax purposes, a corporation into a sole proprietorship or partnership, while still keeping the limited liability of the C corporation. The cost of this tax benefit is reduced flexibility. First, an S corporation can have no more than 75 shareholders. Second, shareholders must be natural persons and cannot be Indian tribes, resident aliens, or other corporations or partnerships. Third, the S corporation can have only a class of voting stock. Just complying with these regulatory requirements can be burdensome for many businesses. For this reason alone, the S corporation is increasingly being supplanted by the limited liability corporation.

Limited liability corporation or limited liability partnerships

A recent innovation in corporate law, the limited liability corporation (LLC), as it is known in the United States, or the limited liability partnership (LLP), as it is called in the United Kingdom, combines the pass-through tax characteristics of a partnership or sole proprietorship with the limited liability of a corporation. Unlike a limited partnership, these attributes are maintained even for those active in the business itself. Unlike a sole proprietorship, an LLC or LLP can have unlimited members. Unlike a C corporation or limited liability company, an LLC or LLP is not subject to double taxation. Unlike an S corporation, an LLC can have not only unlimited members but can have other LLCs, partnerships, corporations, and Indian tribes as members; this is also true for an LLP.

In the United States, LLCs can choose to be taxed either like a C corporation or like a partnership; most LLCs choose to be pass-through entities in which profits are reported by members on their individual tax returns. In the United Kingdom, LLPs can also choose to be either transparent, with taxes being passed through to owners, or opaque, like a limited liability corporation. Owners of an LLC are typically called members and have membership interests in the LLC rather than shares. In the United States, profit of the LLC is not considered to be earned income of the members, as it is in a sole proprietorship, and is not subject to self-employment Federal Insurance Contributions Act (FICA) taxes as a result. The managing member of the LLC can deduct 100 percent of health insurance premiums, again unlike a sole proprietor, up to the extent of the managing member's pro rata share of the LLC's profits.

As with a C or S corporation, US states all require formal articles of organization to be filed for a new LLC. In the United Kingdom, the formation of an LLP requires registration with Companies House. While not every state requires LLCs to have operating agreements, it is advisable to have a formal document articulating how business decisions will be reached, the division of profits and losses, and other administrative matters. One of the strengths of the LLC or LLP form is that the operating agreement can be tailored for the unique needs of a business, avoiding the default oversight of state or national corporate laws and the associated requirements for annual reports, director meetings, and the like. An LLC or LLP operating agreement can also specify a distribution of profits differently than membership interests; corporations, in contrast, must distribute profits according to shareholder interests. In neither the United States nor in the United Kingdom are the operating agreements of LLCs or LLPs required to be made public.

OTHER SOURCES OF LIABILITY AND INSURANCE

Product Safety

Over the past two centuries laws concerning consumers and product safety have evolved from "caveat emptor" to strict liability for manufacturers (Eades, 2008). This governing principle is expressed in Restatement (Second) of Torts, Section 402A (ibid.). According to Eades, "this section provided that a seller of products could be liable for physical harm to persons or property caused by a product sold by that defendant if that product was in a defective condition unreasonably dangerous" (ibid., p. 14). A seller may be liable even if there is no obvious intent to harm, and defective conditions include failure to warn consumers adequately about the proper use of products (ibid.).

This is yet another area of operations where small business owners fail to consider potential liability. What they deem sufficient in terms of warning labels, for example, may be insufficient in the eyes of the law:

Q: Besides insurance, what are other best practices for identifying and avoiding product safety liability?

Tom: Have lots of warning labels and disclosure. Check the product and the packaging carefully. You know, I have people bring me nifty gadgets with tiny parts, and they say, "Isn't this neat?", and I say, "Yep, I bet a toddler could choke on that". They haven't thought about that. You have to put warning labels on everything, including the packaging.

Beyond warning labels, another best practice for this area is risk management. Small business owners may not be aware of risks that exist because of prior claims. Here is the conversation with Chris White and David Holden:

Chris: Product safety is a big area. We have an expert in product safety liability, the warning labels, everything. He gives expert testimony all of the time. Anyway, he assessed a client who had been in business for 20 years and never had a claim. The client wanted to sell the company, and during the time of the sale two claims in a row were made! The kicker is that for the first one it was his competitor who had the problem initially, not him, but it resulted in a claim. This product hasn't changed in 60 years.

David: Maybe even 80.

Chris: There is exposure he never knew about. This is where risk management would be useful. Product labeling is important, too.

David: There is another client who does pressure-drilling for the big oil and gas firms, ConocoPhillips, BP, etc. He has no insurance. If something goes wrong it goes wrong in a big way; the pressure can blow things sky-high. What he does is to fix problems immediately. He is monitoring things, and he just fixes it. Now of course his customers are sophisticated, so he can do that.

Q: Since he has no insurance, his method of handling product liability is rapid response?

David: That's right. He says he could try covering himself and he could cover himself enough with contracts and insurance to win lawsuits, but winning lawsuits would put him out of business. It's much cheaper just to fix the problem straightaway.

Chris: Some of these issues with product specification and safety provide an opportunity to sell. You can consult, provide answers to problems and make money.

Warning labels and a proactive stance towards problems are the best ways to ward off product liability. As Chris White opines, problems may present opportunities for savvy small business owners to earn more profits.

Environmental Liability

Over the past four decades increasing attention has been paid to environmental concerns around the world, which has led to a mushrooming of statutes and regulations to hold polluters accountable. For example, the applicable federal law in the US is the Comprehensive Environmental Response, Compensation and Liability Act of 1980 (CERCLA), which has the scope to designate any owner, user, or other agent associated with a polluted site as a "potentially responsible party (PRP)" (Zuckerman et al., 2007). The all-encompassing nature of this law has made its application highly controversial; to the extent that President George W. Bush signed into law a relief act for small businesses that innocently purchased tainted land (ibid.). This is just the federal statute and doesn't consider the thicket of state and local regulations a small business owner must navigate; moreover, a small business could easily be bankrupted, defending itself in court despite being innocent of any transgression.

As with some other legal areas already mentioned, our experts cited strong leadership as a best practice in this area, along with knowledge of compliance practices and training. Here is an excerpt from Tom Jurgensen:

Q: What about environmental liability for small firms? You've said that your clientele is high-tech; how many of these issues have you seen?

Tom: I do see it on occasion. Some of my firms work with toxic chemicals or bio-hazardous waste, and I also have my own experience in bio-tech. It comes back to cutting corners and the tone from the top. Some entrepreneurs run a tight ship. They say, "We want to make money, and we follow the rules, too." Others simply say, "We want to make money". When it comes to proper disposal of chemicals, bio-medical waste, there is zero tolerance. If people don't follow the rules then they are fired.

Q: So you've seen this? You have clients who have set a clear standard for compliance, and who have fired employees who cut corners?

Tom: Yes, and I've seen the other type, too: the entrepreneurs who want to cut corners and who think it's no big deal to pour chemicals down a drain. In my experience, many of the best entrepreneurs have come from high-quality companies. They may not have fit in there, but they know how a business should be run. Then you have people who are more seat-of-the-pants. They usually have very little experience in the business world. These ones are more likely to cut corners.

Q: Would you say that with regards to environmental liability you have the same three types you described earlier: don't know, know, and don't want to know?

Tom: Yes, although with regard to the environment you don't need to have a PhD in chemical engineering to consider the consequences of dumping chemicals down a drain. Common sense should lead you to know it isn't a good idea. I always ask people who don't want to know about the environmental regs if they would do it in their own home. I say, "Let's go pour that down your drain, or on your couch or carpet, if it's not such a big deal". You can see I don't have much patience with this sort of thing. I also cover myself; I document that I've told them about the environmental regs and other regulations so that they can't later say I didn't warn them.

And this from David Holden and Chris White:

David: It comes down to the culture. Do you have a stainless-steel culture or a cardboard culture? It does cut across so many areas of regulation you're asking about: employees, safety, the environment.

Chris: I have one client, a high-hazard chemical company.

David: If you drop one of their products it just blows up right there – boom!

Chris: They do everything; they have all of the employee training, they have all of the right certifications. That's just an outgrowth of the owner's attitude. The owner doesn't care about whether or not he has insurance, or what the legal nuances are; he just doesn't want people to get hurt. He has the right values. One time he rolled up his sleeve and showed me the scar on his arm from a chemical burn. That's where it comes from. He knows what it's like.

Securities Regulation

According to Mandel (2010), there are two common fallacies among small business owners regarding securities: either they think that securities regulations only apply to large corporations or they narrowly construe securities to mean only stocks. One of our experts echoed this sentiment. Securities regulation is also another area of law that contains both national and subnational governing agencies. Even if small business owners are aware of the reach of the applicable statutes they are probably not au courant about them.

Q: What should small business owners know about securities regulation?

David: There are two big things I find that entrepreneurs don't know about securities. The first is that securities are regulated. The second is that what constitutes a security is very broad; it's not just a paper certificate of stock. Any vehicle that separates investment from management functions as a security. The best practice here is to make my clients aware that there are concentric levels for raising capital (draws circles). The innermost circle is family. The entrepreneur borrows from his mom. There is little risk of suit from failure to comply. It's not that his mom has no right to sue; under the law she does. It's just that the possibility of that happening is remote. Even if his mom did sue, the jury is likely to sympathize with him. . .his own mom suing! The next level is friends. It's the same story; they're not likely to sue. Once you get beyond friends, the picture changes. Here you either must comply with regulations, or you must comply with exemptions. I've made it a practice to help comply with regs, but I will only deal with accredited investors if an entrepreneur wants to comply with exemptions. Other types are too risky and too time-consuming; this is the safe route. As long as you're not committing fraud, you should be legally OK when approaching accredited investors. You are not required to provide offering documents, which are generally complex, to accredited investors. Once you start with offering documents you're approaching what you would need for the SEC (Securities and Exchange Commission). Since accredited investors are sophisticated you don't need them: that's why it's safe. And you have to be aware that there are both federal and state regulations. If someone, based on their need for capital, wants to comply with regs then they have to be aware there are both federal and state.

Q: This dovetails with what the lawyer in San Francisco told me. He said that securities regulation is definitely one area where an entrepreneur shouldn't cut corners.

David: That's right. Both federal and state securities agencies tend to be understaffed, but they're vigorous. They will come after you if you're not in compliance, and non-compliance involves both criminal and civil penalties.

Q: What about raising capital? What regulatory issues do entrepreneurs need to consider?

Tom: Here's an area where it's very tempting for entrepreneurs to cut corners. My advice is: don't cut corners! Whatever you do, make sure that you are in compliance. File all of the paperwork that is required, both federal and state, for the issuance of securities. Also, keep communicating with investors. If you don't, it breeds problems. That's how you wind up with investors getting upset and making those claims of breach of fiduciary duty we just talked about. I try to have my clients avoid equity and use grant money or debt if at all possible.

There are several best practices here worth highlighting. Small business owners should avoid complex financing arrangements with outsiders if possible. Bootstrap or borrow funds from family and friends. If your business requires more capital than these sources can provide, focus on accredited, sophisticated investors for whom the reporting requirements are less onerous. A small business owner should hire a lawyer knowledgeable about securities regulation and stay in compliance. He/she should communicate regularly and thoroughly to investors about the status of the business to reassure them that due care is being exercised.

Insurance

One best practice to mitigate the effects of liability is to purchase insurance. We asked our experts about this topic separately since it is so complex:

Q: What about insurance? What types do you recommend for small firms, and what levels of coverage do you suggest? I know you're not an insurance agent, but I want to know the advice you give.

Tom: I recommend a general liability policy for a start, and also product liability. You can also buy employee-related insurance for the issues we discussed earlier, like discrimination and harassment. I also advise getting director/officer [D&O] insurance.

Q: You mean for malfeasance?

Tom: That's right. D&O insurance protects you for claims of breach of fiduciary duty. This is a big issue, and makes it difficult to find good talent for start-ups. If investors get upset, they typically blame the officers and sue for breach (of fiduciary duty). I do also recommend life insurance, the key person insurance, in circumstances where someone's loss would cripple the start-up.

Here are Chris White's remarks regarding insurance:

Chris: The best thing to do is to hire a risk management specialist. These people examine the entire business and issue a comprehensive report. They are proactive in assessing the safety programs the company has, and they make recommendations about what kinds and levels of coverage. Another good source is an industry association. You join them and you find out who knows about risk management and insurance. This is an ongoing process, staying on top of risks and coverage. You remember the ice storm in 2007? We had 47 companies; not a single one received a penny for that. Some of them had business interruption coverage, but most didn't. Even the ones who had the coverage couldn't collect; the reporting was too onerous. No one knew what to do or how to interpret the policies they had. They would call the agent and the agent would say, "Well, if the policy was written this way, you'd be covered, but it wasn't, so you're not". Insurance is a black hole. Like life insurance and such: no one wants to talk about the events that would trigger a claim.

Q: You have to force them to have that conversation. What coverages do you suggest? Key person, D&O?

Chris: Yes, we recommend key man, D&O, product liability. We make sure for the key man that there's a succession plan in place. That's usually part of risk management. The best practice is to get a specialist; that's what we advise.

There are some standard insurance policies every small business owner should have: key person, general liability, product liability, director/officer (D&O), and employee-related liability. Beyond these, a best practice identified by Chris White is to hire a risk management specialist. This person can identify other areas of exposure that may require insurance, and can also ensure that existing policies give adequate coverage. An issue that small business owners may face is being uncovered when they thought their current insurance was sufficient.

CONCLUSION

The small business owner needs to make hiring competent legal counsel a priority. There are a plethora of legal pitfalls in the normal course of business, and the typical entrepreneur has neither the time nor the expertise to recognize them all. A best practice is to find an attorney who has also operated a small business or at least has devoted his/her practice to advising them.

Adequate documentation is a critical best practice that cuts across many areas of business operations and the law. Although it is tedious, the small business owner must ensure that there are systems in place to monitor compliance with various regulations at the national and subnational levels. Many otherwise thriving small businesses have discovered too late that they have violated statutes in employment, securities, and so on, with catastrophic results.

A third best practice with broad implications is communication. This encompasses a company culture of striving for excellence in all facets, including communication. When employees and investors don't know what the entrepreneur expects, problems invariably ensue. The ultimate best practice is to forestall difficulties, legal or otherwise, before they truly emerge as issues.

REFERENCES

Brown, Robert L. & Alan S. Gutterman (2005), "Non-tax aspects of forming and organizing a new business", in Robert L. Brown & Alan S. Gutterman (eds), *Emerging Companies Guide: A Resource for Professionals and Entrepreneurs*, Chicago, IL: American Bar Association.

Eades, Ronald W. (2008), *Mastering Series: Products Liability*, Durham, NC: Carolina Academic Press.

Eschels, Philip C. & Robert L. Brown (2005), "Human resources", in Robert L. Brown & Alan S. Gutterman (eds), *Emerging Companies Guide: A Resource for Professionals and Entrepreneurs*, Chicago, IL: American Bar Association.

Gregory, David L. (2002), "The road from negligence to negligence in employment", in Alfred G. Feliu & Weyman T. Johnson (eds), *Negligence in Unemployment Law*, Washington, DC: The Bureau of National Affairs, Inc.

Hickson, Charles R. & John D. Turner (2005), "Corporation or limited liability company", in John J. McCusker, Stanley Engerman, Lewis R. Fischer, David J. Hancock & Kenneth L. Pomeranz (eds), *Encyclopedia of World Trade since 1450*, New York, NY: Macmillan Reference.

Holden, David (2010), Interview conducted on 9 June 12 pm–1:40 pm CST. Profiles available at: http://www.mergerservices.com/home.htm and http://www.dwhweb.com/BackgroundInfo/index.cfm; accessed 18 November 2010.

Jurgensen, Tom (2010), Interview conducted on 25 May 4 pm–5 pm CST. Full bio available at: http://www.jurgensenvillasenor.net/about_us.html; accessed 22 November 2010.

Mandel, Richard (2010), "Legal and tax issues", in William D. Bygrave & Andrew Zacharakis (eds), *The Portable MBA in Entrepreneurship*, Hoboken, NJ: John Wiley & Sons, pp. 263–95.

Patrizia, Charles A., Gregory R. Watchman & Elizabeth M. Georges (2002), "Safe workplace issues", in Alfred G. Feliu & Weyman T. Johnson (eds), *Negligence in Unemployment Law*, Washington, DC: The Bureau of National Affairs, Inc.

Petillon, Lee R. & Robert J. Hull (2009), *Representing Start-up Companies*, St. Paul, MN: Thomson Reuters/West.

Presser, Stephen B. (2005), *An Introduction to the Law of Business Organizations*, St. Paul, MN: Thomson West.

White, Chris (2010), Interview conducted on 9 June 12 pm–1:40 pm CST. Profile available at: http://www.mergerservices.com/home.htm; accessed 18 November 2010.

Zuckerman, Tod I., Bois II, Thomas J. & Thomas M. Johnson (2007), *Environmental Liability Allocation: Law and Practice*, St. Paul, MN: Thomson West.

APPENDIX BRIEF BIOGRAPHIES OF EXPERTS INTERVIEWED

Tom Jurgensen Tom, the Chief Executive Officer of Catalyst Law Group, brings more than 18 years of experience in technology-based law and business to his pioneering practice. Tom founded Catalyst Law Group to provide intellectual property, corporate, securities, transactional and regulatory legal counsel to companies seeking collaborative, personalized service. He is a member of several for profit and not-for-profit boards, including Allylix, Inc., a biotechnology company he co-founded with Dr. Joseph Noel of The Salk Institute and Dr. Joseph Chappell of the University of Kentucky.

Tom received a Bachelor of Science in Biology and a minor in Chemistry from the University of Wisconsin, River Falls. He also earned a Master of Science in Animal Ecology from Iowa State University and a Juris Doctorate degree from the University of Oregon. He has published a variety of articles and numerous patents. See http://www.jurgensenvillasenor.net/about_us.html.

David Holden David serves as general counsel for the firm of Merger and Acquisition Services (M&A), LLC and is also the president of his own company, David Holden Consulting, LLC, which he has operated for 15 years. He specializes in developing and evaluating legal structures for M & A transactions and providing project management services during the negotiation, due diligence and closing processes. David has 30 years' experience as a lawyer involved in securities and business transactions and has practiced for over 40 years in total. Prior to founding his own venture he worked for Holliman, Langholz, Runnels, and Dorwart and successor firms from 1968 to 1995, where he served as president and on the Board of Directors. He also was a director, officer, and member of the controlling shareholder group for Flare, Inc. during the 1980s.

He has Bachelors and Juris Doctor degrees from the University of Oklahoma and is a Certified Management Consultant. He is a member in the American and Oklahoma Bar Associations and the Institute of Management Consultants. See http://www.dwhweb.com/BackgroundInfo/index.cfm.

Chris White Chris specializes in developing valuations on closely held companies and intangible assets, in creating financial structures and in developing corporate financial strategies. He previously was a partner in the consulting division of an international accounting firm and has consulted for more than 32 years with businesses in the construction, environmental services, health care, manufacturing, distribution, transportation, and petroleum industries.

He has a BSBA degree in Accounting from the University of Tulsa and an MBA from Indiana University. He is a Certified Public Accountant and a Certified Management Consultant with memberships in the AICPA and the Institute of Management Consultants where he serves as Chair of IMC's Oklahoma Chapter. See http://www.mergerservices.com/home.htm.

8. Health and safety in small businesses

Sharon Clarke

Companies employing fewer than 250 employees constitute 99.9 per cent of UK businesses; they accounted for more than half of employment (59.4 per cent) and turnover (50.1 per cent) in the UK for 2008 (DBIS, 2009). Whilst small and medium-sized enterprises (SMEs) continue to grow and prosper, in terms of occupational safety and health, there is evidence that SMEs experience significantly higher accident rates than large firms (Fabiano et al., 2004; McVittie, et al., 1997). Furthermore, it has been estimated that the rate of workplace injury and ill health in SMEs is approximately twice that found in large organizations (Pearson, 2001). Nevertheless, as noted by Hale (2003) the "vast majority of studies of safety management come from the large, bureaucratic organizations that run high-hazard technologies such as power utilities, process industry, mining, and transport . . . there are relatively few studies of small and medium-sized companies" (pp. 186–7). Thus, although health and safety risks appear to be significantly higher in SMEs, there has been limited research conducted to understand the reasons for these elevated risks. There has also been a tendency for researchers to consider both medium-sized and smaller businesses as a collective, whereas there is evidence that occupational safety and health issues are particularly acute for small enterprises (with fewer than 50 employees) and micro-businesses, and may require different types of solutions (Champoux & Brun, 2003; Micheli & Cagno, 2010). This chapter will review the current literature on health and safety in SMEs, including small and micro-businesses, with particular emphasis on the implications for human resource management, and make recommendations for best practice.

Substantial evidence has been reported, both across countries and industrial sectors, that workplace accident and injury rates are significantly higher in SMEs than in large companies. McVittie et al. (1997) reported a significant trend for injury frequency to decrease with increasing firm size for Canadian construction companies; this trend was significant over a six-year period, including across differing economic contexts (i.e., construction "boom" of the late 1980s and the recessionary period of the early 1990s). The trend for increasing numbers of accidents with decreasing company size was significant within the SME sector, with the smallest companies suffering the highest levels of occupational injuries. Furthermore, the study showed that whilst the construction industry overall had achieved a significant 44 per cent reduction in injuries, injury rate was falling at a faster rate in larger firms compared with SMEs.

A later analysis of accident frequency rates was conducted by Fabiano et al. (2004) across all Italian industries for the period 1995–2000. This study found that the accident frequency rate for small companies (<30 employees) was 47 per cent higher than for large firms. There was a significant trend for increasing injuries and accidents with decreasing firm size across industries; however, for some industries, the risk factor associated with smaller firms was particularly high – for example, the accident frequency rate for small companies was four times higher than large firms in the mining and quarrying sector, and twice that of large firms in construction. Furthermore, the trend was significantly affected by the concentration of employees in larger firms; where large firms dominate an industry (i.e., employ more than 50 per cent of the workforce), these firms had an even lower accident frequency rate compared with smaller companies. Micheli and Cagno (2010) emphasized the importance of differentiating between medium-sized companies (50–250 employees), small companies (10–50 employees) and micro-businesses (< 10 employees) with relation to health and safety issues. The study, conducted in an area of Northern Italy with a high concentration of SMEs, showed that accident and injury rates were significantly higher in micro- and small businesses compared with medium-sized enterprises.

Fabiano et al. (2004) reported a significant negative relationship between fatalities and firm size; for example, in construction, small companies have a fatal accident rate four times higher than large firms. The differentiation between the risk factor for all injuries compared with fatalities highlights the issue of under-reporting in SMEs; this suggests that reported injuries may only indicate the "tip of the iceberg" in terms of safety issues. Indeed, there is evidence to suggest that SMEs, and particularly the smaller companies, are more likely to under-report injuries compared with large firms (Leigh et al., 2004; Oleinick et al., 1995). Leigh et al. (2004) note that there are disincentives for the owners of small firms to report injuries to OSHA (the US Occupational Safety and Health Administration), including the burden of completing the paperwork required, increased premiums paid to worker compensation schemes and the need to maintain a safe company image in order to be eligible for government contracts. Such disincentives are likely to contribute to under-reporting by small firms, in addition to employees failing to report accidents and injuries to their employers.

THE NATURE OF HEALTH AND SAFETY RISKS IN SMEs

Although accident and injury rate is associated with organizational size, the factors that increase the likelihood of workplace accidents and injuries in SMEs have received little research attention. However, the literature highlights a number of factors that are likely to increase the vulnerability of SMEs to accidents. First, the nature of SMEs is that they are often newly formed, have a short life span and less financial stability than large firms. As such, SMEs are less likely to invest substantially in health and safety, given that they will have less certainty about the benefits of such investments, which require a long-term vision.

Second, there is evidence that SMEs tend to operate in more hazardous work environments (Sørensen et al., 2007). In their study of small Danish private-independent enterprises, Sørensen et al. (2007) found that the highest levels of ergonomic strains were reported in small companies: there was a significant trend for smaller companies to have higher levels of back, back/neck and hand strain, which was consistent across all industries (except transportation). They also reported similar significant trends for chemical exposure and hand vibration; however, other work environment factors (such as noise exposure and indoor climate) showed no significant relationship with firm size. These findings demonstrate that several aspects of the work environment, including ergonomic, physical and chemical hazards, are significantly higher in SMEs compared with large firms.

Finally, a number of studies have highlighted a range of management and organizational factors associated with SMEs that appear to contribute to their increased health and safety risk (e.g., Champoux & Brun, 2003; Cheng et al., 2010; Clarke & Flitcroft, 2008; Sørensen et al., 2007; Vassie et al., 2000). The management approach of SMEs has been found to differ significantly in comparison with large firms. Matlay (1999) found that owner-managers of SMEs tended to operate an informal management style: 92 per cent in micro-businesses (< 10 employees), 68 per cent in small businesses (10–50 employees) and 24 per cent in medium-sized businesses (50–250 employees) compared with none of the large firms in the study. In particular, owner-managers of micro-businesses tended to operate highly personalized management styles. These findings have implications for the management of health and safety in SMEs.

In terms of occupational health and well-being, Sørensen et al. (2007)

found that, given their smaller size and lower complexity, psychosocial work conditions were often better in SMEs compared with larger organizations. Their findings demonstrated a trend for higher task and emotional demands in larger companies rather than SMEs, but this trend was only significant for emotional demands. However, most psychosocial factors were found to be unrelated to organizational size. The smaller size of SMEs has been reported to facilitate close social relationships, which support a more positive psychosocial work environment (Hasle & Limborg, 2006). Small-sized workplaces, owned by SMEs, have been found to have the highest levels of perceived job quality; a finding that was not replicated where such workplaces were owned by large firms (Storey et al., 2010). Furthermore, Storey et al. (2010) showed that organizational size was significantly related to perceived job quality, after controlling for formality (e.g., formal versus informal ways of communicating with employees). Although there is evidence supporting the suggestion that SMEs foster more positive working environments, a limited amount of research has been conducted examining the implications for occupational stress and health outcomes.

Absenteeism in SMEs is lower than for large firms; for example, in the UK, for 2007–08, the sickness absence rate was recorded as 2.3 per cent for small workplaces (with fewer than 25 employees) compared with 2.8 per cent for large firms, employing more than 500 employees (Leaker, 2008). Such figures may reflect that the employees of SMEs are more motivated to come to work due to the greater impact of their absence from work in a smaller firm. De Kok (2005) argues that, due to low absence rates, most small firms do not have a deliberate policy of reducing absence rates by improving working conditions, given that there is little financial gain from this investment. Such an attitude is also evident in relation to workplace health promotion activities; SMEs have reported a tendency to focus on occupational safety and health, rather than activities targeted at the personal health and well-being of their employees (Moore et al., 2010).

Health and Safety Issues

Clarke and Flitcroft (2008) conducted in-depth semi-structured interviews with a sample of 19 organizations, all SMEs (with fewer than 250 employees) in North-West England. The sample comprised companies based in the following industries: manufacturing (7), construction (3), distribution (2), transport (2), public administration (2), education (1) and other services (3). The interviewees were health and safety managers or managing directors/senior managers with health and safety responsibility. Thematic analysis of the interview data identified 16 themes:

1. awareness;
2. communication;
3. economic change/pressures;
4. encouragement;
5. flexible management practices;
6. excessive health & safety regulation;
7. human error;
8. job security;
9. management;
10. blame/claim culture;
11. procedures;
12. resistance;
13. resources;
14. safety vs production;
15. supportive environment;
16. workplace pressures.

A further analysis was performed that differentiated the themes into those that promoted workplace safety and those that hindered workplace safety. In total, three of the themes promoted workplace safety, 11 themes hindered workplace safety and two themes applied to both positive and negative aspects of workplace safety (communication and supportive environment).

Promotion of workplace safety

Only three of the 16 themes identified were found to promote workplace safety (awareness, encouragement and flexible management practices), although a further two themes (communication and supportive environment) could also have a positive effect.

Safety training was the main human resource practice aimed at raising awareness of safety and encouraging safe behaviour. Just over half of the organizations, ten (56 per cent) indicated they had a budget for training. The majority of organizations, 16 (89 per cent), indicated that training was conducted both in-house and outsourced. All organizations reported offering induction training to new staff members and maintaining training records. The majority also provided refresher training (83 per cent). There were mechanisms in place for raising and providing feedback within the majority of organizations, with 13 (72 per cent) reporting a set procedure for feedback on health and safety issues. However, only one organization (6 per cent) offered rewards and recognition for safe behaviour, whilst the remainder of the sample reported that they did not acknowledge safe behaviour.

Barriers to improving safety

Those themes that were found to hinder workplace safety included: economic change/pressure, excessive health and safety regulation, human error, job security, management, blame/claim culture, procedures, resistance, resources, safety versus production and workplace pressures. In addition, a lack of communication and organizational support were also highlighted as having a negative effect on safety. Reference to management appeared consistently within all of the transcripts where the interviewee was not the managing director. Furthermore, within the negative themes, the issue of excessive health and safety regulation was evident within interviews from the chemical, transport, manufacturing, construction and service industries.

All organizations reported having an up-to-date health and safety policy, although these policies were not always developed in consultation with relevant staff (this happened in 14 organizations, 78 per cent). In terms of formal procedures, the majority of organizations, 16 (89 per cent) indicated that a formal investigation procedure was in place for use in the event of an accident, with 15 organizations (83 per cent) indicating that the recommendations from such accident investigations had been implemented in the past. In total, 13 organizations (72 per cent) indicated that they reported "near misses" and 15 organizations (83 per cent) reported keeping records of sickness absence. Sixteen organizations (89 per cent) reviewed accident, near misses and sickness reports regularly. Furthermore, 14 organizations (78 per cent) utilized the information gathered from accident, near misses and sickness reports in the identification of hazards within the workplace. Whilst 17 organizations (94 per cent) had an emergency procedure in place, the extent to which it was regularly practised varied considerably between organizations. All organizations reported supplying first aid services, equipment and trained first aid representatives.

Respondents highlighted the prevalence of a "blame/claim" culture, which encouraged employees to claim against the organization. Whilst no organizations reported being prosecuted by the UK Health and Safety Executive (HSE), 12 organizations (67 per cent) reported being in receipt of litigation claims within the last three years, which were related to workplace injuries or illnesses.

HEALTH & SAFETY MANAGEMENT SYSTEMS

The findings of Clarke and Flitcroft's (2008) study suggest that UK-based SMEs have basic safety management systems in place. This is consistent with previous research; for example, Vassie et al. (2000), who found that the majority of UK-based SMEs (80 per cent) had a written safety policy, as well as formal procedures relating to risk assessment and accident reporting. Nevertheless, Sørensen et al. (2007) found that there was a highly significant trend for the quality of occupational safety and health management to increase with increasing organizational size ($p < 0.001$). They also found a similar significant trend for the use of workplace risk assessment.

In a survey of Spanish and UK-based SMEs, Vassie et al. (2000) found that the majority of respondents did not employ a dedicated health and safety manager, with senior managers in 77 per cent of SMEs involved in health and safety. This is likely to be an indicator of the tendency for SMEs to demonstrate "resource poverty" in relation to safety (Clarke & Flitcroft, 2008). Senior managers are often expected to undertake a variety of management functions, including health and safety, where they may have little experience or formal training. Particularly in small and micro-businesses, owner-managers are liable to retain the "final say" in decision-making (Matley, 1999). Champoux and Brun (2003) interviewed owner-managers of small Canadian manufacturing firms (< 50 employees); they also reported that the majority of owner-managers took control of health and safety responsibilities in their company.

Champoux and Brun (2003) found that the minority of their respondents (13 per cent) had written preventive activities, which focused solely on accident prevention, although preventive activities that had a direct bearing on production, such as equipment maintenance, were used routinely by all companies; furthermore, very few (5 per cent) had formal participatory mechanisms (such as health and safety committees) despite these being required by legislation. Clarke and Flitcroft (2008) found more evidence of preventive activities, such as keeping records of "near misses" and feedback to staff on health and safety issues, but still little evidence of employee participation and active involvement. The approach to health and safety management in small firms has been characterized as:

- inactive/uninformed (7 per cent) – where there was essentially no safety management system;
- inactive/traditional/unstructured (52 per cent) – owner-manager responsible for health and safety, but had few formal mechanisms in place, characteristic of micro-businesses (< 5 employees);
- active/participatory/unstructured (18 per cent) – owner-manager responsible for health and safety, but had an informal, participatory management approach to safety (still few formal mechanisms in place);

- active/participatory/structured firms (23 per cent) – had a foreman/manager who took the role of health and safety manager; adopted a participatory management approach, including formal mechanisms such as health and safety committees and prevention activities (Champoux & Brun, 2003).

Similarly to Clarke and Flitcroft (2008), Champoux and Brun (2003) found that owner-managers reported that the most common obstacles to safety were: prevention and production costs, paperwork, lack of training, priority to production and lack of time.

Whilst SMEs considered safety training as important, almost half did not incorporate a training budget within their financial accounts (Clarke & Flitcroft, 2008). Cheng et al. (2010) investigated small construction companies based in Taiwan; they demonstrated that newly hired construction workers were particularly at risk of occupational injury in small companies due to insufficient safety education and training.

The extent of health and safety legislation was perceived to hinder workplace safety, with SMEs struggling to implement what was perceived by some to be "excessive" (Clarke & Flitcroft, 2008). Therefore, whilst the owners of small firms have been described as less responsive to legal regulation compared with large organizations (Bacon & Hoque, 2005), this may reflect the difficulty of responding to a wide range of legislative responsibilities, including health and safety. The UK HSE considers small businesses to be a "hard to reach" sector (HSE, 2004), but continued effort is clearly needed to support such businesses in their efforts to implement regulations. A report conducted by the UK Risk and Regulation Advisory Council (RRAC, 2009) found that SMEs often struggle to implement health and safety measures within their companies as they lack confidence and are confused by regulatory requirements. Such issues are particularly salient within small and micro-businesses. Micheli and Cagno (2010) reported significantly higher deficiencies regarding the provision of financial resources for health and safety, introduction of safer technologies, provision of information and training for employees and the perception that legislative provisions were excessive, for small and micro-businesses, compared with medium-sized enterprises.

In Clarke and Flitcroft's (2008) study, the majority of the organizations were in receipt of litigation claims from employees, which were related to workplace injuries or illnesses; this finding emphasizes the perception of a "blame/claim culture" and the "firefighting" approach to managing safety. Cox et al. (1995) suggest that the promotion of safety performance within the workplace necessitates a combination of the following: hardware (related machinery, tools and facilities that an employee needs to perform their job), software (systems and procedures in accordance with legislative requirements) and the organizational social context. In relation to SMEs, it appears that organizations struggle to implement software and demonstrate a limited understanding of social factors. These are areas for further consideration, both in relation to the regulation of safety within SMEs and in terms of further research.

IMPLICATIONS FOR HUMAN RESOURCE PRACTICES

Research has emphasized the importance of high-quality human resource (HR) practices for positive safety outcomes (Barling et al., 2003; Zacharatos et al., 2005). The management of human resources using high-commitment management practices, rather than focusing on compliance to rules and regulations, can increase employees' identification with organizational goals, generate extra effort to achieve them (Whitener, 2001) and lead to safety improvements (Barling & Hutchinson, 2000). In relation to safety, Zacharatos et al. (2005) found that a high-performance work system (which includes emphasis upon employment security, selective hiring, team-working, extensive training, information-sharing, high-quality work and reward systems) is significantly associated with fewer lost time injuries at an organizational level. The average number of employees in this sample was over 500, indicating the high proportion of large organizations included in the study. Thus, the use of high-quality, commitment-oriented HR practices in larger organizations has been associated with lower accident rates. However, the study of HR practices and safety outcomes in SMEs is lacking in the literature.

SMEs tend to adopt more informal HR practices (e.g., Bacon & Hoque, 2005; Cassell et al., 2002) compared with larger organizations. However, the poor state of HR practices utilized by SMEs has been frequently noted (e.g., Bacon & Hoque, 2005; Dundon & Wilkinson, 2003; Wilkinson, 1999). For example, the majority of SMEs are less likely than larger organizations to have systematic recruitment and selection procedures or conduct formal performance appraisals (e.g., Cassell et al., 2002), or to provide regular formal training (e.g., Holliday, 1995; Storey & Westhead, 1997). Informal procedures and practices tend to predominate in SMEs; for example, Cassell et al. (2002) describe the approach to the use of HR practices as "pick and mix" rather than reflecting a coherent strategy. Such an approach to human resource management would suggest that SMEs are less likely to develop the commitment-based practices associated with positive safety outcomes. Indeed, limited evidence of commitment-based practices, such as employee involvement and participation, has been reported by studies of health and safety in SMEs (Champoux & Brun, 2003; Clarke & Flitcroft, 2008).

Preventive activities in SMEs tend to focus on safety training and emphasize that employees must follow rules and regulations (safety compliance). This may reflect a predominant belief that workplace accidents are caused by employees and a tendency to blame them for accidents, rather than recognize the role of managerial and organizational factors in accident causation (Champoux & Brun, 2003; Hasle et al., 2009). This was described in terms of a "blame-claim" culture by Clarke and Flitcroft (2008). Hasle et al. (2009) conducted interviews with the owners of 22 small enterprises (< 20 employees) within six months of an accident occurring at their company, leading to the absence of a worker for at least two weeks. They found that owners most frequently attributed the accident to unforeseen circumstances, the worker's fault or a combination of both, without any recognition of a possible role for themselves in accident causation. In addition, as owners saw the causes of accidents as beyond their control (defensive attribution), risk control measures were rarely implemented in order to prevent further accidents occurring.

Commitment-based management approaches, which encourage the involvement and participation of employees in safety activities, such as incentive schemes (Vassie et al., 2000) or recognition of safe behaviour (Clarke & Flitcroft, 2008), are rarely used in SMEs. There is also little use of team-working, particularly self-managed teams, in SMEs (Fazzari & Mosca, 2009). Well-managed teams can have safety benefits (Glendon et al., 2006) and self-managing teams, in particular, increase autonomy and employee empowerment, which in turn lead to safety improvements (Hechanova-Alampay & Beehr, 2002; Roy, 2003).

Senior Managers' Attitudes Towards Health and Safety

Research has suggested that senior managers' safety attitudes are crucial to an understanding of the type of safety activities supported by an organization (Flin, 2003). For example, Rundmo and Hale (2003) examined the safety attitudes of senior managers, showing that they were strongly related to the managers' behavioural intentions and self-reported behaviours in relation to safety activities, such as safety communication, motivating workers and improving safety measures. Furthermore, managers' safety attitudes have been found to have a significant effect on the success of safety interventions (Barrett et al., 2005). Thus, the safety attitudes and perceptions of senior managers in SMEs are likely to be particularly important in shaping the company's safety culture.

Table 8.1 SME managers' ranking of the relative importance of safety issues in the organization

	Rank Order	Mean Ranking
Working in a safe manner	1	3.7
Provision of relevant safety training	2	5.3
Minimization of workplace hazards	3	5.7
Provision of safety equipment	4	6.5
Management concern for employee safety	5	6.6
Management involvement in workplace safety	6	6.7
Safety awareness	6	6.7
Management view safety as important	8	7.2
Use of effective procedures and policies	9	9.2
Communication of health and safety issues	9	9.2
Supportive environment	11	9.6
Getting the job done	12	10.2
Involvement in safety issues	13	10.4
Making a profit	14	10.7
Employee risk taking	15	11.8

Source: After Clarke and Flitcroft (2008).

Clarke and Flitcroft (2008) report the results of a safety attitude survey conducted with a sample of senior managers based within 19 UK-based SMEs. A total of 272 questionnaires were distributed to all managers at the companies, of which 63 were returned (a response rate of 23 per cent). Managers were asked to rank safety issues in order of importance within their organization (with 1 = most important, 15 = least important). The mean rankings reported indicated that managers perceived that employee behaviour, training and the minimization of workplace hazards were viewed as most important to maintaining safety (see Table 8.1).

Safety issues related to management concern, involvement and attitudes towards safety were ranked lower, but issues such as effective procedures and policies, communication, supportive environment and employee involvement, were placed towards the lowest end of the rankings. However, the majority of managers perceived that companies prioritized safety issues over productivity, with items such as "getting the job done" and "making a profit" amongst the lowest ranked.

Managers also responded to a number of items regarding their attitudes and perceptions of safety within their organizations. The survey indicated that the majority of managers believed that a basic safety management system was operating effectively.

Items relating to the recording of accidents, reviewing of accident reports, taking action to minimize hazards and keeping up-to-date with safety legislation received high levels of agreement. There was also evidence that managers perceived the operation of other policies and procedures to be effective, such as safety communication and feedback, workplace inspections and the monitoring of sickness absence. However, it was clear that some practices, such as recognizing and rewarding safe behaviour and employee participation in safety, were perceived to be less well-utilized. Lower levels of agreement were reported in relation to the utilization of near-miss reporting, and the assessment of the direct and indirect costs of accidents. Thus, managers perceived that a limited amount of information is considered when evaluating safety priorities and spending. Managers generally agreed that employees were told about workplace hazards and understood the hazards involved in their work. In addition, attitudes towards health and safety within their organizations were generally perceived to be good. However, managers tended to agree somewhat that employees were reluctant to report accidents and found it difficult to understand safety rules. There was some indication that managers perceived that "resource poverty", in terms of staff shortages, and time pressure (deadlines) had an adverse impact on safety, with low levels of agreement that these issues had no effect.

Although managers generally expressed positive attitudes towards safety, they tended to place emphasis on workers' safe behaviour, and also safety training and minimization of workplace hazards, with management-related issues coming further down the list of priorities. This is consistent with research findings that managers of SMEs tend to view employees as the primary cause of accidents (Champoux & Brun, 2003; Hasle et al., 2009). Furthermore, O'Dea and Flin (2001) showed that there can be a considerable discrepancy between managers' awareness of best practice and their ability to apply it in their own organizations. Thus, positive safety attitudes and "good intentions" may not always be translated into practice within SMEs.

Although managers may perceive that safety is important and is well-managed, this is not always a perception shared by employees (Clarke, 1999). Communication to employees about the importance of safety to the company, especially in relation to managing daily conflicts between production and safety (Zohar, 2008), is an important process in shaping the safety culture. Given the nature of SMEs, especially small and micro-businesses, closer social relationships may facilitate enhanced communication and trust in managers, leading to a more positive safety culture. For example, Hofmann and Morgeson (1999) found that close and positive relationships between managers and employees lead to increased safety communication, which in turn was associated with lower accident rates.

However, Jansen et al. (2006) found that, contrary to their expectations, smaller worksites reported significantly more negative perceptions of site management support. The authors suggested that this effect may be due to managers of larger worksites benefiting from more structured communication and support, and therefore fostering more positive employee perceptions. Indeed, Clarke and Flitcroft (2008) reported that these issues featured as aspects of the workplace that could either promote or hinder the development of a positive safety culture. Therefore, there is a need to focus not only on fostering positive managerial attitudes, but to develop effective communication and support systems in order to facilitate a more positive safety culture. Furthermore, as noted earlier, close interpersonal relationships within SMEs can hinder the implementation of risk control measures and organizational learning following accidents (Hasle et al., 2009).

Research has shown that safety leadership can have a profound effect on safety outcomes, in both a positive and a negative way. Safety-specific transformational leadership describes a leadership style characterized by rewarding and encouraging safe behaviour, listening to concerns and encouraging employee safety participation, and demonstrating visible commitment to safety; this leadership style leads to higher safety consciousness in workers and fewer injuries (Barling et al., 2002; Kelloway et al., 2006). Furthermore, Kelloway et al. (2006) found that passive leadership (where the leader waits for things to go wrong before taking action and fails to intervene until safety problems are serious) did not have "null" effects, but had a significant association with *increased* occupational injuries. Given the crucial role played by senior managers in SMEs, particularly owner-managers of small and micro-businesses, adopting a leadership style conducive to safety is particularly important in terms of reducing health and safety risks.

CONCLUSIONS AND RECOMMENDATIONS FOR BEST PRACTICE

A review of the literature indicates that SMEs, and particularly small and micro-businesses, are especially vulnerable to workplace accidents and injuries. Elevated health and safety risks exist within SMEs for a number of reasons including: the nature of SMEs (newly formed, short life span, little financial stability), lack of investment in safety, operation in hazardous work environments and deficiencies in organizational and managerial practices. The latter is the most amenable to intervention and improvement by SMEs themselves. Furthermore, it is also evident that SMEs in many contexts lack support from regulatory authorities to help them understand and implement legal requirements.

Health and safety management systems are less well-developed within SMEs compared with large firms, with less emphasis on formal risk assessment, prevention activities, commitment-based HR practices and employee involvement and participation. The adoption of a "fire-fighting" approach to safety, which involves reacting to safety problems as they arise, and failing to acknowledge the role of managerial and organizational issues in accident prevention, has negative consequences in terms of health and safety risk. A more formal approach to health and safety management, modelled on large firms, may be most beneficial for medium-sized enterprises, where resources may be invested in safety systems. However, smaller firms often simply lack the resources to do this, and further research is needed to identify and develop solutions tailored to their specific needs.

Reason (1997) argues that competence, cognizance and commitment at senior management level, are needed to ensure the development of a positive organizational safety culture. SMEs should make improvements in each of these areas to enhance their safety culture and so reduce the risk of workplace accidents and injuries. Those with responsibility for health and safety require training and support to develop their knowledge and confidence in implementing regulatory requirements. A shift in focus is needed towards both formal and informal mechanisms for encouraging safety participation. Clarke and Ward (2006) found that leader behaviours were significantly related to employee safety participation – these behaviours were not all "transformational", but also related to a wider range of more transactional behaviour, including rational persuasion (using logical arguments and factual evidence), coalition (using coworkers to create pressure to comply) and consultation (involving employees in the decision-making process). Such behaviours need to be visible to employees to demonstrate commitment to safety; this will help to encourage a positive safety culture, in which employees demonstrate higher levels of safety consciousness, willingness to participate and make safety suggestions, and to report minor accidents and injuries. In particular, the management style adopted by owner-managers in small businesses should avoid passive leadership in relation to safety, which has been shown to have damaging effects on accident and injury rates.

REFERENCES

Bacon, N. & Hoque, K. (2005). HRM in the SME sector: Valuable employees and coercive networks. *International Journal of Human Resource Management*, **16**(11), 1976–99.

Barling, J. & Hutchinson, I. (2000). Commitment vs. control-based safety practices, safety reputation, and perceived safety climate. *Canadian Journal of Administrative Sciences*, **17**(1), 76–84.
Barling, J., Loughlin, C. & Kelloway, E.K. (2002). Development and test of a model linking safety-specific transformational leadership and occupational safety. *Journal of Applied Psychology*, **87**(3), 488–96.
Barling, J., Kelloway, E.K. & Iverson, R.D. (2003). High quality work, job satisfaction and occupational injuries. *Journal of Applied Psychology*, **88**(2), 276–83.
Barrett, J.H., Haslam, R.A., Lee, K.G. & Ellis, M.J. (2005). Assessing attitudes and beliefs using the stage of change paradigm–case study of health and safety appraisal within a manufacturing company. *International Journal of Industrial Ergonomics*, **35**(10), 871–87.
Cassell, C., Nadin, S., Gray, M. & Clegg, C. (2002). Exploring human resource management practices in small and medium sized enterprises. *Personnel Review*, **31**(6), 671–92.
Champoux, D. & Brun, J. (2003). Occupational health and safety management in small size enterprises: An overview of the situation and avenues for intervention and research. *Safety Science*, **41**(4), 301–18.
Cheng, C.W., Leu, S.S., Lin, C.C. & Fan, C. (2010). Characteristic analysis of occupational accidents at small construction enterprises. *Safety Science*, **48**(6), 698–707.
Clarke, S. (1999). Perceptions of organizational safety: Implications for the development of safety culture. *Journal of Organizational Behavior*, **20**(2), 185–98.
Clarke, S. & Flitcroft, C. (2008). Regulation of safety in UK-based SMEs: A managerial perspective. The Annual Conference of the British Psychological Society's Division of Occupational Psychology, Stratford-Upon-Avon, UK, January 2008.
Clarke, S. & Ward, K. (2006). The role of leader influence tactics and safety climate in engaging employee safety participation. *Risk Analysis*, **26**(5), 1175–86.
Cox, S., Janes, W., Walker, D. & Wenham, D. (1995). *Office Health and Safety Handbook*. London: Tolley Publishing Company.
de Kok, J.M.P. (2005). Precautionary actions within small and medium-sized enterprises. *Journal of Small Business Management*, **43**(4), 498–516.
Department for Business, Innovation & Skills (DBIS) (2009). SME Statistics 2009. Available at: http://stats.berr.gov.uk/ed/sme/; accessed 20 November 2010.
Dundon, T. & Wilkinson, A. (2003). Employment relations in small firms. In: B. Towers (ed.) *Handbook of Employment Relations: Law and Practice*, 4th edn. London: Kogan Page.
Fabiano, B., Curro, F. & Pastorino, R. (2004). A study of the relationship between occupational injuries and firm size and type in the Italian industry. *Safety Science*, **42**(7), 587–600.
Fazzari, A.L. & Mosca, J.B. (2009). "Partners in Perfection": Human resources facilitating creation and ongoing implementation of self-managed manufacturing teams in a small medium enterprise. *Human Resource Development Quarterly*, **20**(3), 333–76.
Flin, R. (2003). "Danger – Men at Work": Management influence on safety. *Human Factors and Ergonomics in Manufacturing*, **13**(4), 261–68.
Glendon, A.I., Clarke, S.G. & McKenna, E. (2006). *Human Safety and Risk Management*, (2nd edn). Boca Raton, Florida: CRC Press.
Hale, A.R. (2003). Safety management in production. *Human Factors and Ergonomics in Manufacturing*, **13**(3), 185–201.

Hasle, P. & Limborg, H.J. (2006). A review of the literature on preventive occupational health and safety activities in small enterprises. *Industrial Health*, **44**(1), 6–12.
Hasle, P., Kines, P. & Andersen, L.P. (2009). Small enterprise owners' accident causation attribution and prevention. *Safety Science*, **47**(1), 9–19.
Health and Safety Executive (HSE) (2004). Successful interventions with hard to reach groups. Available at: www.hse.gov.uk/research/misc/hardtoreach.pdf; accessed 19 November 2010.
Hechanova-Alampay, R.H. and Beehr, T.A. (2002). Empowerment, span of control and safety performance in work teams after workforce reduction. *Journal of Occupational Health Psychology*, **6**(4), 275–82.
Hofmann, D.A., & Morgeson, F.P. (1999). Safety-related behavior as a social exchange: The role of perceived organizational support and leader–member exchange. *Journal of Applied Psychology*, **84**(2), 286–96.
Holliday, R. (1995). *Investigating Small Firms: Nice Work?* London: Routledge.
Jansen, S.K., Stuebing, K.K., Ekeberg, S. & Sykora, K. (2006). Improving safety outcomes: A multilevel analysis. Paper presented to The 21st Annual Conference of the Society for Industrial and Organizational Psychology, Dallas, TX, USA, May 2006.
Kelloway, K., Mullen, J.E. & Francis, L. (2006). Divergent effects of transformational and passive leadership on employee safety. *Journal of Occupational Health Psychology*, **11**(1), 76–86.
Leaker, D. (2008). Sickness absence from work in the UK. *Economic & Labour Market Review*, **2**(11), 18–22. Available at: http://www.statistics.gov.uk/elmr/11_08/downloads/ELMR_Nov08_Leaker.pdf; accessed 19 November 2010.
Leigh, J.P., Marcin, J.P., & Miller, T.R. (2004). An estimate of the U.S. government's undercount of nonfatal occupational injuries. *Journal of Occupational and Environmental Medicine*, **46**(1), 10–18.
Matlay, H. (1999). Employee relations in small firms: A micro-business perspective. *Employee Relations*, **21**(3), 285–95.
McVittie, D., Banikin, H., & Brocklebank, W. (1997). The effect of firm size on injury frequency in construction. *Safety Science*, **27**(1), 19–23.
Micheli, G.J.L. & Cagno, E. (2010). Dealing with SMEs as a whole in OHS issues: Warnings from empirical evidence. *Safety Science*, **48**(6), 729–33.
Moore, A., Parahoo, K. & Fleming, P. (2010). Workplace health promotion within small and medium-sized enterprises. *Health Education*, **110**(1), 61–76.
O'Dea, A. & Flin, R. (2001). Site managers and safety leadership in the offshore oil and gas industry. *Safety Science*, **37**(1), 39–57.
Oleinick, A., Gluck, J.V., & Guire, K.E. (1995). Establishment size and risk of occupational injury. *American Journal of Industrial Medicine*, **28**(1), 1–21.
Pearson, P. (2001). *Keeping Well at Work*. London: Kogan Page.
Reason, J.T. (1997). *Managing the Risks of Organisational Accidents*. Aldershot: Ashgate.
Risk and Regulation Advisory Council (RRAC), (2009). *Health and Safety in Small Organisations: Reducing Uncertainty, Building Confidence, Improving Outcomes*. Available at: http://www.bis.gov.uk/files/file52340.pdf; accessed 19 November 2010.
Roy, M. (2003). Self-directed work teams and safety: A winning combination? *Safety Science*, **41**(4), 359–76.

Rundmo, T. & Hale, A.R. (2003). Managers' attitudes towards safety and accident prevention. *Safety Science*, **41**(7), 557–74.
Sørensen, O.H., Hasle, P. & Bach, E. (2007). Working in small enterprises – Is there a special risk? *Safety Science*, **45**(10), 1044–59.
Storey, D.J. & Westhead, P. (1997). Management training in small firms – a case of market failure? *Human Resource Management Journal*, **7**(2), 61–71.
Storey, D.J., Saridakis, G., Sen-Gupta, S., Edwards, P.K. & Blackburn, R.A. (2010). Linking HR formality with employee job quality: The role of firm and workplace size. *Human Resource Management*, **49**(2), 305–29.
Vassie, L., Tomàs, J.M. & Oliver, A. (2000). Health and safety management in UK and Spanish SMEs: A comparative study. *Journal of Safety Research*, **31**(1), 35–43.
Whitener, E.M. (2001). Do "high commitment" human resource practices affect employee commitment? A cross-level analysis using hierarchical linear modeling. *Journal of Management*, **27**(5), 515–35.
Wilkinson, A. (1999). Employment relations in SMEs. *Employee Relations*, **21**(3), 206–17.
Zacharatos, A., Barling, J., & Iverson, R.D. (2005). High-performance work systems and occupational safety. *Journal of Applied Psychology*, **90**(1), 77–93.
Zohar, D. (2008). Safety climate and beyond: A multi-level multi-climate framework. *Safety Science*, **46**(3), 376–87.

PART IV

Human resource management and individual challenges

9. Addressing personal and family transitions in small businesses: effective human resource management practices

Kyle Fuschetti and Jeffrey M. Pollack

INTRODUCTION

As the global economy attempts to recover from one of the worst economic downturns in recent memory, some of the most pivotal players on the road to recovery might not be household names like General Electric, General Dynamics, or General Motors. Rather, with small businesses becoming more and more important to the global economy, it might be businesses with names such as Jim's General Store that most aid the economic recovery. In fact, the growing importance of small and medium enterprises (SMEs) is a global trend that drives productivity, innovation, and employment growth in both developed as well as developing nations (e.g., Ayyagari et al., 2007; Van Praag & Versloot, 2007). However, though the importance and the prevalence of SMEs have increased, SMEs still face multiple obstacles.

Globally, failure rates in SMEs within the first three years of operations range from roughly 30 percent to upwards of 50 percent (for an initial review and introduction to relevant controversies see Headd, 2003; Van Praag, 2003). Overall, though it is important for owners as well as stakeholders of SMEs to be aware of the high proportion of failure, it is more important to understand why high numbers of SMEs fail. Multiple categories of reasons exist that attempt to explain the general causes of business failures such as lack of planning and organization (e.g., insufficient business planning, lack of long-term outlook, inaccurate analysis of competitive environment, unrealistic expectations), lack of knowledge or experience (e.g., lack of business expertise in critical areas, unwillingness to seek help), lack of resources (e.g., not enough financial capital, not enough human capital, poor credit or lack of access to debt financing), and personal and family transitions (e.g., role stress, lack of good models and/or support, difficulty dealing with uncertainty, family issues). Overall, considering these factors, the data are clear – due to these liabilities (often termed liabilities of newness and smallness) it is probable that early-stage entrepreneurs will fail (Delmar & Shane, 2004).

Substantial amounts of research have focused on some of these critical risk factors for business failure. However, a notable lack of research has focused on the personal and family transitions entrepreneurs encounter; this chapter, thus, focuses here. Specifically, we focus on two general areas in which entrepreneurs face difficult transitions: (1) stress-related issues and (2) family-related issues. We proceed as follows. First, we discuss the stress-related transition issues entrepreneurs encounter, and then we explore the family-related issues that can arise. Second, consistent with the benchmarking practices in SMEs (Cassell et al., 2001, 2002), we present relevant best practices for dealing with issues in both of these categories (i.e., stress-related, family-related). In conclusion, we provide practical, empirical, as well as theoretically-oriented thoughts regarding the personal and family transitions entrepreneurs face (see Table 9.1).

PERSONAL AND FAMILY TRANSITIONS IN SMALL BUSINESSES

Entrepreneurial Stress

Across the domains of organizational behavior, human resources, and management, occupational stress is a key construct (Barsky et al., 2004; Gilboa et al., 2008). We build on this research in the following section, which provides some insight into the stress-related transitions entrepreneurs encounter. Overall, though, limited research has been conducted in the domain of entrepreneurial stress. The work that has been done in entrepreneurship has focused on two general areas: (1) role conflict, role ambiguity, and role overload (for a review see Wincent & Ortqvist, 2009a, 2009b), and (2) failures (for reviews see Shepherd, 2003, 2004, 2009).

First and foremost, the main transition a person faces when engaging in entrepreneurial activity is the reality of working for yourself (i.e., role issues). Potentially, the days of hour-long lunch breaks, lenient bosses, and the occasional snow day are gone. Your business may now be open (i.e., you can now work) 24 hours per day, seven days per week – and, clients often do not care about extenuating circumstances; they want the work done or service provided efficiently and effectively. This, potentially, can lead to role conflict (i.e., difficulty meeting the demands of

Table 9.1 Transition issues, consequences, and best practices

Transition Type	Specific Transitions	Consequence	Best Practice(s)	Practitioner Exemplar
Stress-related	Role conflict Role ambiguity Role overload	Loneliness Excessive time demands Work overload Conflict with partners & employees Environmental uncertainty Struggles with high need for achievement	*Train others to do what you do*	WhitGroup Consulting
Stress-related	Pressure for success Threat of failure Lack of necessary know-how	Inability to cope Loss of confidence Diminishing self-worth Unfavorable long-term outlook	*Bring in outsiders to fill high-level positions*	Wahoo's Fish Taco
Stress-related	Lack of uniform prescriptions to transitional problems	Applying best practices that don't fit the company Ignoring important issues altogether	*Analyze your specific situation*	Stroller Strides
Family-related	Family members are completely excluded from the business	Mental alienation of family members Lack of quality family time Strain on familial relationships	*Encourage family members to feel as if they are part of the business*	The Road Less Traveled
Family-related	Entrenchment Lack of incentive to share wealth Nepotism Free-riding	Significant knowledge gaps Unsuccessful generational transitions Unfairness toward non-family employees	*Make family members earn their stripes/ engage in open & honest communication with family stakeholders*	Dorothy Lane Markets
Family-related	Lack of distance from family Inability to recognize individual talents	Unrealized potential Unfair business judgments based on family members' past actions Smothering effect: all family, all the time	*Recognize family member strengths and give them room to succeed*	Take-A-Boo Emporium

customers, financiers, licensing agencies, family members), role ambiguity (i.e., difficulty being the salesperson, marketing representative, payroll processer, and chief executive officer), and role overload (i.e., inability to accomplish all that needs to be done) (for reviews see Wincent & Ortqvist, 2009a, 2009b). Specific concerns related to the stressful nature of the entrepreneurial occupation include factors such as loneliness, excessive time demands, work overload, conflicts with partners and employees, environmental uncertainty, and struggles with high need for achievement (Akande, 1994; Buttner, 1992; Harris et al., 1999). Wincent and Ortqvist (2009a, p. 228) present a model and describe how role conflict, role ambiguity, and role overload may lead to both potential rewards and exhaustion – stress-related transition issues can have serious consequences for job performance, work–family conflict as well as job satisfaction and withdrawal (for a review see Wincent & Ortqvist, 2009b).

Though transition-related role issues are a concern, one additional concern is related to the threat of entrepreneurial failure. Specifically, the pressure for success grows and the consequences of failure increase; suddenly poor business performance leaves a small business owner wondering if he or she will be able to put food on the family's table. Generally, this area is substantially under-examined. However, research by Shepherd (2003, 2004, 2009) focuses on the issues related to businesses failure and how this adversely affects entrepreneurs and their families, both pre- and post-failure. As a stress-related issue, owners of SMEs should be aware that performance-oriented pressure can be a substantial concern to an entrepreneur.

Regarding the overall study of stress in entrepreneurs, recent research by LePine et al. (2005) as well as Podsakoff et al. (2007) holds promise as a framework to examine the stress-related transitions of entrepreneurs. This research highlights both the positive and negative effects that stress can have on individuals' performance. Traditionally, stress is viewed as a negative influence – however, this is not how original research on stress emerged. Originally, stress was simply described as a framework involving stimulus and a subsequent response (e.g., Lazarus & Folkman, 1984). Recent conceptualizations have described stress in terms of both feedback loops (e.g., Edwards, 1992) and resource conservation (e.g., Hobfoll, 2002). And, research by LePine et al. (2005) and Podsakoff et al. (2007) focuses on the differences between challenge stressors versus hindrance stressors. Challenge stressors are those influences that can improve performance (e.g., personal development and achievement) whereas hindrance stressors inhibit performance.

Imagine, for a moment, an entrepreneur facing two issues that are causing stress. Issue one is that the bank from which he/she seeks financing is two weeks late in making a decision. Issue two is that it is the end of the month and he/she is behind on sending out invoices to clients. In the challenge stressor–hindrance stressor framework, issue one would be a hindrance stressor – something that inhibits performance. Alternatively, issue two – the invoices – may actually put pressure on the entrepreneur to work efficiently and effectively to mail all the invoices in one day – a performance-enhancing stressor. In the present work, we primarily discuss the negative implications of stress as they relate to personal and family transitions, however, an intriguing line of research for future inquiry relates to how challenge stressors and hindrance stressors differentially affect entrepreneurs. For instance, Hunter and Thatcher (2007) examined a sample of 270 bank employees and found that individuals who felt stress and had higher commitment and higher levels of experience exhibited better performance relative to individuals who felt stress and had lower commitment and experience. Extending this line of research to the domain of entrepreneurship holds both practical and theoretical value.

Family-related Transition Issues

In terms of family-related issues, there are two main types of issues that can arise. On one hand, problems can arise if family members are *not* included in the business. On the other hand, problems can arise if family members *are* involved in the business. Overall, family-related factors influence one's ability to work effectively and are directly related to personal depression (Frone et al., 1992). And, when elements of work interfere with one's family life, overall life satisfaction and work satisfaction of the small business owner may be negatively affected (Adams et al., 1996). In the following section, we first discuss the problems that arise from not having family members involved, then we address the issues that can arise with direct family involvement.

To operate a business in which family members are not explicitly involved creates some important challenges. As an example, for a spouse, when a partner decides to embark on an entrepreneurial endeavor it can be difficult that financial security is no longer assured, set paychecks no longer arrive each month, and personal savings accounts become business reserves. Additionally, time spent together may decrease and some new SME owners have a workaholic mentality that can alienate a partner. Also, for children of entrepreneurs, the transition can be difficult as well (Mendels, 2000). Research has noted that children are actually "silent carriers of family financial stress", and that they are "not only keenly aware of it, but. . . more likely to behave badly and develop emotional problems" (Shellenbarger, 2008). Thus, it is easy to envision the problems that arise in terms of family-related transition issues if members are not involved in the business.

Alternatively, when operating a business in which family members are explicitly involved, some of the above issues may be somewhat alleviated. However, though there are significant benefits, important disadvantages also can also arise (for reviews see Hoy & Sharma, 2009; Nicholson, 2008a, 2008b; Sharma, 2004; Sharma et al., 1997). On the plus side, firms with higher family involvement are typically able to leverage and build strength through their shared life experiences; thus, small businesses with high family involvement may be more able to handle challenges and crises (Nicholson, 2008a). However, overall, Lansberg (1983) found that there are four different types of problems that firms with high family involvement can encounter: (1) employee selection, (2) employee compensation and equity, (3) employee appraisal, and (4) employee training and development. And, these areas manifest themselves as problems with higher levels of entrenchment, special dispensation or compensation, lack of incentive to share wealth, nepotism, and free-riding (Burkart et al., 1997; DeAngelo & DeAngelo, 2000; Gomez-Mejia et al., 2001; Pollack, 1985; Schulze et al., 2003).

Synthesis

Overall, new entrepreneurs in SMEs may encounter substantial difficulties due to the transition. These transition issues can be due to stress-related and/or family-related issues. Transition issues may have serious consequences for job performance, job satisfaction, work–family conflict as well as withdrawal. In the following sections we outline some best practices that focus on addressing some of these transition issues and decreasing the potential negative impacts.

DEALING WITH TRANSITION-RELATED ISSUES: BEST PRACTICES

In order to help smooth personal and family transitions in small businesses, there are several human resource (HR)-related practices that owners of SMEs can follow. By adhering to some of these basic concepts and learning from various small business success stories, a new entrepreneur will be able to avoid some of the common emotional pitfalls discussed earlier and establish an enterprise oriented towards long-term success. In the following examples, we address both how to deal with common stress-related issues as well as common family-related transition issues.

Train Others to Do What You Do

Initially, an entrepreneur in an SME may need to do everything (e.g., marketing, sales, emptying the trash, doing the payroll). However, this is neither sustainable nor realistic in the long run (Gerber, 2001). Eventually, as discussed earlier, role conflict, role ambiguity, and/or role overload create unacceptable levels of stress, which then affect performance. Therefore, as soon as the SME gets to the point where employees can be hired, the entrepreneur has a real opportunity to take a significant amount of the workload off his/her shoulders – generally, adding an employee can pay for itself in terms of efficiency and effectiveness in a short amount of time. Additionally, by investing in employee training, a lot of time can be freed up for the small business owner to devote to his or her family and other commitments; vacations can be planned, school plays can be attended and reasonable work hours can be realized.

A great example of this can be seen by analyzing the story of WhitGroup Consulting LLC (http://www.wgconsult.com/) (see Isidro, 2010). Bianca Whitfield, a newly divorced mother with a one-year-old daughter, made a career choice that few individuals would consider. Instead of playing it safe with a guaranteed paycheck from her corporate accounting job, Whitfield decided to go into business for herself and start an accounting, tax and financial services firm: WhitGroup Consulting LLC. Success came quickly to Whitfield – almost too quickly. WhitGroup Consulting LLC, once a one-woman, home-based operation, soon became a full-fledged small business with its own office and employee base. Though success did come fast, it certainly did not come easy. Early on in the company's existence, Whitfield was forced to work long hours in order to grow her business while remaining a devoted mother. These significant changes in her personal and professional life were becoming hard to deal with so Whitfield took steps to help ease the transition. One of these major moves was her commitment to her employees' training and development. Not only did she want to see these individuals succeed and develop their knowledge bases, but Whitfield also wanted them to learn as much as they could as quickly as possible so that they could help take some of the work off her plate. This additional assistance greatly helped Whitfield with her and her daughter's transition into this new, entrepreneurial life (ibid.).

Encourage Family Members to Feel as if They Are Part of the Business

Completely separating the family and business aspects of entrepreneurial life is difficult. A spouse, partner, or child will often feel like the entrepreneur is living two lives – one at home and one at work. This often can foster resentment and feelings of a lack of appreciation when the entrepreneur chooses to stay late at work instead of coming home for meals or family events.

The entrepreneur can counteract this vicious cycle by engaging family members in the business. Bringing work "home" is often referred to negatively – however, tasks such as stuffing envelopes in the living room, or making the weekly deposit at the bank a family endeavor, can enable members to feel as if they are truly a part of the business. Indeed, enabling family members, especially kids, to be part of the business builds pride, and understanding of the endeavor (Hirshberg, 2010).

The Road Less Traveled (http://www.theroadlesstraveled.com/), a Chicago-based small business, exemplifies the family involvement model. Jim and Donna Stein, the owners and founders of the company, which leads expeditions with high school students around the globe, have three children. Two decades ago, when they started the business, the three kids were just born. Over time, Jim and Donna had a choice – lead the company by keeping work and family separate – or, engage the family in the business and enable all the employees to benefit from the family-oriented culture. Their choice – high involvement of both Jim and Donna, as well as the three kids – has been tremendous for the company. Expedition leaders with the company, who see the kids at all company events and at the annual staff training, have the sense that they are part of a family. And, the kids are now engaged in the business and actually, now that they are old enough, lead trips of their own for the company.

Analyze Your Own Specific Situation

Studying successful small businesses practices and the musings of sage HR professionals is a wise move for any entrepreneur, however, in reality, there is no one-size-fits-all approach to managing personal and family transitions into small business. Rather, each person is different, each family is different, and each business is different. In fact, Edwards and Rothbard (1999, p. 123) noted that "uniform prescriptions for resolving work and family stress are likely to be ineffective". Importantly, they asserted that "Efforts to manage work and family stress should be individualized, based on careful assessment of the fit between the person and his or her own work and family environments". We, accordingly, encourage owners of SMEs to find a way of doing things that works in their particular situation.

A great of example of this can be found by studying Lisa Druxman's company, Stroller Strides (http://www.strollerstrides.com/) (see Pennington, 2005). In 2001, Lisa Druxman, a fitness aficionado, gave birth to her son and made the very tough decision not to return to her general manager position at her California-based health club. Druxman's choice left her with two difficult questions to answer: how could she continue to bring income into the household and how could she be sure to maintain her extremely fit and healthy lifestyle? Druxman, in response, started her own company, Stroller Strides, which provided stay-at-home moms with a work-out program that included their children.

With Stroller Strides, Druxman was able to create a service for the large, underserved market of stay-at-home moms looking to find time to stay in shape without neglecting their children. In addition, Druxman was able to ease her own transition into the world of small business by actually *incorporating* her child into the business. Druxman shows that creativity and out-of-the-box thinking are vital to smoothing out personal and family transitions in entrepreneurial endeavors (ibid.).

Engage in Open and Honest Communication with Family Stakeholders

As with any good peer-review process at a large corporation, small business owners should engage in scheduled, frequent 360 degree reviews with all of their stakeholders, namely, their family members. These candid review sessions give everyone a forum where they are free to speak their mind about their concerns and feelings about their family's transition to a small business lifestyle. These reviews allow the entrepreneur to see where he or she is failing as a boss, partner, spouse, and/or parent as well as where he/she is doing well (Hirshberg, 2010).

It is also prudent to set up certain unbreakable family rules and guidelines, such as non-negotiable partner–partner time or parent–child time, or outlawed use of technology (e.g., phones, computers) at the dinner table. This open and honest communication with one's family will create a more pleasant home environment for everyone, which has far-reaching benefits. Research has shown that a person's overall happiness in life is more closely related to family satisfaction than it is to work satisfaction; even the most dedicated entrepreneur would be wise to make his or her family's happiness his or her top priority (Edwards & Rothbard, 1999).

One HR practice that can be used is to set up specific governance tools for family members that guide actions, set expectations, and provide a forum for feedback. Some tools to consider are regularly scheduled family-only meetings, elected family councils, and collaborative family constitutions (Hoy & Sharma, 2009). By keeping family members constantly engaged and expressing an interest in their feedback, the entrepreneur will ensure his or her management style doesn't appear to be that of a dictatorship. These governance tools will also establish a certain degree of fairness since underlying ground rules are documented for all to see and feedback is routinely being solicited.

Bring in Outsiders to Fill High-level Positions

By putting only family members in high-level positions of power, the entrepreneur misses several significant opportunities. In the realm of HR, engaging a professional employer organization (PEO) can lead to many great benefits for the company. First, this PEO can signify a certain degree of fairness to employees, indicating that HR decisions are being influenced by an outside third party and any sort of family bias that exists with the business owner can be effectively managed (Tansky & Heneman, 2006). Furthermore, bringing in non-family member employees and putting them in positions of power can lead to significant gains in organizational knowledge, efficiency, and effectiveness.

A great example of this can be seen by studying the story of Wahoo's Fish Taco (http://www.wahoos.com/) (see Kilroy, 2009). In 1988, Wing Lam, Ed Lee, and Mingo Lee opened up a small restaurant in Costa Mesa, California. These three brothers, who grew up peeling shrimp in their parents' Chinese restaurant, never dreamed that Wahoo's Fish Taco would become the incredible success that it is today. Early on, as the business demands began to explode, the three brothers were able to recognize their own professional shortcomings. Ed explained, "After we opened our third store, it sort of became a business. I started having to worry about inventory controls, scheduling people. I mean, we didn't have any of those things in place" (Kilroy, 2009). In 1990, the three brothers recognized that they couldn't expand any further without some outside help. As a result, Steve Karfaridis became a partner and COO of Wahoo's and brought with him several years of experience as a consultant to many Orange County restaurants.

Because Wing, Ed, and Mingo were able to recognize their professional shortcomings and solicit outside help, Wahoo's was able to expand geographically and flourish. Wahoo's now has over 50 stores in four different states and continues to grow and gain national brand recognition. Their sage decisions allowed the three brothers to transition smoothly from a small, family-owned operation to a bigger, ever-expanding enterprise (ibid.).

Make Family Members Earn Their Stripes

The majority of businesses do not require family members to have any sort of experience or necessary qualifications when entering the company (Beck, 2009). However, for multiple reasons (e.g., effectiveness, efficiency, employee morale, fairness) it is imperative that family employees receive the necessary training and develop significant knowledge bases before taking on any sort of important role within the firm.

A great case study of this principle can be found with Dorothy Lane Markets (http://www.dorothylane.com/), a small, family-owned Ohio-based supermarket chain (see Fenn, 2005). These markets, owned since 1948 by the Mayne family, provide customers with an incredible environment in which to do their shopping: free cappuccino at the coffee bar, fresh artisanal bread baking in the $60 000 French hearth oven and an incredibly helpful staff, dressed in crisp white shirts and bow ties (ibid.).

Due to the upscale and ultra-welcoming store environment, any customer who spends more than five minutes in a Dorothy Lane Market would leave convinced that, for management, the customer is the number one priority. They would, however, be incorrect in that assumption. In the early years of the business, customer service was certainly the Mayne family mantra, but they soon came to realize that exceptional service starts with exceptional employees (ibid.). As a result, Dorothy Lane spends over $25 000 (and uncountable amounts of time) on employee training each year. The industry average turnover of part-time supermarket employees is around 100 percent – at Dorothy Lane, this number is closer to 25 percent.

As a family-owned business, though, much attention is paid to family employees in addition to part-timers. Older generations want to be absolutely sure that the future of the company is in good hands, so they invest heavily in growing the knowledge base of the younger members of the Mayne family. Norman Mayne, son of founder Calvin and current CEO, spent his youth sweeping floors, stocking shelves, and working the register. Norman's son Calvin is also getting into the act: at 12 years old, Calvin was sweeping the basement floor and stocking shelves during the graveyard shift. He became a specialty food buyer in the mid-1990s and became a general manager in 1996. Calvin understands the need for his years of grunt-work, explaining it was understood that he needed to earn his role in the company. This notion of a successor having to earn his or her stripes is missing from far too many family-owned small businesses. This leads to an extremely high failure rate for inter-generational transitions. By starting employees at a young age and having them truly learn the craft, this risk of uninformed successors can be effectively mitigated in many SMEs (ibid.).

Recognize Family Member Strengths and Give Them Room to Succeed

Family meetings, councils, and constitutions can be very useful governance tools for an entrepreneur, but also must be used in moderation. If too many policies, rules, and regulations are put in place, family member employees may begin to feel overwhelmed and micro-managed. Too much of a family culture can also suffocate employees and have adverse effects on the long-term health of the business. Once employee strengths are identified, they should be given a certain degree of freedom to pursue their objectives and deliver results for the business without interference.

Husband and wife team Martin and Andrea Swinton learned this lesson early on when starting their business: Take-A-Boo Emporium in Toronto, Ontario (http://takeaboo.worldpress.com) (see Ward, 2010). As a married couple, the Swintons quickly came to discover the challenges associated with working with your spouse as a business partner. Every minute of each day was spent with one another – this, they realized, could be difficult for even the most devoted couples. By opening Take-A-Boo together, the Swintons not only had to worry about the health of their business but also the health of their marriage.

Martin and Andrea realized that their business and their marriage would never last if they were constantly in each other's space. They also realized that they had two very different professional backgrounds and skill sets that could complement each other very well. As a result, the Swintons set up clearly defined responsibilities and spheres of action: Martin was responsible for the day-to-day antique-based operations while Andrea managed the business, operated the website, and handled the finances. By being honest and open with each other and recognizing individual strengths, Martin and Andrea Swinton were able to assist each other with their transitions into the world of operating a small business and kept their marriage healthy. These lessons can be applied in almost any family-operated small business and can be utilized to prevent many of the common pitfalls that send these businesses to their demise (ibid.).

CONCLUSION

Research shows that business practices, specifically in the area of human resources, vary substantially among small and medium-sized businesses (Cassell et al., 2002). Not only do the practices show a high degree of variability, but so do the relative levels of success. Overall, existing SMEs can learn from peers, both from within and outside of their own industry. Without positive role models, or benchmarks, for human resource-related best practices the need for a small business owner to figure things out alone will quickly result in elevated difficulty due to stress and family-related issues in the transition to entrepreneurship (e.g., De Grip & Sieben, 2005).

In this chapter we've explored the difficult personal and family transitions that go along with entrepreneurial endeavors. And, in order to smooth these transitions we've concluded that, first and foremost, the business owner must understand the challenges being faced by all involved stakeholders (e.g., owners, managers, family). Accordingly, we have established a series of best practices, based on high-performing SMEs, that business owners can model to help smooth the transition-related issues that result from engaging in entrepreneurial activity.

REFERENCES

Adams, G.A., King, L.A. & King, D.W. (1996). Relationships of job and family involvement, family social support, and work–family conflict with job and life satisfaction. *Journal of Applied Psychology*, **81**(4), 411–20.

Akande, A. (1994). Coping with entrepreneurial stress: Evidence from Nigeria. *Journal of Small Business Management*, **32**(1), 83–7.

Ayyagari, M., Beck, T. & Demirguc-Kunt, A. (2007). Small and medium enterprises across the globe. *Small Business Economics*, **29**(4), 415–34.

Barsky, A., Thoresen, C.J., Warren, C.R. & Kaplan, S.A. (2004). Modeling negative affectivity and job stress: A contingency-based approach. *Journal of Organizational Behavior*, **25**(8), 915–36.

Beck, D. (2009). HR can help ensure the success of family businesses – from mom-and-pop stores to Wal-Mart. *Employment Relations Today*, **35**(4), 31–8.

Burkart, M., Gromb, D. & Panunzi, F. (1997). Large shareholders, monitoring, and the value of the firm. *Quarterly Journal of Economics*, **112**(3), 693–728.

Buttner, E.H. (1992). Entrepreneurial stress: Is it hazardous to your health? *Journal of Managerial Issues*, **4**(2), 223–40.

Cassell, C., Nadin, S. & Gray, M.O. (2001). The use and effectiveness of benchmarking in SMEs. *Benchmarking*, **8**(3), 212–22.

Cassell, C., Nadin, S., Gray, M. & Clegg, C. (2002). Exploring human resource management practices in small and medium sized enterprises. *Personnel Review*, **31**(6), 671–92.

DeAngelo, H. & DeAngelo, L. (2000). Controlling stockholders and the disciplinary role of corporate payout policy: A study of the Times Mirror Company. *Journal of Financial Economics*, **56**(2), 153–207.

De Grip, A. & Sieben, I. (2005). The effects of human resource management on small firms' productivity and employees' wages. *Applied Economics*, **37**(9), 1047–54.

Delmar, F. & Shane, S. (2004). Legitimating first: Organizing activities and the survival of new ventures. *Journal of Business Venturing*, **19**(3), 385–410.

Edwards, J.R. (1992). A cybernetic theory of stress, coping, and well-being in organizations. *Academy of Management Review*, **17**(2), 238–74.

Edwards, J.R. & Rothbard, N.P. (1999). Work and family stress and well-being: An examination of person–environment fit in the work and family domains. *Organizational Behavior and Human Decision Processes*, **77**(2), 85–129.

Fenn, D. (2005). *Alpha Dogs: How Your Small Business Can Become a Leader of the Pack*. New York: HarperCollins Publishing.

Frone, M.R., Russell, M. & Cooper, M.L. (1992). Antecedents and outcomes of work–family conflict: Testing a model of the work–family interface. *Journal of Applied Psychology*, **77**(1), 65–78.

Gerber, M.E. (2001). *The E-myth Revisited: Why Most Small Businesses Don't Work and What to Do About It*. New York: HarperCollins.

Gilboa, S., Shirom, A., Fried, Y. & Cooper, C. (2008). A meta-analysis of work demand stressors and job performance: Examining main and moderating effects. *Personnel Psychology*, **61**(2), 227–71.

Gomez-Mejia, L.R., Nuñez-Nickel, M. & Gutierrez, I. (2001). The role of family ties in agency contracts. *Academy of Management Journal*, **44**(1), 81–95.

Harris, J.A., Saltstone, R. & Fraboni, M. (1999). An evaluation of the job stress questionnaire with a sample of entrepreneurs. *Journal of Business and Psychology*, **13**(3), 447–55.

Headd, B. (2003). Redefining business success: Distinguishing between closure and failure. *Small Business Economics*, **21**(1), 51–61.

Hirshberg, M.C. (2010, 1 March). Minding the kids. *Inc.* Available at http://www.inc.com/magazine/20100301/minding-the-kids.html; accessed 20 November 2010.

Hobfoll, S.E. (2002). Social and psychological resources and adaptation. *Review of General Psychology*, **6**(4), 307–24.

Hoy, F. & Sharma, P. (2009). *Entrepreneurial Family Firms*. Upper Saddle River: Pearson Press.

Hunter, L.W. & Thatcher, S.M.B. (2007). Feeling the heat: Effects of stress, commitment, and job experience on job performance. *Academy of Management Journal*, **50**(4), 953–68.

Isidro, I. (2010, 23 January). Bianca Whitfield: A single parent's success story. *Women Home Business*. Available at: http://www.womenhomebusiness.com/success/bianca-whitfield-a-single-parents-success-story.htm; accessed 20 November 2010.

Kilroy, J. (2009, 27 February). Wahoo's has a birthday party (and I get invited). *Entrepreneur*. Available at http://blog.entrepreneur.com/2009/02/wahoos-has-a-birthday-party-and-i-get-invited.php; accessed 20 November 2010.

Lansberg, I.S. (1983). Managing human resources in family firms: The problem of institutional overlap. *Organizational Dynamics*, **12**(1), 39–46.

Lazarus, R.S., & Folkman, S. (1984). *Stress, Coping, and Adaptation*. New York: Springer-Verlag.

LePine, J.A., Podsakoff, N.A., LePine, M.A. (2005). A meta-analytic test of the challenge stressor–hindrance stressor framework: An explanation for inconsistent relationships among stressors and performance. *Academy of Management Journal*, **48**(5), 764–75.

Mendels, P. (2000, 27 December). Should working parents work less? *Business Week*. Available at http://www.businessweek.com/smallbiz/content/dec2000/sb20001227_601.htm; accessed 20 November 2010.

Nicholson, N. (2008a). Evolutionary psychology and family business: A new synthesis for theory, research and practice. *Family Business Review*, **21**(1), 103–18.

Nicholson, N. (2008b). Evolutionary psychology, organizational culture, and the family firm. *Academy of Management Perspectives*, **22**(2), 73–84.

Pennington, A.Y. (2005, 1 December). Baby steps. *Entrepreneur*. Available at: http://www.entrepreneur.com/worklife/successstories/article81120.html; accessed 20 November 2010.

Podsakoff, N.P., LePine, J.A. & LePine, M.A. (2007). Differential challenge

stressor–hindrance stressor relationships with job attitudes, turnover intentions, turnover, and withdrawal behavior: A meta-analysis. *Journal of Applied Psychology*, **92**(2), 438–54.
Pollack, R.A. (1985). A transaction cost approach to families and households. *Journal of Economic Literature*, **23**(2), 581–608.
Schulze, W.S., Lubatkin, M.H. & Dino, R.N. (2003). Toward a theory of agency and altruism in family firms. *Journal of Business Venturing*, **18**(4), 473–90.
Sharma, P. (2004). An overview of family business studies: Current status and directions for the future. *Family Business Review*, **17**(1), 1–36.
Sharma, P., Chrisman, J.J. & Chua, J.H. (1997). Strategic management of the family business: Past research and future challenges. *Family Business Review*, **10**(1), 1–35.
Shellenbarger, S. (2008, 24 September). When tough times weigh on the kids. *The Wall Street Journal*. Available at: http://online.wsj.com/article/SB122220949327768879.html; accessed 21 November 2010.
Shepherd, D.A. (2003). Learning from business failure: Propositions of grief recovery for the self-employed. *Academy of Management Review*, **28**(2), 318–28.
Shepherd, D.A. (2004). Educating entrepreneurship students about emotion and learning from failure. *Academy of Management Learning and Education*, **3**(3), 274–87.
Shepherd, D.A. (2009). Grief recovery from the loss of a family business: A multi- and meso-level theory. *Journal of Business Venturing*, **24**(1), 81–97.
Tansky, J.W. & Heneman, R.L. (2006). *Human Resource Strategies for the High-growth Entrepreneurial Firm*. Charlotte: Information Age Publishing.
Van Praag, C.M. (2003). Business survival and success of young small business owners. *Small Business Economics*, **21**, 1–17.
Van Praag, C.M. & Versloot, P.H. (2007). What is the value of entrepreneurship? A review of recent research. *Small Business Economics*, **29**(4), 351–82.
Ward, S. (2010, June). Take-A-Boo Emporium: Canadian small business of the month. Available at: http://sbinfocanada.about.com/cs/successstories/a/antiquesuccess.htm; accessed 20 November 2010.
Wincent, J. & Ortqvist, D. (2009a). A comprehensive model of entrepreneurial role stress antecedents and consequences. *Journal of Business and Psychology*, **24**(2), 225–43.
Wincent, J. & Ortqvist, D. (2009b). Role stress and entrepreneurship research. *International Entrepreneurship Management Journal*, **5**(1), 1–22.

10. The challenges for female small business owners and managers: a consideration of the veterinary profession

Colette Henry, Lorna Treanor and Sarah Baillie

INTRODUCTION

Female small business ownership, as a subject of concerted academic research, has attracted considerable attention in recent years (Henry & Johnston, 2007; Marlow et al., 2008; Idris, 2009; Women's Enterprise Task Force, 2009). This is partly due to the continued interest, at both the academic and political level, in entrepreneurship and small business generally, and the growing recognition that female-led businesses make a valuable contribution to the global economy (Prowess, 2007). In addition, as noted by Idris (2009, p. 416), women entrepreneurs add diversity and choice to the broader business environment (Verheul et al., 2006), and, in some respects, can even be considered to contribute to enhancing gender equality. At the academic level, the field has developed significantly from the purely exploratory and descriptive studies characterized by the earlier literature toward more robust evidence bases that further our understanding of complex issues inherent in women's business ownership, management and entrepreneurship (Carter & Shaw, 2006). From a political perspective, the promotion and support of women's business start-ups and growth has become an important area for government, leading, in the UK, to the launch of the Strategic Framework for Women's Enterprise and the establishment of the Women's Enterprise Taskforce.

While there is a significant body of international literature on women as small business owners, managers and entrepreneurs, there are still relatively few studies that explore the challenges women encounter in the context of specific professions, particularly those where women are now, or will soon be, in the majority. In this regard, veterinary medicine is a particularly relevant example, given the unprecedented increase in the number of women entering undergraduate programmes and the imminent gender shift towards a predominantly female practice profession (Henry et al., 2010).

Reflecting the dearth of research in this particular area, we adopt a highly inductive approach, designed to generate new understandings and propositions for further research (Rosa & Dawson, 2006). Our key objective in this chapter is to highlight the types of generic challenges that women business owners and managers currently encounter and discuss how such challenges will inevitably manifest within the veterinary profession, in light of the imminent gender shift in the veterinary workforce. We also explore the impact that these challenges are likely to have on women's future participation in veterinary business ownership and management. Thus, we lay the theoretical foundation for future empirical work in this field and offer suggestions for a new strand of enquiry geared toward exploring the entrepreneurial and business management opportunities available within, what is soon to become, a female-led veterinary sector. We begin by examining some of the recurring themes in the literature in relation to female entrepreneurship and business ownership, paying particular attention to gender-based theories, including stereotypical assumptions and behaviours and their impact. This is followed by a consideration of the veterinary profession, including the make-up of the sector and women's role therein. We then apply some of the key themes from the women's business and management literatures, as presented in the preceding sections, to the veterinary profession, and discuss the particular challenges that will inevitably emerge for future women veterinary business owners and managers. Finally, we explore the likely impact on women's participation levels in veterinary entrepreneurship and business ownership.

WOMEN AS ENTREPRENEURS, BUSINESS OWNERS AND MANAGERS

General Trends and Women's Representation

According to the Global Entrepreneurship Monitor (GEM) report, women are half as likely as men to set up their own business, with the number of women entrepreneurs continuing to lag significantly behind that of men in most developed economies (GEM, 2008). Despite the fact that women make up half of the European population, less than one-third of all businesses in Europe are female-led. In the UK, for example, around 15 per cent of small businesses are led by women, suggesting that there are about

620 000 women-owned businesses in the UK. Collectively, such businesses contribute some £130 billion in turnover to the economy (Women's Enterprise Task Force, 2009). Although there are undoubtedly variations between different regions and countries (GEM, 2008), and particular framework conditions for entrepreneurship in specific economies also have an impact, women are still considered the most under-represented group in entrepreneurship (Delmar, 2001, as cited in Verheul et al., 2006; GEM, 2010).

The literature has reported several reasons for the generally low number of women entrepreneurs and business managers across different sectors. These include social and cultural influences, education and career choices and a lack of self-confidence (Wilson et al., 2007); the nature of women's entrepreneurial motivation (Bruni et al., 2004); attitude to risk (Brindley, 2005) and, fundamentally, the general and stereotypical perceptions relating to the traditional role of women (Henry & Kennedy, 2003; Marlow & Patton, 2005). Terrell and Troilo (2010) also suggest three factors that could help to explain the low number of women business owners globally: the generally lower female (compared with male) labour participation rates, life values and their influence on labour force participation rates, and work values and their impact on a woman's decision to own her own business. Regardless of how women's lower levels of business ownership are explained, women entrepreneurs and business managers do appear to face particular challenges as distinct from those typically encountered by their male counterparts. These include: coping with and appropriately balancing a typically disproportionate share of family responsibilities (Fielden et al., 2003; Jennings & McDougald, 2007); a lack of, or restricted access to, human and financial capital (Orser et al., 2006; Shaw et al., 2009) and engaging in appropriate networks of information and access to assistance (Bruni et al., 2004). We now discuss some of these challenges as well as other pertinent themes in the women's entrepreneurship and business management literatures.

Gender Stereotypes and the Traditional Role of Women in Society

In developed countries around the world women have traditionally been regarded as submissive, sentimental and superstitious, with men considered adventurous, independent and forceful (Williams & Best, 1990). Earlier literature has also assumed that women are less assertive, less ambitious and less career-oriented than men (Kauffman & Fetters, 1980). The impact of these gendered perspectives throughout societies and cultures can produce socially accepted norms and expectations; these, in turn, establish normative institutions that limit the choices, or, at the very least, the perceptions of opportunities open to individuals (Wilson, 2003; Baughn et al., 2006; Welter & Smallbone, 2008).

Gender is explained in the literature as a social construction of sex through which particular masculine characteristics are ascribed to men and particular feminine characteristics are ascribed to women (Oakley, 1973; Ahl, 2004). However, attributing characteristics to women that are deemed to be typical of their sex can often constitute a major barrier to career progression within most industry sectors. As explained by Marlow and Patton (2005, p. 719), a number of stereotypical behaviours are associated with either the masculine or the feminine, where the former is privileged over the latter, thus supporting a hierarchical valuation of traits and characteristics. Attributes often considered essential for promotion within a competitive industry, for example, are typically contrary to those thought to be held by women.

Such stereotypes and perceptions surrounding the capabilities of women are sometimes even internalized by women themselves. For example, Bandura (1992) confirmed that women are more likely than men to limit their career aspirations because of a lack of belief or confidence in their own abilities. Furthermore, the literature has shown consistently over the years that women's career aspirations and choices tend to be significantly lower than those of their male counterparts (Fitzgerald & O'Crites, 1980; Betz & Fitzgerald, 1987; Gatewood et al., 2002). This lack of self-efficacy has also been found to impact upon entrepreneurial career choices (Wilson et al., 2007) and is consistent across countries (Langowitz & Minniti, 2007).

Several studies have shown that men, across different countries, education levels and age ranges, do not perceive or consider women to be "able" managers and, within certain cultures, men are less likely to accept women in management positions (Cordano et al., 2002). This may explain why women managers often report difficulties in gaining respect in managerial positions (Stephens & Greer, 1995), citing stereotypical attitudes, direct challenges of competence by male employees and being spoken to in a patronizing manner by male superiors (Muller & Rowell, 1987; Gowan & Trevino, 1998; Cordano et al., 2002).

Most significantly, in a male-dominated society and workplace, male managers have retained their long-held perception that successful managerial characteristics are more likely to be held by men than women (Schein & Mueller, 1990; Dodge et al., 1995; Schein, 2001). Essentially, men do not consider women to possess the characteristics, traits or skills associated with good managers or entrepreneurs (Schein, 2001; Gupta et al., 2009). This has obvious significance when one considers that men are more likely to be a woman's superior in the workplace, undertaking annual appraisals and making decisions in relation to career progression. Such attitudes and beliefs can lead to women managers and entrepreneurs being regarded as less competent or perceived as being less credible in their work roles than their male counterparts (European Commission, 2008). It is, perhaps, these types of subconscious gender stereotypes that maintain the often cited "glass walls" and "ceilings" in the workplace, a phenomenon that is evidenced by, and perhaps may even explain, women's lack of progression into senior management roles. Indeed, despite a significant increase in the number of women managers in recent years, women continue to be under-represented in managerial positions worldwide (Peus & Traut-Mattausch, 2008). For example, in 2000, the Cabinet Office identified that women held 18 per cent of UK Civil Service management posts and 3.6 per cent of FTSE Directorships. In 2010, the equivalent figures stand at 27 per cent and 12 per cent respectively, indicating a progressive, albeit slow, climb towards parity. Most tellingly perhaps, consecutive *Global Gender Gap Reports* (World Economic Forum, 2006, 2007) highlight that, around the world, women still earn less than men for doing similar or, indeed, the same work.

Management and Leadership Styles

The lower number of female compared with male entrepreneurs and business managers has been attributed by some commentators to a difference in management style, with the underlying assumption that men are more natural and, thus, more effective managers and leaders. However, there does not appear to be any empirical evidence for this assumption (Peus & Traut-Mattausch, 2008). Hofstede (1980), in his study of masculine and feminine roles within organizations, associates interpersonal relationships, the environment and a sense of service as being characteristic of women. Women are also found to adopt less authoritarian management styles and display superior negotiating and diplomatic skills. Furthermore, they tend to be more customer-oriented in their enterprise dealings than their male counterparts, adopting management styles that place greater value on the human capital, cultural and product/service quality aspects of their business (Henry, 2008).

A typology of female entrepreneurs recently constructed by Idris (2009) identified four distinct management and leadership styles: mother, teacher, boss and chameleon. While the style categories are essentially shaped by the individual women's experiences and, to some degree, reflect gendered norms, they are, with the exception of the "boss" category, highly feminine in nature (Foss & Henry, 2010). Indeed, it appears that women often adopt those management styles that best reflect their traditional roles in society, thus, enabling them to fit in and be accepted as managers and leaders by their mainly male peers. On a more positive note, however, evidence is beginning to emerge indicating that the contribution women managers can make in both established corporate and innovative new start-up ventures is significant to the extent that their involvement boosts performance and enhances firm reputation in the stock market (Welbourne et al., 2007; Miller & Triana, 2009).

Confidence, Risk Orientation and Growth

It has been suggested that women often have less confidence than men in their entrepreneurial, business and management abilities (Wilson et al., 2007; Kirkwood, 2009). This has been attributed to a lack of management and related decision-making experience, having fewer resources at business start-up (Orser et al., 2006; Shaw et al., 2009; Watson et al., 2009) and a general perception that women's achievements are, possibly, less valued by society than men's (Reis, 2001). Self-confidence is directly associated with the concept of self-efficacy, which has been shown to contribute to the disparity between men's and women's career choices and progression within the workforce. Wilson et al. (2007) define self-efficacy as "self-confidence in a given domain" and as an element that is "based on individuals' self-perceptions of their skills and abilities" (p. 389); essentially, it reflects one's belief as to whether he/she actually has the specific abilities required to perform a particular task. Overall, the evidence would suggest that women are often less likely to perceive of themselves as entrepreneurs or business managers (Verheul et al., 2006; Wilson et al., 2007).

With seemingly a lower level of confidence in their business and management abilities, it is hardly surprising that the literature depicts women as more risk averse than men. According to Marlow and Carter (2004), women may well be more reluctant than men to take on the burden of business debt but, as explained by Brindley (2005), there may be other factors apart from gender that could account for men's and women's different attitudes towards risk. Confidence levels and risk orientation also tend to impact on one's perception of and attitude to growth. Indeed, according to Wagner (2004), fear of failure is more of a concern for women than it is for men.

Access to Finance, Undercapitalization and Underperformance

While some research has indicated that women are becoming more successful in accessing finance for their start-up and growing businesses (Brush et al., 2003), it is clear that women business owners still face particular financing challenges, especially when attempting to access debt or equity finance (Marlow & Patton, 2005). This would appear to be due, in some cases, to women's difficulty establishing an appropriate credit track record possibly as a result of having a shorter, often broken or part-time (due to maternity and family leave) employment history, or a lack of entrepreneurial or business management experience. Indeed, some studies have found that fewer women than men apply for debt capital as they feel they may not be successful (Buttner & Rosen, 1992; Fielden et al., 2003; Orser et al., 2006), often resulting in them becoming "discouraged borrowers" (Kon & Storey, 2003). This in turn has led to women entrepreneurs under-resourcing and under-capitalizing their business at the start-up stage (Henry, 2008). In comparison with their male counterparts, it has been demonstrated that women seeking to start a new business tend to be more modest and more cautious when determining the amount of finance they require to get their new venture up and running (Carter & Rosa, 1998; Marlow & Carter, 2004). Such undercapitalization has also been shown to have long-term negative impact on the business in terms of firm under-performance in terms of growth, revenues, profits and employee numbers (Carter & Marlow, 2003; Shaw et al., 2009).

Networking Practices

The management and entrepreneurship literature suggest that women may network differently from men (McGowan & Hampton, 2006; Hampton et al., 2009). For example, while men's informal networks comprise a mixture of business and personal/social contacts, women's tend to consist mainly of family and friends and are driven by a need to maintain a strong social affiliation and develop supportive relationships with other women. While such networks can provide valuable emotional support for women in their entrepreneurial or managerial roles, they tend not to have the types of connections typically needed for business success. The all-women style of composition also tends to dominate women's more formal business networks, resulting in networks that lack the appropriate range and quality of contacts (both male and female) critical to long-term business success (Henry, 2008). McGowan and Hampton (2006) categorize the different networking approaches adopted by women entrepreneurs and identify "myopic" and "high-flyer" types at opposing ends of the spectrum. Myopic networking approaches tend to be adopted by those businesswomen who have lower confidence levels, have failed to explore wider networking opportunities and have become almost completely reliant on all-female networks. In contrast, the high-flyer networking approach will typically be adopted by the more established female business owner or manager who strategically utilizes her network to grow the business and builds it on the basis of quality and expertise rather than gender. Typologies of this nature have, however, also been challenged in the literature, with the finding by Foss (2010) that there are no significant differences in the networks of female and male entrepreneurs. Rather, businessmen and women have often been shown to use similar networking channels, such as friends and business associates. Regardless of gender, a collaborative network orientation is positively correlated with business performance for both men and women (Sørenson et al., 2008, as cited by Foss, 2010, p. 88).

THE MAKE-UP OF THE VETERINARY SECTOR AND THE ROLE OF WOMEN

The Changing Veterinary Landscape

The role of veterinary professionals has widened in recent years to include greater involvement in production animals, public health, food hygiene and the protection of the health and welfare of diverse species such as laboratory animals, zoological collections and wildlife (QAA, 2002, p. 1). In addition, there has also been a significant increase in the number of companion animals. As a result, there has been a considerable increase in the number of veterinarians trained and working in the UK, particularly over the last decade. In 1997, for example, there were just over 450 new veterinary graduates registered in the UK; by 2007, this figure had risen to 628, with expectations of a further rise to 800 by the end of 2010.

In terms of the business landscape, the veterinary sector has, traditionally, been characterized by small, owner-managed, private practices, predominately run as partnerships and led by male veterinary surgeons. Large animal work has also traditionally been a key component of the workload. While, more recently, there has been a steady growth in the number of practices working with small and companion animals (Lowe, 2009), in some areas, the smaller independent practices have been replaced by corporate chains or groups comprising much larger practices. Such corporate practices take the form of large, limited companies, often operating a business model similar to that of a commercial franchise (Turley, 2010). Equine services, which were previously incorporated into many traditional or rural practices, now tend to be offered by specialist providers. Difficulties relating to late night and emergency cover have, in many areas, been alleviated through the establishment of dedicated out-of-hours facilities. Finally, the provision of farm animal veterinary services has become problematic due to rural and remote locations, antisocial working hours and, as a consequence, difficulties recruiting new graduates with the relevant specialist expertise (Lowe, 2009).

Entrepreneurship and Business Ownership

As discussed in Henry et al. (2010), given that the majority of veterinary graduates tend to work in general veterinary practice, a relatively small number take up roles in industry, R&D or areas where there are significant opportunities for innovative new venture creation. Despite this, however, veterinary medicine has proven to be a highly entrepreneurial arena, generating a considerable number of scientific research discoveries leading to new product and process developments over many decades. Examples of commercialized research that has led to new venture creation or entrepreneurial spin-off companies include new veterinary vaccines, wormers and mineral supplements; new clinical technologies; surveillance systems for emerging and re-emerging pathogens and diseases such as rabies, bluetongue and African horse sickness; veterinary food products and a range of pharmaceuticals (BVA, 2008b). As the field of veterinary medicine expands alongside the growth in small animal practices, it is expected that the sector will continue to provide an environment conducive to innovation, commercialization and entrepreneurship.

The Feminization of the Sector

The veterinary profession has traditionally been viewed as a male domain but, by 2006, 49 per cent of all working veterinarians were women, employed mostly in companion animal practice, a figure that is expected to reach 51 per cent by end of 2010 (RCVS, 2006). The majority of farm animal work continues to be conducted by male vets. Indeed, as reported by Henry et al. (2010), there has been an unprecedented increase in the number of women entering veterinary medicine in recent years (BVA, 2008a; Lowe, 2009), with females now accounting for almost 80 per cent of veterinary student admissions in the UK (RCVS, 2008). While, in the US, the number of women attracted to the profession has been rising steadily for the last 30 or 40 years, the marked gender shift is still seen as a fairly recent development (Maines, 2007). Several explanations have been offered for the feminization of veterinary medicine, including improvement in chemical restraints available for large animals; the elimination of gender-based admission discrimination and the generally caring portrayal of veterinarians in both the literature and on television (Lofstedt, 2003, p. 534). Controversially, perhaps, the marked increase in women entering the veterinary profession and, in parallel, the decline in men's participation, may also be attributed to the relatively lower salary levels of veterinary professionals (Lofstedt, 2003). This hypothesis builds on Tuchman's (1989) argument that professions deemed to be lacking in appropriate economic incentives and, by association, cultural legitimacy, may quickly lose their attraction for men. It must be noted, however, that despite the increasing number of women entering veterinary medicine and the fact that women now make up half of the veterinary workforce, most veterinary businesses, whether based on traditional practice or the commercialization of scientific research, are still led by men. Thus, to date, women have not featured prominently as business leaders within the veterinary profession, nor have they been perceived as potential entrepreneurs or innovators.

DISCUSSION

Reflecting on what we know about women generally as entrepreneurs, business owners and managers, alongside the changes that are taking place in the veterinary profession, we now focus our attention on the possible future challenges for aspiring veterinary businesswomen. The question immediately arises as to whether the imminent feminization of the veterinary sector will simply exacerbate existing challenges for aspiring women entrepreneurs seeking to establish their own veterinary practices; create an entirely new set of challenges or, potentially, open up new and relatively unexplored entrepreneurial opportunities. In this regard, we are mindful of longstanding concerns suggesting that the feminization of veterinary medicine in itself will be problematic and could, potentially, have a negative impact on the sector as a whole. For example, according to Slater and Slater (2000), the increasing number of women entering veterinary medicine has evoked several fears in relation to the standing of the profession, including a disproportionate increase in the number of small and companion animal practices, a decrease in the level of specialization and, as a result, a possible decline in standards. Further, some reports of lower salary packages being offered to women (Felsted & Volk, 2000; Rubin, 2001) may serve to drive down the average salary level of veterinary graduates, rendering the field economically unattractive. While yet to be supported by empirical evidence, these points again directly link to Tuchman's (1989) "empty field" theory regarding the legitimacy status of particular professions from which men are beginning to withdraw.

Consistent with mainstream gender and career literatures, the increasing number of women entering veterinary medicine may actually serve to further embed some of the gender inequalities reported within the sector to date, including the above-mentioned differences between job offers, pay and benefit packages made to men and women (Felsted & Volk, 2000; Rubin, 2001) and the perspective that women may be unsuitable for leadership or management roles because of concerns around maternity and family responsibilities (Slater & Slater, 2000; Henry et al., 2010). Such inequalities may prevent women from realizing their full potential within the veterinary sector, despite their increasing level of participation in the profession.

We know too that, currently, women are half as likely as men to set up their own business (GEM, 2008) and, as yet, there is no evidence to suggest that women entering the veterinary sector will be any different. For the reasons discussed earlier in this chapter, women across all sectors have simply not been coming forward in sufficient numbers to take on the role of entrepreneur or business manager. One particular reason relates to women's lack of confidence, which stems from their inherent belief that they simply do not possess the skills and abilities required for business or leadership roles. Indeed, it is of some concern that women veterinary students in particular have been found to be lacking confidence in their business, management and financial abilities (Brown and Silverman, 1999). Interestingly, such skills have since been identified as critical to veterinary practice and, as a consequence, to modern veterinary curricula (Kogan et al., 2005). Thus, improving their own level of self-efficacy will pose a particular challenge for future women veterinarians entering a sector where, currently at least, the dominant business model is still that of the small private partnership or limited company.

The longstanding gender stereotypes and the negative perceptions relating to women's perceived capabilities as managers will, no doubt, continue to represent significant challenges for women aspiring to veterinary business leadership roles. In this regard, issues relating to women's attitude to risk and their lack of confidence in their own entrepreneurial abilities pose particular challenges that need attention. From the evidence presented in our review of the literature, it is unlikely that such issues will rectify themselves in the veterinary sector without some sort of structured intervention. Indeed, it is of particular concern that one of the key strategies typically employed by women to overcome such challenges includes simply lowering their career aspirations, that is, "settling" for less, choosing roles that are less demanding, prestigious or rewarding (Slater & Slater, 2000). This type of coping strategy has already been evidenced in human medicine (Driscoll, 2010).

On a more positive note, reflecting on the above challenges from an opportunity perspective, we contend that veterinary business owners and managers will still be very much in demand in the future, and women veterinarians, who will shortly constitute the bulk of the workforce, will be needed to fill such roles. In this regard, the marked difference between men's and women's management styles may prove advantageous. For example, the literature reports women as having superior diplomatic skills, being more customer-oriented and placing greater value on the human capital and quality aspects of their business (Henry, 2008). Such attributes are particularly well suited to the caring and client interaction aspect of veterinary practice. Indeed, women in human medicine have been shown to spend more time in consultations with patients than their male counterparts (Driscoll, 2010). In addition, from a commercial perspective, the emerging evidence in the literature that women managers make a valuable impact in both corporate and small businesses in terms of boosting performance and enhancing firm reputation in the stock market (Welbourne et al., 2007; Miller & Triana, 2009) should be welcome news to existing veterinary businesses struggling to increase profit margins.

Further, it is our view that the future veterinary landscape will offer opportunities for women to create innovative new veterinary practices and to buy into more established practices where senior partners are seeking to retire. In addition, a range of new business and management opportunities will exist within large corporate practices and chains in the form of roles as senior managers, executives or entrepreneurs franchising a branded practice outlet. It is also worth noting that, as evidenced in other sectors where large corporates and multinational companies have entered the market, significant positive "spill-over" effects by way of local supply opportunities, specialist services or spin-out/spin-in niche ventures could also justifiably be anticipated (McKeon et al., 2004).

While other reported challenges for aspiring women business owners and managers have included lower levels of education and work experience, these do not typically feature as issues of concern in veterinary medicine. Third-level veterinary medicine education courses have the highest set of entry criteria of the traditional professions, and students, whether male or female, are required to complete the same amount of experiential learning and clinical placement through the compulsory Extramural Studies (EMS) component of their degrees. Thus, when they enter practice following graduation, there should, in theory, be no difference between males and females in terms of their education and work experience. This latter point, however, has been debated in the literature, with a suggestion that male veterinary students actually get more hands-on experience in their EMS than their female counterparts (Ward, 2004).

Reflecting further on the business, gender and management literatures in the context of the veterinary profession, we contend that one of women's biggest challenges in the future will continue to relate to maternity leave and family responsibilities. We argue this based partly on trends in the closely related field of human medicine (O'Connor, 2009; Driscoll, 2010) and the stark reality that little has changed in recent years by way of support for working mothers. Until a workable solution to this problem is found, women will continue to be faced with the dilemma of whether to simply forego the opportunity to have a family, accept the continuous struggle to balance work and family commitments or lower their career (including business ownership and management) aspirations (Slater & Slater, 2000; Driscoll, 2010). However, the feminization of the veterinary sector along with the changes occurring in the veterinary business landscape could well accommodate this dilemma by opening up opportunities for flexible or part-time working as well as shared business ownership. With more women in the profession there should also be greater recognition and understanding of the challenges facing female veterinary business owners and managers. Indeed, the "empty field" phenomenon should afford women the opportunity to significantly reshape the profession, promoting more family-friendly work practices and creating new business models based on entrepreneurial partnerships.

CONCLUSIONS AND AVENUES FOR FUTURE RESEARCH

This chapter highlighted some of the generic challenges faced by female business owners and managers and discussed these in the context of the veterinary profession. In this regard, particular attention was paid to the imminent gender shift towards a predominantly female-led veterinary workforce. In our review of the literature, we found gender-biased and stereotypical perspectives to have an important impact on the way in which women managers are viewed and, subsequently, the roles they take on in the workforce. Management and leadership styles, confidence, risk-orientation, attitude to growth, access to capital and networking strategies were all identified as pertinent themes in the literature, which pose challenges to women aspiring to business ownership or management.

In our discussion, we were mindful of the changing veterinary business landscape, and so attempted to identify the potential challenges, as well as the opportunities, that might emerge for women veterinarians in the future. The tradition in other industries of women simply not coming forward to take on entrepreneurial leadership roles; the lack of confidence in one's own business, management and financial skills; feminized management and leadership styles and family responsibilities were all identified as current key challenges for women that could justifiably be expected to transfer into the veterinary profession.

It is our view that the feminization of the veterinary sector may serve to further embed some of the traditional gendered perspectives and stereotypical views of women "not being suitable" for management and leadership positions. As evidenced in the literature, the unique challenges faced by women business managers and owners in the small firms context primarily relate to their gender and result from widely held gender stereotypes and assumptions (Brush et al., 2001; Marlow & Patton, 2005). Such assumptions can impact upon women's acceptance as competent managers or businesswomen, which in turn may be detrimental to establishing a client base or recruiting and retaining male staff.

Notwithstanding the above, there would, however, appear to be new opportunities opening up for future women veterinarians to pursue entrepreneurial careers within large veterinary corporates, branded chains or multinationals. In addition, women will still have the option of establishing their own independent veterinary practice. The key question here is how do we best prepare our future veterinary businesswomen to fully exploit such opportunities? Despite the many innovative business and management opportunities we anticipate for the veterinary sector, we expect that many of the gender-related challenges discussed in this chapter will remain. Thus, it is clear that some sort of intervention within veterinary undergraduate education is needed if we are to embrace the imminent changes and avoid the trap of women "settling for less" (Slater & Slater, 2000; O'Connor, 2009; Driscoll, 2010).

The changing veterinary business landscape, coupled with the growing importance of commercial performance in what is fast becoming a highly competitive industry, may encourage women to view partnership forms of entrepreneurship as more suited to their needs. Business structures of this nature may provide women with more flexibility, the option to work part-time as and when required and the opportunity to share both risk and reward. Such partnership-style businesses, which could take the form of traditional partnerships, limited liability partnerships (LLPs) or limited companies, should not only help women overcome some of the key challenges discussed above, but could also help alleviate stress and boost mental health and well-being, a particular concern within the veterinary profession (Bartram et al., 2009). Further, if such partnership arrangements strategically include both male and female veterinarians, additional gendered assumptions and stereotypical views will also be overcome. Of course, this puts further emphasis on the need for educational intervention to boost skills and abilities in business, management and financial areas. Such skills are, with a few exceptions, considered lacking in veterinary undergraduate curricula, despite having been deemed critical to successful veterinary practice (Kogan et al., 2005).

In light of this, we suggest future research focuses on what can be done to help female veterinarians overcome business and management challenges, and explore how future aspiring veterinary entrepreneurs can be encouraged to fully exploit the many opportunities that are beginning to emerge within the sector. In this regard, structured educational programmes that focus on enhancing business and management skills and developing an entrepreneurial mindset will have an important role to play (Henry & Treanor, 2010). Future studies should also seek to assess the economic costs associated with women veterinarians not taking on business management and leadership roles within the sector, or equally, not exploiting the full range of entrepreneurial opportunities that are beginning to emerge. After all, in the case of the veterinary profession, the "empty field" (Tuchman, 1989) might well present a unique opportunity for women to significantly reshape the sector to better meet the needs of its workforce.

REFERENCES

Ahl, H. (2004). *The Scientific Reproduction of Gender Inequality: A Discourse Analysis of Research Texts on Women's Entrepreneurship*, Malmo: Liber.

Bandura, A. (1992). "Exercise of personal agency through the self-efficacy mechanism", in R. Schwartzer (ed.), *Self-efficacy: Thought Control of Action*, Washington DC: Hemisphere, pp. 3–38.

Bartram, D.J., Yadegarfar, G. & Baldwin, D.S. (2009). "A cross-sectional study of mental health and well-being and their associations in the veterinary profession", *Social Psychiatry and Psychiatric Epidemiology*, **44**(12), 1075–85.

Baughn, C., Bee-Leng, C. & Neupert, K.E. (2006). "The normative context for women's participation in entrepreneurship: A multicountry study", *Entrepreneurship Theory and Practice*, **30**(5), 687–708.

Betz, N.E. & Fitzgerald, L.F. (1987). *The Career Psychology of Women*, London: Academic Press.

Brindley, C.S. (2005). "Barriers to women achieving their entrepreneurial potential: women and risk", *International Journal of Entrepreneurial Behaviour and Research*, **11**(2), 144–161.

Brown, J.P. & Silverman, J.D. (1999). "The current and future market for veterinarians and veterinary medical services in the United States", *Journal of the American Veterinary Association*, **215**(2), 161–83.

Bruni, A., Gherardi, S. & Poggio, B. (2004). "Entrepreneur mentality, gender and the study of women entrepreneurs", *Journal of Organizational Change*, **17**(3), 256–68.

Brush, C., Carter, N., Gatewood, E., Green, P. & Hart, M. (2001). *The Diana Project, Women Business Owners and Equity Capital: The Myths Dispelled*, Insight Report, Kansas City, MO: Kauffman Center for Entrepreneurial Leadership.

Brush, C., Carter, N., Gatewood, E., Green, P. & Hart, M. (2003). "Women entrepreneurs who break through to equity financing: The influence of human, social and financial capital", *Venture Capital*, **5**(1), 1–28.
Buttner, E.H. & Rosen, B. (1992). "Rejection in the loan application process: Male and female entrepreneurs' perceptions and subsequent intentions", *Journal of Small Business Management*, **30**(1), 58–65.
BVA – British Veterinary Association/AVS – Association of Veterinary Students (2008a). "Survey 2008", available at: http:www.bva.co.uk/student_centre/Student_survey.aspx; accessed 21 November 2010.
BVA – British Veterinary Association (2008b). "Policy Brief: The relevance of research & development to the veterinary profession", December, available at: www.bva.co.uk, accessed 21 November 2010.
Carter, S. & Marlow, S. (2003). "Professional attainment as a challenge to gender disadvantage in entrepreneurship", paper presented at the 48th International Small Business Conference, June, Belfast.
Carter, S. & Rosa, P. (1998). "The financing of male- and female-owned businesses", *Entrepreneurship and Regional Development*, **10**(3), 225–41.
Carter, S. & Shaw, E. (2006). *Women's Business Ownership: Recent Research and Policy Developments*, Report to the Small Business Service, UK, available at: http://www.berr.gov.uk/files/file38330.pdf; accessed 21 November 2010.
Cordano, M., Scherer, R.F. & Owen, C.L. (2002). "Attitudes toward women as managers: Sex versus culture", *Women in Management Review*, **17**(2), 51–60.
Delmar, F. (2001). "Women entrepreneurship: Assessing data availability and future needs", paper presented at the workshop on Improving Statistics on SMEs and Entrepreneurship, OECD, Paris, 17–19 September.
Dodge, K.A., Gilroy, F.D. & Fenzel, L.M. (1995). "Requisite management characteristics revisited: two decades later", *Journal of Social Behavior and Personality*, **10**(6), 253–64.
Driscoll, M. (2010). "Women doctors: the waste of money you'll be glad to see", *The Sunday Times*, 9 May available at http://www.timesonline.co.uk/tol/life_and_style/health/features/article7120486.ece; accessed 22 November 2010.
European Commission (2008). *Promotion of Women Innovators and Entrepreneurship Final Report*, Enterprise and Industry Directorate General, Brussels, July.
Felsted, K.E. & Volk, J. (2000). "Why do women earn less?", *Vet Economics*, **41**(8), 33–8.
Fielden S.L., Davidson M.J., Dawe, A.J. and Makin P.J. (2003). "Factors inhibiting the economic growth of female owned small businesses in North West England", *Journal of Small Business and Enterprise Development*, **10**(2), 152–66.
Fitzgerald, L.F. and O'Crites, J.O. (1980). "Towards a career psychology of women: What do we know? What do we need to know?", *Journal of Counselling Psychology*, **27**(1), 44–62.
Foss, L. (2010). "Research on entrepreneur networks: The case for a constructionist feminist theory", *International Journal of Gender and Entrepreneurship*, **2**(1), 83–102.
Foss, L. & Henry, C. (2010). "Gender and innovation: Exploring the hegemonic voice", paper presented at the Gender, Work and Organisation Conference, Keele University, 20–23 June.
Gatewood, E., Shaver, K., Powers, J. & Gartner, W.B. (2002). "Entrepreneurial expectancy, task effort, and performance", *Entrepreneurship Theory and Practice*, **27** (2), 187–206.

GEM – Global Entrepreneurship Monitor (2008). *GEM 2007 Report on Women and Entrepreneurship*, available at: http://www.gemconsortium.org; accessed 21 November 2010.

GEM – Global Entrepreneurship Monitor (2010). *GEM 2009 Global Report*, available at: http://www.gemconsortium.org; accessed 21 November 2010.

Gowan, M. & Trevino, M. (1998). "An examination of gender differences in Mexican-American attitudes toward family and career roles", *Sex Roles*, **38**(11–12), 1079–93.

Gupta, V.K., Turban, D.B., Wasti, S.A. & Sikdar, A. (2009). "The role of gender stereotypes in perceptions of entrepreneurs and intentions to become an entrepreneur", *Entrepreneurship Theory and Practice*, **33**(2), 397–417.

Hampton, A., Cooper, S. & McGowan, P. (2009). "Female entrepreneurial networks and networking activity in technology-based ventures: An exploratory study", *International Small Business Journal*, **27**(2), 193–214.

Henry, C. (2008). "Women entrepreneurs", in Charles Wankel (ed.), *21st Century Management: A Reference Handbook*, Vol. 1, Thousand Oaks, CA: Sage, pp. 51–9.

Henry, C. & Johnston, K. (2007). "Introduction", in N.M. Carter, C. Henry, B.O Cinnéide & K. Johnston (eds), *Female Entrepreneurship: Implications for Education, Training and Policy*, Abingdon: Routledge, pp. 1–7.

Henry, C. and Kennedy, S. (2003). "In search of a new Celtic Tiger – female entrepreneurship in Ireland", in John Butler (ed.), *New Perspectives on Women Entrepreneurs*, Vol. 3, in Research in Entrepreneurship and Management Series, Hong Kong: Information Age Publishing, Inc.

Henry, C. & Treanor, L. (2010). "Entrepreneurship education and veterinary medicine: Enhancing employable skills", *Journal of Education & Training*, **52**(8/9), 607–23.

Henry, C., Baillie, S. & Treanor, L. (2010). "Encouraging women's entrepreneurship in the sciences: Women in veterinary medicine", in P. Wynarczyk and S. Marlow (eds), *Innovating Women: Contributions to Technological Advancement*, Bingley: Emerald Publishing.

Hofstede, G. (1980). *Culture's Consequences: International Difference in Work Related Values*, London: Sage.

Idris, A. (2009). "Management styles and innovation in women-owned enterprises", *African Journal of Business Management*, **3**(9), 416–25.

Jennings, J.E. & McDougald, M.S. (2007). "Work–family interface experiences and coping strategies: Implications for entrepreneurship research and practice", *Academy of Management Review*, **32**(3), 747–60.

Kauffman, D. & Fetters, M.L. (1980). "Work motivation and job values among professional men and women: A new accounting", *Journal of Vocational Behavior*, **17**(3), December, 251–62.

Kirkwood, J. (2009). "Is a lack of self-confidence hindering women entrepreneurs?", *International Journal of Gender and Entrepreneurship*, **1**(2), 118–33.

Kogan, L.R, McConnell, S.L. & Schoenfeld-Tacher, R. (2005). "Perspectives in professional education: Response of a veterinary college to career development needs identified in the KPMG LLP study", *Journal of the American Veterinary Medical Association*, **226**(7).

Kon, Y. & Storey, D.J. (2003). "A theory of discouraged borrowers", *Small Business Economics*, **21**(1), 37–49.

Langowitz, N. & Minniti, M. (2007). "The entrepreneurial propensity of women", *Entrepreneurship Theory and Practice*, **31**(3), 341–64.

Lofstedt, J. (2003). "Gender and veterinary medicine", *Canadian Veterinary Journal*, **44**(7), 533–5.

Lowe, P. (2009). *Unlocking Potential – A Report on Veterinary Expertise in Food Animal Production*, DEFRA (Department for Environment, Food and Rural Affairs), UK.

Maines, R. (2007). "Why are women crowding into veterinary medicine but are not lining up to become engineers?", *Chronicleonline*, Cornell University, 12 June, available at: http://www.news.cornell.edu/stories/june07/women.vets.vs.eng.sl.html; accessed 22 November 2010.

Marlow, S. & Carter, S. (2004). "Accounting for change: Professional status, gender disadvantage and self-employment", *Women in Management Review*, **19**(1), 5–16.

Marlow, S. & Patton, D. (2005). "All credit to men? Entrepreneurship, finance and gender", *Entrepreneurship Theory and Practice*, **29**(6), 717–35.

Marlow, S., Carter, S. & Shaw, E. (2008). "Constructing female entrepreneurship policy in the UK: Is the US a relevant benchmark?", *Environment and Planning C: Government and Policy*, **26**(2), 335–51.

McGowan, P. & Hampton, A. (2006). "An exploration of networking practices of female entrepreneurs", in N.M. Carter, C. Henry, B.O Cinnéide & K. Johnston (eds), *Female Entrepreneurship: Implications for Education, Training and Policy*, Abingdon: Routledge, pp. 110–33.

McKeon, H. Johnston, K. & Henry C. (2004). "The role of MNCs in entrepreneurial learning", *Journal of Education and Training*, **46**(8/9), 433–43.

Miller, T. & Triana, M.C. (2009). "Demographic diversity in the boardroom: Mediators of the board diversity–firm performance relationship", *Journal of Management Studies*, **46**(5), 755–86.

Muller, H.J. & Rowell, M. (1997). "Mexican women managers: An emerging profile", *Human Resources Management*, **36**(4), 423–35.

Oakley, A. (1973). *Sex, Gender and Society*, London: Temple Smith.

O'Connor, V. (2009). "Women in the medical profession", unpublished Masters thesis, Dundalk Institute of Technology, Ireland.

Orser, B., Riding, A.L. & Manley, K. (2006). "Women entrepreneurs and financial capital", *Entrepreneurship Theory and Practice*, **30**(5), 643–65.

Peus, C. & Traut-Mattausch, E. (2008). "Factors influencing women managers' success", in Charles Wankel (ed.), *21st Century Management: A Reference Handbook*, Vol. 1, Thousand Oaks, CA: Sage, pp. 157–66.

Prowess (2007). *Under the Microscope: Female Entrepreneurs in SECT*, available at: http://www.prowess.org.uk/documents/UndertheMicroscope_000.pdf; accessed 21 November 2010.

QAA – Quality Assurance Agency (2002), *Veterinary Science – Subject Benchmark Statements*, Quality Assurance for Higher Education, Gloucester.

RCVS – Royal College of Veterinary Surgeons (2006). *The UK Veterinary Profession in 2006: The Findings of a Survey of the Profession, Conducted by the Royal College of Veterinary Surgeons*, June, available at: http://www.rcvs.org.uk/shared_asp_files/uploadedfiles/97d3daf0-9567-4b2f-9972-b0a86cfb13c7_surveyprofession2006.pdf; accessed 21 November 2010.

RCVS – Royal College of Veterinary Surgeons (2008). "Drive to increase diversity of veterinary profession", 8 May, available at: http:www.rcvs.org.uk/templates/Internal.asp?NodeID=307905; accessed 21 November 2010.

Reis, S.M. (2001). "Towards a theory of creativity in diverse creative women",

in M. Bloom and T. Gullota (eds), *Promoting Creativity Across the Life Span*, Washington DC: CWLA, pp. 231–76.
Rosa, P. & Dawson, A. (2006). "Gender and the commercialization of university science: Academic founders of spinout companies", *Entrepreneurship and Regional Development*, **18**(4), 341–66.
Rubin, H.E. (2001). "Generation and gender – a critical mix", *JAVMA*, **218**(11), 1753–4.
Schein, V.E. (2001). "A global look at psychological barriers to women's progress in management", *Journal of Social Issues*, **57**(4), 675–88.
Schein, V.E. & Mueller, R. (1990). "Sex role stereotyping and requisite management characteristics: A cross cultural look", paper presented at the 22nd International Congress of Applied Psychology, Kyoto, Japan.
Shaw, E., Marlow, S., Lam, W. & Carter, S. (2009). "Gender and entrepreneurial capital: Implications for firm performance", *International Journal of Gender and Entrepreneurship*, **1**(1), 25–41.
Slater, R.S. & Slater, M.S. (2000). "Women in veterinary medicine", *Journal of the American Veterinary Medical Association*, **217**(4), 472–6.
Sørenson, R.L., Folker, C.A. & Brigham, K.H. (2008). "The collaborative network orientation: Achieving business success through collaborative relationships", *Entrepreneurship Theory and Practice*, **32**(4), 615–34.
Stephens, J.K. & Greer, C.R. (1995). "Doing business in Mexico: understanding cultural differences", *Organizational Dynamics*, **24**(1), 39–55.
Terrell, K. & Troilo, M. (2010). "Values and female entrepreneurship", *International Journal of Gender and Entrepreneurship*, **2**(3), 260–86.
Tuchman, G. (1989). *Edging Women Out: Victorian Novelists, Publishers and Social Change*, New Haven, CT: Yale University Press.
Turley, G. (2010). "Corporate practice and the generation Y vet graduate", *Veterinary Business Journal* (Personnel), December/January, 38–9.
Verheul, I., Stel, A.J. von & Thurik, A.R. (2006). "Explaining female and male entrepreneurship at the country level", *Entrepreneurship and Regional Development*, **18**(2), 151–83.
Wagner, J. (2004). "What a difference a Y makes: Female and male nascent entrepreneurship in Germany", *Small Business Economics*, **28**(1), 1–21.
Ward, C. (2004). "An insight into gender differences in the next generation of veterinary graduates", *Veterinary Times*, 22 November.
Watson, J., Newby, R. & Mahuka, A. (2009). "Gender and the SME finance gap", *International Journal of Gender and Entrepreneurship*, **1**(1), 42–56.
Welbourne, T.M., Cycyota, C.S. & Ferrante, C.J. (2007). "Wall Street reaction to women in IPOs: An examination of gender diversity in top management teams", *Group & Organization Manag*ement, **32**(5), 534–47.
Welter, F. & Smallbone, D. (2008). "Women's entrepreneurship from an institutional perspective: The case of Uzbekistan", *International Entrepreneurship and Management Journal*, **4**(4), 505–20.
Williams, J.E. & Best, D.L. (1990). *Measuring Sex Stereotypes: A Multination Study*, Newbury Park, California: Sage.
Wilson, F. (2003). *Organizational Behaviour and Gender*, Aldershot: Ashgate Publishing Ltd.
Wilson, F., Kickul, J. & Marlino, D. (2007). "Gender, entrepreneurial self-efficacy, and entrepreneurial career intentions: Implications for entrepreneurship education", *Entrepreneurship Theory and Practice*, **31**(3), 387–406.

Women's Enterprise Task Force (2009). *Greater Return on Women's Enterprise (GROWE)*, available at: http://www.womensenterprisetaskforce.co.uk/growe_report.html; accessed 21 November 2010.
World Economic Forum (2006, 2007). Global Gender Gap Report. Harvard University and University of California, Berkeley, available at: http://www.weforum.org/pdf/gendergap/report2007.pdf; accessed 23 November 2010.

11. Who's minding the kids? Work and family issues among owners of small business enterprises in Ireland

Eileen Drew and Anne Laure Humbert

This chapter addresses the largely under-researched theme of how entrepreneurs in Ireland manage their business lives in parallel with their family commitments, with specific reference to dependent children. Since the emergence of dual-earner couples as "typical", there has been an expanding attention to the working lives of parents and the issue of work–family conflict in the context of employment. This strand of literature sought to explain patterns of working, for example, sector of employment, hours of work and flexibility, in terms of highly gendered preferences. The discourse has moved from woman/mother/family-friendly to more gender-neutral work–life balance (WLB), in tracking the responses of organizations to the needs of their employees, in the broader context of ability to provide family care. Some research examined both sides of the "reconciliation" divide by surveying the needs of employers and employees (Drew et al., 2003; O'Brien & Shemilt, 2003). These and subsequent studies noted that even in organizations with well-developed policies in place, take-up of WLB arrangements was highly gendered and associated with lower-level occupations (clerical/administrative). It has been further observed that, in an Irish context, managers fail to lead by example (Drew & Murtagh, 2005) and often adopt a gatekeeping role in the practice and availability of WLB arrangements for themselves and their staff (Drew & Daverth, 2009). With the growth of smaller enterprises a gap is evident in our knowledge of how entrepreneurs behave in their unique multi-functional roles (as owner employer/employee), particularly when they become parents.

Managers in employment frequently propound their need for WLB in their own lives and those of their staff, however they rarely champion flexible working by working part-time or availing of family-related leave themselves. Indeed, it has been demonstrated that long hours, in employment, are a perceived necessary hallmark of management, and advancement within management ranks. By implication therefore, any deviation towards flexible working by employees can be construed as demonstrating a lack of commitment to their careers. This rigidity in the culture of management (Humphreys et al., 1999; Drew et al., 2003) contributes to the glass ceiling effect that deflects women from aspiring to, or progressing within, the management track.

While there is a growing understanding of these issues in employment, they have seldom been considered within the context of entrepreneurship. With the rising importance of entrepreneurship throughout developed economies, it is important to investigate the degree to which WLB arrangements are created by small business owners. This is especially relevant in an Irish context given the much lower levels of female entrepreneurship compared with other EU countries. Therefore, questions of interest include: do small business owners replicate the HR practices of larger employers, which contribute to gender segregation? Or do entrepreneurs create and avail of alternative working practices that are better suited to WLB? Can running SMEs offer parents a means of better reconciling working and family roles? If so, are there gender differences in the degree of adherence to long hours versus flexible working patterns of entrepreneurs?

Evidence from the literature on women holding management posts in larger organizations suggests that, in response to role conflicts, a higher proportion of women than men exit from the employment sphere in order to escape from the "family-hostile" cultures of many private and public sector organizations. Some of these women take time out to spend with their children while a small, but growing, proportion gravitate to setting up small businesses to allow them to manage their conflicting schedules and spend more time at home/with their child(ren). Are such strategies evident among Irish entrepreneurs? This chapter focuses on work–family issues among small business managers and entrepreneurs in Ireland, with particular attention to their status as parents.

BACKGROUND

In order to understand the conditions prevailing in Ireland, a brief outline is presented of some key demographic and labour market changes along with current levels of entrepreneurship, which form a backdrop to the survey of entrepreneurship among parents of dependent children.

Since the 1970s, Ireland has experienced a major shift from a predominantly agrarian economy to a fast-growing service-led economy. Ireland's entry to the European Union in 1973 marked a transition towards EU norms in terms of fertility rates, rising female labour force participation, accompanied by higher levels of educational attainment by women.

In 1970, Ireland's total fertility rate was 3.87 (Fahy, 2001), the highest rate in the EU, due to the strong influence of the Catholic Church over personal morals and on the political system: contraception, divorce and abortion[1] were still illegal. Following the legalization of contraception, the fertility rate dropped to levels comparable to other EU member states (1.93 in 1997). During the last decade, fertility has risen to 2.01 in 2008, which saw the highest number of births (75000) in the state since 1898, in parallel with a rise in the age of mothers at first birth from 27.5 years in 1955 to 28.9 years in 2008 (CSO, 2010).

Alongside demographic changes, Ireland has experienced a feminization of education, most notably in secondary and tertiary rates of educational attainment. The proportion of the population aged 25–34 years with a third-level qualification is 51 per cent among women compared with 39 per cent for men. Furthermore, only 9 per cent of young women leave the secondary school system early while 14 per cent of young men drop out of school before gaining a secondary qualification (Lunn et al., 2009).

The extraordinary economic growth witnessed in Ireland since the mid-1990s (up to 2008), has been a major factor in women's rising labour market representation. By 2008, Ireland's female employment rate had met/exceeded the Lisbon target of 60 per cent. This is in strong contrast to the female participation of 28 per cent in 1971, when married women were forced out of paid employment due to the existence of the "Marriage Bar"[2] which prohibited their participation throughout the public sector and in many private companies. Despite the abolition of the Marriage Bar in 1973, women's participation in the Irish labour market remained well below the EU average until the 1990s.

According to the Global Entrepreneurship Monitor (GEM, 2009) report for Ireland 2007, the rate of entrepreneurial activity among men has always been higher than for women and a gender gap exists. However, the GEM data show that while the percentage of men engaged in early-stage entrepreneurial activity has been relatively stable (10.6 per cent in 2007) the percentage for women has increased to 5.9 per cent, from 4.2 per cent in 2006. This remains lower than in the US (7.2 per cent). The report flags the factors inhibiting entrepreneurial growth in Ireland that affect women's start-up prospects to a greater extent than men's: fewer women (29 per cent) have a circle of acquaintances who are in business compared with men (49 per cent); more men (56 per cent) are confident about starting/running a business compared with women (42 per cent); perceptions of good business prospects are higher among men (50 per cent) than women (42 per cent) and fear of failure is also higher among women (40 per cent) than men (35 per cent). The GEM predicts that if more women were involved in early-stage entrepreneurship, the rate at which people are setting up new businesses in Ireland would begin to rival that of the US.

Having briefly outlined the altered demographic, educational, economic and entrepreneurial context in Ireland, the next section reviews the international literature on entrepreneurship and family. This examines the existing literature and identifies a gap in the gendering of work–family conflict and how this is addressed (or not) by men and women who run small businesses.

LITERATURE REVIEW

Early research on entrepreneurship, as in management, assumed a "male norm" that ignored any work/business interaction with home/family. The exceptions to this explored family in the context of generational change and the transfer of leadership and ownership within families. The next main body of research concentrated on work–family conflict, usually from the perspective of mothers running/owning SMEs. By the 1990s the theme of work–life balance, and whether entrepreneurship offered women a way of achieving it, became hotly debated.

Compared with the literature on work–family in the employment context, there has been relatively little research on work–family issues among entrepreneurs and what does exist is based mainly on experience in the US and other non-EU states such as Australia, Israel, South Africa and New Zealand (Lerner et al., 1997; Smith, 2000; Schindehutte et al., 2003; Dupuis & de Bruin 2004). Research into family and entrepreneurship stemmed initially from establishing the motivation for business start-up and the influence of "family" connections in spurring business creation and providing support and labour inputs. Having a parent or sibling in business has been noted as a very positive factor in embarking on entrepreneurship (Dyer & Handler, 1994) and may contribute to the viability and/or growth of a family business. There remains a major lacuna in research that examines running a small enterprise ownership in the context of rearing young children and their mutual implications.

With the global surge of women-led business start-ups it became necessary to address this research deficit, hence the next strand of publications that explored women's two *conflicting* roles of work and family. In recognition of their shift from home-based to work-based production, this research assumed that only women experience conflict in their dual roles.

Work–Family Conflict

Stoner et al. (1990) located the critical problem of the tension between personal life and career pursuits as a specifically female one, explained in terms of "interrole conflict". The authors emphasized the lack of research into this topic:

> to date, most entrepreneurial and small business studies have not fully explored the variables influencing work–home role conflict. The existing work–family role conflict literature has a distinctive non-entrepreneurial slant, in that it deals with women who are employees rather than owners/managers, and often employs samples that are predominantly male. (ibid., p. 30)

In their exploratory study of 300 female business owners in the US, Stoner et al. (1990) showed that time pressures (in the form of long working hours) and family size (younger children) and support (from family – most notably their partner) were among the key variables affecting work–home role conflict. "Husbands are often nonsupportive, and may even be obstructive to the careers of their entrepreneurial wives" (ibid., p. 31). Furthermore, the authors noted that the demands of their family role were permitted to intrude into the work role of mothers in business. For men, the opposite was true. Their findings support the belief that female SME owners experience significant interference from, or conflict between, work and home roles. The authors also showed that marital status, number of children and hours worked are not significantly related to work–home role conflict. They ascribe this apparent contradiction to the fact that in running small businesses the women have autonomy and control that "may permit them to structure time to accommodate many dimensions affecting work–home conflict" (ibid., p. 38).

According to Kim and Ling (2001) work–family conflict can be allocated to three broad categories (job–parent conflict; job–homemaker conflict and job–spouse conflict), with some work undertaken on the first category. However, where children are considered to be a significant factor, research has concentrated on women only, rather than entrepreneurial men or parents. Work by Bowen and Hisrich (1986) in the US traced the emergence of the female entrepreneur using a career development perspective. They highlighted the limitations of earlier research in terms of its use of small samples and over-reliance on cross-sectional studies. Noting the lack of even basic demographic information on women small business owners, the authors pointed to Texas-based research showing that female entrepreneurs rated their business as a higher priority than their family. Support for this contention comes from Bourne's (2006) US-based study of ten women entrepreneurs. Contrary to Stoner et al. (1990) who suggested that women allow family to infiltrate business life, the women in Bourne's (2006) study demonstrated primacy to the work sphere.

Aldrich and Cliff (2003) stressed that family and businesses are inextricably linked and urged entrepreneurship scholars to adopt a *family embeddedness* perspective on new venture creation, in recognition of the changes in North America's family system. This dynamic focus acknowledges the shifts that can occur during a life course via changing roles and relationships reflecting the "interweave of work, family, and community role trajectories, the interdependencies of paths among family members, and the changing circumstances and options of both families and family businesses" (ibid., p. 579). The authors traced how changing demographics, most notably in family composition, have implications for the emergence and recognition of entrepreneurial opportunities, for example in stimulating new ventures arising from divorce or other family disruptions. Aldrich and Cliff (2003) also emphasized how women's changing roles (from home- to market-based work) have stimulated new enterprises. In response to the rise in dual-income couples with young children, new products and services have emerged to fill demand, for example, childcare, processed meals, housecleaning (to which Internet online shopping/home delivery might be added). In the authors' view (ibid.) the lingering adherence to the division of labour whereby women continue to have primary responsibility for household chores and childcare even when employed, represents an impediment to the emergence and growth of women-led businesses.

Motherhood and entrepreneurship were explored by Schindehutte et al. (2003) who compared the impacts on children of combining parenting and business in South Africa and the US, but their research largely ignored issues related to fatherhood and entrepreneurship. The study showed that while women-owned businesses are disruptive to family life, children did not resent this. For Schindehutte et al. (ibid., p. 104) the entrepreneurial mother can be viewed as a positive role model, a testimony to "the ability of female entrepreneurs to achieve work–family balance".

Shelton (2006, p. 285) utilized a conceptual framework to predict the effectiveness of strategies for "structurally reducing work–family conflict by manipulating roles, given the salience of work and family roles and resources available to the female entrepreneur". Shelton (2006) places emphasis on work–family management strategies and how these can contribute to the performance and growth of women-led businesses. In outlining appropriate strategies, such as delegating of venture roles through participative management practices and team building, in common with other researchers, Shelton concentrated solely on women-owned business and ignored the behaviour of male partners and entrepreneurs as agents in sharing the responsibilities associated with family care and domestic work. If only women are engaged in addressing work–family conflict (which may even lead them to embark upon entrepreneurship as a coping strategy) this leaves the business world as a male-dominated domain where men need not take on/share responsibility for vital activities that occur outside the business.

Work–Life Balance

An emerging theme in employment and entrepreneurial research during the 1980s was work–life balance or WLB. Some early studies examined this as an issue of concern for both male and female business owners (Goffee & Scase, 1983; Honig-Haftel & Martin,1986), but the topic quickly became relegated to a "woman's issue". For example, one study examined time use patterns and the use of household help by self-employed women, suggesting that increased responsibility for family can provide some explanation for the lower profitability of women's firms (Longstreth et al., 1987).

Since these early studies, achieving better WLB has been systematically associated with motivations and obstacles to female entrepreneurship. In the context of Internet growth, for instance, Abarbanal (2008) highlights the economic conditions in which women are exiting from the constraints of traditional corporate jobs in order to create enterprises. Reasons cited for this exodus relate to: freedom and flexibility, desire for challenge and personal achievement, giving rise to the (derogatory) term "mompreneurs" to facilitate: "creating home-based activities that would allow them control over their time so they could be more available to their young families" (ibid., p. 32). Women's exodus to entrepreneurship was also noted by Buttner and Moore (1997) who claimed that work–life balance emerged among the top four motivators to set up businesses, based on a study involving 129 women in the US who completed a survey questionnaire and attended focus group sessions. Based on a Canadian study, Fenwick (2002) also saw WLB as a positive factor influencing women's choice to enter business enterprise by allowing them more freedom and control over their lives.

Work by Dupuis and de Bruin (2004) referred to blurring of the boundaries and the way work and life traverse, which are not captured in WLB. They challenged the appropriateness of the concept for SME owners, due to the significant personal and business restraints facing them. The authors acknowledge that SMEs could more readily implement flexible policies due to less role specialization and staff who would be more likely to multitask. Yet the authors point out that WLB policies remain more closely associated with larger organizations.

One study explored *both* women and men entrepreneurs in terms of similarity and difference. Among their sample of entrepreneurs drawn from US MBA alumni, DeMartino and Barbato (2003) found that a higher proportion of women become entrepreneurs in order to balance work and family while a higher proportion of men sought wealth creation and/or economic advancement. These gender differences are greater among married entrepreneurs with dependent children. According to DeMartino and Barbato (ibid., p. 816), "entrepreneurship as a career can offer a degree of flexibility and balance that some other careers do not offer". Further support for this comes from Still and Timms (2000) using focus groups with 63 women owners of small businesses in Australia. Their participants were motivated to start a business because of lifestyle issues, that is, flexibility and ability to balance work with their relationships and family. Similar findings were noted by Maysami and Goby (1999) for female entrepreneurs in Singapore.

Posig and Kickul (2004) claim that work/home trade-off for men is "bi-directional" but only "uni-directional" for women. Faced with inter-role conflict, men in their study adjusted one domain to compensate for the other, while women aimed to ensure that while family involvement could impinge on work, the reverse was not allowed to happen. Hence the double/triple shift for women. The authors found that men were primarily motivated by financial imperatives (money, financial security) rather than WLB among those with dependents, while for women with dependents, WLB and lifestyle flexibility were the most important motivations for business ownership. The authors voice caution about small business ownership as an alternative to mainstream employment for women since according to their findings it "may well give them occupation, but does not necessarily give them the financial security that paid employment does" (ibid., p. 270). Furthermore, such women were still responsible for domestic tasks, drawing into question the achievement of WLB and business success.

Walker et al. (2008) also explored the attraction of small enterprise ownership as a solution to achieving WLB. Their study reports on a survey of men and women running home-based businesses in Western Australia showing that while gender was not the major determining factor, having dependent children did influence female business owners towards seeking flexibility via business start-up. Walker et al. (ibid., p. 259) acknowledged that "although men and women both experience inter-role conflicts, it is often more difficult for women to balance their work and home roles".

The search for WLB via entrepreneurship was explored, in the context of New Zealand, by Kirkwood and Tootell (2008), based on interviews with 32 women and 26 men. Like Walker et al. (2008), they are cynical about the view that entrepreneurship might be the much sought-after panacea for WLB. Their study addresses work–family conflict in an entrepreneurial setting and explores how entrepreneurs experience work–family conflict and their strategies for WLB. "The impact of children for women entrepreneurs is significant in their desire to achieve work–family balance" (ibid., p. 288), arising from women's major role in childcare and household management. The study showed that starting a business did not resolve the problem for women in achieving a desired flexibility in relation to work and family – which, in their view, may be unattainable.

Overall, the existing literature highlights some important gaps in our understanding of family and small business management. The shift from ignoring women-led business to looking at women-led business in isolation from men-led enterprises demonstrates the need to examine how family interacts with business life and the ways that male *and* female owners deal with the potential conflicts, in order to understand the requisite supports for existing, or budding, small enterprises. The literature also suggests that other factors, in themselves important proxy markers of family structure, such as marital or parental status, need to be taken into account in further work.

Hence this chapter examines how mothers and fathers assign their time in their business and family lives and whether they have experienced conflict and/or made sacrifices due to work–family demands. Through the study of male and female entrepreneurs with dependent children in Ireland, it illustrates the degree to which flexible working exists in their businesses and the division of labour in their households. The overarching emphasis is on identifying gendered patterns that can be analysed in terms of showing the kind of behavioural shifts that would support more equitable sharing of family/household responsibilities and hence access to business venture creation and growth, for women and men.

SURVEY METHODOLOGY

This chapter draws upon data collected in a national survey of entrepreneurship conducted[3] to obtain information on men and women entrepreneurs. The total sample size for the survey was 3498 entrepreneurs, 924 men and 2574 women, of whom 832 (23 per cent), responded. Of these responses, 440 respondents (207 men and 233 women) had dependent co-resident children. This analysis focuses on the responses of entrepreneurs who were parents of dependent children aged less than 18 years.

The mainly quantitative data collected were analysed using SPSS®. Since most of the variables were categorical, Pearson's chi square test was used, where appropriate, to test for any statistically significant differences in the responses of fathers and mothers. The key measures included: working time arrangements; allocation of childcare within entrepreneurial households; the extent to which respondents and their employees availed of flexible working practices; and the interferences/sacrifices experienced among SME owners in relation to business versus caring demands. In addition, all measures were examined in the context of sex, hours worked, number of dependent children, ability to delegate childcare to another parent and involvement in childcare, using ordinal logistic regression modelling (see Appendix at the end of the chapter).

The remainder of this chapter concentrates on the intersection of work–family in the lives of Irish entrepreneurs with dependent children in terms of: working time arrangements of business owners and their own employees; experiences of conflict between work and family; sacrifices made in relation to time spent with partner, children and friends; and the divisions of labour in the domestic sphere between housework, childcare and leisure.

FINDINGS

This section outlines the profiles of the survey respondents in terms of demographic characteristics, sector of business and family status. It goes on to examine the working time patterns of business owners and their employees. The major focus is on the degree to which entrepreneurs experience conflict between work and family; have made sacrifices in relation to time spent with partner/children/friends; and the divisions of labour in the domestic sphere between housework, childcare and leisure.

In order to draw conclusions about the issues of work and family and how these are handled by entrepreneurs in Ireland, this chapter addresses the following questions:

- How do small business owners allocate their working and non-working time?
- Do these replicate or address work–family conflict in employment?
- Is achieving WLB a priority among small business owners?
- Are there gender differences in the responses to WLB for themselves and their employees?
- To what degree have entrepreneurs experienced interferences from, and/or made sacrifices in relation to, their personal/family lives, in order to grow their businesses?
- Who is responsible for housework/childcare in business owners' homes?

Profile of Entrepreneurial Parents

Of the 440 entrepreneurs in this analysis who had a dependent child/ren, 207 were fathers (47 per cent) and 233 mothers (53 per cent). Three-quarters of mothers were aged less than 45 years while 63 per cent of fathers were in this age range. However, age differences of fathers and mothers were not statistically significant. The majority of parent entrepreneurs were married or living with a partner (91 per cent), though this applied more to fathers (94 per cent) than mothers (82 per cent). There were no significant gender differences in the percentages of mothers and fathers with dependent children under 6 years of age, aged 6–12 years and 13–18 years.

Fathers had been involved in their enterprise for an average of 13.4 years while the average for mothers was 12.7 years. There were major sectoral differences among entrepreneurs with dependent children. These differences were statistically significant ($p < 0.01$). Women entrepreneurs predominantly traded in professional services, catering, education or tourism while men were concentrated in manufacturing, construction, agriculture and fisheries and transport, thereby reflecting the highly gender-segregated sections of the economy. These findings are consistent with SME ownership in Ireland and the EU (GEM, 2009).

Also consistent with the different sectors of trading, fathers employed a much higher percentage of male staff (68 per cent) compared with mothers (26 per cent). In accordance with GEM (2009) patterns in Ireland, in which 27 per cent of women entrepreneurs set up in business to create a job for themselves (compared with 19 per cent of men), mothers were less likely than fathers to have full-time staff, and when they did they employed fewer of them. This points to a very important structural difference in the composition of entrepreneurial mothers' and fathers' businesses that may affect aspects of their entrepreneurial experience, including those examined in this chapter. It is therefore fundamental to consider the findings of this study in light of this structural difference and employment patterns, which are themselves highly gendered. With this in mind, the analysis now compares the entrepreneurial experiences of mothers and fathers.

Childcare Arrangements

Major, and statistically significant, differences ($p < 0.01$) are evident in the childcare arrangements used by fathers and mothers running SMEs. More than half of the fathers who were entrepreneurs (56 per cent) relied on their partners to care for their child/ren, compared with only 21 per cent of mothers ($p < 0.01$). Furthermore, one-third of mothers (34 per cent) were responsible for providing care for their child/ren ($p < 0.01$). Private childcare arrangements were used by 37 per cent of mothers but only 24 per cent of fathers ($p < 0.01$); a baby-sitter or domestic worker provided childcare for 25 per cent of mothers and 18 per cent of fathers ($p < 0.05$). The remaining childcare was by family members (other than partners) for 19 per cent of mothers and 13 per cent of fathers, but the gender differences were not statistically significant.

This major gender divergence in childcare arrangements may help to explain some of the other differences noted among entrepreneurs – namely the greater demand for flexible working hours by mothers, as distinct from fathers, and the stronger likelihood of a child(ren) interfering with the business ventures of mothers. The fact that relatively few fathers provided the primary care for their child(ren) and that more than half of them could rely on their partner to provide this has serious implications for the ability of some parents to commit fully, or even partially, to running and developing their businesses. In contrast to these fathers, a substantial minority (14 per cent) were responsible for childcare alongside running a business.

Working Hours

The working hours of the 440 parents in the sample averaged 49 per week, well above the weekly hours for employees in Ireland. However, fathers worked in excess of 55 hours while mothers worked just under 44 hours per week. The main reasons for working longer than standard hours were: backlog of work, own desire to get job done and temporary increase in workload. There were no significant differences between the reasons given by mothers and fathers.

Given the major commitment to their businesses, as measured by working hours, alongside family demands, parents were asked to cite the degree to which they had experienced conflict in their personal/family lives.

Role Conflict

International literature on women and entrepreneurship has flagged the continuing problem that women (though not men) face when setting up enterprises, particularly when juggling this with raising children. Figure 11.1 illustrates that, in accordance with previous findings, it is women who experience conflict to a much greater degree than men. The gender differences are statistically significant ($p < 0.01$).

While a minority of fathers (10 per cent) and mothers (7 per cent) experienced no conflict between work and their personal life, nearly one-quarter of mothers (23 per cent) compared with 17 per cent of fathers "often"

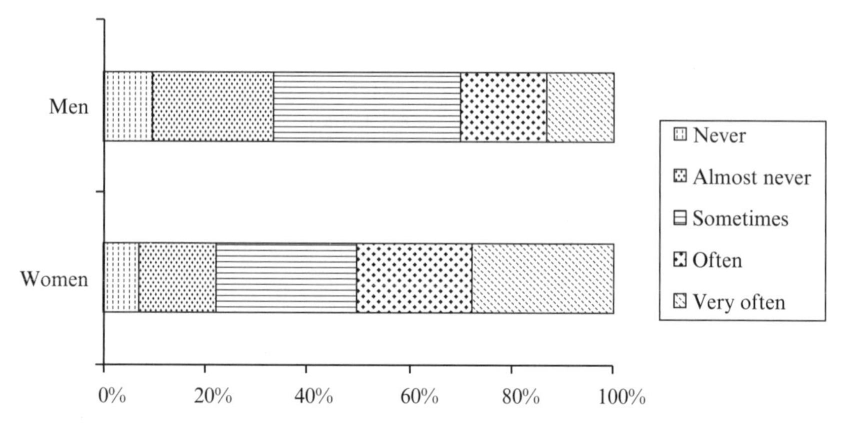

Source: Authors' research.

Figure 11.1 Experience of conflict between work and family according to sex (n = 433)

experienced such conflict. The gender differences were even stronger among parents who "very often" experienced conflict – 28 per cent of mothers and 13 per cent of fathers (Figure 11.1). Overall there were statistically significant differences between mothers' and fathers' experience of conflict ($p < 0.01$). An ordinal logistic regression model showed that both sex and hours worked contributed to the level of conflict experienced.

The following sections examine some of the responses to questions that related to how conflict might be reduced or fuelled in terms of the availability of flexible working and the degree to which different family/partner influences had interfered with their entrepreneurial activities.

Flexible Working Arrangements

Parents were asked whether they offered a range of flexible arrangements to their employees. The most common one available was flexitime, to staff in 179 enterprises, with more women-led owners having it available than men's businesses ($p < 0.05$). This was true to a greater extent with reduced working hours, available to staff in 45 of fathers' and 75 of mothers' SMEs ($p < 0.01$). Parental leave and paternity leave were less commonly available in 56 and 25 enterprises respectively. There were no statistically significant differences between family-related leave availability in the enterprises owned and run by fathers and mothers.

Respondents were asked about the relative importance they attached to flexible working *for their employees* (where relevant) and *themselves*.

For both, the differences in the responses of mothers and fathers were statistically significant ($p < 0.01$). Only a small percentage of entrepreneurs, male and female, ranked the need for flexible working for employees as unimportant or not very important (17 per cent of fathers and 10 per cent of mothers) compared with 54 per cent of mothers who ranked this flexibility as very important and a further 20 per cent as important. The level of agreement that flexibility was important, or very important, among fathers was 57 per cent in total. An examination of this using ordinal logistic modelling showed an effect from both sex and involvement in childcare: the greater the involvement in childcare, the more important flexible working became for employees ($p < 0.01$).

A similar, if more pronounced, gender cleavage exists in relation to the importance of flexibility for entrepreneurs themselves. More than one-quarter of fathers (28 per cent), compared with only seven per cent of mothers, ranked flexibility for themselves as unimportant or not very important. In contrast, 58 per cent of mothers felt that flexibility was very important for them while an additional 18 per cent also ranked such flexibility as important. While more than half of fathers ranked flexibility for themselves as important or very important, only one-third (35 per cent) felt it was very important. Both the hours worked and sex were important in predicting the importance attached to flexibility for themselves. Working longer hours and being male reduced this effect ($p < 0.01$). In addition, involvement in childcare also increased the importance of flexible working for entrepreneurial parents ($p = 0.01$).

Given the different responses from female and male entrepreneurial parents to flexible working, the next section examines a range of possible factors that might have impeded them in their entrepreneurial endeavours.

Interference with Careers in Business

Survey respondents were asked if a number of obligations/circumstances might have interfered with the development and growth of their businesses, namely: care of child/family member; after-school care of children; partner's career; partner's attitude; housework and other family commitments. In each case the gender differences in responses were statistically highly significant ($p < 0.01$) (Table 11.1).

Mothers (32 per cent) were much more likely than fathers (7 per cent) to have experienced some/much interference in their business career stemming from childcare or care of another family member. The ability to delegate childcare to the other parent reduced this level of interference slightly, but was only significant at the 10 per cent level. More than one-third of mothers (35 per cent) claimed that after-school care had interfered

Table 11.1 Experience of interference with business according to sex

Some or Much Interference From:	*n*	Mothers	Fathers
Care of child or other family member**	407	32%	7%
After-school care of child(ren)**	392	35%	16%
Partner's career**	389	18%	5%
Partner's attitude**	393	14%	7%
Housework**	404	16%	3%

Note: ** Denotes a statistically significant difference at the 1% level.

Source: Based on survey data.

(some/much) with their business career, compared with 16 per cent of fathers. This level of interference from after-school care was also highly affected by the number of hours worked ($p < 0.05$) as well as sex ($p < 0.01$).

Partners' careers had interfered much less in the business development of mothers (18 per cent some/much interference) and fathers (5 per cent some/much interference). However, more women claimed that their partner's attitude had interfered some or a lot (14 per cent) compared with the men surveyed (7 per cent). However, when controlling for other variables, it appears that this is closely related to the number of hours worked rather than sex itself: the greater the number of hours worked, the stronger the interference from spousal attitude is reported ($p < 0.01$).

Finally, major gender differences are evident in relation to how much housework had interfered with mothers' and fathers' careers in business. While 16 per cent of mothers claimed that housework had interfered (some/much), this applied to only 3 per cent of fathers (Table 11.1). The level of interference was higher for parents who were involved in childcare ($p < 0.05$).

Personal Sacrifices

Respondents were asked about sacrifices they may have made in progressing their business that would have reduced their own free time, or time spent with friends, partner, child/ren or in postponing having children. There were no statistically significant differences in the responses from fathers and mothers in relation to any of these forms of sacrifice.

Three-quarters of fathers and mothers had sacrificed some/much of their free time (Table 11.2). A higher percentage of mothers (53 per cent) than fathers (45 per cent) had sacrificed a lot of their free time in order to further their business venture.

Table 11.2 *Levels of personal sacrifice according to sex*

Some or Many Sacrifices In:	*n*	Mothers	Fathers
Free time	413	75%	75%
Social time	401	58%	54%
Time spent with children	401	43%	36%
Time spent with partner	395	41%	39%
Delaying having children	351	7%	4%

Source: Based on survey data.

A majority of parents had sacrificed time that they would otherwise have spent socializing in order to succeed in their business venture; 58 per cent of mothers and 54 per cent of fathers.

While mothers in the sample worked shorter hours than fathers it is evident from Table 11.2 that women entrepreneurs felt that they had made more sacrifices in relation to time spent with their child/ren than the men surveyed, though these gender differences were not statistically significant. More than one-third of fathers (36 per cent) had sacrificed some or a lot of time with their children; this applied to 43 per cent of mothers. Similar proportions of mothers (29 per cent) and fathers (28 per cent) felt that they had sacrificed little or no time that would have been spent with their children, due to their business ventures. An ordinal logistic model showed that the level of making sacrifices was highest for those who worked long hours ($p < 0.01$) or did not have any involvement in childcare ($p < 0.01$) in addition to being a mother ($p < 0.01$).

The pattern of responses for sacrifices in time spent with their spouse/partner was very similar for mothers and fathers. Forty-one per cent of mothers and 39 per cent of fathers had sacrificed some/much time with their partners. Levels of sacrifice were highest for those working long hours ($p < 0.01$), not involved in childcare ($p < 0.05$) and being a mother ($p < 0.05$). When asked if they had made sacrifices by delaying having children, only a very small minority of mothers (7 per cent) and fathers (4 per cent) had made major sacrifices in delaying having children and the gender differences were not statistically significant.

CONCLUSIONS

In the face of a culture of long working hours experienced by many entrepreneurial respondents, different attitudes to WLB can be observed among entrepreneurial mothers and fathers. Mothers unsurprisingly attach a greater importance to flexible work arrangements and report putting it into practice in their ventures to a greater extent than fathers.

The study also highlights the greater degree of conflict experienced by mothers, despite the perception of similar levels of sacrifice. Possible explanations could be due to the greater degree of concurrent demands on mothers leading to greater conflict for them, as discussed by Stoner et al. (1990) or in the family-embedded work of Aldrich and Cliff (2003). Alternatively, the results may arise as a direct consequence of the uni-directional work/home trade-off experienced by women (Posig & Kickul, 2004).

Most importantly, the analysis shows that, in some instances, the number of hours worked is critical in understanding the level of conflict and interference experienced, although hours worked are themselves highly gendered. Remarkable by its absence is the lack of effect of both the number of dependent children and the ability to delegate childcare to another parent when used as control variables. The analysis also showed the importance of responsibility for childcare: being involved in childcare decreased some types of sacrifice in time, presumably due to an increased presence within the home, and had little effect on any forms of interference with the business.

This chapter has identified a major gap in the prevailing discourse around gender and entrepreneurship by highlighting the need to take account of divergent childcare arrangements. While societal expectations suggest that women can now progress their careers in the professions, employment and business *on similar terms to men*, this fails to acknowledge the inequitable division of labour in the domestic sphere for many women entrepreneurs once they become mothers – relatively few can expect their partners to provide primary childcare or to share that responsibility equitably.

Divergent childcare arrangements have not been adequately examined in the context of entrepreneurial activity. Research to date that sought to explain women's lower levels of commitment, productivity and business growth has assumed that (1) women choose family over business concerns and (2) that an uneven division of labour within the home is reflected in uneven business venture outcomes. The findings of this chapter challenge the long-term viability of the second assumption. An alternative vision of women and men as entrepreneurs would seek to factor in availability for care and responsibility for child(ren) and other family members – to be shared equally among couples/family members. The current link between care and employment is detrimental to women's equality. These findings suggest that within a more fluid future environment of small businesses and entrepreneurship, a continuation of existing and highly gendered patterns of family care must be challenged. The prevailing discourse of domesticity and motherhood as an impediment to successful business ventures for women needs to be revised to take into account new family roles, especially among fathers, and a shift away from the women = mother = role conflict discourse. With the emergence of more egalitarian gender roles, domesticity and childcare do not have to be seen as exclusively "female" activities that conflict with work and business growth. Doing entrepreneurship differently could mean that men replicate women's patterns (to reduce role conflicts) rather than the (socially accepted) alternative.

In the light of these findings, policy-makers need to re-orient their incentives/measures to encourage entrepreneurship as a means of reconciling work/family life and achieving WLB via more diverse interventions and a broad range of key players: not only government, employers and trade unions but educators and service providers – most notably in early childcare. Irish society has seen major changes in the representation of women in the labour market alongside a virtually privatized system of childcare, which is very expensive for parents. Women's increased participation in the labour market has brought about two jobs for women/mothers while leaving men to pursue serious careers and to build major enterprises. The all too prevailing policy measures have served to "accommodate" Irish women's need for flexibility, hence the status quo that seems self-perpetuating. However, EU countries like Finland that have achieved high levels of female entrepreneurship have done so by diverse and interconnected policies to attain equality in all spheres and have stressed the objective of sharing parenting.

Among the policy implications, key starting points are: parenting skills in the primary and secondary curriculum for boys and girls; broadening career aspirations to reduce gender segregation via work experience/vocational courses (including entrepreneurship) crossing the gender divide; subsidized affordable high-quality childcare with full/part-time options; paid parental and paternity leave to ensure that men can avail; flexible working time options (not just full- or part-time) with rights to access the same at family formation, and family as well as financial/information supports for entrepreneurs wishing to combine business and family.

NOTES

1. While contraception and divorce have since been legalized, abortion remains illegal in Ireland.
2. The Marriage Bar required that women leave paid employment on getting married. It applied mainly to women's white-collar occupations, in both the public and private sector. In Ireland, where labour surpluses have been larger and more long-standing than

in most countries, it persisted until the Marriage Bar was abolished in the public sector in 1973, and discrimination in employment on grounds of sex was made generally illegal in 1977.

3. To give an indication of the reach of this survey, Eurostat (http://appsso.eurostat.ec.europa.eu/nui/setupModifyTableLayout.do) estimates the number of entrepreneurial organizations in Ireland at the time of sending out the survey at approximately 320000 organizations, while the Global Entrepreneurship Monitor (Acs et al., 2005) provides a figure of approximately 250000 "established" organizations for that period.

REFERENCES

Abarbanal, K. (2008), "Women Entrepreneurs: Reshaping the Workplace', *Interbeing*, **2**(2), 31–4.

Acs, Z.J., Arenius, P., Hay, M. and Minniti, M. (2005), *Global Entrepreneurship Monitor, 2004 Executive Report*, Babson College and London Business School, available at: http://www.gemconsortium.org/about.aspx?page=global_reports_2004; accessed 23 November 2010.

Aldrich, H. & Cliff, J. (2003), "The Pervasive Effects of Family on Entrepreneurship: Toward a Family Embeddedness Perspective", *Journal of Business Venturing*, **18**(5), 573–96.

Bourne, K. (2006), "In and Out of Balance: Women Entrepreneurs and the Gendered 'Work' of Work–Family", PhD Dissertation, Isenberg School of Management, Graduate School of the University of Massachusetts, Amherst.

Bowen, D. & Hisrich, R. (1986), "The Female Entrepreneur: A Career Development Perspective", *The Academy of Management Review*, **11**(2), 393–407.

Buttner, H. & Moore, D. (1997), "Women's Organizational Exodus to Entrepreneurship: Self-reported Motivations and Correlates with Success", *Journal of Small Business Management*, **35**(1), 34–47.

CSO (2010), *Vital Statistics*, Central Statistics Office, Dublin.

DeMartino, R. & Barbato, R. (2003), "Differences between Women and Men MBA Entrepreneurs: Exploring Family Flexibility and Wealth Creation as Career Motivators", *Journal of Business Venturing*, **18**(6), 815–32.

Drew, E. & Daverth, G. (2009), "Living to Work. . . .Or Working to Live? The Role of Managers in Creating Work Life Balance in Ireland", Briefing Paper, Irish Congress of Trade Unions, Dublin.

Drew, E. & Murtagh, E. (2005), "Work/Life Balance: Senior Management Champions or Laggards?", *Women in Management Review*, **20**(4), 262–78.

Drew, E., Humphreys, P. & Murphy, C. (2003), *Off the Treadmill: Achieving Work/Life Balance*, Dublin: National Framework Committee.

Dupuis, A. & de Bruin, A. (2004), "Women's Business Ownership and Entrepreneurship", in P. Spoonley, A. Dupuis, A. de Bruin (eds), *Work and Working in 21st Century New Zealand*, Palmerston North: Dunmore Press.

Dyer, W. and Handler, W. (1994), "Entrepreneurship and Family Business: Exploring the Connections", *Entrepreneurship: Theory and Practice*, **19**(1), 71–91.

Fahy, T. (2001), "Trends in Irish Fertility Rates in Comparative Perspective", *The Economic and Social Review*, **32**(1), 153–80.

Fenwick, T. (2002), "Transgressive Desires: New Enterprising Selves in the New Capitalism", *Work, Employment & Society*, **16**(4), 703–23.

Global Entrepreneurship Monitor (GEM) (2009), *GEM Ireland 2008 National Report*, Dublin: Enterprise Ireland.

Goffee, R. & Scase, R. (1983), "Business Ownership and Women's Subordination: A Preliminary Study of Female Proprietors", *Sociological Review*, **31**(4), 625–48.

Honig-Haftel, S. & Martin, L. (1986), "Is the Female Entrepreneur at a disadvantage?", *Thrust: The Journal for Employment and Training Professionals*, **7**(1/2), 49–64.

Humphreys, P., Drew, E. & Murphy, C. (1999), *Gender Equality in the Civil Service*, Dublin: Institute of Public Administration.

Kim, J. & Ling, C. (2001), "Work–Family Conflict of Women Entrepreneurs in Singapore", *Women in Management Review*, **16**(5), 204–21.

Kirkwood, J. & Tootell, B. (2008), "Is Entrepreneurship the Answer to Achieving Work–Family Balance?", *Journal of Management and Organisation*, **14**(3), 285–302.

Lerner, M., Brush, C. & Hisrich, R. (1997) "Israeli Women Entrepreneurs: An Examination of Factors Affecting Performance", *Journal of Business Venturing*, **12**(4), 315–39.

Longstreth, M., Stafford, K. & Mauldin, T. (1987), "Self-employed Women and their Families: Time Use and Socioeconomic Characteristics", *Journal of Small Business Management*, **25**(3), 30–37.

Lunn, P., Fahey, T. and Hannan, C. (2009), *Family Figures: Family Dynamics and Family Types in Ireland, 1986–2006*, Dublin: ESRI.

Maysami, R. & Goby, V. (1999), "Female Small Business Owners in Singapore and Elsewhere: A Review of Recent Studies", *Journal of Small Business Management*, **37**(2), 96–105.

O'Brien, M. & Shemilt, I. (2003), *Working Fathers: Earning and Caring*, Equal Opportunities Commission, Research Discussion Series, Manchester.

Posig, M. & Kickul, J. (2004), "Work-role Expectations and Work Family Conflict: Gender Differences in Emotional Exhaustion", *Women in Management Review*, **19**(7), 373–86.

Schindehutte, M., Morris, M. & Brennan, C. (2003), "Entrepreneurs and Motherhood: Impacts on their Children in South Africa and the United States", *Journal of Small Business Management*, **41**(1) 94–107.

Shelton, L. (2006), "Female Entrepreneurs, Work–Family Conflict, and Venture Performance: New Insights into the Work–Family Interface", *Journal of Small Business Management*, **44**(2) 285–97.

Smith, C. (2000), "Managing Work and Family in Small 'Copreneurial' Business: An Australian Study', *Women in Management Review*, **15**(5/6), 283–9.

Still, L. & Timms, W. (2000), "Women's Business: The Flexible Alternative Workstyle for Women", *Women in Management Review*, **15**(5/6), 272–83.

Stoner, C., Hartman, R. & Arora, R. (1990) "Work–Home Role Conflict in Female Owners of Small Businesses: An Exploratory Study", *Journal of Small Business Management*, **28**(1), 30–38.

Walker, E., Wang, C. & Redmond, J. (2008), "Women and Work–Life Balance: Is Home-based Business the Solution?", *Equal Opportunities International*, **27**(3), 258–75.

APPENDIX

Table 11A.1 Sacrifice of time with partner

	Coefficient Estimate	Significance
Number of children under 18	0.044	0.610
Number of hours worked	*0.031*	*<0.001*
Selves involved in childcare	*−0.566*	*0.012*
Ability to delegate childcare to other parent	0.241	0.236
Men	*−0.496*	*0.021*

Note: Link function: logit.

Table 11A.2 Sacrifice of time with children

	Coefficient Estimate	Significance
Number of children under 18	0.064	0.458
Number of hours worked	*0.035*	*<0.001*
Selves involved in childcare	*−1.127*	*<0.001*
Ability to delegate childcare to other parent	0.105	0.605
Men	*−0.841*	*<0.001*

Note: Link function: logit.

Table 11A.3 Importance of flexibility for employees

	Coefficient Estimate	Significance
Number of children under 18	0.033	0.713
Number of hours worked	0.000	0.973
Selves involved in childcare	*0.746*	*0.002*
Ability to delegate childcare to other parent	−0.081	0.695
Men	*−0.920*	*<0.001*

Note: Link function: logit.

Table 11A.4 Importance of flexibility for selves

	Coefficient Estimate	Significance
Number of children under 18	0.088	0.314
Number of hours worked	*−0.019*	*0.002*
Selves involved in childcare	*0.597*	*0.010*
Ability to delegate childcare to other parent	−0.148	0.464
Men	*−0.677*	*0.001*

Note: Link function: logit.

Table 11A.5 Interference from care

	Coefficient Estimate	Significance
Number of children under 18	−0.027	0.763
Number of hours worked	−0.008	0.201
Selves involved in childcare	0.004	0.984
Ability to delegate childcare to other parent	−0.369	0.073
Men	*−1.129*	*<0.001*

Note: Link function: logit.

Table 11A.6 Interference from after school care

	Coefficient Estimate	Significance
Number of children under 18	0.076	0.382
Number of hours worked	*0.013*	*0.032*
Selves involved in childcare	−0.284	0.215
Ability to delegate childcare to other parent	−0.178	0.382
Men	*−1.018*	*<0.001*

Note: Link function: logit.

Table 11A.7 Interference from partner's attitude to work

	Coefficient Estimate	Significance
Number of children under 18	0.004	0.965
Number of hours worked	*0.021*	*0.002*
Selves involved in childcare	0.312	0.205
Ability to delegate childcare to other parent	0.276	0.214
Men	−0.168	0.473

Note: Link function: logit.

Table 11A.8 Interference from housework

	Coefficient Estimate	Significance
Number of children under 18	0.073	0.432
Number of hours worked	<0.001	0.965
Selves involved in childcare	*0.514*	*0.026*
Ability to delegate childcare to other parent	−0.366	0.096
Men	*−1.305*	*<0.001*

Note: Link function: logit.

12. Entrepreneurial satisfaction: job stressors, coping and well-being among small business owner managers

Magnus George and Eleanor Hamilton

INTRODUCTION

The purpose of this chapter is to consider how job stressors, coping and well-being are relevant to the small business context, and to identify what is known about how they interact to contribute to performance. It is, to a large extent, taken for granted that the entrepreneurial activity associated with running a small business brings with it exposure to psychological pressure and stress. Nonetheless, there are few studies on the occurrence, prevalence or impact of entrepreneurial role stress (Buttner, 1992; Wincent & Ortqvist, 2009, p. 118). This is in marked contrast to the extensive literature addressing organizational stress. Beyond management studies, large and growing bodies of literature from psychology, sociology, medicine, psychotherapy and other fields have considered a multitude of facets of job stressors, coping and well-being. This chapter draws on these concepts in an attempt to better understand small business behaviour and performance.

To achieve that, we address how entrepreneurship differs from other organizational, occupational or workplace settings in regard to stress, health and well-being interactions. We consider features of the entrepreneurial lifestyle and "job" that amplify stressors, increase susceptibility to these, contribute positively or negatively to coping, or that bolster resilience to stress. The lenses of stress and well-being provide a new way of considering the impact of entrepreneurial behaviours.

There is much complexity and ambiguity in the use of the terms stressors, coping and well-being, and we do not attempt here to rehearse a comprehensive review of the current understanding of these inter-linked phenomena. However, in the sections below, we provide an outline of these concepts. We then position small business, the role of employees and family business. This is followed by a comparison of the experience of small business owner managers and corporate managers. Next, we consider some of the studies to date that have examined entrepreneurial stress, followed by sections on how stress affects entrepreneurial satisfaction, job crafting and positive well-being, and the role of social support and networks in entrepreneurial stress. We finish the chapter with a section dealing with practical implications.

THE CONCEPT OF STRESSORS

The stress concept has a long history, though the purely psychological sense of stress only became prevalent during the twentieth century. As early as 1910 Sir William Osler used the term "stress" in his descriptions of medical patients (Cooper & Dewe, 2004). Stress has been described as a general adaptation syndrome, a physiological response mechanism to actual or perceived environmental demands. It is an adaptive survival mechanism, and has been defined as "the non-specific response of the body to any demand placed upon it" (Selye, 1956, p. 1). Further, stress is more than simply nervous tension; it is an inevitable consequence of living, is not necessarily bad and cannot be avoided (ibid., pp. 64–5). It can only be avoided by death; it is not stress itself that is bad but an excess of stress and the consequences that arise. The term is, nowadays, in widespread and general usage, and covers an array of occurrences, syndromes and experiences.

To clarify the potential impact of stress, researchers have introduced, and distinguished between, three linked terms – stressors, stress and strain. Stressors are those things in a person's life or environment that may cause stress as a response. The impact of those stressors is mediated by a host of factors, generally described as buffering mechanisms. Stress results when stressors exceed a person's ability to handle them. Stress may result in strain, the effects of which are moderated, or exacerbated, by coping mechanisms. And strain can negatively affect a person's well-being. Workplace stress can result in a variety of undesired effects, such as increased absenteeism, reduced productivity and disengagement.

Although the stress response has been adaptive in evolutionary terms, the modern disease of psychological stress is an example of the so-called "mismatch paradigm" (Schulkin & Power, 2009). This describes the clash between features that have arisen through time as an adaptive development but which are out of sync with the modern era. Contemporary workplaces and societies provide an abundance of potential stressors.

Many of these are not true corporeal threats, but they still arouse the generalized stress reaction. In abundance and without adequate respite these can, over time and in aggregation, produce the same endocrine resistance and exhaustion effects as mortal dangers. There is an extensive and well-established body of research linking occupational stress to disease and ill health (e.g., Cooper & Marshall, 1976; Shirom, 2003). Statistics about the impact of stress on productivity and national economies are legion (HSE, 2009). Therefore, consideration of stress is important from both human compassion and economic impact perspectives.

THE CONCEPT OF COPING

Coping refers to the processes people use to deal with stress. Both cognitive and non-cognitive components exist. The former includes thought processes and learning, while the non-cognitive element includes automatic responses that seek to reduce discomfort. It has been summarized as "all about what individuals think and do in a particular stress encounter" (Dewe, 2004, p. 139). For a psychologically stressful situation to occur it needs to be assessed as such by a person (Lazarus & Folkman, 1984). There is therefore a role for cognition in the assessment of events in terms of how much a situation constitutes a real or potential threat, is a challenge, or is benign. There is then a role for perception. This primary appraisal triggers an initial coping mechanism, which can be action-based and task or problem-focused, or emotion-focused. Subsequent secondary appraisal involves consideration of resources available to deal with the situation, which can result in a change to the primary appraisal. Coping is therefore flexible, and involves feedback to an individual, who may try different approaches if one does not work as desired.

A number of typologies of coping mechanisms have been produced. One review of stress of "managerial occupations" listed 40 coping strategies (Burke & Weir, 1980). A simple classification distinguishes between action-based, emotion-based and harmful mechanisms. Action-based approaches include time management, exercise, retreats or leaving a job. Emotion-based strategies include, for example, cognitive reframing. Harmful coping includes substance abuse, such as alcohol or drugs. Beyond descriptive studies of coping there remains much debate on how to measure coping and, more importantly, how to apply research findings in practice, that is, their "clinical relevance" (Dewe, 2004). Further, an integrated approach to stress management has been argued for (Arthur, 2004). This would seek first to reduce workplace stressors in organizations and teams and then provide appropriate clinical interventions for affected individuals. This refocuses attention on organizations themselves, and disputes that only solutions addressing individuals are required. That is, it reopens the question about who is responsible in regard to stress interventions: the individual, the organization, or both? Even if it is true that "it is important to recognize that the well-being of individual employees and the well-being or efficiency of their employing organization are often in conflict" (Reynolds, 1997, p. 101), where owner managers are concerned these two priorities need to be aligned.

THE CONCEPT OF WELL-BEING

Considerable richness surrounds the modern concept of well-being, reflecting both its longstanding interest to mankind and its current topicality. Well-being covers both physical and mental or psychological health. It is a state, not a possession, and can be in a positive or good state, or in a negative or poor condition. Happiness and prosperity are other contributors to well-being. Collectively, these aspects give a broad synopsis of how a person's overall life is going. The term "quality-of-life" has been used as a synonym for well-being, and to describe the well-being of individuals or societies.

Positive psychological well-being has been linked to the idea of self-actualization (Maslow, 1954), and to the theory that striving to achieve higher-order goals brings intrinsic reward and positive emotional outcomes from reflecting upon that activity. This is pre-dated by a much earlier view of well-being, which used the Aristotelian concept of eudaimonia, the state wherein a life of virtue, the "good life", would better bring about true happiness than one of mere pleasure seeking. The latter, hedonic view emerged from the philosophy that the fundamental goal of life should be the pursuit of pleasure.

Hedonic psychology assesses subjective well-being, often synonymized as "happiness" and composed of life satisfaction, presence of positive mood, and the absence of negative mood (Ryan and Deci, 2001). The eudaimonic view distinguishes between well-being and happiness per se, emphasizing that even when all desires are satisfied true well-being does not necessarily result. While some human needs are only subjectively felt as desires, others are more fundamental to human nature. Satisfying these deeper needs produces personal growth. These two views remain in play in our contemporary understanding of well-being. Critics note that the eudaimonic view gives experts the power to define well-being, whereas subjective well-being allows individuals to decide this for themselves. In return, subjective well-being has been challenged for its lack of ability to embrace the totality of healthy living.

The consensus is that at the individual level well-being is better suited to a subjective, personal evaluation than to an objective one. Multi-component, holistic measures of subjective well-being have emerged in recent years, which include both the conditions or context in which a person operates and the experience that they have (Searle, 2008, p. 12). By taking account of the psychological and social environments in which a person gains reward or satisfaction from their work and other behaviours, researchers have been better able to understand the stressors they are exposed to and also the types of coping resources available to them.

STRESSORS, COPING AND WELL-BEING IN THE SMALL BUSINESS LITERATURE

Well-being has emerged over recent decades as a significant issue and focus of study in the management literature. In particular, the widely documented and high prevalence of changes to workplaces and their organization, job (in)security, new technology, social changes (such as the rise in number of families where both parents work) and the emergence of globalization, to name but a few, have all been linked to rising levels of workplace stress (see, for example, Cooper & Robertson, 2001) and reduced individual well-being.

Paradoxically, despite the ubiquity of references to the stressors and strains involved in small business management, and the frequent invocation of these as important defining factors, well-being is infrequently mentioned in entrepreneurship literature. Where it does occur it is often in a variety of impersonal contexts, such as "well-being of the business". For example, a study on the "family effect" on firm performance highlighted the potential that, in what were termed self-interested family firms, "family members look after their own and the family's self-interest as opposed to the well-being of the firm", to the detriment of firm performance (Dyer, 2006). Consider the well-being associated with the satisfaction of running a business. This condition, often articulated as "being your own boss", we term "entrepreneurial satisfaction". Having defined stressors, coping and well-being, and the relation between these terms, we now turn to consider their utility in the small business context.

Defining Small Business

An important premise in this chapter is the overlap between the fields of small business and entrepreneurship in terms of theory and practice. We draw on literature that in the main uses the terms interchangeably. There was a key debate in the late 1980s sparked by an article by Carland et al. (1984, p. 12), proposing a conceptual framework for differentiating entrepreneurs from small business owners. Gartner (1988) strongly contested this differentiation proposing that a more fruitful approach was to adopt a behavioural approach, with a particular focus on new venture creation. Whilst this perspective served to move the field on, away from the trait-based quest for "who is the entrepreneur", more recent research has proposed that entrepreneurial activity goes beyond start-up. It is associated, for example, with processes of growth, opportunity seeking and learning from failure. It is a dynamic process embedded in particular social and historical contexts. For the remainder of this chapter we synonymize entrepreneurs with small business owner managers. Implicit in "organizational" literature is the idea that the "norm" is that organizations are big corporations or bureaucracies. Small businesses are therefore often overlooked, or subsumed within the general category.

The Role of Employees in Small Businesses

While this chapter focuses on owner managers, it is important to remember that small- and medium-sized enterprises (SMEs) employ a large percentage of the workforce. In considering the topic of stress we therefore need to consider the extent to which it relates to the business owner (and possibly key managers), or to all workers in an SME. The central role of the owner manager in the small business has been asserted, such that in many respects "the owner *is* the business" (Churchill & Lewis, 1983, p. 32). Such a position justifies a strong focus on the owner in all considerations of the small business. A contrasting opinion would focus instead on the full range of employee relations within an SME. Two polarized views of the experience of work in the SME world have been proposed. Goss (1991) described these as "sweet harmony" and "sweatshop", while Wilkinson referred to "small is beautiful" versus "Bleak House" (Wilkinson, 1999). In either case, the former categorization sees small business as a locus for harmonious relations, little need for excessive formality, and working conditions that typify a "happy family", while the latter sees exploitation, poor and dangerous working conditions, rampant conflict and an authoritarian attitude to employee relations.

The Link Between Family and Small Business

Many small businesses can also be categorized as family businesses (Baines & Wheelock, 1997). In these, family members are not only involved "behind the scenes" (Hamilton, 2006a), but they actively work in the business and may also be co-owners. Children may be immersed in work, though paradoxically their parents may in many ways be absent (Hamilton, 2006b). By definition, family businesses bring the stressor of hierarchies within and between family versus non-family sub-groups. Within the family, the business is omnipresent and demanding of time, attention and financial resources, with resulting potential for conflict between business and family priorities (George & Hamilton, 2010).

Small Business Owner Managers and Entrepreneurs: How do they Differ from Managers and Leaders in Large Organizations?

The study of managerial work has sought to establish what managers "really do", and has focused on executives in large corporations. In contrast, as recently as 2006 it was reported in a review and modest observational study of managerial work in small businesses that "our knowledge of what small business managers really do is limited" (Florén, 2006, p. 272). That study examined time allocation, with whom managers interacted, and the specific elements of their work. It found that the working day of those studied was long, hectic and lacking in routine events. Work was fragmented, interruption-prone and involved frequent redirection and switching of effort. Compared with managers in large organizations, small business managers were found to exhibit greater task brevity and fragmentation. There was little use of recognized managerial procedure tools, and small business managers had less well-developed networks than CEOs from larger organizations. In terms of their work, they took multiple roles, including both technical operational roles in project teams and senior leadership ones. They showed technical, interpersonal and conceptual skills, and operated at all organizational levels. Moreover, they frequently needed to bridge across these skill sets and managerial positions. The owner managers in the study were the "backup" for any contingency, yet they also interpreted their roles according to their inclination, ability and subjective enjoyment. They were found to "gravitate towards the active elements of their work and they prefer current, specific and *ad hoc* activities" (ibid., p. 281), though the extent of actual freedom of choice was suggested to be less than that reported in general managerial work studies.

Organization boundary roles involve working at the interface between an organization and external people, whether customers, suppliers, or other stakeholders. Such boundary spanning has been identified as a workplace stressor and is central to the work of the owner manager (Miles, 1980). Both positive and negative impacts of assuming such job positions have been identified. In them, the owner can both enjoy relatively high levels of power and autonomy, and also be vulnerable to comparatively high levels of stress. Entrepreneurs have also been defined as working with great decision uncertainty and complexity, with greater personal involvement, and with sparse formal management systems relative to other managers (Busenitz & Barney, 1997).

Gender, Ethnicity and Culture

While in this chapter we will not devote our attention to gender, ethnicity or cultural effects on the workplace stress phenomenon, these are each relevant considerations. Regarding gender, the issues surrounding female self-employment and business ownership in regard to, in particular, work–family interactions are complex (Gatrell, 2004). Comparing unemployed, employed and self-employed women in a large sample (n = 1412) over a 20-year period, a US study found that employed women fared far better in health terms than their unemployed counterparts (Dolinsky & Caputo, 2003). Self-employed women exhibited worse health than wage earners, though the underlying explanation of these findings remains obscure. Beyond the entrepreneurial domain, the psychological effects of employment, and their interaction with social roles were compared for men and women (Pugliesi, 1995), and again the importance of family roles on work satisfaction has been emphasized. Among other salient factors were self-esteem, social integration, work complexity and work control – all features relevant to the entrepreneurial context. While the results suggest general well-being impacts of employment and differences between men and women, there clearly remains much to be studied in regard to the influence of these factors on experiences of workplace stress.

WHAT DO WE REALLY KNOW ABOUT ENTREPRENEURIAL STRESS?

While stress experts from disciplines including psychology, sociology and medicine have very well-developed understandings of stress, and substantial research literatures to draw on, very little is known about the occupational stress experiences of small business owner managers. Though they may be "experiential experts" (Morse, 1995, p. 229), how owner managers articulate workplace stress is not well understood. One study (Kinman & Jones, 2005) described stress in three broad ways: as an environmental stimulus, a response to such stimuli and as a relationship between stimulus and response. Participants used a diverse lexicon, rich in metaphor when describing their stress experiences. Salient stress features included both environmental and individual factors, and outcomes included overwork, emotional and psychological turmoil, reduction in physical well-being, impaired cognition, or a combination of these. References were made to being like a taut wire, under oppressive weight, having besieged bodily defences, the depletion of resources and a pressure increase that required an outlet. Such terms will be familiar to many in small business, and lists of stressors can read like the job description for a small business owner manager (see Table 12.1). Some support emerged for the controversial idea that stress can be a positive thing, with some respondents contrasting the motivational quality of some stress with damaging stress.

Perceived outcomes from occupational stress included a wide range of psychological (tension, anxiety, worry, depression and unhappiness), behavioural (irritability and marital difficulties), physical (health, tiredness, aches and pains), and cognitive (poor standard of work, mistakes, poor concentration) complaints. To the extent that these articulations reflect the situation experienced by small business owner managers, then we can assume that they will be detrimental to their psychological well-being; to that of their families, employees and other stakeholders; to their physical health; and to their work performance.

Small business owner managers frequently need to manage how they present themselves to employees, customers, suppliers, funders and their families. This has been described as a facade of confidence (Kets de Vries, 1980). This corresponds closely to some aspects of what has been termed "emotion work", an identified contributor to burnout (Zapf et al., 2001). Emotion work requires that people do more than just suppress their feeling; it requires that they constitute feelings *expected* of them under certain circumstances (Lupton, 1998). Emotion work is most commonly associated with professions such as nursing and teaching where, in addition to the above demands, workers need to actively manage how they display their own emotions (Maslach et al., 2001). Workers in such front line and caring professions often deal with people who themselves are under stress, and being responsible for the welfare of others has been identified as a stressor (Kinman & Jones, 2005), and has been termed "emotional labour" (Lupton, 1998). Owner managers are, at least in the short term, responsible for the jobs, incomes and security of their employees, many of whom may themselves face a range of stressors. We propose that "entrepreneurial emotion work", incorporating notions of emotional labour and emotion work in the context of small business, is a concept that deserves further consideration in order to better understand the experience of entrepreneurship.

A better understanding of how the stress concept is articulated was proposed by Kinman and Jones (2005) as a key tool for the development of more effective workplace stress interventions. Some support was found for an earlier proposition that attitudes to stress would be influenced by

Table 12.1 A summary of key stress features from the literature

Key Attributes of the Small Business Owner Manager Role That Can Contribute Towards Stress	Sources of Stress for Entrepreneurs	Managerial Implications to Assist Entrepreneurs to Cope with Stress
Inherent downsides of the entrepreneurial job: Being exposed to risk by virtue of making a sizeable personal investment in business assets A dominant degree of boundary spanning activity, in excess of that experienced by managers in general A need to take on a multiplicity of roles Simultaneous demands that risk overload High demand on available time and energy, to the detriment of personal and family time Isolation or only a small social support network Rewards implicit in entrepreneurship: The absence of an unreasonable boss and jeopardy of severance Ability to establish their own priorities and allocate time Resulting in reduced role conflict	Role ambiguity Role conflict Role overload Job versus non-job conflict Concern for quality Responsibility pressure Time pressure and deadlines Job insecurity Lack of support Responsibility for others Lack of resources Dealing with stressed people Personality High self-expectations Moderators of the impact of stressors on physical and mental well-being: Personality type Type A and Type B did not significantly affect either job satisfaction or health problems. Type B entrepreneurs were found to find ambiguity stressful, though in general entrepreneurs in the study were found to absorb conflicting work demands[a] without experiencing stress Tension discharge rate Social support	Work pressures often result in the de-prioritization of health issues until they become critical and interfere with work for entrepreneurs Regular exercise, moderation in substance use, and the adoption of relaxation techniques have proven efficacy in stress relief Set a clear corporate direction and strategy Clearly establish duties and responsibilities for all employees More effective delegation of work and pass appropriate routine decision-making to subordinates Advisory boards are a potential useful adjunct to decision-making Networking as a way to share experiences with others, and gain insights into how they manage business problems For entrepreneurs manifesting stress due to work–home demand conflicts, it was suggested that some form of coaching in relaxation would be fruitful

Table 12.1 (continued)

Note: a. This categorization of personality arose from the work of Friedman and Rosenman, who coined the terms Type A and Type B in their study of the links between behaviour and the risk of coronary heart disease. The Type A and Type B behaviour patterns describe two contrasting personality types (which have been joined by others, such as the so-called thrill-seeking personality, or Type T). Type A people typically demonstrate to a high degree a chronic sense of time urgency combined with excessively competitive behaviour. Type A has been defined (Friedman and Rosenman, 1974, p. 67) as "an action-emotion complex that can be observed in any person who is *aggressively* involved in a *chronic, incessant* struggle to achieve more and more in less and less time, and if required to do so, against the opposing efforts of other things or other persons" (emphasis in original). In contrast, "the person with Type B Behavior Pattern is the exact opposite of the Type A subject. He . . . is rarely harried by desires to obtain a wildly increasing number of things or participate in an endlessly growing series of events in an ever decreasing amount of time" (ibid., p. 68).

Source: Adapted from Buttner (1992) and Kinman and Jones (2005).

occupational status. Specifically, people with line management responsibilities tended to favour individual responsibility for stress management, while those with no such responsibility proposed that a combination of efforts by organizations and affected individuals should apply. The authors suggested that the:

> managers' beliefs and attitudes regarding work-related stress and its impact on employees will determine the culture of the organization and inform its policies and practices on dealing with stress, whereas employees' beliefs and attitudes will determine which policies and practices are likely to be resisted and which may be successful. (Ibid., p. 118).

Small business owner managers both determine organizational attributes and are subject to them. They also frequently have high self-expectations. Whether responsibility for stress intervention lies with the organization or the individual, or both, the buck stops with them (Zhang & Hamilton, 2009). Moreover, they also hold considerable influence over the determinants of workplace stress that their employees experience, as well as the response those employees receive should they present with stress complaints.

It can be seen from the above that despite their abundance little is known about stress in small businesses in terms of how owner managers perceive it, its actual prevalence and severity and its impacts on employees. Large-scale surveys of occupational stress typically under-represent or even ignore entrepreneurs. Textbooks on entrepreneurship may explore psychological traits in regard to their contested utility in defining entrepreneurs, and they frequently invoke the heady pressure and exuberance of start-up, but they fail to give appropriate coverage to entrepreneurial stress and well-being.

Empirical Studies of Job Stress in Small Business Owners

There have been a few studies focused on entrepreneurial stress. Rare examples include a case study from Nigeria (Akande, 1992), which examined stressors and coping strategies in a sample of 198 small business owners. It found evidence that stress was seen as having both positive motivational and damaging attributes. A range of both proactive and responsive coping techniques used by respondents was listed. Another study from 1992 addressed the question of how entrepreneurial stress differs from managerial stress (Buttner, 1992). A survey of 68 entrepreneurs and 44 middle and senior managers from large corporations on the east coast of the US identified stressors and moderators listed by each respondent. Key findings include that managers had a faster tension discharge rate than entrepreneurs, suggesting that entrepreneurs find it harder to leave work concerns at work when they come home. This study predates the near ubiquity of modern communication forms such as mobile Internet and Smartphone technology, which has permeated every facet of managerial life. Entrepreneurs' general health problems exceeded those reported by managers; they expressed greater role ambiguity, and less satisfaction with their work than managers. Social support was reported to make little difference to entrepreneurial health, and it was posited that this reinforced earlier findings that entrepreneurs are "autonomous, independent, and have a low need for support" (ibid., p. 232). Buttner concluded that entrepreneurial work does significantly differ from managerial work in terms of stressors and stress outcomes. A final example is of a survey (Tetrick et al., 2000), which compared business owners and non-owners (managers and employees), looking for differences in stressors, strain and coping between these two groups. A key finding was that owners reported greater work satisfaction than non-owners, a phenomenon explained in terms of family business membership satisfaction. The study illustrates the need to consider small business employees as well as owners if a full understanding of workplace stress and performance in small businesses is to be gained.

STRESS, BUSINESS SURVIVAL AND ENTREPRENEURIAL SATISFACTION

Globally, business survival rates are low, and various theories invoking environmental factors for this have been advanced. While the impact of failure as a cause of stress and ill-health has been studied (Whyley, 1998; Shepherd, 2003; Singh et al., 2007; Cope, 2010), the role played by stress in failure has been under-examined.

The direct relationship between entrepreneurial stress and business survival was examined in a ten-year longitudinal study of 201 German small business owners (Rauch et al., 2007). Poor business performance was found to reduce satisfaction and well-being, and to increase strain. Based on this, high levels of strain will reduce what we termed earlier "entrepreneurial satisfaction". However, strain effects for owner managers occur in combination with the high potential for control over work that exists in the entrepreneurial job. Rauch et al. (2007) found strain caused managers to employ coping strategies that resulted in enhanced business performance in terms of survival. Specifically, experiences of strain prompted proactive coping strategies that resulted in behaviours that reduced the causes of strain, leading in due course to improved business performance.

On the other hand, we might speculate that, when the levels of "entrepreneurial strain" exceed the ability to cope, a tipping point might be reached when the strain could prompt a decision to choose to cease trading. Rauch et al. (2007) concluded that the high demands placed on entrepreneurs do not necessarily produce negative outcomes in terms of business survival, though they suggested that some owners and in some conditions, for example, recession, might react to strain by prioritizing survival and not growth. Proactive pursuit of business goals, combined with coping strategies targeted at reducing stress reactions, was suggested as the optimal approach to developing a business, as well as enhancing personal health and well-being. We take from this study the concept of a particular form of strain, namely "entrepreneurial strain", which may have a long-term positive effect on business performance and survival. This concept could be linked to the literature on entrepreneurs' propensity and ability to bear risk.

While entrepreneurship is often described as a stressful and demanding undertaking, several studies have found that in general self-employed people express higher levels of job satisfaction than employees (Blanchflower & Oswald, 1998; Benz & Frey, 2004). Another US study found that self-employed people, working in the "smallest of small businesses" (Clinton et al., 2006), exhibited moderately higher levels of job satisfaction than other workers, higher self-efficacy values and lower rates of depression (Bradley & Roberts, 2004).

The reason for "choosing" an entrepreneurial career has been investigated for its impact on entrepreneurial satisfaction (Cooper & Artz, 1995). In a study of 777 Finnish micro-businesses, a necessity-based (as opposed to an opportunity-based) start-up was found to moderately reduce satisfaction and to increase the likelihood of a subsequent return to paid employment, though this effect was reduced if a satisfactory income was achieved through entrepreneurship (Kautonen & Palmroos, 2009). The negative effect on satisfaction was reduced when the entrepreneur was happy with the level and regularity of income that they were achieving through self-employment. A policy recommendation was that there should be training in business skills that could enhance business viability and success for necessity-based entrepreneurs. We add that stress awareness and management training would be a valuable component of such provision.

ENTREPRENEURIAL JOB CRAFTING AS A CREATIVE COPING STRATEGY

In light of the complexity involved in the stress and coping interaction, and the role that workers themselves have in shaping their own stress experiences, there have been suggestions that there needs to be a reconsideration of the theoretical basis used to address these issues (Briner et al., 2004). The job crafting concept has expanded the theme of workers exploiting the scope available to them to determine how they actually undertake their duties. Defined as "the physical and cognitive changes individuals make in the task or relational boundaries of their work" (Wrzesniewski & Dutton, 2001, p. 179), job crafting has been identified as a creative coping approach that some workers use to reduce their workplace stress, which may or may not benefit their employer. It explains the common observation that two people who ostensibly fill identical roles carry out their work differently, and experience different levels of workplace stress. Job crafting has been identified as a contributor to personal work identity and how people derive meaning in their work.

Entrepreneurs heavily invest emotionally in their status as business owners, and derive considerable personal meaning from what they do, a form of what we are terming "entrepreneurial satisfaction". We also suggest here that the concept of job crafting may be a helpful conceptual framework to understand how levels of entrepreneurial satisfaction may be created and maintained.

For many entrepreneurs, for whom work *is* leisure, well-being is strongly affected by their own crafting of their own work. Put another way, the practice of entrepreneurship is, in itself, deeply rewarding for many entrepreneurs. When employment has fallen short of expectations, entrepreneurial and lifestyle job crafting are the tools used by entrepreneurs to construct their own careers and lives. Job crafting has been viewed as a way to align motivations and experiences in the pursuit of callings (Hall & Chandler, 2005), and this activity has been described as bringing both enjoyment and meaningfulness (Berg et al., 2010), two components of psychological well-being (Ryan & Deci, 2001).

Job crafting has been primarily associated with workers who have a high latitude for workplace creativity, freedom and discretion to choose how they conduct themselves, though it has also been studied in other, apparently more controlled settings too (e.g., hospital cleaners or call centre workers). It is not uncommon to hear entrepreneurs describe their chosen work in terms of vocation or "the only thing I could really do". Organizational managers have also been described as job crafters insofar as they undertake job role design and influence employee morale, motivation and satisfaction by altering job specifications. Small business owner managers thus have considerable job crafting scope both in terms of designing and enacting their own entrepreneurial careers and as managers of their employees. The potential for job crafting to foster entrepreneurial careers, especially for employees who have been frustrated in their previous jobs, was identified in Wrzesniewski and Dutton's (2001) seminal paper. While the job crafting concept has been adopted as an explicator for corporate entrepreneurship (Kuratko et al., 2004), it has received little attention as a lens to study general small business entrepreneurship. Further consideration of "entrepreneurial job crafting" should further elucidate the complex relationships between entrepreneurial motivations, entrepreneurial stress, coping, satisfaction, business success and entrepreneurial well-being. Indeed, entrepreneurship might be the ultimate expression of job crafting in the twenty-first century.

WHAT CONTRIBUTES TO FLOURISHING AND POSITIVE WELL-BEING FOR SMALL BUSINESS OWNERS?

Existing studies have identified the potential for entrepreneurship to contribute to positive psychological well-being (Schindehutte et al., 2006). The concept of entrepreneurship as an expression of job crafting opens up links to ideas of self-actualization (Maslow, 1954), optimal experience and flow (Csikszentmihalyi, 1990).

How entrepreneurs experience and respond emotionally to their work might have a strong bearing on how they invest themselves in their venture, and affect their "propensity to pursue growth, recognize emerging opportunities, or achieve balance between work and family or personal demands" (Schindehutte et al., 2006, p. 350). These responses, therefore, can have a major impact on company performance and are not of merely philosophical interest. New venture creation can be conceived of as an example of self-actualization. Peak performance describes instances where people are motivated by circumstances to surpass their normal levels of achievement. Flow is used to describe the positive experiential state when a person is fully engaged in a task where their skills match the significant challenges it poses. The experience of entrepreneurship can provide all of the above. Indeed, not only does entrepreneurship feature numerous highs and lows, the choices made by entrepreneurs can increase the prevalence of these (Shane et al., 2003). Where positive experiences occur, the desirability of such events increases and they become a source of motivation to the entrepreneur. Entrepreneurship takes place in a context of abundant stressors, many challenges and competing demands, and much uncertainty about what action to take or its likely outcomes. Achieving success in such an environment can provide peak experiences, performance in that arena can be self-actualizing and flow states can arise periodically (Schindehutte et al., 2006). These aspects of entrepreneurial experience may provide entrepreneurs with the psychological resources necessary to endure in the face of obstacles, in turn contributing to personal and organizational performance.

THE ROLE OF SOCIAL SUPPORT CAPITAL

Entrepreneurs have been called a product of their social environment, background, networks and interactions (Anderson & Miller, 2003), echoing the psychodynamic approach to understanding entrepreneurial motivations (Kets de Vries, 1980). We suggest that a hitherto underexplored but important aspect of social interactions in entrepreneurial networks is their potential role in buffering stress. The mechanism for this is social support, the network manifestation of which is conceptualized as social capital.

The role of social support as a buffer of stress has been widely studied. Social support in organizations has been found to come from supervisors, colleagues, family and a participative leadership style. According to the model of optimal stress–support matching, the effect of social support is moderated by its fit to the situation (Thoits, 1995). That is, specific types of support are most beneficial to specific outcomes only. While acknowledging the universal beneficial nature of support, proponents of this model argue that work stress can be most strongly buffered by supervisors. Social support is an important potential buffering factor in entrepreneurial stress because owner managers typically report isolation as a key factor of their working lives (Zhang & Hamilton, 2009, 2010).

It has been suggested that people who perceive that they receive high levels of social support assess their environment as less stressful than others, and that social support conveys protection from future stressful events, promotes well-being and buffers against the impact of events. While empirical evidence for the protective and promotive effects has been found, the so-called "buffering effect" has been subject to much debate and dispute about empirical evidence for its validity (Luszczynska & Cieslak, 2005). Social support is clearly an important consideration in regard to the well-being of small business owner managers. They typically lack internal mentors, and have no superior, but might rely instead on peers and networks.

Numerous studies have examined the link between networks and entrepreneurship (Hansen, 1995; Chell & Baines, 2000; Dodd & Patra, 2002; Jack et al., 2008); and entrepreneurship has even been described as a "social undertaking" that should be "understood within the context of social systems" (Sarason et al., 2006). Most small business owners are involved in micro-businesses, and they typically have relatively small networks with low diversity (Curran et al., 1993; Taylor et al., 2004), consisting of customers, suppliers, competitors, professional advisers and funders. Moreover, the intensity of the day-to-day requirements of small business management limits their potential exposure to wider networks, with the exception of personal social networks.

Lists of entrepreneurial coping mechanisms often include networks and social capital, which have been described as crucial to entrepreneurial processes. Gordon & Jack (2010) reviewed the importance of the social relations and networks in which an entrepreneur is immersed. They listed a range of benefits, including that they are valuable in enterprise formation; extend the potential resource base of the entrepreneur; provide a learning environment; are a source of information on opportunities and resources; increase the probability of venture success; and enhance venture survival. However, their potential role as an effective component of entrepreneurial coping strategies has been underplayed. It is at least partly through their impact on coping that entrepreneurial networks can help overcome start-up concerns, underpin motivation and improve survival.

Social capital has been described as a resource of personal ties used by people for their development (Anderson & Jack, 2002; Casson & Giusta, 2007). It facilitates activity in particular social contexts, and its features include social interaction, social ties, trusting relationships and value systems (Nahapiet & Ghoshal, 1998). Social capital arises by a process involving learning about others, developing knowledge of them and learning to trust another person (Jack & Mouzas, 2007). Trust is a crucial contributor to building relationships with others (Zhang & Hamilton, 2010), and has been called a "coin of social exchange" (Anderson et al., 2007, p. 246). It is therefore a vital element in establishing social capital.

It is taken as axiomatic that small business owners often have few people with whom they can openly and honestly discuss issues of concern to them, and research provides many examples to validate that assumption (for example, Zhang & Hamilton, 2010). The world of the owner manager has been described as a lonely place. Dealings with traditional entrepreneurial network members – suppliers, customers, funding organizations and family – may all invoke the facade of confidence that Kets de Vries (1980) described. That leaves the entrepreneur without the pressure release valve of a trusted confidante. To provide that, while simultaneously maintaining sufficient levels of challenge to keep a purposeful focus on goals, requires a particular type of *challenging* social support. Combining the concepts of social capital and social support we suggest that, in the context of stress and coping, "social support capital" is an important resource for entrepreneurs. This parallels the suggestion by Jack and Mouzas (2007) that entrepreneurs should discriminate between general network relationships and ones that provide timely opportunities to learn or obtain resources appropriate to their business. This analysis of the benefit derived from networks further strengthens their importance in the entrepreneurial context, and brings to light their potential role in stress moderation. Indeed, the historic fixation on the putative material benefits from networks and social capital has resulted in a failure to realize the huge psychological benefits that these can provide to owners of small businesses.

PRACTICAL IMPLICATIONS FOR SMALL BUSINESS OWNERS

The entrepreneurial lifestyle is invariably subject to a wide range of stressors, and entrepreneurial behaviour can exacerbate those. There is also considerable ongoing debate in the literature on the applicability of research findings in practical and effective interventions (Dewe & Trenberth, 2004). Furthermore, the evidence base for the experience of workplace stress in small businesses, its occurrence and how it is handled in practice is very weak. The number and diversity of small businesses means that no single approach is likely to suit them all (Black, 2008), yet they make an enormous contribution to the economy and employ a large proportion of the workforce. What, then, should the small business owner manager do? Research from many fields gives considerable insight into ways in which practitioners can respond positively and creatively to the challenge of workplace stress. This section contains a selection of examples.

Commenting on the comparatively high rates of entrepreneurship typically demonstrated by immigrant communities in the UK, Dewhurst (1996) identified hardship and cultural dislocation as key motivators to enterprise. He suggested that:

> Perhaps in the UK, we should encourage small business training schemes which are themselves tough and which emphasise the characteristics of toughness and discipline required to succeed in this area. Perhaps we still tend to featherbed "start-ups", to encourage new businesses with financial support in the early months which subtly deprives the entrepreneur of the need to fight hard for survival in a hostile business environment. If this, too, is true, we have some clear guidelines on how to encourage small business entrepreneurship in the UK: we need to make small business entrepreneurs realise that self-reliance, hard work and discipline are necessary factors for success. (Dewhurst, 1996, pp. 107–8).

While we do not wholly concur with Dewhurst's "tough love" approach, we do believe that entrepreneurs, their advisers and entrepreneurship scholars need to pay more attention to the concept of stress. Entrepreneurial stress remains poorly understood, yet clearly has substantial impacts upon the effectiveness of entrepreneurs, the performance of their businesses, their own psychological and physical health and their family relationships. Merely stating that business founders need to take risks and work hard is not enough. Aspiring entrepreneurs should be better educated on how to understand the ways in which stress can become manifest, to develop their own suitable coping approaches and to appreciate the importance of workplace stress among their staff.

The Value of Respite

The pervasive nature of entrepreneurship, which can monopolize financial and emotional resources, intrude into home life, and come to dominate every waking hour, has been well documented. While in many ways that reflects the due care and attention business ownership demands, it leaves open the question of how should owner managers re-energize themselves or "sharpen the saw" (Covey, 1989)? Put another way, entrepreneurs need to focus as much on their own performance as on that of their business. The value of leisure as a restorative coping strategy for stress in general (Haworth, 1997; Haworth & Veal, 2004) and workplace stress (Kabanoff, 1982; Trenberth et al., 1999) in particular has been comprehensively studied. Active (e.g., sport) and passive (e.g., television viewing) leisure modes have been distinguished, and serious leisure (engaging in amateur, hobbyist or volunteer activities) and optimal leisure lifestyles have been defined (Stebbins, 2004).

Contrary to the view that leisure is a trivial concern, it has been described as having a huge therapeutic effect (Caldwell, 2005), often producing the types of peak experience and flow states mentioned earlier in this chapter. Leisure has protective features, and has been identified as providing protective, coping and transcending effects in regard to stress. In regard to burnout, it has been found that actual leisure behaviour, not just leisure attitudes, is inversely related to burnout and that "there is a reason to believe that simply taking 'time-out' through any leisure activity is important in the reduction of burnout, at least in the short run" (Iso-Ahola & Mannell, 2004, p. 192).

The work–leisure patterns of workers in different occupations have been examined. One study of workplace stress and leisure (Kabanoff & O'Brien, 1986) found that "for managers stress was associated with recuperative leisure (reactive compensation), but for professionals stress was associated with both recuperative and active-compensatory leisure". Entrepreneurs were not directly identified.

Vacations as a form of respite have been found to have recuperative value, though with a marked half-life of diminution upon return to work and much complexity in regard to how they match expectations, or cause further stress themselves (Eden, 2001). Among more frequent and episodic forms of leisure buffer, exercise is a much-promoted coping strategy that provides many people with a leisure activity of choice. Links between entrepreneurship and physical fitness (Goldsby et al., 2005), and between exercise and mental well-being in corporate employees (Thogersen-Ntoumani et al., 2005) have shown some of its benefits on performance (Neck & Cooper, 2000) and psychological health (Rippe, 1989). Though by no means a panacea for everyone, exercise has even been viewed as a maintenance function that itself becomes part of work:

> Many entrepreneurs realise that the extraordinary workloads that their way of living imposes on them means that they have to be fit to be able to take the strain. Many entrepreneurs monitor what they eat and drink. Some establish exercise routines. Jogging, keep-fit classes, aerobics, swimming, walking and weight lifting are their favoured activities for what little "leisure" time they allow themselves. In such circumstances leisure itself is little more than an extension of time dedicated to work. (Dewhurst, 1996, p. 101)

The Role of Positive Psychology

The discipline of positive psychology (Seligman & Csikszentmihalyi, 2000; Aspinwall & Staudinger, 2003) brings many lessons that can be applied to the small business stress context. In particular, empirical validation of interventions has shown that many variables of expressed personality are malleable, and can be trained (Seligman et al., 2005). One such factor is locus of control (Rotter, 1966), which has been described as a key component of well-being (Spector et al., 2002), and studies made in terms of its contribution to entrepreneurial behaviour (Rahim, 1996). Locus of control describes beliefs about how strongly behaviour will be likely to produce a rewarding outcome. People with an internal locus of control believe that they can influence the likelihood of receiving desired outcomes. People with an external locus of control see a far weaker link between their behaviour and the likelihood of being rewarded.

An example of the practical relevance of locus of control comes from a study of over 100 small business owners who had been affected by a US hurricane, an event reasonably assumed to "contribute to abnormal stress levels" (Anderson, 1977, p. 447). The study looked at subsequent business performance and the impact that locus of control had on long-term performance. As expected, those with strong internal locus of control perceived lower stress levels than those with a stronger external locus of control, and they responded with more task-oriented coping behaviours than externals. It was suggested that locus of control orientation influences performance outcomes, providing a feedback that contributes to future locus of control orientation. Identifying a practical application in stress training for entrepreneurs, he concluded that "an internal locus of control orientation is a prerequisite of success for entrepreneurs" (p. 450).

Better awareness of the role that stress can play in small business performance, and openness to the value that leisure can bring as a coping mechanism, are both instances of where self-leadership falls firmly under the remit of the small business owner manager. Other aspects of self-leadership that can impact on the stress that owner managers and their employees experience include emotional intelligence (Goleman, 1996), which can allow people to better sense their own stress responses and allow for a more proactive approach to coping (Aspinwall & Taylor, 1997). However, some authors from the clinical psychology domain have cautioned that the control of one's thoughts and feelings advocated by emotional intelligence can be disadvantageous for mental well-being compared with psychological acceptance. Acceptance refers to willingness to "experience thoughts, feelings, and physiological sensations, especially those which are negatively evaluated (e.g. fear), without having to avoid them, or let them determine one's actions" (Donaldson-Feilder & Bond, 2004, p. 188).

Supporting Owner Managers to Develop as Leaders of Small Businesses

Our institution has a decade-long history of working closely with small business owner managers on their personal and business development and growth. Two of our programmes provide good examples of the ways in which targeted business support can provide owner managers with a set of valuable tools to address entrepreneurial job stress. The LEAD programme (Zhang & Hamilton, 2009, 2010) is a ten-month-long business growth initiative, built around what we call an integrated learning model. Cohorts of 20–25 owner managers work together in a peer-to-peer network that features high levels of inter-personal trust. Delegates attend an initial two-day experiential event at an off-campus location, during which a variety of devices are used to engender mutual trust and sharing. Initial individualized feelings of isolation and context-specific problems are soon realized to have broad general occurrence, common ground is established, and delegates begin to build a trust platform important for the remainder of the programme. Subsequent activities include business and leadership masterclasses, action learning, coaching, business shadowing and exchanges, and feedback and reflection sessions. A strong focus is placed on the role of the owner manager as leader of their business (Kempster & Cope, 2010), their impact on their employees and how to implement effective task delegation practices. LEAD provides an opportunity to work "on the business, not in the business", encourages reflection, provides respite, gives strategic space (Jones et al., 2007) and offers a trust-based peer-to-peer environment that provides support *with* challenge. It generates social support capital of the sort we described above, and provides purposeful high-order network learning. Initially funded by the Northwest Regional Development Agency, the LEAD model has now been deployed across the North West of England, and in Wales. By 2012 there will be in excess of 2000 LEAD graduates.

Since our first LEAD delegates graduated in 2004 we have also always offered a post-LEAD programme. The current version of this is GOLD, a non-executive director simulation (George et al., 2010). Working in their now-familiar action learning set groups of six or seven members, GOLD participants come together to work as if they were boards with non-executive directors. An overnight experiential is used to establish trust as well as explain the procedural elements of GOLD. All participants begin to work on a five-year development for themselves and their businesses. Meeting on a rotating basis at each other's premises, the host for each meeting circulates, in advance, a full board briefing. One member acts as chair for the meeting and they agree with the host what strategic issue the board needs to work on. Meetings conclude with action points, which are revisited at future meetings for progress reports. The aim is to both challenge and support owner managers as they focus on the survival, development and growth of their businesses, while being simultaneously mindful of the need to devote due attention to their own personal aspirations, motivations and growth.

Neither of these two programmes was designed to address stress and well-being issues. However, they include elements such as strategic planning, realistic but challenging goal setting, peer-to-peer learning, social support capital, delegation and related time and task management issues, self-reflection and appropriate development of organizational procedures to support business growth. These features have all been identified in the main part of this chapter as being important facets of entrepreneurial satisfaction, stress interactions and well-being in the entrepreneurial context.

CONCLUSION

Cooper and Dewe (2004, p. 118), in answering their own question "Why study stress?", stated that "if stress is an important factor in illness today, then society should expect 'those who know something about its antecedents and its mediators to do something about it'". It is in the spirit of that challenge, and recognition of the role that stress plays in organizational performance, that we offer this chapter as a contribution to the small business literature. This chapter explored the concepts of job stressors, coping and well-being in the context of small business. It considered ways in which stressors, coping and well-being might contribute to understanding the experience of small business owners and their employees.

Despite the recognition that small business management involves certain unique stresses and strains in individual and organizational terms, it appears that there is a dearth of empirical research in this important area. This is a major omission as, through their interaction with emotion and behaviour, stress and well-being have a huge impact on entrepreneurial satisfaction and motivation, personal and business performance and the health and well-being of entrepreneurs, their employees and their families. Entrepreneurial job stress affects performance, and performance affects stress. These, in turn, influence entrepreneurs as they decide how to launch, develop, grow or close their businesses.

This chapter contributes four concepts adapted from other literatures, to help frame our thinking in terms of the small business and entrepreneurial context. First, we introduced the idea of "entrepreneurial satisfaction" to capture well-being associated with running your own business, derived from relatively high levels of power and autonomy, and freedom; the ability to job craft; and responding to and overcoming challenges. Second, and linked to this, is the concept of "entrepreneurial strain". Specifically, experiences of entrepreneurial strain can prompt proactive coping strategies that result in behaviours that reduce the causes of strain, leading in due course to improved business performance. Third, we identified that the concept of "entrepreneurial emotion work" could provide a fruitful theoretical framework to help us understand the underlying experience of being a small business owner manager. Finally, we articulated "social support capital", whereby networks provide a type of support that is sufficiently, but not overly, challenging and have the potential to enhance individual and organizational performance. There is the potential for these concepts to add substantially to our understanding of small business behaviour and performance.

Small businesses are a major constituent of national economies, and great hopes are pinned on their potential to deliver economic growth, innovation and employment in the future. Stress and well-being issues are central to our understanding of how owner managers experience entrepreneurship, its challenges and rewards. There remains a huge opportunity to research the experience of entrepreneurial stress, employee stress in small businesses, and to identify appropriate workplace interventions that will assist owner managers to deal with stress in ways that foster their own well-being as well as that of their businesses.

REFERENCES

Akande, A. (1992), Coping with entrepreneurial stress: A Nigerian case study. *Leadership and Organization Development*, **13**(2), 27–32.

Anderson, A.R. & Jack, S.L. (2002), The articulation of social capital in entrepreneurial networks: A glue or a lubricant? *Entrepreneurship & Regional Development*, **14**(3), 193–210.

Anderson, A.R. & Miller, C.J. (2003), "Class matters": Human and social capital in the entrepreneurial process. *Journal of Socio-Economics*, **32**(1), 17–36.

Anderson, A., Park, J. & Jack, S. (2007), Entrepreneurial social capital: Conceptualizing social capital in new high-tech firms. *International Small Business Journal*, **25**(3), 245–72.

Anderson, C.R. (1977), Locus of control, coping behaviors, and performance in a stress setting – longitudinal-study. *Journal of Applied Psychology*, **62**(4), 446–51.

Arthur, A.R. (2004), Work-related stress, the blind men and the elephant. *British Journal of Guidance & Counselling*, **32**(2), 157–69.

Aspinwall, L.G. & Staudinger, U.M. (eds) (2003), *A Psychology of Human Strengths: Fundamental Questions and Future Directions for a Positive Psychology*, Washington DC, American Psychological Association.

Aspinwall, L.G. & Taylor, S.E. (1997), A stitch in time: Self-regulation and proactive coping. *Psychological Bulletin*, **121**(3), 417–36.

Baines, S. & Wheelock, J. (1997), A business in the family: An investigation of the contribution of family to small business survival, maintenance and growth. Institute for Small Business Affairs, *Research Series Monograph No. 3.*

Benz, M. & Frey, B.S. (2004), Being independent raises happiness at work. *Swedish Economic Policy Review*, **11**(1), 95–134.

Berg, J.M., Grant, A.M. & Johnson, V. (2010), When callings are calling: Crafting work and leisure in pursuit of unanswered occupational callings. *Organization Science*, **21**(5), 973–94.

Black, C. (2008), *Working for a Healthier Tomorrow – Dame Carol Black's Review of the Health of Britain's Working Age Population*, Presented to the Secretary of State for Health and the Secretary of State for Work and Pensions, London.

Blanchflower, D.G. & Oswald, A.J. (1998), What makes an entrepreneur? *Journal of Labor Economics*, **16**(1), 26–61.

Bradley, D.E. & Roberts, J.A. (2004), Self-employment and job satisfaction: Investigating the role of self-efficacy, depression, and seniority. *Journal of Small Business Management*, **42**(1), 37–58.

Briner, R.B., Harris, C. & Daniels, K. (2004), How do work stress and coping work? Toward a fundamental theoretical reappraisal. *British Journal of Guidance & Counselling*, **32**(2), 223–34.

Burke, R.J. & Weir, T. (1980), Coping with the stress of managerial occupations. In C.L. Cooper & R. Payne (eds) *Current Concerns in Occupational Stress.* Chichester: John Wiley & Sons.

Busenitz, L.W. & Barney, J.B. (1997), Differences between entrepreneurs and managers in large organizations: Biases and heuristics in strategic decision-making. *Journal of Business Venturing*, **12**(1), 9–30.

Buttner, E.H. (1992), Entrepreneurial stress: Is it hazardous to your health? *Journal of Managerial Issues*, **4**(2), 223–40.

Caldwell, L. (2005), Leisure and health: Why is leisure therapeutic? *British Journal of Guidance & Counselling*, **33**(1), 7–26.

Carland, J.W., Hoy, F., Boulton, W.R. & Carland, J.A.C. (1984), Differentiating entrepreneurs from small business owners – a conceptualization. *Academy of Management Review*, **9**(2), 354–9.

Casson, M. & Giusta, M.D. (2007), Entrepreneurship and social capital: Analysing the impact of social networks on entrepreneurial activity from a rational action perspective. *International Small Business Journal*, **25**(3), 220–44.

Chell, E. & Baines, S. (2000), Networking entrepreneurship and microbusiness behaviour. *Entrepreneurship & Regional Development*, **12**(3), 195–215.

Churchill, N.C. & Lewis, V.L. (1983), The five stages of small business growth. *Harvard Business Review*, **61**(3), 30–50.

Clinton, M., Totterdell, P. & Wood, S. (2006), A grounded theory of portfolio working – experiencing the smallest of small businesses. *International Small Business Journal*, **24**(2), 179–203.

Cooper, A.C. & Artz, K.W. (1995), Determinants of satisfaction for entrepreneurs. *Journal of Business Venturing*, **10**(6), 439–57.

Cooper, C.L. & Dewe, P. (2004), *Stress: A Brief History*, Malden, MA: Blackwell Publishing.

Cooper, C.L. & Marshall, J. (1976), Occupational sources of stress: A review of the literature relating to coronary heart disease and mental ill health. *Journal of Occupational Psychology*, **49**(1), 11–28.

Cooper, C. & Robertson, I.T. (eds) (2001), *Well-being in Organizations: A Reader for Students and Practitioners*, Chichester: John Wiley & Sons Ltd.

Cope, J. (2010), Entrepreneurial learning from failure: An interpretative phenomenological analysis. *Journal of Business Venturing*, in press.

Covey, S.R. (1989), *The 7 Habits of Highly Effective People*, London: Simon & Schuster UK Ltd.
Csikszentmihalyi, M. (1990), *Flow: The Psychology of Optimal Experience*, New York: Harper Perennial.
Curran, J., Jarvis, R., Blackburn, R.A. & Black, S. (1993), Networks and small firms: Constructs, methodological strategies and some findings. *International Small Business Journal*, **11**(2), 13–25.
Dewe, P. (2004), Work stress and coping: Theory, research and practice. *British Journal of Guidance & Counselling*, **32**(2), 139–42.
Dewe, P. & Trenberth, L. (2004), Work stress and coping: Drawing together research and practice. *British Journal of Guidance & Counselling*, **32**(2), 143–56.
Dewhurst, J. (1996), The entrepreneur. In P. Burns & J. Dewhurst (eds) *Small Business and Entrepreneurship*, 2nd edn. London, Macmillan Business.
Dodd, S.D. & Patra, E. (2002), National differences in entrepreneurial networking. *Entrepreneurship & Regional Development*, **14**(2), 117–34.
Dolinsky, A.L. & Caputo, R.K. (2003), Health and female self-employment. *Journal of Small Business Management*, **41**(3), 233–41.
Donaldson-Feilder, E.J. & Bond, F.W. (2004), The relative importance of psychological acceptance and emotional intelligence to workplace well-being. *British Journal of Guidance & Counselling*, **32**(2), 187–203.
Dyer, W.G.J. (2006), Examining the "Family Effect" on firm performance. *Family Business Review*, **19**(4), 253–74.
Eden, D. (2001), Vacations and other respites: Studying stress on and off the job. In C.L. Cooper & I. Robertson (eds) *Well-being in Organizations: A Reader for Students and Practitioners.* Chichester: John Wiley & Sons Ltd.
Florén, H. (2006), Managerial work in small firms: Summarising what we know and sketching a research agenda. *International Journal of Entrepreneurial Behaviour & Research,* **12**(5), 272–88.
Friedman, M. & Rosenman, R.H. (1974), *Type A Behaviour and Your Heart*, London: Wildwood House.
Gartner, W.B. (1988), "Who is an entrepreneur?" Is the wrong question. *American Journal of Small Business*, **13**(1), 11–32.
Gatrell, C.J. (2004), *Hard Labour: The Sociology of Parenthood*, Maidenhead: Open University Press.
George, M.J.A. & Hamilton, E. (2010), Exploring the concept of "well-being" in the context of family business. Long Term Perspectives on Family Business, 10th Annual IFERA World Family Business Research Conference, Lancaster, England.
George, M.J.A., Hamilton, E. & Gordon, I. (2010), Case study: What is (the point of) an entrepreneur in residence? A description of the Lancaster University experience, plus some worldwide comparisons. *Industry and Higher Education*, **24**(6), 495–503.
Goldsby, M.G., Kuratko, D.F. & Bishop, J.W. (2005), Entrepreneurship and fitness: An examination of rigorous exercise and goal attainment among small business owners. *Journal of Small Business Management*, **43**(1), 78–92.
Goleman, D. (1996), *Emotional Intelligence: Why it Can Matter More than IQ,* London: Bloomsbury Publishing PLC.
Gordon, I. & Jack, S.L. (2010), HEI engagement with SMEs; Developing social capital. *International Journal of Entrepreneurial Behaviour and Research*, **16**(6), 517–39.

Goss, D. (1991), *Small Business and Society*, London: Routledge.
Hall, D.T. & Chandler, D.E. (2005), Psychological success: When the career is a calling. *Journal of Organizational Behavior*, **26**(2), 155–76.
Hamilton, E. (2006a), Narratives of enterprise as epic tragedy. *Management Decision*, **44**(4), 536–51.
Hamilton, E. (2006b), Whose story is it anyway?: Narrative accounts of the role of women in founding and establishing family businesses. *International Small Business Journal*, **24**(3), 253–71.
Hansen, E.L. (1995), Entrepreneurial networks and new organization growth. *Entrepreneurship Theory & Practice*, **19**(4), 7–19.
Haworth, J.T. (1997), *Work, Leisure and Well-being*, London: Routledge.
Haworth, J.T. & Veal, A.J. (eds) (2004), *Work and Leisure*, London: Routledge.
HSE (2009), Health and Safety Statistics 2008/09. London: Health and Safety Executive.
Iso-Ahola, S.E. & Mannell, R.C. (2004), Leisure and health. In J.T. Haworth & A.J. Veal (eds) *Work and Leisure*, Hove: Routledge.
Jack, S.L. & Mouzas, S. (2007), Entrepreneurship as renegotiated exchange in networks. Paper presented at the 23rd IMP conference, Manchester.
Jack, S., Dodd, S.D. & Anderson, A.R. (2008), Change and the development of entrepreneurial networks over time: A processual perspective. *Entrepreneurship & Regional Development*, **20**(2), 125–59.
Jones, O., Macpherson, A., Thorpe, R. & Ghecham, A. (2007), The evolution of business knowledge in SMEs: Conceptualizing strategic space. *Strategic Change*, **16**(6), 281–94.
Kabanoff, B. (1982), Occupational and sex differences in leisure needs and leisure satisfaction. *Journal of Occupational Behavior*, **3**(3), 233–45.
Kabanoff, B. & O'Brien, G.E. (1986), Stress and the leisure needs and activities of different occupations. *Human Relations*, **39**(5), 903–16.
Kautonen, T. & Palmroos, J. (2009), The impact of a necessity-based start-up on subsequent entrepreneurial satisfaction. *International Entrepreneurial Management Journal*, **6**(3), 285–300.
Kempster, S. & Cope, J. (2010), Learning to lead in the entrepreneurial context. *International Journal of Entrepreneurial Behaviour and Research*, **16**(1), 6–35.
Kets De Vries, M.F.R. (1980), Stress and the entrepreneur. In C.L. Cooper & R. Payne (eds) *Current Concerns in Occupational Stress*. Chichester: John Wiley & Sons.
Kinman, G. & Jones, F. (2005), Lay representations of workplace stress: What do people really mean when they say they are stressed? *Work & Stress*, **19**(2), 101–20.
Kuratko, D.F., Ireland, R.D. & Hornsby, J.S. (2004), Corporate entrepreneurship behavior among managers: A review of theory, research, and practice. In J. Katz & T. Lumpkin (eds) *Entrepreneurship, Firm Emergence and Growth*. Bingley, UK: Emerald Group Publishing Limited.
Lazarus, R.S. & Folkman, S. (1984), *Stress, Appraisal and Coping*, New York: Springer.
Lupton, D. (1998), *The Emotional Self*, London: Sage Publications Ltd.
Luszczynska, A. & Cieslak, R. (2005), Protective, promotive, and buffering effects of perceived social support in managerial stress: The moderating role of personality. *Anxiety, Stress & Coping*, **18**(3), 227–44.
Maslach, C., Schaufeli, W.B. & Leiter, M.P. (2001), Job burnout. *Annual Review of Psychology*, **52**(1), 397–422.

Maslow, A.H. (1954), *Motivation and Personality*, London: Harper Collins.
Miles, R.H. (1980), Organization boundary roles. In C.L. Cooper & R. Payne (eds) *Current Concerns in Occupational Stress.* Chichester: John Wiley & Sons.
Morse, J.M. (1995), Designing funded qualitative research. In N.K. Denzin & Y.S. Lincoln (eds) *Handbook of Qualitative Research.* Thousand Oaks, CA: Sage.
Nahapiet, J. & Ghoshal, S. (1998), Social capital, intellectual capital, and the organizational advantage. *The Academy of Management Review*, **23**(2), 242–66.
Neck, C.P. & Cooper, K.H. (2000), The fit executive: Exercise and diet guidelines for enhancing performance. *Academy of Management Executive*, **14**(2), 72–83.
Pugliesi, K. (1995), Work and well-being: Gender differences in the psychological consequences of employment. *Journal of Health and Social Behavior*, **36**(1), 57–71.
Rahim, A. (1996), Stress, strain, and their moderators: An empirical comparison of entrepreneurs and managers. *Journal of Small Business Management*, **34**(1), 46–58.
Rauch, A., Unger, J. & Rosenbusch, N. (2007), Entrepreneurial stress and long term survival: Is there a causal link? *Frontiers of Entrepreneurial Research*, **27**(4), Article 2.
Reynolds, S. (1997), Psychological well-being at work: Is prevention better than cure? *Journal of Psychosomatic Research*, **43**(1), 93–102.
Rippe, J.M. (1989), CEO Fitness – the Performance Plus. *Psychology Today*, **23**(5), 50–53.
Rotter, J.B. (1966), Generalized expectancies for internal versus external control of reinforcement. *Psychological Monographs*, **80**(1), 1–28.
Ryan, R.M. & Deci, E.L. (2001), On happiness and human potentials: A review of research on hedonic and eudaimonic well-being. *Annual Review of Psychology*, **52**(1), 141–166.
Sarason, Y., Dean, T. & Dillard, J.F. (2006), Entrepreneurship as the nexus of individual and opportunity: A structuration view. *Journal of Business Venturing*, **21**(3), 286–305.
Schindehutte, M., Morris, M. & Allen, J. (2006), Beyond achievement: Entrepreneurship as extreme experience. *Small Business Economics*, **27**(4–5), 349–68.
Schulkin, J. & Power, M.L. (2009), *The Evolution of Obesity*, Baltimore: The Johns Hopkins University Press.
Searle, B.A. (2008), *Well-Being: In Search of a Good Life?*, Bristol: The University of Bristol.
Seligman, M.E.P. & Csikszentmihalyi, M. (2000), Positive psychology: An introduction. *American Psychologist*, **55**(1), 5–14.
Seligman, M.E.P., Steen, T.A., Park, N. & Peterson, C. (2005), Positive psychology progress – empirical validation of interventions. *American Psychologist*, **60**(5), 410–21.
Selye, H. (1956), *The Stress of Life,* New York: McGraw-Hill Book Company.
Shane, S., Locke, E.A. & Collins, C.J. (2003), Entrepreneurial motivation. *Human Resource Management Review*, **13**(2), 257–79.
Shepherd, D.A. (2003), Learning from business failure: Propositions of grief recovery for the self-employed. *Academy of Management Review*, **28**(2), 318–28.
Shirom, A. (2003), The effects of work stress on health. In M.J. Shabracq, J.A.M. Winnubst & C.L. Cooper (eds) *The Handbook of Work & Health Psychology.* London: Wiley.

Singh, S., Corner, P. & Pavlovich, K. (2007), Coping with entrepreneurial failure. *Journal of Management & Organization*, **13**(4), 331–44.

Spector, P.E., Cooper, C.L., Sanchez, J.I., O'Driscoll, M., Sparks, K., Bernin, P., Bossing, A., Dewe, P., Hart, P., Lu, L., Miller, K., De Moraes, L.R., Ostrognay, G.M., Pagon, M., Pitariu, H.D., Poelmans, S.A.Y., Radhakrishnan, P., Russinova, V., Salamatov, V. & Salgado, J.F. (2002), Locus of control and well-being at work: How generalizable are Western findings? *Academy of Management Journal*, **45**(2), 453–66.

Stebbins, R.A. (2004), Serious leisure, volunteerism and quality of life. In J.T. Haworth & A.J. Veal (eds) *Work and Leisure*. Hove: Routledge.

Taylor, D.W., Jones, O. & Boles, K. (2004), Building social capital through action learning: An insight into the entrepreneur. *Education & Training*, **46**(4/5), 226–35.

Tetrick, L.E., Slack, K.J., Da Silva, N. & Sinclair, R.R. (2000), A comparison of the stress–strain process for business owners and nonowners: Differences in job demands, emotional exhaustion, satisfaction, and social support. *Journal of Occupational Health Psychology*, **5**(4), 464–76.

Thogersen-Ntoumani, C., Fox, K.R. & Ntoumanis, N. (2005), Relationships between exercise and three components of mental well-being in corporate employees. *Psychology of Sport and Exercise*, **6**(6), 609–27.

Thoits, P.A. (1995), Stress, coping, and social support processes – where are we – what next. *Journal of Health and Social Behavior*, **35**(Extra Issue), 53–79.

Trenberth, L., Dewe, P. & Walkey, F. (1999), Leisure and its role as a strategy for coping with work stress. *International Journal of Stress Management*, **6**(2), 89–103.

Whyley, C. (1998), *Risky Business: The Personal and Financial Costs of Small Business Failure*, London: Policy Studies Institute, University of Westminster.

Wilkinson, A. (1999), Employment relations in SMEs. *Employee Relations*, **21**(3), 206–17.

Wincent, J. & Ortqvist, D. (2009), Role stress and entrepreneurship research. *International Entrepreneurial Management Journal*, **5**(1), 1–22.

Wrzesniewski, A. & Dutton, J.E. (2001), Crafting a job: Revisioning employees as active crafters of their work. *The Academy of Management Review*, **26**(2), 179–201.

Zapf, D., Seifert, C., Schmutte, B., Mertini, H. & Holz, M. (2001), Emotion work and job stressors and their effects on burnout. *Psychology & Health*, **16**(5), 527–45.

Zhang, J. & Hamilton, E. (2009), A process model of small business owner-managers' learning in peer networks. *Education & Training*, **51**(8), 607–23.

Zhang, J. & Hamilton, E. (2010), Entrepreneurship education for owner-managers: the process of trust building for an effective learning community. *Journal of Small Business and Entrepreneurship*, **23**(3), 249–70.

PART V

Improving human resource management practices in small businesses

13. A comprehensive approach to promoting justice in SMEs

Andrew Noblet and Denise Jepsen

INTRODUCTION

Employees' perceptions of how fairly they're treated in the workplace (also referred to as organizational justice) have long been known to impact on a range of outcomes critical to organizational functioning including employee motivation, labour turnover, deviant work behaviours (e.g., theft, sabotage) and employee performance (e.g., Adams, 1965; Colquitt et al., 2001; Greenberg, 1990; Leventhal, 1976). The literature examining the strategies organizations can adopt to prevent and reduce perceptions of injustice is less developed (Greenberg, 2009) and what information is available tends to assume that organizations have a team of professionally trained human resource (HR) specialists to address justice-related issues (Cropanzano et al., 2003; Posthuma & Campion, 2008). However, smaller firms are far less likely to have dedicated HR personnel, with owners and managers often performing key HR functions (Forth et al., 2004; Saru, 2009), and there are strong indications that these and other common characteristics of SMEs (e.g., decreased spatial and organizational distance between members) may make them especially vulnerable to both the sources and ill-effects of unfair treatment.

The central question addressed in this chapter is, what strategies can SMEs adopt in order to promote organizational justice in their workplaces? We present a framework that SMEs can use to develop a comprehensive approach to promoting fairness in their organizations. This framework consists of strategies that operate at three inter-related levels (primary, secondary and tertiary) and is aimed at providing owners, managers and other personnel with people-management responsibilities with practical guidance on how they can address the causes and consequences of injustice in the workplace. Before discussing this framework, we will first describe the different forms of organizational justice and expand on how perceptions of justice (and injustice) can impact on outcomes important to both employers and employees. This discussion will be followed by a more detailed explanation of the reasons why SMEs are particularly susceptible to perceptions of injustice and will highlight why smaller firms need to pay close attention to their employees' fairness perceptions.

WHAT IS ORGANIZATIONAL JUSTICE?

The concept of justice is not a uni-dimensional construct and there are different forms of justice that have been found to have different effects on employee-level outcomes (Bies & Moag, 1986; Colquitt, et al., 2001). The four main forms of justice referred to in recent justice research are distributive, procedural, informational and interpersonal justice (Colquitt et al., 2001).

Distributive justice focuses on the individuals' perception of how fairly their "inputs" (i.e., effort, experience, education) are rewarded in comparison to referent others (e.g., co-workers). These rewards are referred to as "resources" and can come in many forms including pay increases, promotions, new work roles and/or improved physical working conditions (such as office space). While distributive justice captures employees' perceptions of how fairly resources are allocated, procedural justice refers to the perceived fairness of the procedures used to make justice-related decisions (Cohen-Charash & Spector, 2001). Assessments of procedural justice take into account the extent to which the resource-allocation decision was clear and transparent, incorporated accurate information, was impartially applied and provided employees with the opportunity to contribute to the decision-making process – sometimes referred to as process control or "voice" (Leventhal, 1976). Interpersonal justice and informational justice (Greenberg & Baron, 2008), often seen as interactional forms of justice, refer to the interpersonal conduct and communication of the parties in charge of the resource allocation decisions (Bies & Moag, 1986; Cohen-Charash & Spector, 2001). Interpersonal justice focuses on the degree to which people are treated with respect and dignity, while informational justice refers to the extent to which employees receive timely and accurate information about the decision-making processes, or the outcomes of those processes (Colquitt, 2001).

Although the four forms of justice have been found to be independently associated with a range of outcomes (see following section), they have also been shown to interact with one another. For example, Brockner and Wiesenfeld (1996) reviewed research involving 45 independent samples of employees and found that, generally, procedural justice buffered the negative effects of unfair distribution of resources (a relationship commonly referred to as the "fair process effect"). While this buffering effect was thought to be the result of procedural justice, more recent research suggests that interactional fairness (and their component forms, interpersonal and informational justice) can also moderate the negative influence of distributive justice (Bies & Moag, 1986; Colquitt, 2001).

WHAT ARE THE EFFECTS OF JUSTICE?

Perceptions of justice can have far-reaching implications for the attitudes and behaviours of individual employees as well as the functioning of work groups and entire organizations. In terms of employees, perceived injustice has been associated with a range of health-related measures including lower well-being, reduced job satisfaction and increased emotion-related responses including anger, depression and anxiety (e.g., Kivimaki et al., 2004; Schmitt & Dorfel, 1999). Other research shows that more specific forms of fairness, namely distributive and procedural fairness, are closely associated with stress-related outcomes, including psychosomatic health complaints and emotional exhaustion (e.g., De Boer et al., 2002; Tepper, 2001).

The health effects of injustice suggest that fairness perceptions would also impact on the ability of employees to perform roles central to organizational functioning. Indeed, perceptions of justice are associated with in-role performance, citizenship behaviours, commitment to the organization, and withdrawal behaviours such as a lack of effort, absenteeism and turnover (e.g., Ambrose, 2002; Cropanzano et al., 2007; Moliner et al., 2008). Counterproductive (e.g., tardiness, lack of cooperation) and retaliatory (e.g., theft, sabotage) behaviours are also potential outcomes of injustice (Fox et al., 2001; Greenberg, 1990). For example, Fox et al. (2001) found that perceptions of procedural and distributive justice were associated with increased counterproductive behaviour including arriving late, avoiding work and criticizing the organization.

Just as unfair treatment can lead to negative outcomes for individuals and organizations, there is also evidence linking fair treatment to worthwhile benefits. For example, supervisors and managers who are regarded as fair, both in the way they allocate resources and the processes used to make justice-related decisions, may strengthen their credibility and power-base in the eyes of employees. A reputation for fairness is particularly valuable when important decisions are to be made, and employees are uncertain about the outcomes (Greenberg, 1988). In such situations, employees may accept the manager's decision more readily and be more committed to taking the required actions. The positive benefits of fairness have also been found in studies focusing on leader–member exchanges where perceptions of justice improved the quality of leader–member relationships (e.g., Masterson et al., 2000; Rupp & Cropanzano, 2002). Other research indicates that trust in the leader is central to building cooperative relations in work teams and in order to generate this trust leaders need to employ practices that promote a sense of procedural fairness, including giving members greater say in the decisions that affect them (Korsgaard et al., 1995).

WHY SHOULD SMEs CARE ABOUT JUSTICE?

The human and economic costs associated with perceptions of justice indicate that all organizations should be concerned about developing and maintaining a high level of justice in the workplace irrespective of their size, industry type or occupational profile. However, small-medium firms face unique challenges both in terms of the conditions that give rise to fairness perceptions and their ability to address the sources and/or effects of justice. As a result, there are strong indications that smaller firms should pay particular attention to the levels of justice/injustice that exist in their workplace.

One of the commonly recognized advantages of small firms is that members of the organization are more likely to be in close proximity to each other, both in terms of organizational and spatial distance (Mayson & Barrett, 2006; Wilkinson, 1999). Although a more compact size and structure offers considerable advantages (e.g., speed of communication, less bureaucratic decision-making and more hands-on managerial support) this close proximity also means that employees will be more aware of the resources each other receives relative to their contributions (Wilkinson, 1999). Workers in SMEs are also in a much better position to observe the procedures authority figures use when making resource allocation decisions (particularly in terms of accuracy of "data" and degree of bias) and to witness the information and treatment workers receive both during and after the decision-making has been completed. This raised awareness not only increases the likelihood that breaches of justice will be detected by the people directly involved in the resource-allocation decision, but any ill-feeling, frustration, suspicion and other negative outcomes will quickly spread throughout the organization and impact on the attitudes and behaviours of other staff.

The close vertical distance between leaders and their followers also increases the likelihood that line managers will be the targets of any negative outcomes associated with injustice. In larger organizations, justice-related decisions such as salary increases, promotions and transfers are generally handled by HR personnel and selection panels (Behrends, 2007). Line supervisors and team leaders are often excluded from this process and, as a result, people's perceptions of how fairly they've been treated by their direct report can be quite different from perceptions of justice directed at the organization overall (Behrends, 2007; Colquitt et al., 2005). However, in smaller firms, where owners and senior managers are much more likely to take direct responsibility for HR functions (e.g., staff recruitment and remuneration), staff's views on how they've been treated by the organization and by their direct manager are more likely to be one of the same. There is therefore greater propensity for the quality of leader–member relationships to be adversely affected in resource-allocation decisions within smaller organizations.

Another key reason why SMEs need to be acutely aware of employees' perceptions of justice is that smaller organizations are less capable of absorbing the negative outcomes of organizational justice. Withdrawal behaviours such as absenteeism and turnover are particularly problematic for small firms who generally don't have the systems and resources to cover for absent workers or to quickly replace employees who have left the organization (Behrends, 2007). Declining levels of motivation, commitment and employee engagement can also cause problems, as more employees are directly involved in the production of goods and services. Any fluctuations in employees' attitudes and behaviours are therefore likely to impact on quality standards, customer satisfaction and other indicators of company performance more quickly than in larger organizations.

The vulnerability of SMEs to perceptions of injustice may be further exacerbated by the approach smaller firms typically adopt when dealing with labour management issues. There is a great deal of variation in how smaller firms are structured and managed, however, two of the common characteristics shared by many SMEs is an informal approach to employee relations and a strong trend towards adopting people management practices based on owner idiosyncrasies (Forth et al., 2004; Marlow, 2006). Coupled with the financial constraints experienced by many smaller firms (Patel & Cardon, 2010), this informality mitigates the adoption of professionally informed policy and practice that can play a key role in preventing/reducing injustice. For example, there is ample evidence that high levels of procedural justice can off-set the negative effects associated with unfavourable resource-allocation decisions (e.g., Brockner & Wiesenfeld, 1996), however, developing clear guidelines on when and how resources are allocated requires an investment of both time and HR expertise, both of which are often in short supply within smaller firms. Similarly, strategies such as appeals systems and grievance procedures can be used to restore perceptions of justice, following unfavourable outcomes and/or treatment, yet these restorative strategies are time-consuming to develop, and, in order to comply with relevant employment legislation, may require the guidance of professionally qualified employment relations specialists. In both these cases, larger organizations have the benefit of "economies of scale", as any systems and policies that are developed to combat the sources and symptoms of injustice will be utilized more frequently in a large corporation than in a smaller firm.

A COMPREHENSIVE APPROACH TO PROMOTING JUSTICE IN THE WORKPLACE

Given that SMEs may be particularly susceptible to higher levels of injustice, a key challenge for smaller firms is to develop strategies that can prevent/reduce cases of injustice, but at the same time, minimize the negative outcomes associated with breaches of fairness. In the following section, we describe a framework that SMEs can use to help guide the development of a comprehensive approach to promoting justice within their organizations. Although this framework can be applied to organizations of all sizes, the specific strategies have been tailored to take into account the constraints and opportunities typically experienced by smaller enterprises.

Developing and maintaining organizational justice requires a comprehensive, well-informed set of strategies that operate at three inter-related levels, namely primary, secondary and tertiary. Strategies at the primary level target the systems, practices and dominant values that influence how the organization operates, what it considers to be important and how people interact with each other. The overriding aim at this level is to build fairness into the culture of the workplace, to ensure there is a consistency of purpose across the whole organization and to use this widespread appreciation for fairness as a foundation for developing more specific, justice-oriented strategies. These more specific strategies are covered at the secondary level and focus on the resource-allocation decisions that are typically associated with justice including reward and recognition systems and performance reviews (Cropanzano et al., 2005). In contrast to the first two levels, which have an emphasis on the prevention and reduction of injustice, the tertiary level strategies recognize that justice breaches will occur from time to time and hence strategies need to be in place to ensure perceptions of fairness are quickly restored (Vermunt & Steensma, 2005).

Irrespective of the particular combination of strategies used to manage justice perceptions, these need to recognize and build on the prescriptive approach to justice. The prescriptive elements of organizational justice are represented in various industrial relations laws and codes of practice and, in many respects, articulate the minimum standards that need to be achieved in order to protect workers' rights, minimize exploitation and harassment and generally uphold fair standards of workplace practice. These laws are present in all industrialized countries and are critical for maintaining a fair and just society. However, employment relations laws generally represent the minimum that is required in order to build fair working environments and organizations need to go well beyond these in order to meet employees' fairness perceptions.

Primary-level Interventions

Managing organizational justice at the primary level recognizes that people's perceptions of fairness are heavily influenced by the extent to which they have access to the resources required to complete required tasks, to fulfil fundamental human needs and to realize a high level of satisfaction and positive well-being. The resources that are critical for achieving these outcomes include support from supervisors and colleagues, participatory decision-making and job control and information and skill development. In the following section we will discuss the implications these resources can have for employees' perceptions of fairness and outline strategies SMEs can take to ensure workers have adequate levels of control, support and information and development.

In practical terms, ongoing access to these resources will determine whether employees have the information, assistance and feedback to perform their job well or whether they are frequently "thrown in the deep-end" with little guidance and support; whether employees have a genuine say in what happens in the organization or whether they are helpless to decisions and actions of people higher up the organizational hierarchy; whether they deal with supervisors and managers who understand the importance of human needs or whether they are at the beck and call of superiors who focus on the task, but not the people performing the task. The key point here is that employees can feel let down, hard done by, under-valued and unfairly treated in everyday situations, not just when reward-allocation decisions are made. An important aim of the primary-level interventions is therefore to develop fairer and more satisfying working environments where positive outcomes such as trust, mutual respect and a spirit of cooperation are hallmarks of how the firm operates.

Enhancing social support

One of the most consistent findings identified in the HRM and organizational psychology literature is the strong relationship between work-based support and a range of important outcomes including job satisfaction, employee well-being, commitment to the organization and absence behaviours (e.g., House, 1981; Humphrey et al., 2007; Noblet et al., 2007). There are a number of different forms of support – including informational (e.g., providing advice and guidance), instrumental (e.g., helping a colleague to complete their work), appraisal (e.g., providing performance feedback) and emotional support (e.g., showing empathy and trust) – and each can be provided by one or a number of sources (managers, team leaders, colleagues, subordinates) (House, 1981).

A major reason why the support provided by managers and colleagues is so influential in shaping people's attitudes and behaviours at work is because each form of support can play a very functional role in helping workers to complete assigned tasks (Humphrey et al., 2007). For example, a supervisor provides an employee with timely guidance on how to operate a new piece of equipment or a colleague helps a worker meet a tight deadline by providing "hands on" assistance. In each of these cases the recipient would have difficulty performing assigned tasks, or at least performing them to the required standard, if the appropriate form and level of support was not available. The supportive resources provided by supervisors and colleagues can also play key roles in helping to protect employee well-being (Karasek & Theorell, 1990). The information, advice and assistance provided by significant others can be used by employees to prevent or reduce common sources of job stress, including role ambiguity, high job demands or interpersonal conflict (e.g., feedback and information from the unit manager helps clarify key work tasks, thereby reducing the stress associated with role ambiguity). At a more symbolic level, the support provided by leaders and fellow workers conveys the message that the recipient is worthy of the information and guidance, that they can add value to the effectiveness of the group and, that the organization cares about their well-being and is looking out for their interests (Lind & Van den Bos, 2002). These messages not only enhance the individual's self-esteem and sense of belonging, but can also serve to generate high levels of trust and reciprocal commitment.

The connections between social support and organizational fairness are best illustrated when the support is lacking. Employees who are required to perform roles where they don't have the necessary information, guidance and assistance are likely to feel unfairly treated and aggrieved. They are also likely to experience a high level of stress and frustration, particularly when the situation is ongoing, and prompt employees to question whether they deserve to receive such treatment. Perceptions of deservingness lie at the heart of organizational fairness and a heightened sense of injustice will occur when employees believe they are undeserving of the treatment provided (Vermunt & Steensma, 2005).

The close relationship between the support and perceptions of fairness raises the question of what organizations can do to ensure employees have adequate levels of support. One of the prerequisites to boosting employee support is for managers to have an accurate understanding of (1) the demands faced by workers – in terms of the volume and complexity of work required, and (2) the skills, guidance, assistance and other resources required to address these demands (Noblet & LaMontagne, 2009). The relative levels of demands and resources will be subject to ongoing change and hence managers need to closely monitor employees' situation and be prepared to quickly address any imbalances.

In the case of SMEs, managers and supervisors working in smaller firms are often in close proximity to their team members and will therefore be in a good position to see, first-hand, if employees are experiencing demand-resource discrepancies. However, senior personnel may be operating under heavy time and resource constraints themselves and organizations therefore need to have two-way communication systems in place to ensure they maintain a clear understanding of their employees' needs. These communication systems include regular team meetings that facilitate open dialogue regarding current and future work demands; one-on-one discussions with staff that provide the opportunity to identify where additional support may be required; conducting regular "shop-floor" visits that provide managers with a practical understanding of the types of constraints and challenges faced by workers and keeping an "open door policy" that gives staff the chance to raise any issues or ideas as they arise.

Involving and engaging employees

The organizational justice literature indicates that giving employees a "voice" in resource-allocation decisions is critical for developing fair procedures, which, in turn, can abate the adverse consequences of unfavourable distributive justice outcomes (Brockner & Wiesenfeld, 1996). However, as pointed out by Gilliland (2009), the importance of decision-making influence was known 50 years before the term organizational justice was coined. Research dating as far back as the Hawthorne studies (see Mayo, 1949) has shown that giving employees greater autonomy in how they complete their work and providing them with opportunities for having a say in how the organization operates can increase their acceptance of, and commitment to, the outcomes of those decisions (Hackman & Oldham, 1976; Maier, 1970; Mayo, 1949). Participatory decision-making and shared leadership can also lead to more creative and innovative problem-solving, especially in situations involving complex issues, and can generate higher levels of motivation and performance (Carson et al., 2007).

Like social support, job control can impact on perceptions of fairness via the functional and stress-buffering routes. In relation to the former, decision-making influence enables the worker to decide which particular skills, methods or processes are required to complete assigned tasks and is therefore instrumental in helping employees fulfil key job responsibilities (Humphrey et al., 2007). However, when job control is low, and employees are expected to take responsibility for decisions made by others, the lack of genuine decision-making authority can leave employees feeling unjustly treated. This sense of inequity is likely to be accentuated in situations where the decisions lead to more complicated work processes, increase customer complaints or otherwise contribute to a more stressful and dissatisfying working environment. In these situations, the inability to change the conditions that caused the stress simply amplifies the frustration, resentment and other negative outcomes.

At a symbolic level, being denied decision-making opportunities can convey the message that employees' ideas and insights are secondary to those of organizational leaders and that, intellectually, they have little to offer the organization. Critical assessments such as this are less likely to be made in situations that are one-off or irregular. However, control and influence are omnipresent in organizational life and, as almost every task involves an element of decision-making input, employees are continually reminded of how much (or how little) decision-making influence they have. Levels of decision-making influence can therefore have a lasting impact on how employees see themselves, their standing in the organization and the organization itself.

In view of the importance of employee involvement, action should be taken to ensure that the level of employee input or control closely matches the demands and pressures faced by employees. Mechanisms for improving participatory decision-making such as semi-autonomous work teams, problem-solving groups and democratic leadership styles can help enhance people's sense of influence and control at both an individual and a group level.

Information and skill development

Although participatory decision-making is a valuable means of tapping into the ideas of employees and generating higher levels of motivation and commitment, employees will not be in a position to take advantage of these opportunities and make sound decisions if they don't have the relevant background information. Likewise, enhancing employees' control over when and how they complete their tasks is likely to prove counterproductive if they don't have the skills and expertise required to complete these tasks. Employees need to feel as though they are making well-informed decisions and that they have the abilities to perform required roles. If they don't have this prerequisite knowledge/skill, the anticipated improvement in motivation and commitment is likely to be replaced by high levels of uncertainty and demotivation, as well as a strong sense of unfair treatment. Before delegating decision-making responsibility to employees, the managers and supervisors in SMEs need to therefore make sure that they've provided the information needed to make well-informed decisions. They also need to ensure that workers have the skills needed to take on more self-directed, autonomous work roles and, where there is a skills gap, that appropriate training and development is provided.

Adopting more supportive, participatory leadership styles will not come naturally to many managers and an important step towards enhancing the support, control and information available to employees is to ensure leaders have the skills needed to utilize this more people-focused approach. Implementing training and development programs for managers and ensuring there are ongoing opportunities for boosting people-management capacities (e.g., coaching and mentoring programs, 360 degree feedback systems) represent valuable mechanisms for helping managers enhance their social support and participatory decision-making skills.

Secondary-level Interventions

The primary-level interventions are aimed at creating working environments where fairness is integrated into the day-to-day transactions between employers and employees and where employees have the fundamental resources – support, control, information and skill development – required to fulfil their job descriptions and to meet basic human needs (respect, belonging, competence). Organizational justice strategies at the secondary level build on these primary-level interventions and address more specific resource-allocation decisions, including those involving reward and recognition, performance appraisal, conflict management and organizational change. Detailed descriptions on how organizations of all sizes can address these types of decisions are covered elsewhere (e.g., Cropanzano, et al., 2007; Posthuma & Campion, 2008; Sidle, 2003). In the following section we will draw on this and other relevant literature to illustrate how the more specific resource-allocation decisions involving reward and recognition and performance reviews can be addressed by SMEs.

Reward and recognition

How SMEs reward their employees can have rapid, far-reaching consequences for the attitudes and behaviours of their workforce. The close spatial proximity between workers means that employees will not only have a better idea of what others receive in relation to their inputs (i.e., the basis for distributive fairness), but they are also more likely to know whether the criteria for making reward-allocation judgements was applied without bias (i.e., key component of procedural justice). Furthermore, employees in smaller organizations are more likely to be aware of the treatment people receive during and after rewards have been allocated (interpersonal justice) – if not through first-hand observations, then certainly via the company "grapevine" – and be cognizant of how widely reward-related information was shared among workers leading up to these decisions (informational justice).

The more compact size of SMEs also means that any news of unfair treatment can quickly spread throughout the organization and impact on the overall climate within the organization in a relatively short space of time. Even if employees have not been wronged themselves, witnessing unfair treatment can impact negatively on their perceptions and attitudes and ultimately undermine their commitment to the firm (Cropanzano et al., 2007; Mollica, 2004). Smaller organizations rely more heavily on achieving an above-average level of motivation and drive from their employees, hence they need to give careful consideration to how they recognize and reward staff (Behrends, 2007). Further, this consideration applies as much to informal reward methods (i.e., showing gratitude, appreciation) as it does to the formal systems (i.e., pay and promotions).

SMEs typically lack formality in how they manage human resources and whilst this does have its advantages , the absence of clear policies and procedures involving reward and recognition could be particularly problematic (Saru, 2009). For many people, work helps fulfil extrinsic and intrinsic needs (e.g., for economic security, to be esteemed and valued by others) and as one's level of remuneration is often closely linked to both sets of needs, employees are generally very sensitive to how financial rewards are allocated and what procedures have been followed when making these decisions. Smaller organizations simply cannot afford to have employees withdrawing their effort or becoming demotivated because of injustice and they therefore need to reassure their employees that the organization takes justice seriously and are following appropriate guidelines when making reward-allocation decisions. Appropriateness in this context takes into account whether there is equity and equality in the distribution of salaries, bonuses and other financial incentives (i.e., distributive justice), as well as the extent to which the procedures used to make those decisions have been applied consistently across individuals, are based on accurate information, are free of bias and have given employees the opportunity to clearly "state their case". For SMEs, these decisions are often made by busy managers, rather than dedicated HR personnel, and there is a risk that inaccurate and/or inconsistent decisions are made if these processes are not clearly documented (Mayson & Barrett, 2006). Furthermore, looking fair is as important as being fair (Greenberg, 1988) and, at the very least, SMEs should be able to show their employees what steps have been taken to promote high levels of fairness when allocating financial rewards.

Although monetary rewards often figure prominently in what people want from a job, employees still derive high levels of motivation and satisfaction from non-financial forms of recognition such as a verbal thank you, a note of appreciation or a simple pat on the back. Of course managers and supervisors need to communicate these messages in a sincere way, but when done properly, informal recognition can reinforce the recipient's value to the group whilst also providing more immediate feedback on the work undertaken. Providing this more informal and impromptu recognition is a good example of where the specific resource-allocation decisions intersect with and build on the primary-level strategies. The ongoing feedback, recognition, encouragement and other support provided by managers (i.e., "enhancing social support") helps to ensure employees "know where they stand" on a daily basis. The formal and informal rewards are therefore an extension of this broader level of support and help to ensure that employees have the feedback, guidance and emotional support required to meet instrumental and non-instrumental needs.

Performance appraisals

Reviewing employee performance also consists of formal and informal components. In relation to the formal component, this should follow a "due process approach" that consists of three elements: adequate notice, just hearing and judgements based on evidence (Cropanzano et al., 2007). "Adequate notice" refers to letting people know in advance when they will be appraised and making sure they are clear about the criteria on which they will be evaluated. Support for the criteria and the overall appraisal system can be enhanced by getting employees involved in developing the performance standards and making sure these are widely available. "Just hearing" includes basing reviews on performance (rather than personal attacks), and gathering data from multiple sources. Receiving a just review also involves taking into account the employee's perspective of how they've performed and builds on the more general participatory decision-making systems that are already in place (i.e., "involving and engaging employees"). The final element, "judgement based on evidence", involves ensuring that reviews are based on accurate information and that employees themselves have ready access to this information.

The extent to which formal performance reviews impact on salary levels, promotions and other financial rewards will vary between organizations. Where they are closely linked, it is particularly important that reviewers are trained in how to administer performance appraisals and both the processes for undertaking the review as well as the results themselves should be documented (Posthuma & Campion, 2008). The fall-out associated with a negative review could be compounded many times if the employee suffers financially and the organization cannot demonstrate that due diligence has been applied. An appeal mechanism should also be built into the review process and, in accordance with both procedural and restorative justice, managers need to be willing to correct their decision if wrong (see following section for more details on this issue).

Regardless of whether the outcomes of the review are positive or negative, performance appraisals must support employees' developmental needs (ibid.). This approach is consistent with the previous points regarding "information and skill development" (see primary-level interventions) and seeks to ensure employees are given clear, detailed explanations on what they are doing well, where they need to improve and, most importantly, what steps they need to take in order to achieve the desired level of performance. Training opportunities should also be identified in this process and employees should be given the chance to specify other forms of support that may be required to enhance performance.

A common criticism of typical performance review systems is that they operate as a stand-alone process disconnected from other less formal appraisal and support mechanisms (Ivancevich et al., 2011). Such an approach can lead to high levels of uncertainty and stress, especially in situations where the overall tenor of the review is negative and this contrasts with what the employee is hearing on a day-to-day basis. Rather than see the review as an annual or bi-annual ritual that is set apart from the experiences of everyday work-life, the formal performance review process needs to be closely tied to the broader feedback and support strategies discussed in the primary-level interventions. Specifically, the more formal review should represent one component of a comprehensive approach to employee support and development that provides workers with ongoing feedback and guidance regarding their performance. With this approach in mind, employees should be aware of their contributions at all stages of the year, the results of formal appraisals should hold no surprises (particularly in terms of negative feedback) and employees should come away from their review discussions feeling as though they've been treated in a fair, consistent and constructive manner.

The owners and managers of SMEs may feel daunted by the level of formality reflected in the "due process approach" to performance appraisals. However, combining this approach with broader feedback and support initiatives can make the often difficult task of appraising workers' performances much more comfortable and mutually beneficial.

Tertiary-level Interventions

Many of the strategies mentioned thus far have focused on creating fairer working environments and taking steps to prevent or reduce cases of injustice. In contrast, tertiary-level interventions centre on what happens when employees are the recipients of unfavourable resource-allocation decisions; the promotion application was unsuccessful, the much sought-after role was given to a colleague or the performance review was less than flattering. Unfavourable decisions can arouse a range of adverse emotions – feelings of failure, insecurity, suspicion and resentment. When left unabated, these reactions can be very damaging, both for the individual and the organization. Fundamentally, perceptions of injustice can undermine the trust between authority figures and the employee (Vermunt & Steensma, 2005). When the authority figure is also the owner of the firm or the company CEO, as is the case with many SMEs, the employee's view of the entire organization can become quickly tainted. Firms therefore need to have strategies in place to quickly restore the trust and to minimize negative responses to unfavourable decisions. These strategies include justification, counselling, compensation and corrective action.

Justification

The impact of an undesirable decision can be much more severe when recipients aren't fully aware of the reasons why a particular course of action was taken (ibid.). In the absence of detailed explanations, employees can jump to the wrong conclusions or be misguided by rumours, "half-truths" and "office gossip". Authority figures therefore need to quickly follow-up resource-allocation decisions with an open and honest explanation of how the decision was made and what factors were taken into account (Cropanzano et al., 2007; Folger & Cropanzano, 1998). In the case of reward-allocation decisions involving specific employees, such as applications for promotion or performance reviews, these explanations should be made at the time employees learn of the decision. Employees accept that not every decision is going to favour them, however they will think the worst if decision-makers aren't "up-front" with their rationale and appear to be hiding something.

Counselling

Allocating valued resources to some people, but not to others, is an inherently threatening exercise and workers on the receiving end of negative decisions will inevitably question their sense of self-worth and standing in the organization. These negative thoughts must be quickly addressed and managers can do this by reassuring employees that they do have an important role to play in the future of the firm and that their knowledge, skills and contributions are valued (Mollica, 2004). An effective way of reinforcing this message – especially in situations where an individual employee was not successful receiving a promotion, pay rise, or other desired outcome – is to map out a plan to help him/her achieve the desired goal. Clarify what standards of performance are expected and help the employee identify the training or developmental opportunities that can help them acquire the necessary skills or experience. Above all, managers need to show that they do have the employee's best interests in mind and that they are willing to work with the employee to help realize his/her goals and aspirations. Although the initial decision may have been a major disappointment, reinforcing the person's value to the organization and giving them the direction and support needed to "turn this negative into a positive", can go a long way to restoring lost faith and confidence.

Compensation

Another strategy that can help repair strained relationships and to reaffirm the person's value to the firm is to consider offering other desired outcomes; a strategy Vermunt and Steensma (2005) refer to as "compensation". For example, the employee may not have been ready for a promotion, but identifying a project or set of tasks that could help them build the skills and experience needed to move up to the next level, could help re-establish a sense of distributive justice. In this case, firms can demonstrate their support for the employee whilst at the same time, helping to ensure any loss in self-esteem and motivation is minimized.

Corrective action

There will always be times when authority figures make incorrect decisions during the resource-allocation process – they miss relevant information, misinterpret important achievements or circumstances, or make hasty judgements. While the possible fall-out associated with these types of errors reinforce the need for SMEs to adopt a more thorough approach to resource-allocation decisions, these instances also highlight the importance of building "correctibility" into the process (Greenberg & Baron, 2008). Employees need to have the opportunity to appeal justice-related decisions (consistent with procedural fairness) and, where errors in judgement are identified, managers need to be prepared to change their decision. Of course, where individual employees elect to lodge an appeal, he/she should not be made to feel guilty or rebellious (Mollica, 2004).

SUMMARY AND CONCLUDING COMMENTS

The results of organizational justice research indicate that both the employee and the employer can suffer as a result of unfair policies, systems and practices. SMEs appear to be more vulnerable to the sources and effects of employees' fairness perceptions and, in view of their heightened need to maximize workers' capacities and contributions, smaller firms need to pay particular attention to how they manage perceptions of organizational fairness. The organizational justice management framework presented in this chapter has been designed to assist SMEs develop a comprehensive approach to promoting justice within their organizations. The strategies operate at three interrelated levels – primary, secondary and tertiary – and are aimed at preventing/reducing cases of injustice, but at the same time, minimizing the negative outcomes associated with breaches of fairness.

Employees take into account a wide range of resources when assessing the extent to which an organization treats them fairly. Although there is a tendency to focus on the more discrete resource-allocation decisions such as reward and recognition and performance reviews (i.e., secondary-level strategies), the justice management framework underlines the need to also consider the more ubiquitous features of the way work is organized and people are managed, including employee involvement, supervisory support, information sharing and skill development opportunities (i.e., primary-level strategies). Perceptions of injustice at both the primary and secondary levels can damage trust between between managers and employees and an important goal of the tertiary-level strategies is to restore this trust and to quickly re-establish effective leader–member relations.

A key principle highlighted in much of the organizational justice literature is that "means" are as important as "ends". That is, the procedures used to decide who receives important resources, and the manner in which people are treated during and after resource-allocation decisions have been made, are as central to building fair workplaces as the outcomes of the decisions themselves. One area where SMEs need to adhere to this principle very closely is when identifying policies, systems or practices that are considered unfair (Noblet & Rodwell, 2008). Employees are the ones who appraise situations or conditions as fair/unfair, and hence they need to be heavily involved in pinpointing areas where fairness can be improved. Finally, whatever justice management strategies are developed, these need to be closely monitored to ensure they have the desired effect. Assessing the impact of these initiatives, and then using the results to inform subsequent modifications (or new approaches), can help to make sure justice promotion strategies continue to meet the needs and expectations of employees.

REFERENCES

Adams, J.S. (1965). Inequity in social exchange. In L. Berkowitz (ed.), *Advances in Experimental Social Psychology*. New York: Academic Press, pp. 267–99.

Ambrose, M.L. (2002). Contemporary justice research: A new look at familiar questions. *Organizational Behavior and Human Decision Processes*, **89**(1), 803–12.

Behrends, T. (2007). Recruitment practices in small and medium size enterprises. An empirical study among knowledge-intensive professional service firms. *Management Revue*, **18**(1), 55–74.

Bies, R.J. & Moag, J. (1986). Interactional justice: Communication criteria of fairness. In R. Lewicki, B. Sheppard & M. Bazerman (eds), *Research on Negotiation in Organizations*. Greenwich, CT: JAI Press.

Brockner, J. & Wiesenfeld, B. (1996). An integrative framework for explaining reactions to decisions: Interactive effects of outcomes and procedures. *Psychological Bulletin*, **120**(2), 189–208.

Carson, J.B., Tesluk, P.E. & Marrone, J.A. (2007). Shared leadership in teams: An investigation of antecedent conditions and performance. *Academy of Management Journal*, **50**(5), 1217–34.

Cohen-Charash, Y. & Spector, P.E. (2001). The role of justice in organizations: A meta-analysis. *Organizational Behavior and Human Decision Processes*, **86**(2), 278–321.

Colquitt, J.A. (2001). On the dimensionality of organizational justice: A construct validation of a measure. *Journal of Applied Psychology*, **86**(3), 386–400.

Colquitt, J.A., Greenberg, J. & Zapata-Phelan, C.P. (2005). What is organizational justice? A historical overview. In J. Greenberg & J.A. Colquitt (eds), *Handbook of Organizational Justice*. Mahwa, New Jersey: Lawrence Erlbaum Associates, pp. 3–56.

Colquitt, J.A., Conlon, D.E., Wesson, M.J., Porter, C.O. & Ng, K.Y. (2001). Justice at the Millennium: A meta-analytic review of 25 years of organizational justice research. *Journal of Applied Psychology*, **86**(3), 425–45.

Cropanzano, R., Bowen, D.E. & Gilliland, S.W. (2007). The management of organizational justice. *Academy of Management Perspectives*, **21**(1), 34–45.

Cropanzano, R., Goldman, B.M. & Benson III, L. (2005). Organizational justice. In J. Barling, E.K. Kelloway & M.R. Frone (eds), *Handbook of Work Stress*. Thousand Oaks, CA: Sage Publications.

Cropanzano, R., Rupp, D. & Byrne, Z. (2003). The relationship of emotional exhaustion to work attitudes, job performance, and organizational citizenship behaviors. *Journal of Applied Psychology*, **88**(1), 160–69.

De Boer, E., Bakker, A.B., Syroit, J. & Schaufeli, W.B. (2002). Unfairness at work as a predictor of absenteeism. *Journal of Organizational Behavior*, **23**(2), 181–97.

Folger, R. & Cropanzano, R. (1998). *Organizational Justice and Human Resource Management*. Thousand Oaks, CA: Sage.

Forth, J., Bewley, H. & Bryson, A. (2004). *Small and Medium-sized Enterprises: Findings from the 2004 Workplace Employment Relations Survey*, University of Westminster.

Fox, S., Spector, P.E. & Miles, D. (2001). Counterproductive work behavior (CWB) in response to job stressors and organizational justice: Some mediator and moderator tests for autonomy and emotions. *Journal of Vocational Behavior*, **59**(3), 291–309.

Gilliland, S.W. (2009). More application than acknowledged. *Industrial & Organizational Psychology*, **2**(2), 199–200.
Greenberg, J. (1988). Cultivating an image of justice: Looking fair on the job. *The Academy of Management Executive*, **8**(2), 155–8.
Greenberg, J. (1990). Employee theft as a reaction to underpayment inequity: The hidden cost of pay cuts. *Journal of Applied Psychology*, **75**(5), 561–8.
Greenberg, J. (2009). Everybody talks about organizational justice, but nobody does anything about it. *Industrial & Organizational Psychology*, **2**(2), 181–95.
Greenberg, J. & Baron, R. (2008). *Behavior in Organizations* (9th edn). New Jersey: Pearson Prentice Hall.
Hackman, J. & Oldham, G. (1976). Motivation through the design of work: A test of a theory. *Organizational Behavior and Human Performance*, **16**(6), 250–79.
House, J.S. (1981). *Work Stress and Social Support*. London: Addison-Wesley Publishing Company.
Humphrey, S., Nahrgang, J. & Morgeson, F. (2007). Integrating motivational, social, and contextual work design features: A meta-analytic summary and theoretical extension of the work design literature. *Journal of Applied Psychology*, **92**(5), 1332–56.
Ivancevich, J., Konopaske, R. & Matteson, M. (January 2011). *Organizational Behavior and Management* (revised 9th edn). Boston: McGraw-Hill.
Karasek, R. & Theorell, T. (1990). *Healthy Work: Stress, Productivity, and the Reconstruction of Working Life*. New York: Basic Books.
Kivimaki, M., Ferrie, J.E., Head, J., Shipley, M.J., Vahtera, J. & Marmot, M.G. (2004). Organisational justice and change in justice as predictors of employee health: The Whitehall II study. *Journal of Epidemiology & Community Health*, **58**(11), 931–7.
Korsgaard, M.A., Schweiger, D.M. & Sapienza, H.J. (1995). Building commitment, attachment, and trust in strategic decision-making teams: The role of procedural justice. *Academy of Management Journal*, **38**(1), 60–84.
Leventhal, G.S. (1976). Justice in social relationships. In J.W. Thibaut, J.T. Spence & R.C. Carson (eds), *Contemporary Topics in Social Psychology*. Morristown, NJ: General Learning Press.
Lind, E.A. & Van den Bos, K. (2002). When fairness works: Toward a general theory of uncertainty management. In B.M. Staw & R.M. Kramer (eds), *Research in Organizational Behavior*, Vol. 24. Boston: JAI Press, pp. 181–222.
Maier, N. (1970). *Problem Solving and Creativity in Individuals and Groups*. Belmont, CA: Brooks/Cole.
Marlow, S. (2006). Human resource management in smaller firms: A contradiction in terms? *Human Resource Management Review*, **16**(4), 467–77.
Masterson, S.S., Lewis, K., Goldman, B.M. & Taylor, M.S. (2000). Integrating justice and social exchange: The differing effects of fair procedures and treatment on work relationships. *Academy of Management Journal*, **43**(4), 738–49.
Mayo, E. (1949). *Hawthorne and the Western Electric Company, The Social Problems of an Industrial Civilisation*. London: Routledge.
Mayson, S. & Barrett, R. (2006). The "science" and "practice" of HRM in small firms. *Human Resource Management Review*, **16**(4), 447–55.
Moliner, C., Martínez-Tur, V., Peiró, J.M., Ramos, J. & Cropanzano, R. (2008). Organizational justice and extrarole customer service: The moderating role of wellbeing at work. *European Journal of Work and Organizational Psychology*, **17**(3), 327–48.

Mollica, K. (2004). Perceptions of fairness. *HRMagazine*, **49**(6), 169–78.
Noblet, A. & LaMontagne, A. (2009). The challenges of developing, implementing, and evaluating interventions. In S. Cartwright & C. Cooper (eds), *The Oxford Handbook of Organizational Well-being*. Oxford: Oxford University Press.
Noblet, A. & Rodwell, J. (2008). The relationship between organisational justice and job stress: Insights, issues and implications. In J. Houdmont & S. McIntyre (eds), *Occupational Health Psychology: European Perspectives on Research, Education and Practice* (Vol. 3). Castelo da Maia: ISMAI Publishers.
Noblet, A., Cooper, C., McWilliams, J. & Rudd, A. (2007). Wellbeing, job satisfaction and commitment among Australian community health workers – the relationship with working conditions. *Australian Journal of Primary Health*, **13**(3), 40–48.
Patel, P.C. & Cardon, M.S. (2010). Adopting HRM practices and their effectiveness in small firms facing product-market competition. *Human Resource Management*, **49**(2), 265–90.
Posthuma, R. & Campion, M. (2008). Twenty best practices for just employee performance reviews. *Compensation and Benefits Review*, **40**(1), 47–55.
Rupp, D. & Cropanzano, R. (2002). The mediating effects of social exchange relationships in predicting workplace outcomes from multifoci organizational justice. *Organizational Behavior and Human Decision Processes*, **89**(1), 925–46.
Saru, E. (2009). HRM in SMEs: Linking embedded human resources practices to performance and employee wellbeing. In M. Fink & S. Kraus (eds), *The Management of Small and Medium Enterprises*. Hoboken: Routledge, pp. 80–94.
Schmitt, M. & Dorfel, M. (1999). Procedural injustice at work, justice sensitivity, job satisfaction and psycho-somatic well-being. *European Journal of Social Psychology*, **29**, 443–53.
Sidle, S.D. (2003). Best laid plans: Establishing fairness early can help smooth organizational change. *Academy of Management Executive*, **17**(1), 127–8.
Tepper, B. (2001). Health consequences of organizational injustice: Tests of main and interactive effects. *Organizational Behavior and Human Decision Processes*, **86**(2), 197–215.
Vermunt, R. & Steensma, H. (2005). How can justice be used to manage stress in organizations? In J. Greenberg & J.A. Colquitt (eds), *Handbook of Organizational Justice*. Mahwa, New Jersey: Lawrence Erlbaum Associates, pp. 383–410.
Wilkinson, A. (1999). Employment relations in SMEs. *Employee Relations*, **21**(3), 206–17.

14. E-coaching for women small business owners and managers

Carianne Hunt and Sandra Fielden

INTRODUCTION

This chapter presents an evaluation of an online coaching initiative Tailored E-Coaching – (TEC), designed to increase the success of women small business owners and managers in the UK.[1] Forty-four women took part in the programme and they received online coaching over a six-month period from an experienced woman business owner. Their progress was compared with a control group of 26 women, who were also entering small business ownership but did not participate in the TEC initiative. This chapter will detail the rationale behind the TEC programme and provide an outline of the programme, including the recruitment and matching process, pre- and post-events, the website and evaluation. It will then examine the impact of the programme, specifically examining the self-efficacy, locus of control and general entrepreneurial attitudes of coachees compared with a control group, and then explore the general benefits of the programme for all participants, coaches and coachees. It will conclude with a summary and recommendations for programme improvement.

RATIONALE FOR ONLINE COACHING

Women business owners often lack the support, guidance and experience that they require to be successful in business ownership. However, women are not accessing the business support that is currently available, particularly when compared with their male counterparts (Carter et al., 1997; Fielden et al., 2003; Harding, 2004, 2006; Stranger, 2004). Despite the relatively low number of women accessing business support and the importance of providing support for women business owners, there appears to be a lack of research examining what women actually want from business support services, both in terms of content and delivery of support.

Solutions to support and educate entrepreneurs appear to be a primary objective for both academics and policy-makers (Greene, et al., 2004). Despite this, barriers and obstacles to appropriate support remain. The main barriers faced by women business owners appear to be based on access to funding and finance (Carter et al., 2001, 2003; Shaw et al., 2001), balancing domestic responsibilities and work (Holmquist & Sundin, 1988; Aldrich, 1989; Parasuraman et al., 1996; Shelton, 2006), a lack of human capital (Cromie & Birley, 1991; Kalleberg & Leicht, 1991; Chaganti & Parasuraman, 1996; Carter & Williams, 2003) and a lack of social capital (Katz and Williams, 1997; Verheul et al., 2001). Women also often dismiss entrepreneurial endeavours because they believe that they do not have the required skills and therefore lack confidence (Chen et al., 1998; Wilson et al., 2007) and it is evident that women business owners frequently lack familiarity with the business world (Harding, 2006). Women business owners' low self-efficacy regarding entrepreneurial success may indeed be a barrier to their own development. This may also be a contributing factor to the decline of total early stage entrepreneurial activity in the UK in 2006 (ibid.).

There is a wealth of evidence to show that women small business owners lack the support, guidance and experience that they require to be successful in business ownership. However, research has suggested that women are not accessing support because of issues such as a lack of confidence, lack of knowledge, lack of physical access and a lack of understanding about the relevance of the services (Ram and Smallbone, 2001; Fielden et al., 2003). However, women business owners do not lack drive or ambition, although they tend to see fewer opportunities and rate their abilities lower than men (Harding, 2003). Thus, women who are deciding to enter into business ownership are, on the whole, likely to be in greater need of relevant training and support (Stranger, 2004).

One form of professional one-to-one support that has the potential to overcome these barriers to entrepreneurial activity is coaching. Coaching is defined as "a process that enables learning and development to occur and thus performance to improve" (Parsloe, 1999, p. 8). Information technology can help to enhance development tools such as coaching, as Bierema and Merriam (2002, p. 214) state, "all sorts of barriers such as time, work responsibilities, geographical distance and lack of trust often reduce if not halt interaction". Coaching is a highly personalized form of development activity (O'Connor & Lages, 2004), which can be tailored specifically to relevant aspects of women's business ownership. Information technology can open numerous avenues for business support and has an array of benefits for developmental tools such as coaching.

There is a wide range of material relating to the process of coaching, including numerous frameworks and models, which can be used to facilitate executive coaching (Kenton & Moody, 2001; Zeus & Skiffington,

2003; O'Connor & Lages, 2004). In contrast, there is an absence of literature and empirical studies focusing on coaching in an entrepreneurial setting, with the available literature tending to focus on mentoring schemes (Evans & Volery, 2001; Stokes, 2001). The majority of coaching literature typically focuses on large organizations (Megginson & Clutterbuck, 1995; Whitmore, 2002; Zeus & Skiffington, 2003). An explanation for this is that the UK has tended to be relatively slow to focus and capitalize on the SME sector, unlike in the US and Japan (Nancarrow et al., 1999; Peel, 2004). As a result, academic researchers are only now beginning to focus their attention on the SME research agenda (Hill, 2001).

OUTLINE OF THE TAILORED E-COACHING (TEC) PROGRAMME

Based on the above rationale the TEC programme initiative sought to bridge the gap between coaching and the development of women's small business ownership. This section looks at the programme objectives and details key elements of the programme, including recruitment and selection, pre- and post-events, the website and the evaluation process.

Objectives

The main objective of the TEC programme was to develop and deliver a programme of support for women small business owners in the North West of England during the business start-up process. The specific objectives were to:

- provide individualistic support through a one-to-one coaching relationship;
- provide women-only support – coaching provided for women by women;
- provide longer-term support – coaching relationship lasted approximately six months;
- bring together a group of women to enable networking and provide mutual support;
- provide access to online support to overcome physical barriers – online coaching provided and online networking discussion forum.

The TEC programme commenced in January 2006 and was completed in September 2007. Figure 14.1 outlines the implementation of the TEC programme. The majority of coaching relationships lasted approximately

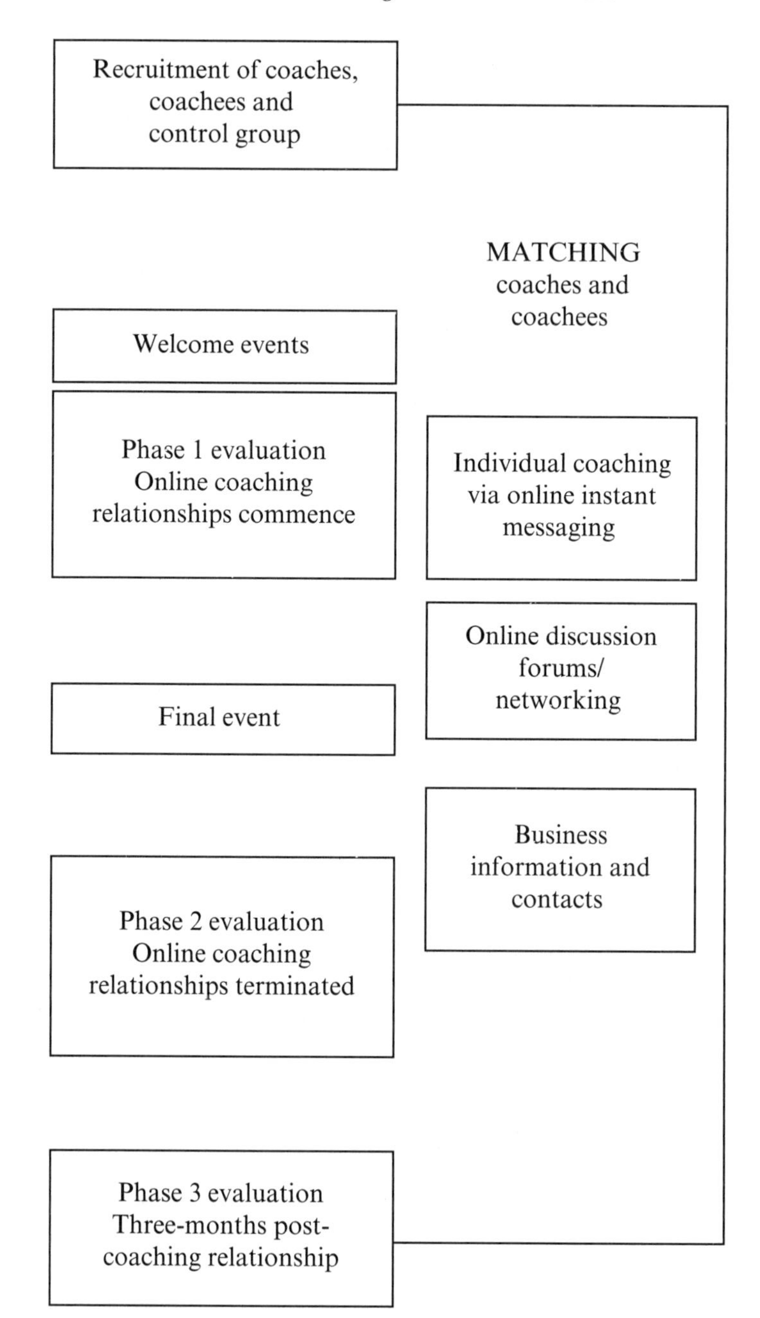

Figure 14.1 Programme model

six months and coaching was primarily delivered via instant messaging software. This method was supplemented with face-to-face and telephone sessions. The control group participated in phase 1 and phase 2 of the evaluation process.

Recruitment and Matching Process

Coachees were defined as women business owners who were at the start-up stage of small business ownership. Coaches were defined as women who were established and experienced business owners, with a minimum of two years' business experience. Women were recruited through a wide variety of networks and open advertising.

A matching form was crucial for the research team to ascertain the suitability of participants and to provide information regarding the criteria used in the matching process. There is little available research examining the matching of coaches and coachees. However, mentoring research focusing on matching has shown that mentees who are demographically different from their matched mentor tend to rate the relationship as unsatisfactory (Kram, 1985). Demographics factors such as age, gender and ethnicity, as well as business and personal development requirements, were therefore used as matching criteria.

The matching form asked coachees to state what their coaching needs were and similarly coaches were asked what they felt their strengths were with regard to coaching. Cohen and Light (2000) state that matching solely on the mentees' needs and the mentors' skills may not be sufficient in order to ensure a successful match and suggests that one must also consider personality factors. In light of their recommendation, the matching forms also asked participants to complete questions examining their attitudes and preferences. These questions enabled the programme team to gain some insight into personality types. Matching computer software was considered, but the programme team felt that hand matching was a more suitable method to employ. The depth of the information utilized in the matching process would have been difficult to summarize using computer software and may have had a negative impact on the matching of coaches and coachees.

One hundred and three participants signed up to the programme (51 coachees and 52 coaches): once the matching criteria was applied only 44 coaching pairs could be successfully matched. The majority of coaches and coachees were between 30 and 49 years of age, married and educated to a good standard. A control group of 26 women were also included in this study. The control group had similar characteristics to the coachees but did not receive the coaching intervention.

Welcome Events

Coaches and coachees were invited to attend a networking event, which was held before the formal commencement of the online coaching relationships. Participants were invited to attend one of two networking events, which enabled them to meet face-to-face with their respective coach/coachee. The events provided an opportunity for participants to discuss the programme model, the research and any hopes and fears regarding the coaching relationships. Participants were also provided with a programme pack, which included a coaching handbook.

The Website

Once participants had registered on the programme and had been assigned a coach/coachee, they were then provided with a username and password to gain entry to the website. Participants were provided with information as to how to download the Spark software onto their home/work computers. The Spark software enabled participants to have instant online coaching sessions with their coach/coachee. Spark software is similar to that of MSN and Skype in that it allows individuals to communicate online.

Alongside the coaching relationships, coaches and coachees were also provided with the opportunity to chat with other participants on the programme. All participants had access to a discussion forum on the website, where they could post suggestions, topics of interest, or create discussion threads with other programme participants. Participants were also provided with contact details for a variety of business support organizations and an area where participants could advertise their business/products or services, or an event/conference or activity. Finally, there was a help area and contact details section that provided contacts for all relevant project team members.

Programme Evaluation

The evaluation was undertaken at three time points: phase 1 baseline (i.e., before commencing the coaching relationship), phase 2 (at the completion of the coaching relationship), phase 3 (coaches/coachees only) (follow-up three months post-programme completion).

Three questionnaires were used to examine the impact of the TEC programme, focusing specifically on a number of key areas: self-efficacy, locus of control and general entrepreneurial attitudes. An additional questionnaire was distributed at phase 2, which was aimed at monitoring and evaluating the TEC programme. Rating scales (seven-point) were used in the questionnaires to measure the skills development of coachees. The areas covered in the questionnaire included marketing, innovation, management, risk-taking, finance, work/life balance and networking.

At phase 3, 18 (coachees $n = 11$: coaches $n = 7$) semi-structured interviews were conducted to explore the impact and efficacy of the programme in more depth.

Final Event

Participants were invited to a celebration networking event at the end of the programme. This provided an opportunity for participants to meet face-to-face and to share their coaching stories with the rest of the group. The event included inspirational speakers, who were all women business owners, and presentations from coaches and coachees.

TEC PROGRAMME OUTCOMES

The findings of the programme evaluation are detailed in this section, which will analyse the questionnaire data for phase 1 and 2 comparing the coachees and the control group. It will then examine the general benefits of the programme reported by coaches and coachees, followed by an evaluation of the specific elements of the programme.

Impact of the TEC Programme

This section compares the questionnaire data collected at phase 1 and phase 2 for coaches and the control group on self-efficacy, locus of control and entrepreneurial attitudes.

Self-efficacy

At time phase 2, coachees had significantly improved their self-efficacy levels in the following areas:

- conducting market research ($p < 0.023$);
- networking with other women business owners ($p < 0.026$);
- defining short-term business goals ($p < 0.015$);
- defining long-term business goals ($p < 0.007$);
- making business decisions under risk and uncertainty ($p < 0.008$);
- confidence in business ability ($p < 0.012$);
- balancing work and home life ($p < 0.024$);
- ability to achieve business goals ($p < 0.038$).

For the control group there was no statistical significance between self-efficacy of each task at phase 1 and phase 2. Coachees appeared to have increased levels of self-efficacy across the key areas when compared with the control group.

In general, coachees had stronger internal locus of control at phase 2 than phase 1. There was an increased number of coachees showing stronger internal locus of control in the following questions:

- My business success depends on whether I am lucky enough to be in the right place at the right time.
- It is not wise for me to establish long-term business plans because things may turn out negatively.
- Success in business is mostly a matter of luck.

However, in general, there was not a statistical significance between phase 1 and phase 2. The only question that showed statistical significance was "When I achieve my business goals it is usually because I worked hard for it". Coachees were more likely to strongly agree, or agree with this question ($p < 0.049$).

The control group appeared to have stronger external locus of control at phase 2, specifically in response to the following questions:

- My business success depends on whether I am lucky enough to be in the right place at the right time.
- To a great extent my business is controlled by accidental happenings.
- When I achieve my business goals it is usually because I worked hard for it.
- It is not wise for me to establish long-term business plans because things may turn out negatively.
- Success in business is mostly a matter of luck.
- I feel that what happens in my business is mostly determined by people in powerful positions.

General entrepreneurial attitudes

The entrepreneurial attitudes questionnaire appeared to show some statistical significance between phase 1 and phase 2. Coachees appeared to feel more self-confident ($p < 0.002$), more satisfied with business progress ($p < 0.049$), satisfied with work life balance ($p < 0.001$), aware of business support available ($p < 0.036$), confident of their marketing ability ($p < 0.012$) and confident about their financial/accountancy ability ($p < 0.036$).

At phase 2 the control group was statistically significantly less likely to feel positive about their future business plans ($p < 0.054$), supported in their business ($p < 0.054$) and self-confident ($p < 0.055$). The findings also show that the control group was less likely to feel motivated to fulfil business goals and objectives ($p < 0.068$), ambitious for greater success and satisfied with work/life balance.

There was a significant increase in the number of coachees reporting stronger internal locus of control in the following questions:

- When I achieve my business goals it is usually because I worked hard for it ($p < 0.049$).
- Whether or not I am successful in business depends mostly on my ability ($p < 0.090$).
- I feel in control of my business ($p < 0.096$).

In contrast, the control group appeared to have stronger external locus of control at phase 2, specifically in response to:

- My business success depends on whether I am lucky enough to be in the right place at the right time ($p < 0.096$).

The General Impact of the TEC Programme

This section examines the TEC programme benefits reported at phase 2 of the evaluation, utilizing quotes from phase 3 of the evaluation to provide more depth and understanding.

Coachees

Over 80 per cent of coachees strongly agreed or agreed that they had benefited from the programme and 87 per cent of coachees were satisfied with the support that they received from their coach. Figure 14.2 illustrates the variety of ways in which coachees benefited from the TEC programme.

On the whole, participants believed that the coaching relationships had helped to clarify business and personal development goals and had provided them with more direction for their business and for their own personal development. Over 75 per cent strongly agreed or agreed that they had improved in the skills they originally highlighted at the start of the programme:

> She (coach) was able to take confused ideas and make it very plain, without changing the nature of what I was doing. . . providing clarity and allowed me to see what I was actually trying to do. (Coachee)

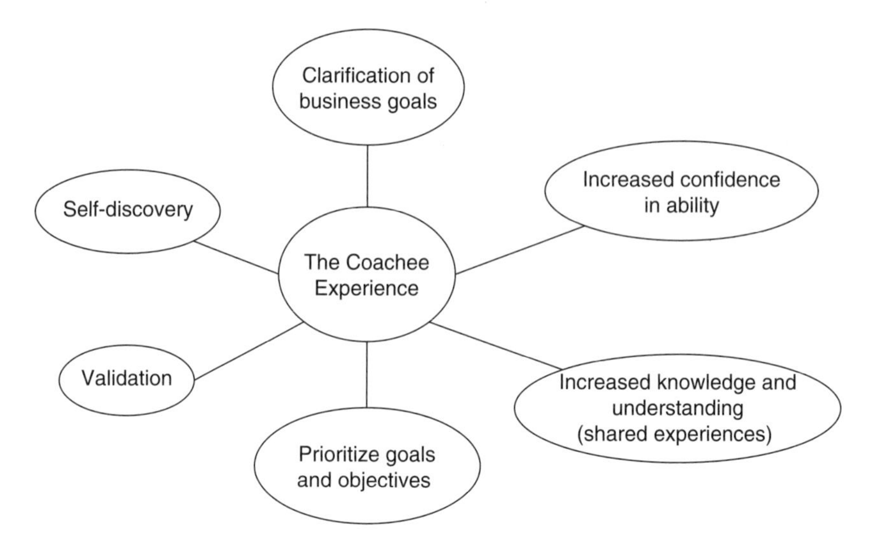

Figure 14.2 Benefits for coachees

The coaching relationships enabled coachees to prioritize their business goals and objectives. Coaching conversations helped to clarify issues and in doing so enabled coachees to prioritize short- and long-term business and personal objectives:

> She helps me to get my priorities sorted out. (Coachee)

Prioritizing goals and objectives was particularly important for a majority of coachees in this study. At baseline only 40 per cent of coachees felt that they were able to strategically plan for the long term; this may be due to their inability to prioritize efficiently and effectively. It is also interesting to note that approximately 90 per cent of coacheees stated that they would expect their coach to help them to define their long-term business goals.

Over 75 per cent of coachees strongly agreed or agreed that the programme had helped them to develop personally. One of the coachees referred to this development as "self-discovery". This appears to be a fitting description for the personal development experienced by the coachees:

> I think probably my self-discovery of me finding out the core truth about myself really. It was like I said like peeling an onion really where you thought there was a problem and then delving a bit deeper until you get to that core. (Coachee)

The coaching relationships helped women to develop their business and also gave them confidence in their own abilities. Having one-to-one support provided women with an insight into the issues that needed to be addressed. This ongoing support helped to reduce the fear that many women faced when starting out in business.

Coachees emphasized the importance of their coaches sharing their experiences with them. This was seen as invaluable and a resource that was not available elsewhere. Sharing experiences was a key part of the coaching process that benefited coachees and this also helped to build rapport. Having a coaching relationship enabled coachees to build up a relationship with one individual:

> She was willing to share her own experiences with me. I benefited from her knowledge. She was also incredibly supportive. (Coachee)

Obtaining guidance from one individual helped to provide some consistency and continuity of advice. Because the coaching relationships were individual, whereby each coach coached one coachee, coaches were able to gain an in-depth understanding of their coachee's business and their strengths and weaknesses. This individual relationship enabled coaches to tailor the coaching relationship to the individual coachee.

Coaches

The main objective of the programme was to provide development for coachees, however, findings show that the coaches also benefited from the relationships. Figure 14.3 shows the range of benefits experienced by the coaches. Findings from the evaluation questionnaire show that 58 per cent of coaches strongly agreed or agreed that they had benefited from the programme.

Evaluation of Specific Elements of the TEC Programme

This section will look at programme specifics regarding time and duration of meetings, main method of meeting and the suitability of online methods for coaching. From the evaluation questionnaire 74 per cent of coachees and 68 per cent of coaches strongly agreed or agreed that they would participate in a similar programme in the future. Furthermore, 87 per cent of coachees and 58 per cent of coaches strongly agreed or agreed that they would recommend this programme to other business owners and 78 per cent of coachees and 47 per cent of coaches strongly agreed or agreed that they had an effective relationship with their coach/coachee.

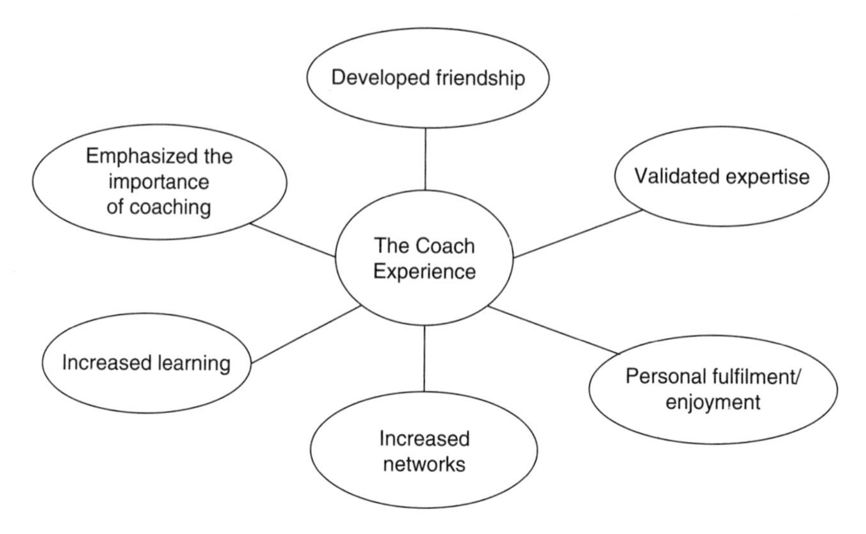

Figure 14.3 Benefits for coaches

Frequency and duration of coaching sessions

On average, coaches and coachees met online once a fortnight for one-and-a-half hours, however, this did vary between pairs. Approximately 74 per cent of coachees strongly agreed or agreed that they were satisfied with the frequency of contact with their coach/coachee.

Main method of meeting (face-to-face, telephone, online)

The TEC programme was designed so that coaching pairs would conduct the majority of their coaching online; therefore, it was important to explore the main method of meeting between coaches and coachees. As the main element of this programme was to provide women business owners with support via a coaching programme, coaching pairs were not prevented from taking a blended approach to their coaching relationship, that is, telephone, or face-to-face, however, participants were encouraged to use the instant messaging software for online coaching. For coaching pairs who did not have any problems using the online system, or pairs who had previous experience of using online methods the majority of coaching was conducted online.

Experience of the online element

Opinion was divided as to whether the online element of the programme suited coaches and coachees' individual styles. Individuals who experienced some problems with the software still made reference to the benefits of online coaching. Women also stated that online coaching may help coachees who are less confident in communicating verbally and may help to facilitate effective communication. Coaches and coachees stated that when using the Spark software to conduct their coaching sessions it was important to be focused and disciplined and experience of using the software impacted on the effectiveness of the online communication. The importance of structure when conducting online conversations was also emphasized. Coaches stated how it was important to consider the questions that were asked at the start of the session so as to gauge how the coachee was feeling.

One important benefit of the online software was that it provided coaches and coachees with an opportunity to reflect on what they were saying and how they would formulate and respond to questions. This thinking time also allowed coaches and coachees to clarify their thoughts. However, some coaches thought that this could be perceived as a negative as it reduced spontaneity and allowed coachees to retype what they were saying numerous times, which may have covered up the real issues and prevented coachees from being totally honest. Coachees also used the instant messaging software as a way of recording what was said in coaching meetings so that they could refer back to the information. This is difficult to do in a face-to-face or telephone session; therefore, this was seen as a benefit of online coaching.

SUMMARY AND RECOMMENDATIONS

Coaching was seen as a valuable tool for participants and the evaluation of the TEC programme clearly demonstrates that a coaching relationship, provided by established women business owners for new women business owners, has significant benefits. Online coaching is an excellent way of providing business support with an array of developmental benefits at both the entrepreneurial and personal level. The evaluation has provided some valuable insights into the development and management of an e-coaching programme and Figure 14.4 shows a revised model for future coaching programmes.

Matching

The matching of coaches and coachees was an important stage of the project. Coaches and coachees were matched based on the completion of an application form. The matching forms asked coachees and coaches to answer a range of questions examining their coaching needs/experience and what they hoped to gain from the programme. This form of hand matching was time consuming, but it did provide excellent results. Hand

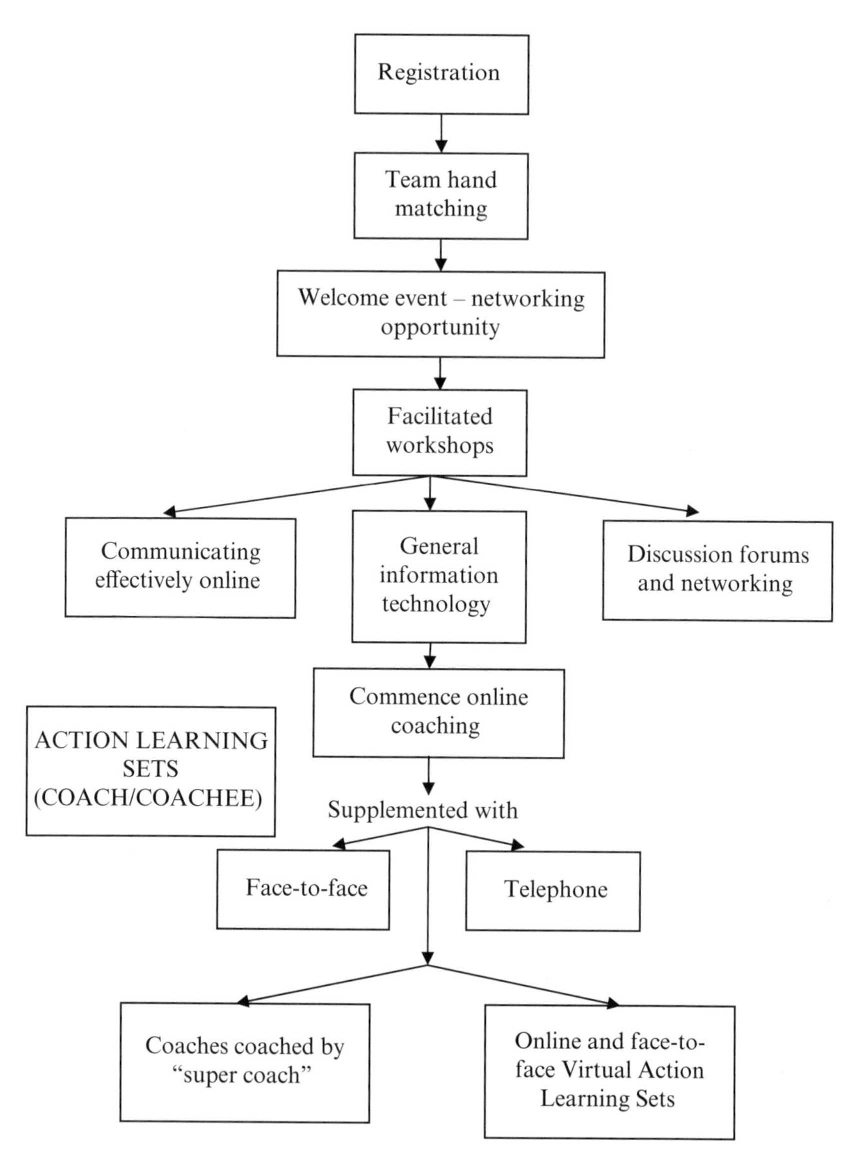

Figure 14.4 Revised model for future coaching programmes

matching can be particularly effective if there is a team available to help to discuss and evaluate forms.

Information technology support

IT support needs to be provided for each individual at the start of the programme. An overview of the TEC programme website and how to use the Spark software was provided at the welcome event, however, not all women were able to attend the networking events that were organized. IT support was on hand for all participants; but it required participants to contact the IT helpline. On reflection, it may have been useful to make training and support a formal part of the programme, rather than something that was provided on an ad hoc basis.

Facilitated workshops

It may have been useful to hold facilitated workshops during the initial stages of the coaching relationships, so as to provide participants with examples of how they could use the discussion forms, that is, discussion threads and so on. In addition, it may have been useful to allow more networking time at the welcome events. Providing such time may have enabled women to start networking face-to-face, which then may have continued online. Furthermore, it may have been useful to run a facilitated workshop on how to build rapport online and how to communicate more effectively using online methods.

Blended approach

The majority of coaching pairs supplemented online coaching with either telephone or face-to-face sessions. This would suggest that a blended approach is more suitable for women business owners. The study found that face-to-face meeting was an essential part of the initial coaching process. Coaches and coachees met face-to-face either at one of the two welcome events, or at an individual meeting arranged by the research team. This enabled the pairs to have a general discussion and to look at coaching objectives and plans for the relationship. A face-to-face meeting was seen as crucial for building rapport.

Support for coaches and coachees

For some coaches it was the first time that they had experienced an online programme and therefore they felt that extra support may have been useful. Therefore, on future programmes a "super coach" could be employed to coach a group of coaches throughout the duration of the programme. Alternatively, it may have been useful to set up action learning sets for coaches and coachees. This may have helped to establish networks and to provide a sounding board and guidance, particularly for coaches.

NOTE

1. This research programme, which was funded by the European Social Fund and Manchester Business School, was designed to explore the most appropriate form of support for women entrepreneurs that utilizes e-coaching.

REFERENCES

Aldrich, H. (1989) Networking among women entrepreneurs. In O. Hagen, C. Rivchum and D. Sexton (eds) *Women-owned Businesses*. New York, NY: Praeger.

Bierema, L.L. & Meriam, S.B. (2002) E-mentoring: Using computer mediated communication to enhance the mentoring process. *Innovative Higher Education*, **26**(3), 211–27.

Carter, N.M. & Williams, M.L. (2003) Comparing social feminism and liberal feminism: The case of new firm growth. In J.E. Butler (ed.), *New Perspectives on Women Entrepreneurs*. Greenwich, CT: Information Age Publishing, pp. 25–50.

Carter, N.M., Williams, M. & Reynolds, P.D. (1997) Discontinuance among new firms in retail: The influence of initial resources, strategy and gender. *Journal of Business Venturing*, **12**(2), 125–45.

Carter, N.M., Brush, C.G., Greene, P.G., Gatewood, E. & Hart, M.M. (2003) Women entrepreneurs who break through to equity financing: The influence of human, social and financial capital, *Venture Capital*, **5**(1), 1–28.

Carter, S., Anderson, S. & Shaw, E. (2001) *Women Business Ownership: A Review of the Academic, Popular and Internet Literature*. London: Small Business Service.

Census (2001) http://www.statistics.gov.uk/census2001/default.asp; accessed 24 November 2010.

Chaganti, R. & Parasuraman, S. (1996) A study of the impacts of gender on business performance and management patterns in small businesses. *Entrepreneurship Theory and Practice*, **21**(2), 73–5.

Chen, C.C., Greene, P.G. & Crick, A. (1998) Does entrepreneurial self-efficacy distinguish entrepreneurs from managers?, *Journal of Business Venturing*, **13**(4), 295–316.

Cohen, K.J. & Light, J.C. (2000) Use of electronic communication to develop mentor–mentee relationships between adolescent and adult AAC users: Pilot Study, *Augmentative and Alternative Communication*, **16**(4), 227–38.

Cromie, S. & Birley, S. (1991) Networking by female business owners in Northern Ireland. *Journal of Business Venturing*, **7**(3), 237–51.

Evans, D. & Volery, T. (2001) Online business development services for entrepreneurs: An exploratory study, *Entrepreneurship and Regional Development*, **13**(4), 333–50.

Fielden, S.L., Davidson, M.J., Dawe, A. & Makin, P.J. (2003) Factors inhibiting

the economic growth of female small business owners, *Journal of Small Business and Enterprise Development*, **10**(2), 152–66.
Greene, P.G., Katz, J.A. & Johannisson, B. (2004) From the guest co-editors, *Academy of Management Learning and Education: Special Issue on Entrepreneurship Education*, **3**(3), 238–41.
Harding, R. (2003) *Global Entrepreneurship Monitor*, UK.
Harding, R. (2004) *Global Entrepreneurship Monitor*, UK.
Harding, R. (2006) *Global Entrepreneurship Monitor*, UK.
Hill, J. (2001) A multidimensional study of the key determinants of effective SME marketing activity: Part 1, *International Journal of Entrepreneurial Behaviour and Research*, **7**(5), 171–204.
Holmquist, C. & Sundin, E. (1988) Women as entrepreneurs in Sweden – conclusions from a survey, *Frontiers of Entrepreneurship Research*. Wellesley, MA: Babson College.
Kalleberg, A.L. & Leicht, K.T. (1991) Gender and organizational performance: determinants of small business survival and success, *Academy of Management Journal*, **34**(1), 136–61.
Katz, J.A. and Williams P.M. (1997) Gender, self-employment and weak-tie networking through formal organizations. *Entrepreneurship and Regional Development*, **9**(3), 183–97.
Kenton, B. & Moody, D. (2001) *What Makes Coaching a Success?* Horsham, UK: Roffey Park Institute.
Kram, K.E. (1985) *Mentoring at Work: Developmental Relationships in Organizational Life*. Glenview, IL: Scott, Foresman.
Megginson, D. & Clutterbuck, D. (1995) *Mentoring in Action: A Practical Guide for Managers*. London: Kogan Page.
Nancarrow, C., Attlee, C. & Wright, L.T. (1999) Weaknesses in the marketing and the adoption of independent inventors with implications for international competitiveness. *Journal of Enterprising Culture*, **7**(3), 233–56.
O'Connor, J. & Lages, A. (2004) *Coaching with NLP*. London: Element.
Parasuraman, S., Purohit, Y. & Godshalk, V.M. (1996) Work and family variables, entrepreneurial career success and psychological well-being, *Journal of Vocational Behavior*, **48**(3), 275–300.
Parsloe, E. (1999) *The Manager as Coach and Mentor*. London: CIPD.
Peel, D. (2004) Coaching and mentoring in small to medium sized enterprises in the UK – factors that affect success and a possible solution, *International Journal of Evidence Based Coaching and Mentoring*, **2**(1), 46–56.
Ram, M. & Smallbone, D. (2001) *Ethnic Minority Enterprise: Policy in Practice*. London: Small Business Service.
Shaw, E., Carter, S. & Brierton, J. (2001) *Unequal Entrepreneurs: Why Female Enterprise is an Uphill Struggle*. The Industrial Society, London.
Shelton, L.M. (2006) Female entrepreneurs, work–family conflict, and venture performance: New insights into the work–family interface, *Journal of Small Business Management*, **44**(2), 285–97.
Stokes, A. (2001) Using telementoring to deliver training to SMEs: A pilot study, *Education and Training*, **43**(6), 317–24.
Stranger, A.M.J. (2004) Gender-comparative use of small business training and assistance: A literature review, *Education and Training*, **46**(8/9), 464–73.
Verheul, I., Uhlaner, L. & Thurik. R. (2005) Business accomplishments, gender and entrepreneurial self-image, *Journal of Business Venturing*, **20**(4), 483–518.

Whitmore, J. (2002) *Coaching for Performance: Growing People, Performance and Purpose*. 3rd edn. London: Nicholas Brealey.
Wilson, F., Kickul, J. & Marlino, D. (2007) Gender, entrepreneurial self-efficacy, and entrepreneurial career intentions: Implications for entrepreneurship education. *Entrepreneurship Theory and Practice*, **31**(3), 387–406.
Zeus, P. & Skiffington, S. (2003) *The Complete Guide to Coaching at Work*. New York, London, Sydney: McGraw-Hill.

15. WestJet Airlines Ltd.: a case study of a successful business that highlights HRM and strategy

Gerard H. Seijts

It's a tough business trying to run a profitable airline. A recent 2010 *Bloomberg Businessweek* article concluded (based on data from the Air Transport Association, a Washington trade group), the US airline industry, over the last decade, has amassed no less than $60 billion in red ink and shed 160 000 jobs (Barrett, 2010). Many airlines have come and gone. For example, since 2000 alone, 37 airlines have filed for Chapter 11 bankruptcy protection from creditors. The situation in Canada is no less dramatic. However, while some Canadian airlines have been struggling (e.g., Air Canada) and failing (e.g., JetsGo, SkyService Airlines, Canada3000, Royal Airlines and Zoom Airlines), one airline in particular has flourished – WestJet Airlines Ltd. Observers credit the success of WestJet to two key success factors: the low cost structure and its relentless focus on customer service. More importantly, the airline's organizational culture helps to drive down costs (e.g., individuals won't make photocopies single-sided) and execute on achieving a great customer experience (e.g., accompanying a person who has a fear of flying).

The objective of this chapter is four-fold. First, to provide a short overview of WestJet and its ongoing successes. Within this is what makes the company so successful. Second, to describe WestJet's culture and the ways the culture manifests itself. Third, to explain how the organization's leadership and human resource approaches contribute to building and sustaining the culture. Fourth, to explore how WestJet can continue to build its high-engagement culture as it continues to rapidly grow.

A SHORT HISTORY OF WESTJET AIRLINES

In 1994, Clive Beddoe, an entrepreneur active in real estate, purchased an aircraft for his weekly business travels between Calgary and Vancouver.

Beddoe made it available for charter to other cost-conscious business people through Morgan Air, owned and operated by Tim Morgan. The response to this venture caused Morgan – along with Calgary businessmen Donald Bell and Mark Hill – to realize there was an opportunity to satisfy the need in Western Canada for affordable air travel by starting an airline.

The odds appeared stacked against launching a successful airline. The airline industry is a tough business. The founders were aware of dozens of failed airlines in Canada. For example, historical data show 97 per cent of start-up airlines fail within the first seven years of operation. They also understood that many people dread airline travel: delayed or cancelled flights; lineups at the counter; cranky flight attendants; lost or damaged luggage; overbooked airplanes; inconsistent pricing; and so on. Beddoe and his colleagues realized they had to approach the task of building a successful airline in an unconventional manner.

The founding team developed a simple, one-line mission statement for their new enterprise named WestJet Airlines Ltd.: to enrich the lives of everyone in WestJet's world by providing safe, friendly and affordable air travel. The team relied on a simple belief: if we as a corporation take care of our people, then our people will take care of our guests, and our guests will take care of our profits. A culture of care was regarded as necessary for providing good customer service. For example, in 2009, WestJet published a set of customer standards – known as the WestJet Care-antee – setting the airline apart from rivals that had little or no hope of matching its offer (Figure 15.1).

Bob Cummings, the Executive Vice-President, Guest Experience and Marketing, said:

> The WestJet Care-antee is a set of promises we vow to uphold in good times and bad. . . So many things are changing right now and people are uncertain about what they can expect from the companies they deal with in their lives. . . The WestJet Care-antee is about showing our guests in a very real way that these are the things they can expect from their airline. (Tradingmarkets.com, 2009)

WestJet commenced operations on 29 February, 1996, flying to Vancouver, Kelowna, Calgary, Edmonton and Winnipeg. It started with approximately 200 employees. WestJet's initial strategy was to use low prices and unrestricted tickets to lure people who would otherwise drive, take the bus or train or stay home. The airline started in an ideal environment – Western Canada – where the main competitor was the financially troubled Canadian Airlines. Canadian Airlines could not compete against the upstart's low-cost structure. For example, WestJet offered no paper tickets, in-flight meals, and frequent flyer programs; and

The WESTJET
Care-antee

We will not charge you for call centre bookings.
We will not charge you to change or cancel your flight for 24 hours after you book.
We will not overbook your flight.
We will not charge you for two checked bags.
We will have the lowest change, cancel and pre-reserved seating fees in Canada.
We will accommodate you if your flight is delayed. Even if it's Mother Nature's fault.
We will fly you in the youngest all-jet fleet in North America.
We will provide live seatback TV on our flights.
We will give you ample legroom and overhead bin space.
We will publish our on-time, lost baggage and cancellation rates.
We will always let you know how we're doing as a company.
We will offer free online check in and seat selection 24 hours before departure.
We will allow you to transfer your credit files to friends or family for free.
We will give you free snacks and refreshments on your flight.
We will always include smiles and thank yous. Always.
And most importantly:
We'll always care. Because that's what owners do. Care-anteed.

Visit westjet.com for full details.

Source: All figures and tables are taken from company sources, use approved by WestJet.

Figure 15.1 The Care-antee

there was only one class of seating. WestJet uses one type of airplane – the Boeing 737. Hence, stocking cost of spare parts and training costs for pilots and employees are lower than airlines with multiple types of airplanes. The company also used a one-destination-to-another-destination model, rather than a web and spokes model. Of course, higher infrastructure and logistical costs are involved with the web and spokes model.

These (and other) strategic choices allowed WestJet to keep its fares competitive compared with the car or train.

In late 1999, taking advantage of turmoil in the Canadian airline industry, WestJet expanded its service across Canada. WestJet continued its expansion despite slowdowns in the industry in 2001. These slowdowns were due to an economic downturn as a result of the dotcom bust and terrorist attacks of September 11.

In 2003, WestJet captured 25 per cent of the domestic Canadian market despite two SARS outbreaks, the North American appearance of mad cow disease and higher fuel prices. It added additional destinations in Canada. In 2004, WestJet began to offer transborder flights from Canada to several US cities, including Los Angeles, San Francisco, Tampa and Orlando. WestJet added its first international service to Nassau, Bahamas in 2006; and other international destinations soon followed including Maui, Honolulu, Montego Bay, Mazatlan and St. Lucia.

WestJet had a record-breaking year in 2007 when revenues exceeded $2 billion and earnings were $193 million. The year 2008 was difficult and WestJet was just one of a few airlines worldwide that were profitable. While other airlines had cut their available seats, WestJet had continued to expand its reach. Revenues grew another 20 per cent in 2008 to $2.5 billion and, despite tough economic conditions, WestJet earned $178 million in net income. 2009 was a tougher year for the airline industry than 2008. Yet WestJet fared well.

The average age of the workforce at the end of 2009 was 34. WestJet employed 7800 people in 2010 (6900 full-time equivalent employees including approximately 1000 pilots and 2300 flight attendants). The days where the senior leadership could get all WestJetters into one room for a fireside chat and explain how and where the business was going were long gone. In 2010, WestJet flew to 69 destinations in Canada, the US, Mexico and the Caribbean.

WESTJET'S PERFORMANCE

Since its inception, WestJet has consistently ranked among the most profitable airlines in North America. The airline had grown revenues at an average annual rate of 37.4 per cent between 1996 and 2008. During the same period, net profit had grown at an average annual rate of 35.8 per cent. By the end of 2009, WestJet had captured 36 per cent of the domestic market for air travel. For perspective, Air Canada had 57 per cent of the domestic market.

WestJet had enjoyed net profits in every year of operation except for fiscal year 2004. And, even in 2004, it had positive cash flow from operations of $144 million. It reported its twentieth consecutive quarter of profitability in May 2010.

WestJet takes pride in its customer service to guests. Since the Air Travel Complaints Commission began tracking passenger complaints in 2000, WestJet had fewer complaints than Air Canada, its main domestic rival. Therefore, it appeared the airline had executed well against the differentiator that the founding team had envisioned: a caring attitude.

In 2010, for the fourth year in a row, WestJet was awarded the title of Canada's Most Admired Corporate Culture by Waterstone Human Capital, an executive search firm. This program recognizes Canadian corporations for having a culture that helps them to achieve a competitive advantage and great financial performance. WestJet was elected into the Corporate Culture Hall of Fame in 2010. Interestingly, it was not the leadership of the company that went down to accept the award. The leadership team sent people from all aspects of the organization – its WestJetters – to accept the award. According to the senior leadership, "It is not about them or us – it is about what we do as an organization and what our people do every single day" (personal conversation, 15 April with Executive VP Ferio Pugliese). The company spends a lot of time recognizing and rewarding the achievements of its people.

WESTJET'S GOALS

WestJet has an ambitious goal. By 2016, the airline aims to be one of the five most successful international airlines in the world, providing its guests with a friendly and caring experience that will change air travel forever. WestJet began to benchmark itself against leading airlines on criteria such as on-time performance, guest satisfaction and people- and culture-related variables. For example, just on the basis of its bottom line, WestJet had already achieved its vision. In 2008, WestJet ranked as the fifth most profitable airline in the world, behind Panama's Copa Airlines, Malaysia's AirAsia, United Arab Emirates' Air Arabia and Republic Airways in the US; its operating margin was 12 per cent.

CORPORATE CULTURE

Beddoe insisted WestJet's corporate culture is the primary reason for the airline's superb performance. He stated, "The entire environment is conducive to bringing out the best in people. It's the culture that creates the passion to succeed." Sean Durfy, who succeeded Beddoe as CEO in 2008, echoed a similar sentiment, "For us, that's the key driver to success" (Verburg, 2000).

Culture can be described as the set of beliefs, values and norms that represents the unique character of a company. These beliefs, values and norms influence the decision-making process and thus guide behaviour; and they are associated with words such as "should" and "ought."

WestJetters are encouraged to ask themselves the question, "Do my behaviours and actions live up to the values of the company or contravene them?" WestJet defines its core values as:

- commitment to safety;
- positive and passionate in everything we do;
- appreciative of our people and guests;
- fun, friendly and caring;
- align the interests of WestJetters with the interests of the company;
- honest, open and keep our commitments.

Building and maintaining the processes that nurture the WestJet culture is a task that management and staff take very seriously. Perhaps the WestJet ad campaign sums up the culture best: "Because owners care" (Figure 15.2). A WestJetter opined, "It's pretty simple. Everyone, and I mean everyone, is a customer, including your fellow employees. We all help each other out. And this creates a culture of always helping out the guest, our bottom line. 'It's not my job', or, 'I don't know' are not acceptable" (AUCANADA Forum, 2007).

The most recent employee engagement survey indicated satisfaction with and loyalty to the organization are strong. For example, 97 per cent of employees surveyed "strongly agreed" or "somewhat agreed" with the statement, "I work hard to continuously improve my productivity and quality," and 91 per cent "strongly agreed" or "somewhat agreed" with the statement, "I would recommend WestJet to friends and family as a great place to work."

Satisfaction with the organization manifests itself in numerous ways: high individual performance, better communication, low turnover, low absenteeism, more organizational citizenship behaviours, helping out colleagues, and so forth. These behaviours benefit the organization in tangible ways. For example, the ground crew raised an issue about the absence of an external sight gauge to read the water level of the potable water tank that supplies the aircraft with water. The crew would always fill the tank regardless of its destination. This added to fuel costs. The installation of an external sight gauge allowed the crew to determine how much potable water was used on a specific flight or route. This procedure led to fuel savings and reduced fuel burn and emissions. WestJet also got a

Figure 15.2 The "Because owners care" campaign

great response around its "Ideas that make cents" campaign (Figure 15.3) – an initiative to strive toward further cost efficiencies. This campaign was launched during the height of the recent financial crisis when domestic and international travel were impacted. The initiative brought savings forward in the order of $80 million.

Every WestJetter is expected to help out and contribute to the organization's success. WestJet's pilots often go into the cabin and help clean it between flights. They pack bags on the aircraft when necessary. Even the CEO helps out when he is on board. These behaviours sharply contrast the industry standard union arrangement where jobs are very clearly defined and employees are forbidden to perform cross-functional tasks, even if colleagues in another department are short-staffed or behind schedule. For WestJet this means annual savings of millions of dollars in grooming and enables quick turnarounds – usually within a half hour. Quick turnarounds were important at WestJet. First, the airline makes no money when aircraft sit on the ground – utilization of aircraft is critical. Second, to deliver a positive guest experience – guests like leaving early and arriving on or before schedule.

To take the pulse of its employees, WestJet conducts an internal biannual

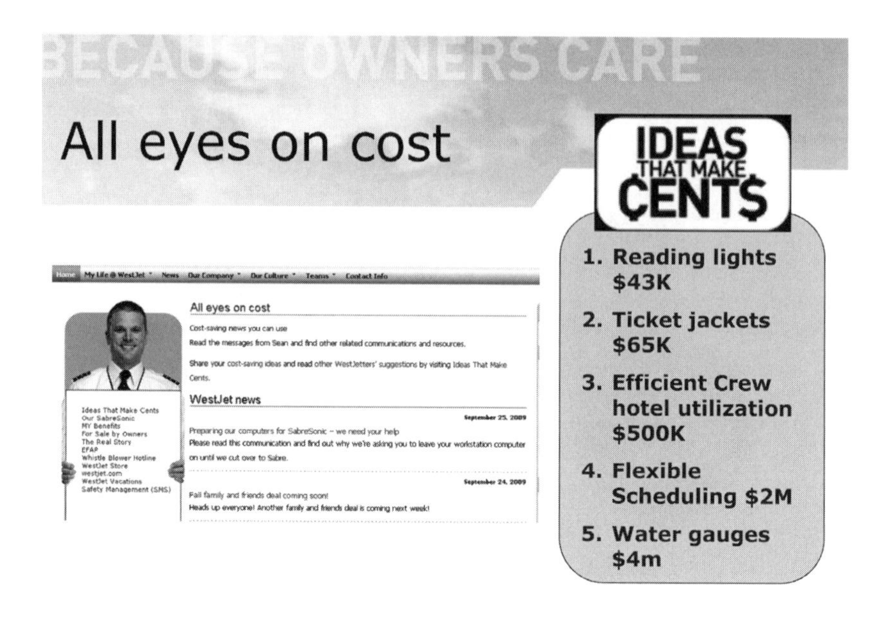

Figure 15.3 Ideas that make cents

survey called WHY (which stands for We Hear You) that measures culture and employee engagement, and encourages feedback so leaders can make improvements in processes and behaviours. The results are disclosed to everybody. The expectation is that leaders will get information relevant to their group (e.g., people, marketing, maintenance, dispatch, information technology, etc.) and they will go and talk to their people. The subsequent discussion is based around, "Ok, we're doing great here; we're not doing so well here; and as a group, let's talk about the things that we can do to improve." The culture emphasizes that everybody should have an active role in solving challenges, whatever the issue is. Therefore, through these types of discussions will come mutually agreed-upon objectives, specific action items, and planning around execution and accountability.

WHAT LEADERSHIP PRACTICES SUSTAIN THE CORPORATE CULTURE?

To management, culture is defined by executives' actions. Some executives focus on empowerment and trust, others on profit sharing. The combined actions of the executives contribute to and form part of the WestJet brand. If executives do things that are not aligned with WestJet's values, then that, too, has an effect on the culture.

Many organizations have value statements. WestJet is set apart from other organizations because everybody at WestJet – including senior executives – live the espoused values. The senior leadership team lives the values of the company in many ways. For example, every two weeks, the CEO and executives hold informal meetings with a group of staff members. Executives make it a habit to connect with employees during airport visits. For example, in November 2003, Beddoe was invited to give a presentation to the Canadian Club of London. He showed up late, a few minutes before he was to deliver his speech. Beddoe had met with WestJet employees at the London Airport to explain the corporate direction and some new initiatives. He also answered employees' questions and was interested in whether they had any concerns. To paraphrase Beddoe, "We had a great discussion that took a bit longer than I had anticipated." These days communication also takes place through social media forums – blogs, video messages, Facebook, and so on. These vehicles are important because WestJet has what is known as an absentee workforce, spread across the country.

Management is seriously committed to recognizing employees for their hard work. For example, Durfy and his team could be spotted at the Calgary Airport distributing buttercream cupcakes to WestJet employees. Traveling through the entire airport with the cupcakes stacked on luggage carts, they made sure every employee – from ticket counters to baggage handlers – received a cupcake.

The Executive Vice-President, People and Culture, has an important voice in the company. The people department is seen as an enabler of high performance. The people department is not seen or treated as an independent business group – it is a business partner. For the people, or human resources management role, to be an enabler it requires the following:

- A change in mindset from more traditional views of HRM as supporters, employee advocates and administrators, to strategic thinkers who ally themselves with the executives they work with to assist them in achieving their business goals.
- The development of business acumen and skills. This includes financial acumen, an understanding of strategy and an awareness of other management functions and the ways they contribute to strategic formulation and execution.
- A primary focus on building organizational capabilities through their pivotal role in talent development.

Figure 15.4 The cultural balance

- The people department has organized itself around five fundamentals when it approaches any people-related initiative:
  - Is it easy to understand?
  - Does it fulfil a need?
  - Is it timely?
  - Does it support WestJet's strategic vision?
  - Will our people feel better off having dealt with us?

The conversation at the executive level always looks at the balance between the needs of the business (to make money) and the needs of the people (both the guests and WestJetters). If the decisions focus too much on one aspect, the others suffer. Thus, WestJet needs to take care of the business so that it remains profitable and hence can provide a great guest experience to the guest and offer a world-class employment experience to WestJetters. It also needs to take care of its guests and WestJetters to remain a profitable organization. Decisions are made with this delicate balance in mind. Executives focus on the question, "How does this decision impact our guests, our WestJetters, our bottom-line?" (Figure 15.4).

There are, of course, situations where things need to be done for the business, perhaps at the expense of the guests or WestJetters. In such cases, executives must communicate why particular actions were initiated. For example, several years ago the company decided to begin charging for head-sets to listen to the in-flight entertainment system – Live TV. Being so customer focused this decision was immediately met with resistance from WestJetters, in particular the in-flight crew. People viewed this as taking advantage of the customer, which would invariably lead to a reduction in the quality of the guest experience. However, this was a change initiative that was necessary to ensure that the company could grow another source of revenue – an area known as ancillary revenue. These are revenues common to the airline industry but that are not part of the ticket purchase. Since the entire WestJet employee base are owners, management had to spend time explaining how the change would grow revenue that would, in turn, impact margin. Margin growth keeps the airline strong. It also contributes to an increase in the profit share.

CARE

WestJet has a group called CARE, or, Creating A Remarkable Experience. It supports and propagates the culture throughout WestJet's operations. CARE helps WestJetters produce videos and plays that inform and entertain staff. It plans more than 250 parties a year, including the profit-sharing parties. These are twice-annual events where WestJetters receive profit-sharing cheques face-to-face from a WestJet executive as a personal thank you. These profit-sharing parties have been a point of contention with the accountants (or, as they are known at WestJet, bean counters) – these parties cost money! WestJet can, but doesn't, electronically deposit the profit-sharing cheques into the bank accounts of all WestJetters. The CEO and executives want to shake people's hands, say thank you, or give them high fives. The actual celebration of success is important.

On only one occasion, no bonus payout was given. This was because the airline had two unprofitable quarters. However, a party was still organized to thank all WestJetters for their hard work. The company places a premium on business literacy among employees of all functional backgrounds and ranks, so the leadership team also used the event to help people understand why the company was unable to provide bonuses.

CARE organizes a number of other events to celebrate and recognize achievements. If a WestJetter is getting married, the leadership sends a gift. If a WestJetter loses an immediate family member, it sends flowers. There will be a celebration if a WestJetter is retiring or reaches a milestone, such as ten-year tenure. If a WestJetter passes away, the company has a commemoration program and dedicates one of its aircrafts to that person. All these initiatives show the leadership cares!

CARE organizes events such as breakfasts, Christmas parties, barbecues and the "Dirty Bird Wash" fun day. WestJetters bring family and friends to these events. CARE helps to create an environment where WestJetters are encouraged to thank one another even for the simplest things. An example would be putting Smarties on people's desks because they had smart ideas. CARE's goal is to make WestJetters feel that even little things matter because they make for a memorable experience from an employment standpoint.

Each airport has a culture committee; and CARE connects into them. These committees approach CARE if they need help with an event or suggestions or direction for interesting or innovative ideas.

THE ROLE OF HRM

The senior leadership at WestJet maintains that the brand and people are its competitive advantages. They believe anyone can put planes in the air; and any airline can compete on price or frequency of flights. At WestJet, the people and their behaviours set the company apart. WestJetters are the faces of the brand. Their interaction with guests helps them to deliver on the brand. Therefore, the company carefully recruits people to the organization and develops them. WestJet wants to be recognized as one of Canada's top ten employers. To do that, the company needs to provide a world-class employment experience.

How do human resource approaches contribute to the building and sustaining of the culture? And how can WestJet continue to build its high-engagement culture as it continues to experience high rates of growth?

TALENT SELECTION

Despite a sluggish 2008 economy, WestJet continued to hire staff. However, like many other organizations, it eventually slowed its growth and workforce plans. A hiring freeze was implemented in 2009 with a call to WestJetters to look for additional cost savings in the company in support of its low cost roots. Through 2009, WestJet also did not experience any reductions in the workforce. In the first few months of 2010, it received 7000 resumés for 272 advertised flight attendant positions, from which a handful of applicants were shortlisted for screening interviews. As WestJet's unique corporate culture is well known, many applicants knew what to expect from their potential future employer.

WestJetters want to be proud of the colleagues with whom they are working. How to recruit and select such individuals? WestJet posts advertisements for frontline positions (e.g., flight attendants, call centre agents, ground handlers and customer service agents) on its website – both internally and externally. It gets enough traffic through the website to receive a significant number of applications. Then how do recruiters narrow down the search for their top candidates and new colleagues?

Knock-out questions

The application form contains several questions; and individuals complete these online. If applicants answer these questions incorrectly, or they don't have the qualifications, they are excluded from the process. Examples of knock-out questions are: Are you a Canadian citizen or eligible to have a Canadian passport? Are you able to lift 50 pounds over your head continuously? Are you able to pass an airport restricted-area clearance? People need to have these (and other) requirements and abilities to get the job.

Nice to haves

If the applicant answers the knock-out questions correctly, there will be a series of nice-to-have questions. These questions focus on an individual's background and work experience. An example of a nice-to-have question is: Give me an example of when you have gone above and beyond to help a customer or client? The recruiter thus explores whether the applicant has any relevant skills or experiences for the job. The answers are submitted online.

Background on the resumé

The recruiters screen the answers and resumés. Given the nature of the business, customer service, years of experience and guest- or customer-facing roles are of interest.

Initial phone interview

If the applicant is of interest, a short five- to 30-minute phone interview is scheduled between the applicant and the recruiter. The person's background is discussed in more detail. An example of a typical question is: Tell me about a time when you dealt with an irate person? The questions asked at this stage of the recruitment and selection process focus on the job-related skills that the applicant needs to bring to the position.

Realistic job previews

The recruiter provides the applicant with the harsh realities of the position. For example, flight attendants could be away from home for five days in a row, with the same pilot, first officer and flight attendants. They might have to work at 4 a.m. Weather could interrupt the schedules, resulting in delays and more time away from home. Details about total compensation are discussed. The rigorous training modules are described. If the applicants are still interested, have relevant skills and experiences and communicated well during the interview, they are invited for a group interview.

Group interview

WestJet uses an interesting approach to the interview sessions to better identify those inherently cheerful, outgoing people who are not afraid to inform and entertain a large group of people, such as those seated together in an airplane. Between 15 and 25 people are brought into a three-hour session. The applicant gets a chance to introduce him or herself to the other applicants and the recruiters and explain why he or she wants to work at WestJet. Typically, the applicants are given a small group assignment (e.g., write and sing a song, present a solution to a challenging work-related problem to the group, or build an airplane from materials that are provided). These assignments are designed to reveal whether or not the candidates fit into WestJet's culture. WestJetters serve as observers. Typically, there are between four and six observers. The recruiters want their opinions. Do they believe they are going to be able to work with this person one-on-one? Are applicants asking good questions? Do they get bored? Do they smile? Do they listen to their colleagues? Are they demonstrating cooperative behaviours? Observers take detailed notes that are then used when applicants are evaluated. The session ends with a behavioural interview. An example of an interview question is: Tell me about a time when you worked in a team where one member wasn't pulling his weight? Tell me what the situation was? How did you deal with it? How did you communicate with him? And what was the overall team result? The recruiters and observers then go through each candidate and compare impressions and notes. The hiring decisions tend to be unanimous.

References

The process concludes with reference checks. The company checks at least two business references for every candidate; and does criminal background checks on candidates before they receive job offers.

The recruitment and selection process shows a number of things. First, it is a rather elaborate process. There are three buckets of criteria: corporate values, team values and technical skills. The company wants to make sure – maybe more so than any other organization – that it identifies those individuals who will thrive in the airline's culture. WestJet's approach is to identify candidates whose personalities fit with the airline's culture and then train them for the jobs in which they are interested. Second, peers help recruiters in the recruitment and selection process. WestJet posts advertisements for these positions. Candidates will go through an interview. Those who are selected will serve a one-year term. These individuals get extensive training. How to interview? How to take notes during an interview? How to phone screen? What can you legally ask? And what should you avoid asking?

The company benchmarks its efforts against other great Canadian companies. It is interested in the question: What does excellence look like in Canadian organizations? WestJet therefore continuously assesses both its processes and outcomes of its various tools. For example, it looks at such measures as roles filled with internal talent, voluntary and involuntary turnover during the first six months, attrition of top performers, performance ratings spread, number of people that fail to pass the checkpoints and exams during the initial training, and how the new employees experience the first 90 days.

Each recruiter is responsible for a particular group of recruits – for example, the call centre. Monthly discussions among recruiters discuss the successes, the individuals the leaders are concerned about, attrition, and so forth. If, for example, the recruits have had difficulties with the technical aspects of the job, this suggests the selection and training processes need closer examination. WestJet is always looking to improve its processes.

ON-BOARDING PROCESS

The objective of the on-boarding process is to create a seamless experience from the recruitment and selection stage to the job-performance process. First, WestJet wants the newcomers to say, "Yes I made the right decision." Second, the company wants these individuals to be ready to perform sooner, both from a cultural perspective and in their functional roles. The on-boarding process has two main pieces.

The new employees come to Calgary and have a two-day orientation program. This orientation is quite a bit different than a traditional orientation where individuals are completing the paperwork, find out about their benefits, are given information about harassment and absenteeism policies, and so forth. WestJet focuses on the cultural piece – explaining the values and showing individuals what those values look like in action. Individuals are told they are owners. They own how they interact with people. Thus, starting on day one, WestJet creates an experience for people where they can quickly understand what is allowed, what is expected and what is encouraged from a behavioural point of view. People walk away from the orientation understanding that they are now ambassadors or stewards of the culture.

Subsequent to the orientation, the initial training at one of the training centres takes place. This training will take several weeks to learn the knowledge, skills and abilities required for being an effective member of the WestJet organization, such as a customer service agent or a flight attendant. Extensive simulations and role-plays are part of the training. For example, individuals could be confronted with a scenario where there is a storm and all the planes are grounded. The agent has a very angry guest in front of her. How would the person defuse that anger? Trainers will observe how individuals react under pressure; that is, whether they are able to deliver the great experience that defines WestJet. Next comes extensive coaching on the required behaviours to be successful in customer-service roles, and goal-setting to improve on behavioural performance.

WestJetters are expected to take initiative and resolve issues themselves. WestJet's founders had set out to create a company that was managed from the bottom-up. WestJet gives employees a high degree of latitude to perform their jobs without too much interference from leaders. Decision-making responsibility is pushed as far down to the front line as possible. For example, representatives from the sales centre have the authority to override fares, make decisions not to charge fees for cancellations and bookings, and waive fees for unaccompanied minors. To ensure that there are checks and balances in place, employees are trained to understand the ramifications of the decisions they make. Senior management trusts the representatives in looking out for the interests of the company, customers and shareholders. Nevertheless, overrides are tracked and monitored each month. Additional training and one-on-one coaching are provided if patterns emerge (e.g. a particular employee consistently waives extra baggage fees).

PERFORMANCE CONVERSATIONS

When they come to work, WestJetters expect their colleagues to support them, help them, give them feedback, help them reach their career goals and help them understand how to make their best contributions. Leaders engage in performance conversations because they care about great performance; and because WestJetters indicated – through the WHY survey – that feedback motivates them to do a good job. They want to understand how their behaviours and actions support the organization and its brand of creating a great guest experience. Since they are owners, this is relevant to them!

The formal performance management program is called Targeting Optimum Performance. Performance conversations take place on a quarterly basis. Both performance and developmental goals are discussed. The performance goals focus on what individuals commit to deliver. Broad organizational goals are translated into individual performance objectives. The traditional SMART approach to goal setting is used – performance goals should be specific, measurable, attainable, relevant and time-based.

Developmental goals focus on the skills WestJetters want to hone in on. What support or development do WestJetters need from their leaders to do well on the job, taking into account the current challenges and those anticipated in the near future?

A second objective of these conversations is for WestJetters to raise issues with their leaders. The idea behind these frequent conversations is, should something go wrong in the job (e.g., someone is making a mistake or not doing as well as she should), the managers and WestJetters should not wait for the annual review to address opportunities for improvement. The culture at WestJet is one of trust so formally scheduled conversations take place quarterly or as needed.

To have such conversations in the in-flight world is a bit more challenging because of the largely absentee workforce. WestJet has recruited top-performing flight attendants who are well respected by the flight attendant group. The company provides leadership training and developmental opportunities to these individuals. They are, therefore, equipped, in the moment, to have performance conversations. They take the same concepts regarding how to have effective conversations that isn't about, "I need to give you some feedback, let's sit down and have this conversation," but instead, "Hey, are you okay? Is there anything I can do to help?"

The organization has a developmental bias. WestJet has some examples of significant failure; the recent implementation of its new reservation system is an example. The reservation system was started in October 2009 and, almost immediately, the company suffered delays at the airport, frustration at the check-in counters, gridlock at the sales centre and the crash of the reservation system. The implementation was anything but smooth and a lot of guests were disappointed with the service. However, several important learnings came from this implementation that are now carried forward.

WestJetters have a mentality of, "Hey, people are going to make mistakes," but how you treat people and help them prevent making such mistakes is going to be the difference. Again, this approach or orientation can be tied back to taking care of the people – something that is at the core of the company. However, when the person keeps making the same mistake two or three times in a row, tolerance goes down. The tolerance level is also lower for people that aren't culturally aligned.

TALENT ORIENTATION AND TALENT MANAGEMENT

Once hired, WestJetters are immediately welcomed into the company. WestJetters are assigned a sponsor who acts as a mentor, teaching them about the organization, helping them work through any issues in their jobs, and making sure they made the right contacts within the organization. If some WestJetters are identified as high-potential employees, a more formalized mentoring program is designed for them so they can gain additional skills and knowledge to be effective in their new roles and beyond.

The Targeting Optimum Performance and talent reviews or succession planning go hand in hand. Individuals who have contributed great performance and have done so in a way that aligns with the values and culture, are identified as high potentials. The nine-box grid is used as a talent management tool; one axis assesses performance and the other assesses leadership potential. WestJet identifies those people with high performance and potential. These individuals will be put in a comprehensive development program where the focus is on building depth and breadth in skills in a constructive fashion. Leadership development is a critical issue for WestJet – the senior leadership understands that a shortage of leadership talent should never be allowed to interfere with growth.

The leadership development program is a recent initiative. WestJet had people that were great doers and these individuals were put into leadership roles. It has begun to take a more systematic approach toward leadership development and the focus now is on making sure individuals are ready to be leaders, not just great doers in a new role.

SHARING THE SUCCESS

Figure 15.5 shows that total compensation at WestJet consists of five elements. The Employee Share Purchase Plan (ESPP) and profit sharing are the unique features.

WestJetters have access to an ESPP, allowing them to accumulate an equity stake in the firm. Contributions of up to 20 per cent of an employee's salary are matched dollar-for-dollar by WestJet.

In addition, each year, between 10 and 20 per cent of pre-tax operating income is set aside for the employee bonus pool. As the airline's profit increases, the employee's bonus increases. The profit-sharing pool amounts and shares per employee over the past 12 years are shown in Table 15.1.

Employees have the option of directing their bonuses toward their ESPP contributions. In 2009, about 84 per cent of WestJetters participated in the ESPP and contributed, on average, 14 per cent of their pre-tax salary toward the purchase of shares. The resulting ESPP funds were used to buy voting shares in the open market during each calendar

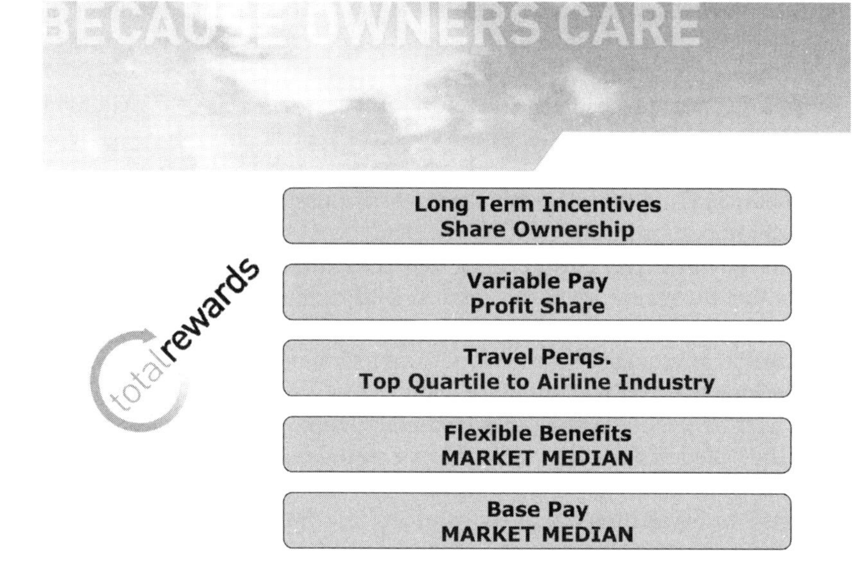

Figure 15.5 Rewarding success – total compensation

Table 15.1 Profit-sharing pool amounts and average shares per employee over the last 12 years

Year	Profit Sharing Pool ($)	Avg. Profit Share per Employee ($)
1998	1 500 000	2 256
1999	6 600 000	7 491
2000	13 500 000	10 449
2001	10 300 000	5 586
2002	15 200 000	5 609
2003	15 000 000	4 417
2004	2 900 000	721
2005	6 000 000	1 400
2006	20 300 000	4 081
2007	46 700 000	8 219
2008	33 400 000	5 398
2009[a]	14 675 000	2 332

Note: a. Full-time employees at 31 December 2009 = 6291.

Source: WestJet.

month. WestJet implemented these structures because the founders felt that owners try harder (e.g., to improve the guest experience, and to save costs) than employees.

Employees need to be in the plan for a full year to receive the matching contribution. If they need to withdraw money prior, they don't get the company's match. Since the inception of the plan, WestJetters have earned more than $155 million in profit sharing. Cheques are cut twice-yearly at profit-share parties in May and November.

WestJet considered cutting back the company's contribution to the ESPP after the recent financial crisis to save millions of dollars. But the company quickly abandoned the idea. Both these programs – profit share and ESPP – have created the "we are owners" mindset. And this mindset is something the company does not want to lose – ever.

As well as cash rewards and personal thank yous, WestJet runs a program called Kudos that recognizes employees internally and externally for outstanding accomplishments or deeds. Notable employees are rewarded with vacations. And WestJetters and their families are invited to the annual "Dirty Bird Wash." Planes are brought into the hangar and kids are given water and soap to clean the aircraft. Celebrating is important at WestJet.

BENEFIT PLANS

WestJet implemented a flexible benefits plan in 2010. Surveys had shown great dissatisfaction with the traditional plan where all WestJetters received the same benefits. Now individuals can choose from a number of options regarding what kind of coverage they need given their specific circumstances depending, for example, on the health plans their spouses have. Individuals also receive flex dollars; and they get to choose where they want to spend them (e.g., buy more dental coverage; or direct money to a wellness account).

The revised program was designed in the traditional WestJet manner – with a lot of consultation and input from WestJetters to make sure the company understood which of its programs the employees valued; and what sort of things they need that are not yet in place.

PACT AND COMMUNICATION

To ensure WestJetters, collectively, have a voice at the management level, WestJet's senior management created the Pro-Active Communication

Team (PACT), an employee association that allows management to keep in touch with the rank and file. This allows management to address concerns before they become a problem. PACT provides WestJet employees with the services they might want to receive through a union – without the hassles, work rules and adversarial environment that a union typically brings.

PACT covers the entire company with a number of chapters representing the different work groups. Each chapter has one or more representatives, who sit on a council. Besides dealing with personnel issues, PACT aids in setting salary scales. WestJet's founder, Clive Beddoe, had opted for PACT because, in his view, this structure reduces the likelihood of conflict because employees are part of the solution, not the problem. Every year, management nominates a representative from PACT to sit on WestJet's board of directors. If an employee group, such as flight attendants, wants to leave PACT, it needs approval from 75 per cent of its members.

As a testament to PACT's effectiveness, three attempts by unions to organize WestJet flight attendants – in 2003, 2006 and 2008 – had failed. The main issues WestJetters brought up were the usual suspects: scheduling, wages and pensions.

CONCLUSION

In 2006, Waterstone Human Capital concluded that, "there is a problem in Corporate Canada when it comes to culture – a glaring disconnect between the beliefs and actions of leading executives." The authors of the report argued that business leaders are ignoring something they believe is in fact important to organizational success – culture. The report articulates the seven forgotten principles of health and performance.

- *Define*. While business leaders know what culture means to them, they do not always take the natural next step: defining – preferably in a clear and concise statement – exactly how their own culture should look and how employees should behave on a day-to-day basis.
- *Align*. It is important that organizations ensure everything – from strategy to processes to training procedures – is aligned with the company's culture.
- *Leaders in action*. Leaders need to set the tone for their organizations through their communication and behaviours. They must have a strong presence for all members of the company, and must exhibit its vision, mission and values through their own behaviours and actions.

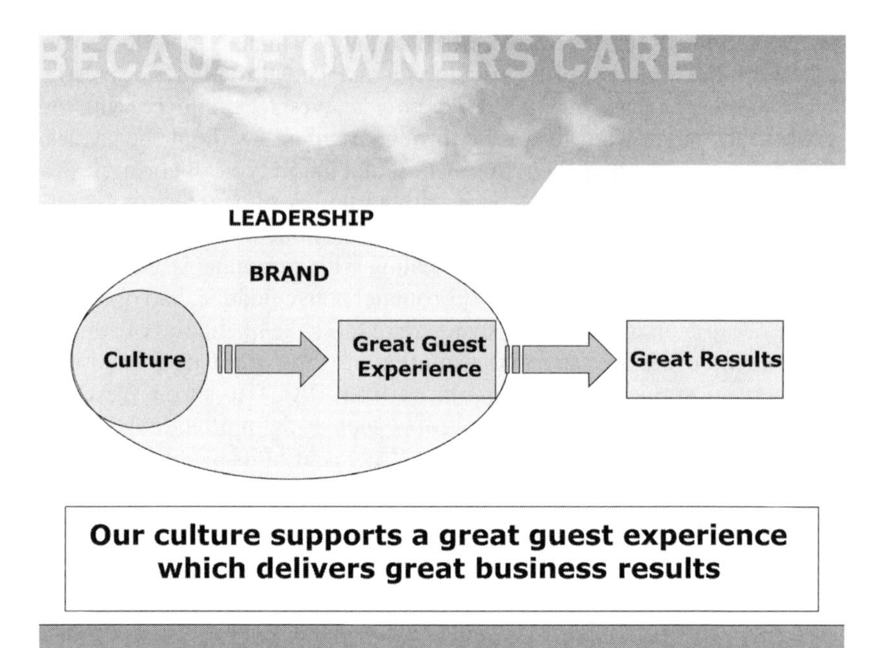

Figure 15.6 A unique culture of care

- *Measure.* Organizations need to take the right steps to ensure their cultures are strong. Just as people need to pay regular visits to the doctor, organizations should also regularly diagnose the health of their corporate cultures. The results need to be communicated.
- *React.* The internal and external business environment is always in flux. Organizations thus need to respond in a positive and productive way to feedback from measurements, both to problems within their culture and changes in the operating environment, as they arise.
- *Reward.* Results are important to any organization's success. But, if having a strong culture drives organizational performance, leaders should focus on adjusting their awards and recognition programs. Reward actual behaviours in addition to results that foster an improved corporate culture.
- *Sustain.* Leaders must ensure the organization's core values and culture – and all of the systems supporting these – are reinforced and extended over the long term. Thus, organizations should recruit and promote the right people; ensure the new hires are successfully integrated into the company's culture; continue to look for better

processes, continue to communicate about the culture and train people, and so forth.

WestJet does well on all of these principles and hence it is no surprise that its culture is a strong contributor to its ongoing success. The culture is in fact required to execute on the brand (Figure 15.6).

But creating this culture is hard work and something WestJet works on day in and day out! Various processes including HRM practices and measurement approaches play a key role in reinforcing and extending the culture. And so does leadership behaviour.

REFERENCES

AVCANADA Forum (21 December 2007) available at: http://www.avcanada.ca/forums2/viewtopic.php?f=36&t=38128; accessed 29 November 2010.

Barrett, P.M. (10–16 May 2010) The departed. *Bloomberg Businessweek*.

Tradingmarkets.com (21 April 2009) The WestJet "Care-antee", available at http://www.tradingmarkets.com/.site/news/Stock%20News/2282291/; accessed 29 November 2010.

Verburg, P. (2000) Prepare for take-off, *Canadian Business*, available at: http://www.myleadership.com/index.php?title=Prepare_for_Takeoff; accessed 29 November 2010.

Index